Developing Amazonia

CONTEMPORARY ISSUES IN DEVELOPMENT STUDIES
General editors F. I. Nixson and C. H. Kirkpatrick

Books previously published in the series

Perspectives on development: cross-disciplinary themes in development
  edited by P. F. Leeson and M. M. Minogue
Development policies: sociological perspectives
  edited by Anthony Hall and James Midgley

Developing Amazonia

Deforestation and social conflict in Brazil's Carajás programme

Anthony L. Hall

Manchester University Press

Manchester and New York

Distributed exclusively in the USA and Canada by *St. Martin's Press*

Published by Manchester University Press
Oxford Road, Manchester M13 9PL, UK
and Room 400, 175 Fifth Avenue,
New York, NY 10010, USA

*Distributed exclusively in the USA and Canada
by* St. Martin's Press, Inc.,
175 Fifth Avenue, New York, NY 10010, USA

Reprinted in paperback, with postscript, 1991

British Library cataloguing in publication data
Hall, Anthony, *1947–*
    Developing Amazonia: Deforestation and social conflict in Brazil's
    Carajás programme
    1. Brazil. Amazon River Basin. Economic
    development, to 1984
    I. Title
    330.981′1

Library of Congress cataloging in publication data
Hall, Anthony L., 1947–
    Developing Amazonia: deforestation and social conflict in Brazil's
    Carajás programme.
    Anthony L. Hall.
        p.   cm.
    Includes bibliographical references.
    ISBN 0–7190–3550–3
    1. Programa Grande Carajás.   2. Regional planning – Brazil – Carajás
    Mountains Region.   3. Human ecology – Brazil – Carajás Mountains
    Region.   4. Man – Influence on nature – Brazil – Carajás Mountains
    Region.   I. Title.
    HT395.B72C3643   1989
    338.981′15 – dc20   89–36252

ISBN 0 7190 3550 3 *paperback*

Phototypeset in Hong Kong
by Best-set Typesetter Ltd.

Printed in Great Britain
by Biddles Ltd, Guildford and King's Lynn

Contents

About the author

Anthony Hall has had wide experience of development issues and problems in Brazil. He has undertaken extensive field research in Amazonia and the North-East, and was OXFAM's representative in the country for several years. Since 1983 he has been Lecturer in Social Planning in Developing Countries at the London School of Economics and Political Science. His major publications include *Drought and Irrigation in North-East Brazil* (Cambridge University Press, 1978), *Community Participation, Social Development and the State* (with J. Midgley and others, Methuen, 1986), *Development Policies: Sociological Perspectives* (with J. Midgley, Manchester University Press, 1988) and *The Future of Amazonia: Destruction or Sustainable Development?* with D. Goodman, Macmillan, forthcoming 1990).

Illustrations

Tables

Acknowledgements

During my research I received invaluable assistance from many quarters. On three field trips to Brazil I consulted a host of officials, development practitioners, churchpeople, peasant farmers and other informants, whose help it is not possible to acknowledge individually. To these sources in Brasília, Rio de Janeiro, Belém, São Luís, Marabá and Açailândia I am deeply indebted and offer my sincere thanks, confident that their contributions to this book have helped fuel the ongoing debate over appropriate development paths for Amazonia. I should also like to express my gratitude to the British Academy, the Nuffield Foundation and the London School of Economics and Political Science for essential funding.

I wish to dedicate this piece of work to my wife, Rejane, in appreciation of her support and patience during its completion; and to our two children, Julie and Joseph, in the hope that they can eventually look forward to a brighter future for their Brazil.

Acronyms and abbreviations

ABRACAVE	Associação Brasileira de Carvoeiros Vegetais (Brazilian Association of Vegetable-Charcoal Producers)
AEA	Associação dos Empresários da Amazônia (Association of Amazon Businessmen)
ALBRAS	Alumínio do Brasil (Aluminium Company of Brazil)
ALCOA	Aluminium Company of America
ALUMAR	Alumínio do Maranhão (Aluminium Company of Maranhão)
ALUNORTE	Alumínio do Norte (Aluminium Company of the North)
AMCEL	Amapá Florestal e Cellulose (Amapá Timber and Cellulose Company)
AMZA	Amazônia Mineração SA (Amazon Mining plc)
BASA	Banco da Amazônia SA (Bank of Amazonia plc)
BCB	Banco de Crédito da Borracha (Credit Bank for Rubber)
BNCC	Banco Nacional de Crédito Cooperativista (National Bank of Co-operative Credit)
BNDE	Banco Nacional de Desenvolvimento Econômico (National Development Bank)

BRASAGRO	Companhia Brasileira de Participação Agrícola (Brazilian Company for Agricultural Participation)
CAMTA	Cooperativa Agrícola Mista de Tomé Açú (Tomé Açú Mixed Agricultural Co-operative)
CAPEMI	Caixa de Pecúlio dos Militares (Military Pension Fund)
CEB	Comunidade Eclesial de Base (Community Religious Group)
CEDI	Centro Eucumênico de Documentação e Informação (Ecumenical Centre for Documentation and Information)
CEPAC	Centro Piauiense de Ação Cultural (Piauí Centre for Cultural Action)
CEPASP	Centro de Educação, Pesquisa e Assessoria Sindical (Centre for Education, Research and Union Advice)
CGT	Confederação Geral do Trabalho (General Labour Confederation)
CHESF	Companhia Hidroelétrica do Vale do São Francisco (São Francisco Valley Hydroelectric Company)
CIMA	Comissão Interna do Meio-Ambiente (Internal Commission for the Environment)
CIMI	Conselho Indigenista Missionário (Indian Missionary Council)
CLT	Consolidação dos Leis de Trabalho (Brazilian Labour Code)
CMM	Companhia Meridional de Mineração (Southern Mining Company)
CNBB	Conferência Nacional dos Bispos do Brasil (National Conference of Brazilian Bishops)

CNI	Conferência Nacional da Indústria (National Council for Industry)
CNPq	Conselho Nacional de Desenvolvimento Científico e Tecnológico (National Council for Scientific and Technological Development)
CNS	Conselho Nacional de Seringueiros (National Rubber Tappers' Council)
CODEVASF	Companhia de Desenvolvimento do Vale do São Francisco (São Francisco Valley Development Company)
COMARCO	Companhia Maranhense de Colonização (Maranhão Colonisation Company)
CONCLAT	Conferêncial Nacional das Classes Trabalhadoras (National Conference of the Working Classes)
CONSAG	Construtora Andrade Gutiérrez (Andrade Gutiérrez Construction Company)
CONSIDER	Conselho Siderúrgica Nacional (National Steel Council)
CONTAG	Confederação Nacional dos Trabalhadores na Agricultura (National Federation of Agricultural Workers)
COSIPAR	Companhia Siderúrgica do Pará (Steel Company of Pará)
CPA	Companhia de Promoção Agrícola (Agricultural Promotion Company)
CPI	Comissão Pro-Índio (Pro-Indian Commission)
CPP	Comissão Pastoral dos Pescadores (Church Fishermen's Commission)
CPT	Comissão Pastoral da Terra (Church Land Commission)
CRID	Centre de Recherche et d'Information pour le

	Développement (Centre for Research and Information on Development)
CSN	Conselho de Segurança Nacional (National Security Council)
CUT	Central Única do Trabalho (Unified Labour Centre)
CVRD	Companhia Vale do Rio Doce (Rio Doce Valley Company)
DNER	Departamento Nacional de Estradas e Rodagem (National Roadworks Department)
EDF	Environmental Defence Fund
ELETROBRAS	Centrais Elétricas Brasileiras (Brazilian Electricity Board)
ELETRONORTE	Centrais Elétricas do Norte (North Brazil Electricity Board)
EMATER	Empresa de Assistência Técnica e Extensão Rural (Technical Assistance and Rural Extension Company)
FASE	Federação de Órgãos de Assistência Social e Educacional (Federation of Organisations for Social and Educational Assistance
FETAGRI	Federação dos Trabalhadores na Agricultura (Federation of Agricultural Workers)
FINAM	Fundo de Investimento da Amazônia (Investment Fund for Amazonia)
FND	Fundo Nacional de Desenvolvimento (National Development Fund)
FTI	Fundação de Tecnologia Industrial (Industrial Technology Foundation)
FUNAI	Fundação Nacional do Índio (National Indian Foundation)
GEAMAM	Grupo de Estudo e Assessoramento Sobre o

	Meio-Ambiente (Environmental Study and Advisory Group)
GEBAM	Grupo Executivo do Baixo Amazonas (Executive Group for the Lower Amazon)
GETAT	Grupo Executivo de Trabalho do Araguaia-Tocantins (Executive Group for the Araguaia-Tocantins)
GETSOP	Grupo Executivo das Terras do Sudoeste do Paraná (Executive Group for the Lands of South-West Paraná)
GTPI	Grupo de Trabalho Política Indigenista (Working Group on Indian Policies)
IBASE	Instituto Brasileiro de Análises Sociais (Brazilian Institute for Social Analysis)
IBDF	Instituto Brasileiro de Desenvolvimento Florestal (Brazilian Institute of Forestry Development)
IBGE	Instituto Brasileiro de Geografia e Estatística (Brazilian Institute of Geography and Statistics)
IDCJ	International Development Corporation of Japan
INCRA	Instituto Nacional de Colonização e Reforma Agrária (National Institute for Colonisation and Agrarian Reform)
INPA	Instituto Nacional de Pesquisas da Amazônia (National Institute for Amazonian Research)
ITTO	International Tropical Timber Organisation
JADECO	Japan-Brazil Agricultural Development Corporation
JICA	Japan International Co-operation Agency
KTS	Korf Tecnologia Siderúrgica (Korf Steel Technology)

LAAD	Latin American Agribusiness Development Corporation
MASTER	Movimento dos Agricultores Sem Terra do Rio Grande do Sul (Landless Workers' Movement of Rio Grande do Sul)
MEB	Movimento de Educação de Base (Popular Education Movement)
MER	Movimento de Evangelização Rural (Rural Evangelical Movement)
MINTER	Ministério do Interior (Ministry of the Interior)
MIRAD	Ministério da Reforma e do Desenvolvimento Agrário (Ministry of Agrarian Reform and Development)
MNDDH	Movimento Nacional da Defesa dos Direitos Humanos (National Movement for the Defence of Human Rights)
MR-8	Movimento Revolucionário 8 de otubro (Revolutionary Movement of 8 October)
MST	Movimento dos Trabalhadores Rurais Sem Terra (Landless Workers' Movement)
NAAC	Nippon Amazon Aluminium Company
OAS	Organisation of American States
PCB	Partido Comunista Brasileiro (Brazilian Communist Party)
PC do B	Partido Comunista do Brasil (Communist Party of Brazil)
PCN	Projeto Calha Norte (Calha Norte Project)
PDAM	Plano do Desenvolvimento da Amazônia (Development Plan for Amazonia)
PDS	Partido Democrático Social

	(Social Democratic Party)
PGC	Programa Grande Carajás (Greater Carajás Programme)
PGCA	Programa Grande Carajás Agrícola (Greater Carajás Agricultural Programme)
PIC	Projeto Integrado de Colonização (Integrated Colonisation Project)
PIN	Plano de Integração Nacional (Plan for National Integration)
PMDB	Partido do Movimento Democrático Brasileiro (Party of the Brazilian Democratic Movement)
PND	Plano Nacional de Desenvolvimento (National Development Plan)
PNDR	Plano Nacional de Desenvolvimento Rural (National Plan for Rural Development)
PNRA	Plano Nacional de Reforma Agrária (National Plan for Agrarian Reform)
POLAMAZONIA	Programa de Polos Agropecuários e Agrominerais da Amazônia (Programme of Agro-Livestock and Agro- Mineral Poles for Amazonia)
PROALCOOL	Programa Nacional do Álcool (National Alcohol Programme)
PRODIAT	Projeto de Desenvolvimento Integrado da Bacia do Araguaia-Tocantins (Integrated Development Programme for the Araguaia-Tocantins River Bain)
PROTERRA	Programa de Redistribuição de Terras e Estímulos à Agroindústria do Norte e Nordeste (Programme of Land Redistribution and Stimuli to Agro-Industry in the North and North-East)
PROVARZEAS	Programa Nacional de Aproveitamento Racional de Várzeas Irrigadas

	(National Programme for the Rational Utilisaton of Irrigated Valleys)
PT	Partido dos Trabalhadores (Workers' Party)
RIMA	Relatório de Impacto Ambiental (Environmental Impact Report)
SBPC	Sociedade Brasileira para o Progresso da Ciência (Brazilian Society for the Progress of Science)
SEMA	Secretaria Especial do Meio-Ambiente (Special Secretariat for the Environment)
SEPLAN	Secretaria de Planejamento da Presidência da República (Planning Secretariat of the Presidency of the Republic)
SNCR	Sistema Nacional de Crédito Rural (National System of Rural Credit)
SNI	Serviço Nacional de Informação (National Intelligence Service)
SPDDH	Sociedade Paraense Para a Defesa dos Direitos Humanos (Pará Society for the Defence of Human Rights)
SPVEA	Superintendência do Plano de Valorização da Amazônia (Superintendency for the Economic Valorisation of Amazonia)
STR	Sindicato dos Trabalhadores Rurais (Rural Workers' Union)
SUDAM	Superintendência do Desenvolvimento da Amazônia (Superintendency for the Development of Amazonia)
SUDENE	Superintendência do Desenvolvimento do Nordeste (Superintendency for the Development of the North-East)

SUMEI	Superintendência do Meio-Ambiente (Superintendency for the Environment)
SURALCO	Surinam Aluminium Company
TDA	Título de Dívida Agrária (Agarian Debt Bond)
UDR	União Democrática Ruralista (Farmers' Democratic Movement)
UNEP	United Nations Environment Programme
UNI	União das Nações Indígenas (Union of Indigenous Peoples)
USAID	United States Agency for International Development

Preface

Tropical rainforests present a major opportunity, and a major challenge, to development policy-makers. Their abundant natural resources and vast areas of largely unpopulated land have offered Third World governments an apparently easy route for tackling a range of social, economic, political and geopolitical problems. Showing little or no regard for longer-term consequences, many countries have embarked on rapid and poorly-planned programmes of wealth extraction and farmer resettlement with a view to maximising immediate advantage. Such strategies, usually pursued by a combination of domestic and foreign interests, are driven by motives which range from the simple generation of foreign exchange or supply of cheap raw materials, to the diffusion of land pressures and social conflicts in longer-settled regions. Brazil has been a major proponent of this approach and has sought to use its vast area of Amazonian rainforest, the largest in the world, for the purposes of economic development and national integration.

This book is about Brazil's most recent and most ambitious attempt to harness Amazonia's potential, the Greater Carajás Programme (*Programa Grande Carajás*–PGC). Officially inaugurated in 1980 as the most ambitious development programme ever devised for any area of tropical rainforest in the world, the PGC's area of jurisdiction covers most of eastern Amazonia, or about one-quarter of Brazil's Amazon Basin. The focus of the present study is an examination of the combined impact upon the people and the environment of the region which has resulted from the programme's huge and distinctive pattern of industrial, agricultural and infrastructural investments.

Although estimates of deforestation in Brazilian Amazonia vary, it is generally agreed that, overall, tree cover has remained relatively intact when compared with other areas of the globe. This is because, until fairly recently, the Amazon Basin was relatively isolated from the mainstream of Brazilian life, populated only by the remaining indigenous Amerindians, their descendants and a small number of new settlers on the fringes. The officially-sponsored, systematic occupation of the region by small farmers and larger commercial interests only started in the late 1950s, taking off after the coup of 1964 with the ambitious settlement policies of successive military administrations. Yet if Brazil has been something of a late starter in exploiting the potential of Amazonia, which covers no less than 40% of the country, it has been trying hard to make up for lost time. Over the past twenty-five years, under both military rule and, since 1985, under the civilian leadership of the 'New Republic', Brazilian governments have followed an aggressive strategy of integrating the region into the process of national development. Its perceived importance is illustrated by the recent words of President José Sarney (Brazil, 1986), 'Who has Amazonia need not fear the future'.

This process of State-backed incorporation has been undertaken through a variety of policies, which are outlined in the first chapter of this book. Chapter 2 goes on to describe the Carajás Programme in detail, including its genesis as a combination of pre-existing and new ventures, its major industrial, infrastructural, lumbering and agro-livestock components, funding sources, administrative structure and the official rationale behind the scheme. Chapters 3 and 4 offer a detailed examination of the social and environmental repercussions of official development policy for eastern Amazonia, concentrating on the Carajás region and the influence of this 'mega-project'. Perpetuating Brazil's *latifúndio*-biased model of frontier settlement (that is, a frontier development strategy heavily biased in favour of large estates, either individually or corporately owned), the PGC has, it is argued, severely exacerbated the region's emerging agrarian crisis; this is characterised by a rapid escalation in land conflict and rural violence, growing polarisation of landownership and landlessness, environmental destruction and localised food deficits. The following chapter considers how the affected populations, in particular peasant farmers and Amerindians, have responded to this growing threat to their livelihoods and, in some cases, their very existence. After examining the impact of countervailing pressures exerted through institutional channels such as political parties, trades unions, the Catholic Church and non-government organisations (at national and international levels), attention is focused on the nature and scope of more spontaneous forms of protest such as armed resistance, estate occupations and other demonstrations of popular opposition to both land concentration and the frequently hostile official policies which exacerbate this process.

Finally, Chapter 6 looks at some of the implications of the Carajás Programme for the future development of eastern Amazonia. It briefly summarises the major impacts of the PGC and suggests that, despite their destabilising influence on local rural populations, the State, as the major formulator of development policy in the region, not only has a responsibility towards the poor but is, indeed, under increasing pressure, principally from small farmers themselves, to take greater account of their interests. The Amazonian peasantry, it is suggested, will not disappear, but will remain an important economic and political force in the forseeable future of Amazonia which policy-makers would be extremely short-sighted to ignore. Sustainable, peasant-based agriculture, extractivism and other activities, while problematic are, nonetheless, feasible development options. Although so far largely ignored by development policy-makers, they could help to guarantee a more secure living from the land for those groups currently under threat. The most crucial challenge facing the victims of official development policy in eastern Amazonia, as well as all those involved in its formulation is, therefore, how to ensure that a much wider section of Brazilian society actually benefits from the transformation currently under way.

Anthony Hall
London, 1988

1

The development of Brazilian Amazonia

The Treaty of Tordesillas (1494) first established Portuguese sovereignty over a large part of what eventually became Brazilian national territory. Penetration of the Amazon Basin, however, began only in 1616 with the building of the *Forte do Presépio* on the river estuary, around which grew the city of Belém, to guard against British, French and Dutch incursions. In 1637 Philip IV of Castile granted Portugal sovereignty over the Lower Amazon. Subsequent expeditions up the rivers Negro, Solimões, Tapajós, Tocantins and Madeira by explorers such as Pedro Teixeira and Antonio Raposo Tavares gradually pushed the effective boundary further westwards, as forts were built at strategic points such as Manaus, Óbidos and Santarém. Luso-Brazilian 'unofficial' methods of colonising Amazonia proved very effective and were eventually legitimised in the Treaty of Madrid (1750) which defined the boundaries of Brazilian Amazonia much as they are today (Bruno, 1967: Tambs, 1974). In fact the concept of actual possession (*uti possidetis de facto*) rather than legal title (*uti possidetis de jure*), which formed the historical basis for land occupation, is still the principal method of occupying frontier lands in the region.

In the eighteenth century the state of Pará was an important source of forest products for export such as drugs, timber, cocoa, vanilla, cinnamon, cloves and aromatic resins which were harvested with the aid of forced indian labour. In addition to extractive activities, some cultivation of sugar-cane, coffee, cotton and tobacco as well as some cattle-raising on Marajó Island took place (Furtado, 1968; Reis, 1974). However, the first significant penetration of Amazonia for economic purposes came with the nineteenth-century rubber industry, whose heyday lasted from 1870s until 1912. *Hevea Brasil-*

iensis is native to Amazonia and had been used by native indians for waterproofing. A significant industrial demand for latex arose after Charles Goodyear discovered the vulcanisation process in 1839.

Demand shot up further following the invention of the pneumatic tyre in 1888, the bicycle craze in the USA during the 1890s and the expansion of the automobile industry. The Emperor, Dom Pedro II, had opened the Amazon to international shipping in 1866, directly linking the region to the world economy. There was a rush for land accompanied by penetration of the Amazon headwaters where the best quality rubber trees could be found. This extended as far as Acre, which was annexed from Bolivia in 1903 and which, in 1899, supplied 60% of all the rubber produced in Amazonia. Lack of an adequate labour supply had imposed a limit on the expansion of rubbertapping and several abortive attempts were made to attract Japanese and European immigrants and even Confederate exiles following the end of the American Civil War (Melby, 1942). The problem was solved by nature which forced the migration in droves of semi-starved peasants from the arid interior or *sertão* of north-east Brazil, expelled from their lands by periodic droughts, particularly that of 1877–79, and transported by ship to Amazonia at government expense. Vast sums of money were made by rubber barons exploiting the cheap labour of rubber tappers or *seringueiros* attracted to Amazonia by the boom and subsequently kept in their place by a savage and merciless system of debt slavery known as *aviamento*. Brazilian rubber enjoyed a twenty-year boom period from 1890 to 1910. Magnificent private mansions and public buildings were constructed, including the US$2 million Manaus Opera House where Caruso performed, as well as a slightly less grandiose version in Belém. European imported goods were available to the wealthy as far up the Amazon as Iquitos in Peru. Such were the profits being made that in 1906 the revenue from rubber paid off 40% of Brazil's annual debt.

The botanist and failed planter (later Sir) Henry Wickham helped lay the foundation for the collapse of the Brazilian rubber boom when in 1876, attracted by the high price of the commodity on the world market, he smuggled out seeds and took them to Kew as the raw material for British plantations, initially in Ceylon and eventually in Malaya, Dutch Java and Sumatra (Melby, 1942; Dean, 1987). Rubber trading had always been speculative and prices erratic, subject to rapid rises and equally dramatic falls, whose warning signals went unheeded by traders and authorities alike. The Amazon industry's fate was sealed, however, by the steady increase in Asian production during the first decade of the century. Rubber production in the much more efficient Far Eastern plantations soon outstripped that of Amazonia and, in a general situation of oversupply, prices fell by two-thirds. 'Buildings were deserted, elaborate mansions were left vacant, parks and avenues were abandoned, and grass again grew in many streets' (Melby, 1942, p. 459). In 1912 the government of Hermes da Fonseca instituted the Rubber Support Plan, aimed principally at strengthening Brazil's position in the international rubber market. Having failed miserably, the plan was abolished in 1914 and Amazonia entered a thirty-year period of stagnation in which rubber production and exports continued to decline and the regional economy collapsed (Mahar, 1979). Whether due to social and economic factors or whether, as argued by Dean (1987), the decline was attributable to the spread of South American Leaf Blight (*Microcylus ulei*), Amazonia's rubber production never recovered its former position.

A second attempt to revive the flagging fortunes of Amazonia and the rubber industry occurred during the Second World War. In a famous speech in Manaus in 1940 President Getúlio Vargas indicated that the government was thinking about opening up and developing the Amazon Basin. He affirmed that, 'The Amazon, under the impact of our will and our labour, shall cease to be a simple chapter in the history of the world and, made equivalent to other great rivers, shall become a chapter in the history of civilisation...Everything which has been up to now done in Amazonas, whether in agriculture or extractive industry...must be transformed into rational exploitation' (quoted by Davis, 1977, pp. 21–2). From 1940 diplomatic links between Brazil and the USA were becoming stronger; the alliance was sealed by the entry of the United States into the War and the Washington Accords of 1942 in which Brazil agreed to supply the Allies with strategic raw materials such as rubber. A major effort was made to increase production, labelled the 'Battle for Rubber' (*A Batalha da Borracha*), and an administrative structure was set up around the Rubber Credit Bank (the *Banco de Crédito da Borracha* – BCB), a forerunner of the present regional development bank, BASA. The American-owned Rubber Reserve Company (later renamed the Rubber Development Corporation) established a US$5 million fund to stimulate production, while the Export–Import

Bank offered Brazil a US$100 million credit for general economic development (Davis, 1977; Mahar, 1979). Yet despite these efforts their impact on rubber production was fairly modest.

The only other significant accomplishment related to Amazonian development during the Vargas period was the setting up, in 1951, of the National Institute for Amazonian Research (INPA) in Manaus. Vargas had in fact alluded to such principles in his famous speech in Manaus in 1940 when he called for an international conference of countries such as the USA with an interest in 'collaborating with us in the development of Amazonia, where their capital and technical resources will find a secure and remunerative application' (quoted by Davis, 1977, p. 23). Although the conference never took place, the idea of international co-operation in the study and development of the region persisted and after the War the Brazilian delegation to the first general UNESCO conference suggested the setting up of an institute to promote these ends. Nationalist hostility to the proposal was so great within Brazil, however, that the idea of a UNESCO body controlled from outside by the UN was also quashed, but INPA was created soon after as a result of the associated technical and scientific debates.

The SPVEA, 1953–64

In recognition of the failure of past attempts to boost the rubber industry and the economy of Amazonia, Article 199 of the new Brazilian Constitution of 1946 provided for the establishment of a regional development programme and special fund to be financed through a 3% share of total tax revenues over a twenty-year period (Cardoso and Muller, 1977; Mahar, 1979). After a long delay, a law was passed in 1953 approving the creation of a regional development plan and a development agency in the form of the Superintendency for the Economic Valorisation of Amazonia (SPVEA), based in Belém. Linked directly to the Presidency of the Republic, the SPVEA was designed to stimulate 'extractive, agricultural, livestock, mineral and industrial activities' (Bonfim, 1958, p. 24). A heated debate ensued over the SPVEA's geographical area of jurisdiction. As a result of political pressures and possibly in order to conform to economic realities, this was changed from the 'classic Amazon' to the much expanded notion of 'Legal Amazonia', which is fully one-third larger than the traditional definition and covers an area of five million square kilometres, or 60% of Brazilian territory. The longer-term regional development goals of the SPVEA were to be achieved through a series of five-year plans, the first of which was published in 1955. First priority was given to agriculture in order to make the region self-sufficient in food and to increase production of raw materials for export and domestic consumption. This would be achieved through research, colonisation and production incentives. Second priority was given to improving river transport and port facilities and, thirdly, the region's health problems were highlighted (SPVEA, 1955; Bonfim, 1958).

Yet the agency encountered fundamental problems from the outset. Some common criticisms of the SPVEA are based rather too heavily on conventional excuses such as lack of managerial expertise and trained technicians (Batista, 1976). While these certainly were contributory factors to the ineffectual nature of the SPVEA, other more fundamental constraints need to be considered. As Mahar (1979) observes, for example, Congress was sceptical about the five-year plan and did not approve it, opting instead to finance development schemes on an annual basis, a procedure which was incompatible with the notion of longer-term planning. Neither did the SPVEA ever have effective control over allocation of its own funds, 85% of which were spent through contracts with other institutions. In addition, substantial budget cuts by Congress undermined project implementation; the SPVEA in fact received and spent only 60% of the budget allocated to the agency during 1955–59. Even then, much of the credit disbursed had gone into the extractive rubber sector and for short-term commercial operations rather than more social or developmental activities.

After ten years of operation in Amazonia the SPVEA's successes had been modest, to say the least. Apart from modernising port facilities and setting up some large industries, its major achievement was the construction of the 2,000-kilometre highway linking the city of Belém to the new capital, Brasília. Originally conceived in 1947 and finally mapped out in 1956, the dirt road was finished in 1960, officially inaugurated five years later, and paved by 1973. Supposedly inspired by pressure from Brazil's nascent automobile industry lobby rather than from a desire to settle the interior *per se*, it has been estimated that the highway attracted some 174,000 migrants during 1960–70, in a very disorderly and unplanned fashion (Martine, 1980), although others (e.g. Katzman, 1977) have suggested a much higher figure of up to 320,000 settlers. The Belém–Brasília was in fact the first of several major highways which now cross the Amazon Basin and which have facilitated the significant penetration and occupation of the region.

The move to develop Amazonia, 1964–70

The 1964 military takeover in Brazil marked a watershed in policy-making for Amazonia. Until then public initiatives to exploit the region's resources, culminating in the ill-fated five year plan of the SPVEA, had been piecemeal, narrowly focused and inconclusive. Possibly because the military authorities were more sensitive to the geopolitical importance of integrating the Amazon Basin into the national economy than their civilian predecessors in government, a new and more aggressive occupation strategy soon became apparent. A speech by the first military president, Castello Branco, in 1965, stressed the need to promote greater efficiency in regional planning and to promote an expanded role for private enterprise in colonising the region. He spoke of widening the tax incentive scheme as 'a sure stimulus to businessmen from all over the country to reinvest their profits in Amazonia' (CNI, 1969, p. 33). In their turn, entrepreneurs saw for themselves a new dynamic role and promised to 'respond to this historic call . . . and repeat the pioneering feat of the conquering of the Western USA during the first decades of the last century' (CNI, 1969, p. 34). A new five-member committee was set up by presidential decree whose recommendations led to the formulation, in 1966, of what became known as 'Operation Amazonia'.

To replace the discredited SPVEA a new agency was created that same year within the Ministry of the Interior, the Superintendency for the Development of Amazonia (SUDAM), modelled along the lines of its sister organisation set up in 1959 for the North-East, SUDENE. The policy of fiscal incentives, originally introduced in 1963 to attract private capital, was significantly widened in 1966, through Law 5174, to grant 50% exemption from income tax liabilities until 1982 for investors into agriculture, livestock, industry and basic services such as education, transport, colonisation, tourism and public health; this increased to 100% exemption for those who put their money into Amazonian projects, either new ones or existing schemes, by 1974 (Cardoso and Muller, 1977). For the first time subsidised credit was given for land acquisition on a substantial

scale, setting a precedent whose social and environmental consequences have been felt to the present day. In addition, foreign
corporations became eligible for these benefits, although their participation in agricultural investment in Amazonia has in fact been
relatively small. The incentive scheme was to be funded through the
new regional development bank, which still exists, the Bank of
Amazonia (BASA). A special new credit fund was created for
investment into private firms and for research relevant to Amazonia,
while further income-tax credits and import/export tax exemptions
were also granted by SUDAM. Multilateral aid money was also
made available for agricultural development through the Inter-
American Development Bank.

'Paulista' businessmen from the South had been investing their
own capital in Amazonian cattle ranches since the 1950s; two huge
estates of 400,000 and 700,000 hectares were set up in 1957, while
the 600,000-hectare Suiá-Missú ranch set up by Ometto and Ariosto
da Riva, subsequently the recipient of millions of dollars of subsidised funding and later sold to the Italian company Liquigas, was
in fact established in 1961 (Pompermayer, 1979). However, the
generous terms granted to private investors in Amazonia led to
a dramatic rise in the number of livestock projects approved by
SUDAM, jumping from only four in 1966 to a total of 162 by 1969,
enjoying tax rebates of over £75 million (Branford and Glock, 1985).
This in fact reflected the global emphasis being given at the time by
multilateral bodies such as the World Bank and the Inter-American
Development Bank to investment in the Third World livestock
sector; these two organisations alone made loans of US$1·3 billion
for cattle-rearing in the 1960s and 1970s.

Cattle ranching was given much publicity as the most profitable
business activity in Amazonia and the president of BASA proclaimed,
in 1969, that 'Ranching... is an activity that has all the necessary
conditions to be transformed into a dynamic sector of the northern
economy' (quoted by Hecht, 1985, p. 671). Development took place
in an uncoordinated and seemingly unplanned fashion, with SUDAM
approving virtually every project put before it. Gestures were made
towards comprehensive planning for Amazonia. In fact SUDAM's
first regional plan (1968) called for immediate government action
in Amazonia through massive public investment, with preferential
treatment for the neglected western portion of the Basin (Amazonas,
Acre, Rondonia and Roraima). Yet this first plan was never approved

by the federal government and, although the Manaus Free Trade Zone was set up in 1967 in an effort to stimulate growth in the western portion of the Amazon Basin, until the 1970s development initiatives in the region were undertaken mainly by the private sector with State backing.

An early project was the Jarí scheme, set up in 1967 by the American billionaire, Daniel K. Ludwig. Occupying some 3·6 million hectares of land near the mouth of the River Amazon it had, by the early 1980s, built up a diverse range of operations: 100,000 hectares of two fast-growing foreign varieties of tree (*Gmelina Arborea* from Africa and *Pinus Carybea* from Honduras); a massive cellulose plant floated from Japan; timber production for plywood and furniture; one of the largest high-yielding rice paddies in the world, covering 12,000 hectares; soybean, sugar-cane, castor-oil and palm-oil plantations; and a livestock project with 50,000 head. It also included a company town with a 40,000 workforce. Ludwig put his total investment in Jarí at US$600 million (Pinto, 1986c; The Economist, 27.9.80). However, owing to a combination of economic setbacks attributed to substantial shortfalls in rice and timber production due to the limitations imposed by the fragile environment, together with growing public concern over the secretive nature of Ludwig's operations, Jarí was eventually purchased in 1982 by a consortium of twenty-two Brazilian businessmen led by A. T. Azevedo Antunes (Rocha, 1982). Some implications of Jarí's experience for Carajás reforestation potential are explored in Chapter 4.

In general terms 'Operation Amazonia' was geared towards establishing 'development poles' such as Manaus, encouraging immigration and the formation of self-supporting groups, providing incentives to private investment, encouraging infrastructural development and research into resource potential. Yet these apparently disparate measures already fell within a broader economic and geopolitical strategy of Amazonian development. Economically speaking, it implied the promotion of an import-substitution industrialisation model funded by both domestic capital from the Centre-South as well as foreign funds. To traditional economists and regional planners the pattern of Amazonian occupation at this time seemed chaotic, unplanned and unable to fulfil its stated objectives when judged by conventional criteria.

However, other observers question such a politically neutral analysis and view the policy established by Operation Amazonia as a deliberate one of reserving land for exploitation by commercial interests at the expense of the mass of land-hungry Brazilian farmers, who started flocking to the region during the 1960s. Ianni describes the policy as one of active official 'blocking, suppressing or controlling spontaneous colonisation, that is, *de facto* agrarian reform, in order to serve the interests of businessmen' (1979a, p. 235). Mahar also criticises heavily subsidised cattle ranching which 'would effectively pre-empt land that could be forseeably utilised for settling new migrants (1979, p. 25). In a similar vein, Branford and Glock see 'Operation Amazonia' essentially as a process of 'pre-emptive occupation, that is, a holding operation by which it could keep out peasant families and reserve the land for capitalist farming' (1985, p. 23). This theme will be taken up again in the final chapter in a discussion of the theoretical context of Amazonian development policy. A basic point, however, is that by adopting a blatantly *latifúndio*-biased strategy during the 1960s, which subsidised the gradual monopolisation of increasingly large areas of tropical rainforest for commerical and speculative exploitation, the Brazilian State has made violent rural conflict an inevitable feature of life in the Amazon Basin.

In an era when neighbouring countries such as Peru, Venezuela and Bolivia had made advanced plans to occupy and develop their own Amazonian rainforest areas, the geopolitical significance of 'Operation Amazonia' becomes apparent in terms of securing Brazilian territorial sovereignty. Even the construction of Brasília in its central location was seen as part of the same strategy (Tambs, 1974), as was the later building of roads such as the Trans-Amazon highway and the *Perimetral Norte*. Such international confrontation along the rim of the Amazon Basin is viewed somewhat anachronistically by Tambs, for example, as 'a continuation of the struggle between Portugal and Castile for pre-eminence in South America' (1974, p. 79). Brazilian nationalist fears over the intentions of suspected predatory foreign interests towards Amazonia had, however, already been emphatically expressed by Reis, originally in 1968, in a well-known and much-quoted book which condemned 'international greed'; significantly, the work was re-issued years later (Reis, 1982). Yet even before the 1964 coup military officers shared a conviction that permanent occupation of national territory was a top priority, and such consolidation was endorsed by the major military college, the *Escola Superior de Guerra*, at the time as a 'Permanent National

Objective' (Branford and Glock, 1985, p. 43). Economic, commerical and geopolitical motives thus played important complementary roles in Amazonian occupation and development from an early stage, and have continued to do so.

National integration: integrar para não entregar, 1970–74

The year 1970 saw the dawn of a new era in Amazonian occupation characterised by a major road-building programme, directed colonisation for small farmers, and concern for tapping natural resources, in addition to the continuation of subsidies to cattle ranchers. A host of reasons have been cited by many authors for this upsurge in federal activity in Amazonia, ranging from the humanitarian to the economic and geopolitical. If popular accounts are to be believed, it was apparently sparked off by forces outside the region, in the North-East, where in 1970 yet another drought had catastrophic economic and social consequences. The government in Brasília intervened with emergency assistance, employing 500,000 men on 112 'work fronts' building roads, which made some 20% of the entire north-eastern population dependent on drought relief (Hall, 1978a). In a dramatic and emotional speech to SUDENE in June of that year, after visiting drought-stricken areas, President Médici affirmed, 'I want to say to the people of the North-East that I do not promise you anything. I do not promise miracles or transformations, nor money nor favours, nor do I solicit sacrifices or votes, nor organisation of charity. I only say that everything has to begin to change' (Médici, 1970).

Nine days later the Plan for National Integration (PIN) was launched by Decree-Law 1106 which would, with a 30% share of fiscal incentive funds, finance a 5,000-kilometre Trans-Amazon highway (BR 230) linking the North-East and Amazonia. The PIN fund provided some US$100 million for the highway, and USAID even donated US$10 million in the form of PL-480 wheat to be sold to finance the scheme (Smith, 1982, p. 14). This whole exercise encouraged the appealing if simplistic notion that the problems of the North-East could be largely resolved by exporting its 'surplus' labour to the rainforest frontier; in the catchphrase of the day, this would 'unite men without land to land without men'. PIN also envisaged a north-south highway linking the *Transamazônica* with the Centre-South, from Santarém to Cuiabá (BR 165), as well as colonisation projects and irrigation in the North-East itself.

The complementarity of Amazonian and north-eastern development was stressed by the First National Development Plan, PND I (Brazil, 1971) and by the Amazon Development Plan – PDAM (SUDAM, 1971). Also stressed was the importance of developing links with the Centre-South not only to provide easy access to Amazonia's raw materials but also to open up new markets for southern goods (Mahar, 1979). In 1971, PIN was complemented by the so-called Land Redistribution Programme (PROTERRA). While PROTERRA did envisage the redistribution of unutilised lands, its major objective seems to have been that of promoting agroindustry and creating a new class of 'modern' small and medium farmers to replace subsistence production. A revitalised National Institute for Colonisation and Agrarian Reform (INCRA) was given the task of settling thousands of immigrants along the Trans-Amazon and Cuiabá–Santarém highways. In 1972 additional funds were provided for a 2,700-kilometre northern perimeter road (the *Perimetral Norte*, BR 210) along the northern bank of the River Amazon. PIN/PROTERRA was seen as an attempt by the government to redirect development strategy in Amazonia and the North-East away from import-substitution industrialisation and towards rural development (Mahar, 1979).

This emphasis on roadbuilding, colonisation and agribusiness went hand in hand with a major expansion of the road network by a federal government which was anxious to occupy the region as quickly as possible. It also implied something of a preoccupation with social issues and, in what appeared to be a significant policy change at the time, seemed to accord a much higher priority to small farmer interests than had been evident previously. Work on the Trans-Amazon highway started in earnest, a mere three months after its official announcement. Strong protests were made by north-eastern politicians resentful of the transfer of federal funding from their region, as well as by environmentalists fearful of the ecological consequences, for no technical or economic feasibility studies had yet been undertaken (Mahar, 1979). Such haste and apparent short-sightedness seem less irrational, however, when viewed in terms of the varied military, commercial and political interests that would be conveniently served by this grandiose scheme, which captured the domestic and international imagination alike.

A major initial stimulus came from transport officials and their allies in the private road-building sector. There was intense federal pressure from the national roadworks department (DNER) and the

Ministries of Transport and Planning to expand the road network; regional politicians in Amazonia were, on the other hand, more concerned about improving river communications. As early as March 1969 the head of the DNER, Eliseu Resende, had written a newspaper article in the *Jornal do Brasil* calling for a Trans-Amazon highway as a vehicle for encouraging Amazonian settlement, an idea quickly sized upon by the Minister of Transport, Mário Andreazza, and by President Médici a year later following the north-eastern drought. Although military personnel and army engineers were used, most construction work was entrusted to private enterprise. Several major engineering companies won contracts to assist in building the Trans-Amazon, including Camargo Correa, Andrade Gutiérrez and Mendes Junior. In the case of Mendes Junior, according to Bourne (1978), the *Transamazônica* accounted for no less than 20% of its annual turnover in 1972.

Yet even if the road construction companies gained prestige and profited economically, Resende himself openly captured the essence of the *Transamazônica* when he stated that it was 'a political decision of the Brazilian government'. Delfim Neto spoke of federal intentions in Amazonia, describing PIN as 'the conquest of a new country within the Brazilian nation' (quotes from Bourne, 1978, pp. 73 and 278). Promoted by a glossy national propaganda campaign during 1970–71, the new highway and PIN symbolised, in a spectacular fashion, the concept of Brazilian national integration and economic progress, thus helping to diffuse internal political conflicts (Kleinpenning, 1975) and certainly diverting public attention away from the brutal political repression which was characteristic of the military regime throughout the 1970s. More specifically, it would allow the issue of land reform in the North-East and South to be bypassed. Amazonia would be offered up as a promising new land ready for occupation by a hard-pressed peasantry, which was being progressively expelled from its traditional homes not only by drought and demographic pressures but by agrarian stagnation and the advance of commercial farming for industrialised agricultural products such as soybean and sugar-cane. As Costa (1979) has noted, an additional advantage was that, by attracting north-eastern migrants to Amazonia, the pressure on urban resources and growth of shanty towns in the South would also be alleviated to some extent.

The armed forces' long-standing preoccupation with establishing a military presence on the Amazonian frontier continued to be important. Integration was seen as a precondition for national security; to 'integrate in order not to forfeit' (*integrar para não entregar*). The 'expansionist threat' presented by neighbouring countries who share the Amazon rainforest, whether real or imagined, had been a preoccupation for Brazilian governments since the early 1900s. But perhaps more importantly in this modern era was the need to strengthen regional integration among Amazonian countries and to increase bilateral trade, opening up new markets for Brazil's expanding industries. Geopolitical considerations also embraced problems much closer to home. Since 1972 eastern Amazonia had become the focus of military intervention against a band of sixty-nine Maoist guerrillas in the Araguaia region of southern Pará. Formed by refugees from repression of urban guerrilla activity in São Paulo after 1968, the movement was finally crushed in 1975 by three military campaigns which reputedly mobilised a total of 20,000 soldiers (Bourne, 1978; Dória *et al* 1978; Portela, 1979). Although the significance of the Araguaia conflict is often played down, it cannot be lightly dismissed. Official sensitivity on the subject is illustrated by the fact that, when an article on the guerrilla movement appeared in the *Estado de São Paulo* on 24 September 1972, six months after the army arrived in the region, rigid censorship was introduced and no further mention of the issue was allowed until 1976, when senator Jarbas Passarinho referred to it during a debate in the national Congress.

If plans for Amazonia's integration could satisfy not only Brazilian geopolitical and counter-insurgency interests, but also the desire of some planners to relieve the suffering of starving north-eastern peasants, then yet another simultaneous economic aim was to unlock the region's vast store of natural resources. The Carajás iron-ore deposits, discovered in 1967, as well as other reserves of cassiterite, gold and copper were already known. Ministers at the time constantly referred publicly to the possibility of discovering ever more minerals and portrayed Amazonia as a 'new Eldorado' (Cardoso and Muller, 1977, p. 171). The RADAM radar survey was started in 1970 to map 1·5 million square kilometres south of the River Amazon from 1972–74 using infra-red survey techniques. Although its results arrived too late to assist in the routing and building of the *Transamazônica*, it was the first systematic aerial survey of Amazonia's natural resources and went a long way towards confirming the vast mineral wealth in the subsoil as well as the extent of timber reserves and land available for livestock production, thus setting the stage for later commercial expansion in the region.

A major tool of frontier expansion and occupation during the early 1970s was directed colonisation for small farmers along the two major new highways, the Trans-Amazon and the Cuiabá–Santarém route. Until then colonisation had remained limited in scope and confined largely to the Belém–Brasília highway. Once again, several objectives appeared to be served simultaneously. If President Médici had created the impression that official colonisation in Amazonia was essentially a humanitarian response to a natural calamity (the north-eastern drought), the military saw it in geopolitical terms of filling Amazonia's vast empty spaces with Brazilian settlers. The State also believed that the schemes would produce a surplus of staple foods such as beans and rice to compensate for the loss of production as southern Brazil was increasingly devoted to soybean production for export. In addition, as already mentioned above, the pressure for agrarian reform arising from growing land concentration in longer-settled regions could be relieved.

A first decree in 1971 expropriated 64,000 square kilometres of land along the *Transamazônica* between Altamira and Itaituba, which were to be the sites of the first colonisation projects. A further law (1.164) in the same year expropriated all lands within one hundred kilometres of existing or planned federal highways in Amazonia in an attempt to prevent land speculation, declaring them 'indispensable to national security and development' (Ianni, 1979b, p. 39). Virtually overnight INCRA, created in 1970 by merging three smaller agencies, was thus made responsible for distributing 2·2 million square kilometres of Amazonian territory, an area ten times the size of the UK (Smith, 1982). The first 1,200-kilometre stretch of the 5,400-kilometre Trans-Amazon highway between Estreito and Itaituba was finished in 1972, followed by a further 1,000 kilometres in 1974 and the Cuiabá–Santarém road in 1976 (Mahar, 1979). In order to attract settlers, not just from the North-East but also from southern Brazil, the government undertook a massive TV, radio and press campaign to transform the popular image of Amazonia from that of an essentially hostile region to one full of opportunities for enterprising individuals. Chartered jets and air force transport planes were used to ferry migrants to the colonisation schemes at Altamira, Itaituba and Marabá. Many arrived independently by bus or lorry at considerable personal sacrifice, illustrating the degree of hope placed by the land-hungry in this new government initiative.

The incentives offered to potential migrants were indeed considerable and this, together with the mounting problems faced by small farmers back home, helps to explain the enthusiastic initial response. Land was allocated to INCRA-approved families in 100-hectare plots at the heavily subsidised price of US$750, payable over twenty years at 7% interest annually and with a four-year grace period. A monthly subsistence allowance, agricultural production credit and housing were all made available on the same generous terms (Kleinpenning, 1975; Smith, 1982). Settlers would live in a series of communities designed by INCRA: the *agrovila* is a small village for up to seventy families placed at ten-kilometre intervals along the main highway and side-roads, designed to provide a medical post, school and government general store as well as offices for INCRA and the extension service, EMATER; the *agrópolis* is a small town for up to 600 families built every twenty kilometres as a intermediate administrative centre, provided with a small hospital and other services; finally, the *rurópoli*, comprising from eight to twelve agropoles with up to 20,000 people, were to be the main administrative and commercial centres, with facilities such as banks, a hospital, an airport, hotels and restaurants (Camargo, 1973).

The strength of official support for directed colonisation along the *Transamazônica* may be gauged by the huge estimated cost to the government of US$2·3 billion at 1984 values (Rich, 1985). Yet the scheme's disappointing results are well known. By 1974 less than 6% of the goal of 100,000 families had been accommodated (5,717 families), this figure increasing to under 8% or 7,647 households by 1978 (Smith, 1982; Fearnside 1984a). INCRA made no attempt to colonise the more westerly Itaituba–Humaitá stretch of the highway, although it was completed by early 1974. Only twenty-seven of one hundred or more planned *agrovilas* and three of the projected *agrópoli* were built. Of these three none functioned properly and only one *rurópolis* prospered, the Vila Presidente Médici, due to its prime location at the junction of the Trans-Amazon and Cuiabá–Santarém highways (Smith, 1982). Had the official targets been reached, directed colonisation may have had an impact in terms of absorbing the drought-vulnerable north-easterners, highlighted by President Médici as the scheme's major beneficiaries. As events turned out, not only was there a vast discrepancy between official and actual targets, but less than half (3,125 families) of those settled were from the North-East. Smith calculated (1982, p. 24) that the Trans-Amazon absorbed a total of 23,000 directed and spontaneous migrants, or under 3% of the North-East's population increase during this period. It is also worth noting that irrigation projects in the North-East itself, which were also funded by PIN after 1971 with the aim of absorbing the 'excess' rural population and creating rural employment, had similarly negative results (Hall, 1978a, 1978b, 1981).

Various reasons have been advanced to explain the 'failure' of official colonisation policy along the *Transmazônica* highway. These range from the purely technical or administrative, to the socio-cultural and political. All of them probably contain an element of truth. Initial criticisms were directed either at the executing agency, INCRA, or the intended beneficiaries themselves. There can be little doubt that INCRA was poorly equipped to tackle the vast influx of aspiring colonists in the early stages. The administration could not process the large number of applications quickly enough, while bureaucratic delays prevented newly recruited colonists from preparing their fields in time, disrupting the agricultural calendar and causing disillusionment (Smith, 1982). Furthermore, as has been well documented by many researchers, the basic infrastructural, educational, health, credit, extension and other services promised to the colonists in the planned settlements, were simply not forthcoming, and land on its own was not enough to secure a livelihood in such difficult circumstances (Kleinpenning, 1975; Bourne, 1978; Martine, 1980; Moran, 1981; Smith, 1982).

A combination of over-centralised planning and rigid management structures resulted in many basic errors being committed by INCRA and other government bodies (Bunker, 1985; Moran, 1989); the construction of roads which were impassable in the rainy season, the provision of fast-growing seed varieties which matured at the wettest time of the year in Amazonia, the allocation to farmers of infertile areas, and rigid credit mechanisms which were not adapted to farmers' needs in the agricultural calendar. Delays by INCRA in providing small farmers with land titles, essential for obtaining subsidised credit, which was being monopolised by larger commercial producers, fuelled colonists' mistrust of government. As disillusionment set in, exacerbated by inadequate official support and increasing indebtedness, many sold their plots, capitalising on the already increasing land values. Fewer and fewer migrnts chose the

Transamazônica, opting instead either for the newer frontier zones of Rondônia and Acre or for spontaneous forms of colonisation locally. As Martine has pointed out (1980), for every official colonist there were four or five who set themselves up with no government assistance.

The situation for settlers on the Trans-Amazon highway has not changed much since the 1970s and observers highlight the continued absence of official support for small farmers. Contemporary accounts of life on the *Transamazônica* abound with familiar themes (*Jornal do Brasil*, 24.5.87): the road itself is frequently impassable, especially in the rainy season, making crop marketing almost impossible, while there are few essential services such as domestic electricity supplies, schools and health clinics. High rates of diseases such as malaria, leichmaniasis, Hansen's disease (leprosy) and parasitic infections, together with constant threats from land-grabbers and INCRA's failure to provide land titles, contribute towards a pronounced exodus of poor cultivators to the burgeoning squatter settlements of Amazonia's expanding local towns and cities.

Although INCRA was subjected to much criticism during the early 1970s, the initial reaction was to 'blame the victims' (Wood and Schmink, 1978) by suggesting that the colonists themselves were primarily responsible for the débâcle and were unprepared for life in Amazonia. Over half of the settlers, it is true, were from outside the region and these optimistic migrants tended to be ignorant of local conditions and agricultural practices (Kleinpenning, 1975; Moran, 1983a). The 'poor and ignorant peasants' were surely an easy target for propagandists anxious to discredit the policy of directed settlement. Yet such accusations conveniently forgot the omissive and irresponsible role of government planning or, more appropriately, the lack of it, in this whole exercise. The high priority accorded to short-term economic and political as well as strategic goals in development policy-making for Amazonia after 1964 and, more particularly, after 1971, meant that planners went ahead with their ambitious proposals without carrying out a proper appraisal. Data from belated feasibility studies were made available too late to affect settlement policy, as a consequence of which much time and money was wasted resettling farmers on poor, unproductive soils.

If officials had taken the trouble to assess the region's agricultural potential in a rational manner, they would have discovered that Amazonia was not quite as propitious for directed colonisation as had been imagined. While there is tremendous scope for small-farmer development on Amazonia's relatively acidic, patchy upland soils in spite of the fragile ecological balance, as shown in Chapter 6, the process is not quite as straightforward as was at first imagined. Without the use of carefully adapted agroforestry techniques and the application of large quantities of expensive fertiliser, long-term cultivation of neither permanent commercial varieties nor short-cycle subsistence crops is possible without causing severe environmental damage through deforestation and soil exhaustion. The Itaituba colonisation project, for example, was severely hampered by such poor soils while the more fertile alfisols (*terra roxa*) of Altamira, itself a region of almost uniquely fertile terrain in Amazonia, were of highly variable quality and gave differential results to farmers. The mass transfer to Amazonia of inappropriate farming systems, by small and large farmers alike, combined with the failure of official research and extension agencies either to direct colonists onto fertile soils or to study and incorporate indigenous techniques for the benefit of colonists (Moran, 1981, 1982, 1983a) has resulted in a mutually reinforcing pattern of declining yields and ecological damage.

Agribusiness reaffirmed, 1975–81

Yet although problems of a technical and administrative nature undoubtedly help to explain this poor performance, they do not provide anything like a total picture or suggest why the government chose, in 1974, to abandon its policy of State-directed colonisation in favour of private enterprise. An increasingly large body of research (discussed in Chapter 6) has shown that properly selected and experienced farmers, given adequate official support can, despite the numerous adaptation problems, achieve increasing yields and secure a stable livelihood in Amazonia. An answer to this question must, therefore, be sought in terms of the political interests that were being served by existing Amazon settlement policies. From the early 1970s strong pressure was exerted by certain State sectors operating in alliance with business interests to alter development priorities in favour of big business. On the State side the Minister of Planning, Reis Veloso, the Bank of Amazonia (BASA) and SUDAM were firmly in favour of such a change. Private enterprise was represented by the São Paulo-based Association of Amazon Businessmen (AEA), which was set up in 1968 as a pressure group for southern industrial interests lobbying for subsidised funding for their new cattle-ranching ventures on the frontier.

The AEA exerted a strong influence on official policy-making for the region and the pressure it applied was crucial in bringing about the renewed emphasis on ranching, at the expense of small farmers (Pompermayer, 1984). The Ministry of Planning, in association with BASA, organised several major tours to Amazonia for southern businessmen, who were encouraged to invest in livestock and private colonisation projects on the grounds that only large companies 'can take rational advantage of the Amazon's huge potential'. During such a trip in 1973 for twenty of Brazil's leading businessmen, including the head of Volkswagen do Brasil (Wolfgang Sauer) and of BRADESCO (Amador Aguiar), civil servants defended the role of private enterprise. Planning Minister Reis Veloso criticised the 'predatory occupation' of small farmers and called upon large firms 'to assume the task of developing the region'. The Minister of the Interior, General José Costa Cavalcanti endorsed these ideas, claiming that, 'The future of the Amazon lies in the hands of businessmen, whether Brazilian or foreign, for Brazil has lost its fear of foreign capital' (quotes from Branford and Glock, 1985, pp. 70–1).

A marked division of opinion became apparent at this time between INCRA (Ministry of Agriculture) and its 'social colonisation' policy on the one hand and, on the other, SUDAM (Ministry of the Interior) which supported private enterprise as represented by the AEA. Towards the end of the Médici government José Francisco Moura Cavalcanti, the new Minister of Agriculture and former director of INCRA, and Walter Costa Porto, the new head of INCRA, attempted to defend the policy of directed colonisation in terms of defusing unrest and using Amazonia as an 'escape valve' for social pressures building up in other areas of Brazil (Foweraker, 1981; Branford and Glock, 1985). But SUDAM continued its attacks on INCRA policy and, in 1973, its recently appointed superintendent, Colonel Câmara Sena, described Amazonia as, 'a region made for cattle-rearing, with excellent natural pastures and plenty of space for the expansion of this sector which, for this reason, will form the mainstay of its economic integration' (quoted by Cardoso and Muller, 1977, p. 158). Although this renewed emphasis on livestock as the answer to Amazonia's development problems was rationalised on technical grounds such as 'economies of scale', in fact much pressure was exerted on SUDAM through the AEA by businessmen anxious to gain access to generous fiscal incentives and subsidised credit (Pompermayer, 1984; Bunker, 1985). As early as December 1972 INCRA had started to sell off 3,000-hectare plots to medium-sized farmers near Marabá (250,000 ha) and in Rondônia (500,000 ha), prompting the Minister of Agriculture, Cirne Lima, to resign in protest at interference with official colonisation projects (Cardoso and Muller, 1977; Bunker, 1985). The oil price rise after 1973 also indicated a much larger Brazilian foreign debt in future and generated further pressure for a policy switch in favour of foreign exchange-earning production in Amazonia.

This debate was resolved by the coming to power of the Geisel government in 1974, whose Second National Development Plan (PND II, 1975–79) based the future development of Amazonia on extending transport and communications, on expanding export-oriented activities such as beef, timber and minerals, and on the geographical concentration of investments in specific areas of the region. This last proposal was formalised in the POLAMAZONIA programme of 1974 (SUDAM 1976a), based on selective invest-ment in fifteen major 'growth poles', of which Carajás was one. The Second Amazonian Development Plan (PDA II) stressed national economic priorities and the role of Amazonia in generating foreign exchange through the export of those natural resources in which Brazil enjoys a 'comparative advantage'. Pursuing the by now familar theme of condemning outright the allegedly negative impact of small farmers in Amazonia, SUDAM emphasised large-scale, export-oriented corporate enterprises: mining would receive 34% of funding, modern agriculture and livestock 31% and industry 21% (SUDAM 1976b).

The sale to large farmers of INCRA lands destined originally for poorer migrants, a reversal so vehemently opposed by Moura Cavalcanti, was now in full swing. Cavalcanti himself was replaced as Minister of Agriculture by Alysson Paulinelli following the change of government in 1974. Paulinelli was 'a fanatical defender of capitalist farming' who opposed the allocation of frontier lands to small culti-vators (Branford and Glock, 1985, p. 72). Under new direction, between 1975–79 INCRA sold off a total of 1.7 million hectares in plots of 500 to 3,000 hectares, or twice the amount distributed to smallholders up to 1974 (Cardoso and Muller, 1977; Bourne, 1978; Fearnside, 1984a). Through the 'Voice of Brazil' national radio network the government, in May 1974, announced its goal of building a 'solid agribusiness sector' as 'the only type of farming which can produce an agile response to the need to increase national production of foodstuffs' (cited by Branford and Glock, 1985, p. 73). This sentiment was echoed by a representative of Swift-Armour who noted that the world food shortage could be alleviated in Amazonia, which was 'destined to be the great meat-exporting centre of the world' (Anderson, 1972, p. 63).

Such enthusiasm for cattle ranching during the early 1970s could lead to the mistaken impression being given that INCRA's 'social colonisation' phase had represented a major departure from previous Amazonian development strategy and that the task now facing government was to bring about a sudden reversal in favour once again of commercial interests. While there is no doubt that PDN II and POLAMAZONIA did represent a more systematic and larger-scale drive to encourage private enterprise in the Amazon Basin, it merely re-emphasised the role of private capital which had always enjoyed top priority, even during the early 1970s. 'Social colonisation' had been at best, perhaps, a temporary hiccup in the major thrust of frontier integration and economic development policy. Even during the Médici government moves were afoot by SUDAM technocrats, under the new direction of Colonel Câmara Sena, to establish a new and more aggressive Amazonian development policy in order to maximise the region's economic contribution to national progress. In 1973 the Minister of Planning, Reis Veloso, had condemned directed colonisation as leading to 'predatory occupation'. A confidential report prepared by SUDAM called 'Studies for the Amazon Development Plan', which laid the basis for PDA II under Geisel, scorned INCRA's resettlement schemes and small farmers in general as unsuited for agricultural activities in Amazonia, accusing them of being the main agents of environmental destruction and a drain on government resources.

SUDAM data show not only how capitalist farming had always been the major beneficiary of official support but also how resources were more selectively concentrated in fewer hands after 1974. From 1970–74, the period of so-called 'social colonisation', 169 cattle projects were approved with tax rebates of £152 million, an average of just under £1 million per project. This compares with twenty-seven projects approved during the 'commercial' 1975–79 period enjoying rebates totalling £212 million, an average of £7·85 million per project. Investment for the two phases is comparable, the major difference being the concentration of funds in a few larger projects in the later period. The average size of cattle ranch approved by SUDAM stood at almost 19,000 hectares and later on the agency refused on consider schemes with less than 25,000 hectares (Cardoso and Muller, 1977). Of the £444 million authorised by SUDAM by 1978, some 10% was concentrated in four large projects: the 678,000-hectare Suiá-Missú ranch set up by the Ometto family from São Paulo and later sold to Liquigas of Italy (£19·7 million); Campo Alegre, owned by the São Paulo construction company, Cetenco (£7·1 million); Codeara, with 600,000 hectares, which belongs to the National Credit Bank or BCN (£8·1 million); and Vale do Rio Cristalino, owned by Volkswagen (£12·4 million), covering 140,000 hectares (Cardoso and Muller, 1977; Branford and Glock, 1985). Many industrial groups, both national and foreign, own land in Amazonia including Georgia Pacific (500,000 ha), Toyomenka of Japan (300,000 ha), Bruynzeel (500,000 ha), Anderson Clayton, Goodyear and Swift Armour amongst others,although the importance of foreign capital in this context should not be exaggerated. By the mid-1980s, SUDAM had approved 469 ranching enterprises which benefited from fiscal incentives, in nominal values, of some US$565 million (Hecht *et al*, 1988b), although this figure could be more than doubled if adjusted to current values. In addition, other concessions have allowed the generation of high institutional rents to corporate landowners.

The World Bank loaned US$6 million to Brazil in 1974 for cattle-raising to boost exports of processed meat, in line with its policy during the early 1970s of encouraging investment in seemingly profitable, large-scale cattle ranches during a period of high beef prices. Brazil has in fact been the Bank's fourth largest Latin American recipient of livestock loans after Mexico, Colombia and Paraguay, with some US$150 million going to Bank-assisted cattle projects (at constant 1980 prices) by 1983. After 1974, however, Bank lending for large-scale commercial livestock diminished for several reasons, including a substantial drop in world beef prices, a switch in Bank policy towards 'poverty-targeted', integrated rural development programmes and internal reorganisation within the institution itself (Jarvis, 1986). During the early 1970s the Food and Agriculture Organisation (FAO) also funded the Suiá-Missú ranch to the tune of US$10 million. What has been happening in Brazilian

Amazonia parallels to some extent a similar process in Central America, where deforestation has taken place to meet US demand for beef as part of the 'hamburger connection' (Veiga, 1975; George, 1976; Caulfield, 1986). However, caution must be exercised in making comparisons with Central America, for Brazilian cattle production has never been as closely integrated into international markets and Amazonia itself remains, in fact, a net beef importer (Hecht, 1985).

Not only the Brazilian but also foreign governments encouraged their entrepreneurs to invest in agribusiness. From the mid-1960s, for example, the US, under Lyndon Johnson's presidency, extolled the virtues of exporting mechanised farming and cattle ranching to developing countries in order not just to boost company profits but ostensibly also to alleviate world hunger by increasing food supplies. This was, and still is, a popularly held misconception but one that received undue support from commercial, academic and aid circles; it was epitomised in the setting up of the Agribusiness Council in 1967, whose 1974 conference in London on 'Science and Agribusiness in the Seventies' warned of the Malthusian dangers of population growth outstripping food stocks as a major determinant of malnutrition; it placed its hopes squarely on private investment into industrialised farming as the solution (The Agribusiness Council, 1975). The Latin America Agribusiness Development Corporation (LAAD), comprising thirteen major US industrial and financial corporations, was set up with US$15 million capital in 1970 with help from the Bank of America to assist such enterprises (Ortiz Mena, 1975). Not only was cheap credit made available but US federal tax laws gave generous incentives to investors overseas. Baker (1973) notes, for example, that payment of corporate income taxes could be deferred until profit repatriation took place, and even then at lower domestic rates. The Western Hemisphere Trade Corporation also allowed companies investing overseas in the Americas to have their income taxed at 34% rather than the standard 48%. Such was the level of subsidy that, in 1972, Del Monte paid only 1.3% in taxes on earnings of US$820 million (Baker, 1973). As well as the generous tax and other incentives offered by the Brazilian government, US companies saw an added advantage in Amazonia's absence of a drought season (compared with other South American countries), which meant that livestock matured faster. A representative of the American company, Swift Armour, noted that the world's hunger crisis could be alleviated in the Amazon Basin which, he optimistically predicted, 'was destined to be the great meat-exporting center of the world' (Anderson, 1972, p. 63).

If the early 1970s were characterised by unqualified official optimism and financial support for cattle-raising as the most productive, profitable and environmentally-appropriate economic activity for Amazonia, by the end of the decade a certain amount of disillusionment had set in. About ten million hectares of Brazilian Amazonia have been converted from forest to pasture and estimates of how much has been severely degraded range from 20% to 50% (Hecht, 1985). Many studies have shown that the thin, relatively poor *terra firme* Amazonian soils, once exposed to the elements by extensive deforestation are, without large inputs of fertilisers, pesticides and herbicides, prone to rapidly declining fertility, erosion, compaction, leaching and weed invasion (Goodland and Irwin, 1975; Sioli, 1985; Caulfield, 1986). The use of chains pulled by a pair of bulldozers (the *correntão*) as well as chemical defoliants have also helped speed up environmental degradation (Branford and Glock, 1985). A combination of fragile ecology and drastic methods of converting the forest give Amazonian pastures a life of ten years (Hecht, 1985). Despite the earlier optimistic predictions that cattle pasture would actually improve soil fertility (Falesi, 1976), thus lending support to government priorities, cattle yields fell far short of official projections and proved to be far more problematic than had been realised, for large and small farmers alike (Fearnside, 1979; Hecht, 1981; Smith, 1982). Added to these problems were the difficulties of efficiently administering vast cattle estates without proper managerial expertise.

A further criticism of cattle-rearing, although this has never seemed to worry Brazil's major policy-makers is that, in a land of chronic rural underemployment and increasing landlessness, it creates very little employment in relation to the total amount invested by the government. Livestock production generates a mere one job per two thousand head of cattle or per twelve square miles, in contrast to the one hundred people per square mile which can be supported by appropriate peasant agriculture in the rainforest (Caulfield, 1986). Local field studies confirm this generalisation. In the municipality of São Félix, in eastern Amazonia, for example, twenty-nine cattle ranches with one and a half million hectares of pasture generated only 200 permanent and 750 temporary jobs

(Wagner, 1985). Another survey of a group of ranches in Mato Grosso, covering 336,000 hectares, found that they generated only 267 permanent jobs (Branford and Glock, 1985). Those few long-term jobs which are created cost on average US$63,000 each, or double that of a job in the industrial sector (Skillings and Tcheyan, 1979).

In 1979 SUDAM stopped granting new fiscal incentives for pasture formation in the 'high forest' part of Amazonia, but allowed new projects only in areas of 'transition forest' (Fearnside, 1985a). The government appeared to want to curtail cattle-raising in Amazonia on the grounds that it had not proved as economically successful as had been hoped. Cattle production in Amazonia before 1974 had been encouraged by high world beef prices, triple those of the early 1960s. Brazilian exports of processed meat quadrupled during the 1970s. In 1975, however, prices dropped by over 50% and have continued at a significantly lower level compared with the boom years of the early 1970s (Jarvis, 1986). Amazonia's unprofitable cattle ranches were subsequently only kept alive by generous State subsidies under the FINAM (Investment Fund for Amazonia) system of fiscal incentives and the economic justification for these enterprises was questioned in the face of declining beef prices. Observers reasoned that in economic, social and environmental terms it made far more sense to develop the savanna grasslands of the *cerrado* to the south rather than to destroy the rainforest (Goodland, 1980; Jarvis, 1986).

In addition to these technical, social and ecological objections, it was realised that many so-called 'entrepreneurs' had been using the scheme as a front for obtaining cheap money which was diverted into other activities, a not uncommon feature of agricultural credit disbursement in Brazil generally. Branford and Glock (1985) estimated, for example, that these Amazonian ranches actually possessed only 36% of the cattle stated in their project proposals. Subsidised funding had totally distorted the market, creating an artificial explosion of cattle enterprises that could not be justified on production grounds. A property boom rather than a cattle boom was the result, with land values increasing by 100% p.a. in real terms (Hecht, 1985). Clearly, land was in demand for its speculative rather than its production value, leading one analyst to conclude that, 'Recent land speculation in Amazonian pasturelands probably could be counted as among the most profitable investments on earth' (Fearnside,

1986a, p. 30). Although some owners genuinely tried to put the land into productive use, even the largest and most efficient estates such as Volkswagen's Vale do Rio Cristalino, the Italian Liquigas Suiá-Missú and the National Credit Bank's Codeara ranch, have struggled and have had to diversify their activities as beef prices have fallen and official subsidies reduced.

A study published by IPEA (Gasques and Yokomizo, 1985) of the FINAM fiscal incentive scheme unequivocally demonstrated the scale of 'leakages' and the extent to which land speculation has been fuelled by SUDAM's policies. After examining a sample of thirty-three long-standing projects, implemented between 1968–71, the report concludes that only 10–30% of the proposed investments funded had in fact been realised. Cattle ranches were found to have achieved only 16% of their production and sales targets, while only three schemes out of ninety-four in the agricultural sector were commercially profitable. A large number of projects are non-existent and registered only to avoid a larger official failure rate. The authors confirm the widely-held view that fiscal incentives have been a 'speculative business and an instrument for guaranteeing occupation of the land' (p. 49), having brought few tangible benefits for Amazonia's economy.

In addition to these problems, Amazonia remained a net importer of beef and thus unintegrated into foreign markets; the goal of generating foreign exchange through exports of processed meat also remained unfulfilled. As Hecht notes, 'the exchange value of the land itself was far higher in this speculative context, than any commodities it could produce... pastureland created from forests is expensive to implant and to maintain, and the value of the animal product does not recompense its production, even with large subsidies' (1985, p. 678). Another researcher has also observed, 'The lure of speculative profits hinders agricultural development by raising land prices to a point where more productive small farmers are excluded, and by chanelling land-use decisions toward unproductive pasture rather than intensive management of smaller areas' (Fearnside, 1985b, p. 398). The existence of loopholes in the law and the practical difficulties of inspecting cattle ranches have meant that the 1979 changes have not in practice significantly curtailed livestock expansion. On the contrary, new fiscal incentives and subsidised credit under the Carajás scheme seem to have given it a fresh boost. As will be argued in Chapter 3, the market distortions generated by government subsidies for cattle ranching have exacerbated land concentration, discouraged rational land management and encouraged speculative exchange and social conflict rather than productive activities and employment generation.

As tax rebates for cattle ranching became more difficult to obtain, private colonisation schemes became an attractive alternative to large companies wishing to realise quick profits from the resale to small farmers of land acquired from the government at nominal prices. In particular, it has enabled enterprises which have been less successful than anticipated at rearing cattle to earn money from their otherwise unproductive land. Just as the Association of Amazon Businessmen (AEA) had been instrumental in persuading the Brazilian government to switch from INCRA-directed small farmer colonisation in the mid-1970s so, towards the end of the decade and into the 1980s, it exerted pressure to obtain official support for a policy of establishing large-scale, integrated private colonisation schemes. By 1982 in fact twelve of the AEA's 250 members were investing in such enterprises with SUDAM backing (Pompermayer, 1984). Private colonisation schemes in Amazonia have attracted increasingly large numbers of small farmers, almost exclusively from the southern states of Rio Grande do Sul, Paraná and Santa Catarina rather than the impoverished North-East. A combination of land concentration and fragmentation has forced small-scale farmers to look towards the Amazonian frontier, where land can be purchased at perhaps one-fiftieth of its price in the South. Between 1968 and 1984 INCRA approved seventy-one private colonisation projects, of which sixty-six were located in Mato Grosso, three in Maranhão and two in Pará (Wagner, 1988). Although the economic performance of these schemes is somewhat mixed, the pace of such resettlement is quickening and is being hastened by continued government incentives.

Branford and Glock (1985) provide a detailed survey of several of the first such schemes. Pioneered in 1973 by the 400,000-hectare Sinop project in Mato Grosso, a more ambitious sale in the same year of two million hectares in the Aripunana area led to the setting up of three major colonisation schemes. By 1984 the 400,000-hectare Indeco project, started by the businessman Ariosto da Riva, which had attracted several thousand families from the South, was generating £1.2 million annually from coffee, cocoa and Brazil nut exports, and had given rise to three small towns including Alta

Floresta with a population of 45,000. Cotriguaçú was set up in 1982 with one million hectares of land and eventually hopes to settle 15,000 families from Paraná. In 1981 the Canarana scheme in Mato Grosso covered 700,000 hectares and included fifteen separate projects but its fortunes were more mixed and by 1983, 25,000 hectares had been abandoned due to soil exhaustion, 300,000 hectares had been turned over to cattle pasture and only 150,000 hectares remained under crops, largely of the subsistence variety. Other schemes in Mato Grosso and Pará include Terra Nova, Cooperlucas, Cotia, Tucumã, Campo Alegre and Colider.

The economic fortunes of these projects have varied considerably. Many have made rapid progress after a faltering start, particularly when due attention has been given to researching appropriate farming techniques and the provision of adequate infrastructure. Some, such as Indeco, have been relatively successful while INCRA has had to intervere in others, such as Terra Nova, due to mismanagement. Tucumã, established on fertile soils within the Carajás Programme heartland has been, as described below in greater detail, thrown into disarray after being invaded by small farmers, large land-grabbers and gold prospectors, leaving the colonisation company CONSAG with little choice but to abandon the scheme in the hope that the Land Reform Ministry will intervene to regulate the situation and offer them some form of indemnity.

A distinct feature of the more successful private colonisation schemes in Amazonia is the vertical integration of the farmers into agro-industrial production chains and the establishment of meat-packing, food-processing plants and alcohol distilleries, and their inclusion into national schemes for the production of cash-crops such as rubber and cocoa. What official propaganda does not mention is that many schemes have only been implemented after native indigenous groups had been driven out; well-publicised cases have involved 10,000 members of the Sururú and Cintas Largas tribes in Aripuana (Branford and Glock, 1985) and the Txukarramãe and Kreen-Akarore in Colider (Speller, 1987). Companies selling lands to would-be colonists have reaped large profits. In Tucumã, for example, land bought by the Andrade Gutiérrez Construction Company (CONSAG) for an average US$0·87 per hectare was resold for prices ranging from US$44 to US$87 per hectare (Butler, 1985), although one project director claimed subsequently in an interview that the firm had projected a profit margin of only 14% on total investment there (*Jornal do Brasil*, 31.5.87). At Indeco land purchased for £3.45 per hectare in 1973 was resold in 1979 for £120 per hectare (Branford and Glock, 1985). Another distinguishing feature of these private schemes is that colonists require a significant amount of capital in order to make the initial investment. Thus most beneficiaries are small farmers from the South who have sold off part of their valuable holdings there in order to gain a foothold in Amazonia.

While the government is actively encouraging southern co-operatives to establish more private colonisation schemes, and large southern companies have discovered a new source of profits, the mass of landless labourers and small cultivators with few resources remain firmly excluded both by lack of capital and, frequently, by security systems which prevent their physical entry into the project areas. However, in the face of increasingly intense competition for land in Amzonia, such pretensions towards exclusivity are becoming more and more difficult to realise and sustain for any length of time. A case in point is the Tucumã private colonisation scheme, set up in 1980 by the Andrade Gutiérrez Construction Company (CONSAG) as one of the pioneering initiatives. By 1987 only 250 of the intended 1,771 plots (over 140,000 hectares) planned for the first phase of the scheme had been sold. The entire project area of 400,000 hectares had been illegally occupied by a total of some 12,000 families unwilling or unable to pay the company asking price for the land.

The newcomers have been attracted by a combination of factors. Some are peasants expelled from other regions desperate for a piece of land on which to make a living. Others have a more clearly speculative and commercial interest in Tucumã. Some larger land 'owners' have accumulated substantial plots through violence and illicit purchases and either produce a variety of profitable cash crops and livestock, or resell the property at a huge profit. Many sawmills have been set up to exploit valuable mahogany reserves, the companies in question encouraging land invasions by small farmers who clear the area and supply them with timber, keeping prices down and speeding up the process of deforestation. In 1986 alone 60,000 cubic metres of timber (15,000 trees) were extracted from Tucumã. About 15,000 gold prospectors have also established themselves in the area, with fourteen of the forty-one registered workings possessing their own landing strips for light aircraft. Even some indigenous groups, who are normally so adversely affected by these developments, have managed to profit. The chief of 400 Kayapó indians in the Tucumã area charged a tax of CrZ2,500 (£40) on every pair of water pumps brought in by gold panners and CrZ800 (£15) for each light aircraft which lands. Further income is provided by sales of timber to the sawmills but the Kayapó, because they charge per cubic metre rather than per tree, reputedly make three times as much profit as the small farmers from the same quantity.

The violence and climate of insecurity which engulfed the project has forced many smaller colonists to leave and the company has abandoned the scheme. Small farmer success at Tucumã was also hampered by technical and organisational difficulties, comparable with problems experienced on the official Trans-Amazon highway (Moran, 1989). Settlers had poor knowledge of local soil conditions and applied inappropriate farm management techniques brought from the South; fertility and erosion problems were compounded by the unwise use of mechanical deforestation; in addition, plots were badly sited and roads badly constructed. These dificulties resulted in low yields, decapitalisation of many small cultivators, indebtedness and farmer turnover. In 1987 the company was negotiating with MIRAD, the Land Reform Ministry, for the area to be expropriated, land titles to be distributed and compensation paid for the estimated US$30 million invested by CONSAG on infrastructural development in Tucumã (*Jornal do Brasil*, 16.3.87, 10.5.87, 31.5.87; *O Liberal*, 19.8.87).

However, despite the publicity attached to recent events on projects such as Tucumã, directed colonisation has never formed more than a small fraction of the total movement of rural migrants to frontier zones in Brazil. Most migration is of the 'spontaneous' variety, which receives no direct protection or financial assistance from either government or private companies. However, directed settlement schemes have often acted like magnets, attracting would-be colonists with vague promises of cheap land and infrastructural support, which implementing agencies such as INCRA have often been unable to fulfil.

Until the late 1950s the southern states of Paraná, São Paulo, Santa Catarina and Rio Grande do Sul were the most popular destinations for poor north-eastern peasant farmers. By the late 1950s and 1960s, encouraged by the building of the Belém–Brasília highway, the most rapidly expanding frontier became the centre-west states of Mato Grosso and Goiás and, by the mid-1960s,

Table 1.1 Total net migration to Amazonia, 1970–80

Region	Volume	% Change
Amazonia		
Acre, Amapá, Roraima,		
Rondônia	+355,890	+203·5
Amazonas	+32,351	+3·4
Pará	+378,194	+17·5
Total	+766,435	+21·3
Centre-west		
Mato Grosso	+418,428	+26·2
Goiás	−135,138	−4·6
Total	+283,290	+6·2
Grand Total	+1,049,725	+ 12·9

Source: Adapted from Wood and Wilson (1984), p. 148.

southern Pará (Goodman, 1978; Foweraker, 1981). During the 1970s, as this frontier gradually closed with the monopolisation of land by large estates (see Chapter 3), so small migrant farmers have moved further west to Rondônia, which became more easily accessible after completion of the BR 364 highway in 1965 linking the capital, Porto Velho, with Cuiabá and the rest of the country. Most recently, in the 1980s, small cultivators are moving increasingly to Acre and Roraima which are, arguably, among the very 'last frontiers' in Brazilian Amazonia.

Data provided by the National Census, as well as local studies, illustrate these trends. Table 1.1 shows that, from 1970–80, net migration to the Centre-West rose by 6·2% and to Para by 17·5%. The most dramatic increase has taken place in Acre, Rondônia, Roraima and Amazonas, which together experienced a 203% rise (386,000 people). However, given the serious problems of census data collection in Amazonia and the dispersed nature of the migrant population, these figures probably underestimate the true increases. Another study of development on the north-west frontier concluded, for example, that net migration to Rondônia alone amounted to some 375,000 during the same decade, and yet another put the net population gain for Rondônia from 1970 to 1982 at some 600,000 (Branford and Glock, 1985). The World Bank (1981a, p. 13) also highlights the particular importance of Rondônia as a destination for migrants; its population grew at an annual rate of 21·3% from 1970–78, compared with 9% for Mato Grosso. This accelerated pace during the 1970s has been attributed in part to the collapse of directed colonisation along the Trans-Amazon highway after 1974 as well as to pressures on small farmers in southern Brazil as mechanised agribusiness has monopolised landownership in the region, and of course to growing rural violence in older frontier zones of southern and eastern Amazonia itself (Martine, 1980, 1987).

Rondônia is INCRA's most successful example of organised colonisation, having settled an estimated 50,000 families or 300,000 to 350,000 people by 1983, with another 30,000 families awaiting plots (Branford and Glock, 1985). However, this influx has far oustripped the capacity of INCRA to absorb new colonists, particularly during the 1975–79 period when land was reserved for more 'modern' farmers from the South possessing some capital, rather than the impoverished mass of landless or quasi-landless peasants. But a continuing influx of 'gusher proportions' dictated that INCRA initiate a process of 'Rapid Resettlement' from 1979 which effectively legitimated the widespread existing spontaneous settlement in the state. A subsequent phase of World Bank-funded Integrated Rural Development under the POLONOROESTE programme absorbed a further 5,000 families on directed colonisation schemes (PICs), in addition to an estimated 18,000 new farms set up outside official control between 1980–85 (Martine, 1987).

As Rondônia has become saturated and land monopolised, reproducing the familiar pattern of land-grabbing, rural violence and land concentration, so the frontier has extended westwards to the unusually fertile soils of Acre, facilitated by extension of the BR 364 from Porto Velho to Rio Branco in 1971. Large financial groups from the South, attracted by SUDAM incentives, bought out rubber estate owners and sought to evict the squatter population and rubber tappers, generating violent clashes in the countryside. Large tracts were bought up by companies such as Coopersucar (sugar), Atlantica Boa Vista (insurance), Cacique (coffee), Bordon (meatpacking) and Viação Garcia (coach transport); by 1975 four fifths of the land belonged to investors from southern Brazil (Branford and Glock, 1985). Five million hectares, or one-third of the surface area of Acre, changed hands between 1971–75, often with the aid of forged titles, while prices of land close to the highway rose by 1,000% to 2,000%. INCRA started two directed colonisation schemes to diffuse land conflicts but these were implemented very slowly so that, by 1980, only 1,400 families had been settled, mainly non-Acreans (Bakx, 1987). By allowing Acrean territory to be taken over by large-scale commercial enterprises from such an early stage in its development, a significant opportunity has been forfeited to undertake the sort of large-scale colonisation by small farmers which failed along the *Transamazônica* but which has been at least partially successful in Rondônia.

The occupation of Amazonia has been characterised by a process of step migration in which many small farmers appear to move on from one frontier, as opportunities diminish, to the next where virgin land is available. This is partly the result of harrassment by land-grabbers but is also the product of small-scale settlers themselves participating in land speculation, albeit on a minor scale when compared with corporate interests. The World Bank (1981a) study cited above found that 71% of settlers on one directed scheme had lived in at least two places, and 27% in three locations, before entering Roraima. These data suggest that, while a substantial number of migrants has been able to secure a livelihood in Amazonia, even larger numbers fail to gain permanent access. It has been estimated that, overall, Amazonia has absorbed a mere 6% of Brazil's rural exodus from 1970–80 (Wood and Wilson, 1984). Thus, the relatively limited numbers involved compared with the size of the problem, as well as the extreme violence associated with the settlement process, must give rise to serious doubts about the region's capacity to fulfil the so-called 'safety-valve' function.

Mining, agribusiness and land reform in the 1980s

Within what might be termed the latest phase of Amazonian development, mining rather than cattle ranching is seen as the leading sector in official plans. As early as the mid-1970s the Second Development Plan for Amazonia and the POLAMAZONIA proposals emphasised the importance attached to mineral extraction, citing the Trombetas bauxite and the Carajás iron-ore reserves (SUDAM, 1976a, 1976b). At the same time, however, the increasingly serious problem of rural violence could not be ignored for, not only was it counter-productive for the ruling military regime at a time of gradual liberalisation or *abertura*, but it also gave Brazil much unfavourable international publicity. In 1980 the government therefore set up two special bodies in areas of intense conflict in an ostensible attempt to diffuse tensions in the countryside.

The Executive Group for the Araguaia-Tocantins Region (GETAT) was created by presidential Decree No. 1767 of 1 February, 1980 and made responsible for land-titling and colonisation over an area of forty-five million hectares. Another group, GEBAM, was responsible for the Lower Amazon, including the Jarí scheme. Covering an area equal to roughly half of the Carajás programme, GETAT originally formed part of the Ministry of Land Affairs, now the Ministry of Rural Development and Agrarian Reform (MIRAD) and was directly subordinate to the National Security Council. Its area of activity centred on the most volatile land conflict zone in Brazil where the states of Maranhão, Goiás and Pará meet, popularly known as the 'parrot's beak' (*bico do papagaio*) due to its distinctive shape. The impact of GETAT will be more closely examined in Chapter 3. Suffice here to say that, rather than effectively redistributing land to the needy, its titling activities have consolidated a polarised structure of ownership and reinforced the view of GETAT as yet another example of increasing military and State intervention on behalf of large capital enterprises which denies permanent access to the peasantry; furthermore, its colonisation schemes (Carajas I, II and III), have resettled few landless farmers. As a result of growing dissatisfaction with GETAT's failure to tackle successfully the problems of land redistribution and rural violence, as well as for deeper political reasons, it was eventually abolished in May 1987.

Potentially of far greater importance in restructuring landownership is the National Agrarian Reform Plan (PNRA), instituted by Decree No. 91.766 of 10 October, 1985 by the Democratic Alliance government of President José Sarney. Based on the Land Statute (*Estatuto da Terra*, Law 4.504) of 30 November, 1964, its main objective is the redistribution of under-utilised public and private lands to small farmers and landless labourers, particularly in areas of acute polarisation and land conflict. It was officially estimated that, by 1984, 41% of all land held under *latifúndia* (itself some 60% of the total agricultural area in Brazil) was unproductive and constituted a valuable resource for absorbing the 10·6 million landless rural labourers in the country (MIRAD, 1985a). Nationally, from 1985–2000, it was hoped to resettle 7·1 million families, with 1·4 million in the short-term from 1985–89. Other complementary measures include resettlement and the provision of agricultural services such as credit and extension. Regional reform plans drawn up state by state would highlight priority areas for expropriation and redistribution.

The original proposals of May 1985 were, by Brazilian standards, quite radical and, following Article 20 of the 1964 statute, provided for the expropriation of all privately-owned *latifúndia* if local circumstances dictated, irrespective of whether the land was 'productive' or not (MIRAD, 1985a; Campanhole, 1969). However, reaction to these initial proposals from the landed oligarchy was considerable. Its main pressure group, the *União Democrática Ruralista* (UDR), mounted a strong lobby in defence of private property; landowners strengthened their private militia, entering into physical conflict with the peasantry which, in the changed political circumstances, had started to invade and occupy large holdings in the southern states of Santa Catarina, São Paulo and Paraná, as well as in southern Pará and northern Goiás in Amazonia (*Veja*, 12.6.85; *Folha de São Paulo*, 8.4.86). As political pressure mounted in Brasília and violence in the countryside escalated the original reform proposals of May 1985 were significantly watered down, and fresh plans published in October of that year.

The reformulated proposals appeared after the Sarney government had 'learned new lessons' from the ensuing debate on the agrarian reform question (MIRAD, 1985b, p. 7). Its major difference was to make ineligible for expropriation two major categories of large estate which previously would have qualified; firstly, all 'rural enterprises' (*empresas rurais*), that is, productive farms and, secondly, all properties smaller than three times the INCRA 'module' size for the region (MIRAD, 1985b, Articles 1.2, 1.3 and 1.4, p. 13). The landowners' lobby, the UDR, made further protests in early 1986 about measures contained in the detailed regional agrarian reform plans being drawn at state level by 'agrarian commissions', publication of which was delayed while changes were instituted at the landowners' insistence (*Folha de São Paulo*, 10.4.86). These modifications severely limited the potential impact of the PNRA and left the head of MIRAD, Nelson Ribeiro, with little option but to resign in protest (*The Guardian*, 30.5.86). His successor, Dante de Oliveira, had a similarly uphill struggle and he too resigned after a year in office, to be replaced by Marcos Freire. The new minister soon agreed, in September 1987, to yet another concession to the UDR which would exclude from expropriation any area of land 'effectively worked' by the owner (*Folha de São Paulo*, 3.9.87).

Taken together with other limitations of the plan, which will be considered at greater length in Chapter 3, these changes have meant that the PNRA will not bring major benefits to small cultivators in Amazonia or anywhere else in Brazil and may, indeed, even exacerbate their position in an already polarised and conflict-ridden rural structure. The initial promise of the agrarian reform as a development initiative which potentially could improve both the productivity and well-being of the Brazilian peasantry in Amazonia and elsewhere, however marginally, thus shows little sign of being fulfilled, not least of all because of its slow progress; by the end of 1986 the plan had succeeded in resettling a mere 1·3% of the target number of families for the year (Pereira, 1987), and the plan's original targets have been revised substantially downwards. Progress has also been slowed down by the rapid turnover of Ministers of Agrarian Reform due to political pressures and, of course, the tragic and untimely death on 9 September, 1987 of Marcos Freire and his team of advisers in a still unexplained plane crash, seconds after take-off from the Carajás project airport.

The latest major official policy initiative for Amazonia concerns a scheme for the systematic occupation of strategic areas north of the Rivers Amazon and Solimões, the *Projeto Calha Norte* (PCN). An interministerial study group was set up in 1985, under the direction of General Rubens Bayma Denys, Secretary General of the National Security Council (CSN), and under the direct control of the President of the Republic. It met in great secrecy and its initial report, given limited internal circulation, was completed in December of that year (PCN, 1985). The PCN covers a vast area of 6,500 kilometres along Brazil's borders with Colombia, Venezuela, Guyana and Surinam, amounting to 1·3 million square kilometres altogether, or 14% of Brazil's territory (and 24% of Legal Amazonia). Originally conceived essentially as a military project, eight new bases will be established; the army, navy and airforce are allocated 78% of the total budget for 1986–89. The stated objectives of Calha Norte are, through a series of 'special projects', to establish a permanent military presence in the region, to improve bilateral relations with neighbouring countries, to define new indian policies 'appropriate to the region' and to set up 'development poles' with adequate infrastructure such as roads and hydroelectric power (PCN, 1985, pp. 2–5).

During this initial phase (1985–6), and despite many public denials by military personnel, the PCN was clearly preoccupied mainly with strategic concerns of securing Brazil's borders against possible subversive infiltration from the Cooperativist Republic of Guyana and from Surinam, both deemed to be 'vulnerable' to Cuban influence. Drugs trafficking and gold smuggling were also highlighted as major problems which demanded a stronger official presence (*Folha de São Paulo*, 1.11.86, 3.12.86). Geopolitical considerations, so prominent in the 1970s, therefore re-emerged as a major influence on official policy for Amazonia. Although vague suggestions have been made of the development potential of the region and the availability of land for resettling landless farmers (*Folha de São Paulo*, 1.11.86), agriculture was in fact accorded a low priority on the grounds of poor soils and the likely competition from coca-leaf cultivation in neighbouring countries. In the most recent phase of policy-making for Calha Norte, in addition to geopolitical concerns, the government has devoted a major effort to facilitating commercial exploitation of the area's enormous mineral wealth. One report described the region as an 'Eldorado' with untapped reserves of oil, gold, diamonds, cassiterite, manganese and uranium, conservatively estimated by the Rio Doce Valley Company, (CVRD) to be worth US$250 million (*Jornal do Brasil*, 30.11.86; *Folha de São Paulo*, 3.12.86).

It has become increasingly clear that the Calha Norte project is designed to limit access by migrant farmers and small prospectors to these strategic areas and reserve land either for large commercial agro-livestock and lumbering enterprises, or for mining companies. These suspicions are reinforced by the stipulation in the Calha Norte project which would prohibit the demarcation of indian territory within a 160 kilometre-wide strip along the entire northern border. This goes against the directives issued to a 1983 group set up by President Figueiredo specifically to draw up boundaries for indigenous reserves, and has prompted strong protests from organisations representing indians' interests (*Folha de São Paulo*, 1.11.86). Since there are an estimated 50,000 indians in the project area, including some 7,500 Yanomami in northern Roraima and Amazonas on the border with Venezuela, the repercussions of such measures could be extremely far-reaching.

More recent government measures have confirmed the State's manifest desire to strengthen its economic and political control over this northern border region, and to mould indian policy in accordance with State and private interets, both commercial and political. Two presidential decrees, issued in October 1987 (Nos. 94.945–6), moved clearly in this direction. Firstly, flexibility was to be allowed in the demarcation of indian lands within the PCN so that they could be reduced in size where this was considered appropriate in order to satisfy regional political–commercial interests. Secondly, the concept of the 'indigenous colony' (*colônia indígena*) was created; this allows indians who are considered acculturated, according to guidelines laid down by the National Indian Foundation (FUNAI) in May 1988, to be permitted to enter into contractual agreements with State and private mining interests. This would enable previously inaccessible mineral resources to be effectively exploited, while appropriate compensation would be channelled back to the groups thus affected in the form of special development projects. Not unsurprisingly, the vast majority of indians in the PCN region fall into this category (Pacheco de Oliveira, 1988). At the same time, although the government has made a commitment to the setting up of a Yanomami reserve, a sixty-kilometre strip along the border would remain under military control. Nevertheless, the project is consistently opposed by a hard-line section of the armed forces which perceives a threat to national sovereignty and the danger of a separatist 'Yanomami State' (*Folha de São Paulo*, 21.1.87; Pacheco de Oliveira, 1988).

The Calha Norte area is something of a 'last frontier' in Brazilian Amazonia which has the potential to absorb many land-hungry small farmers. Yet while detailed plans for developing the region have not yet emerged, the initial proposals in this latest scheme suggest that the bias in favour of large, export-oriented commercial mineral and farming enterprises, strongly supported by and in close alliance with the State, will be continued even here. Initial nationalistic, geopolitical preoccupations have gradually been complemented by a widening of goals to encompass commercial mineral exploitation, with possible future foreign participation, in spite of seemingly restrictive provisions under the new constitution. This has been a consistent theme in official Amazonian development policy-making for almost three decades and is entirely consistent with priorities expressed in a number of regional development plans. Another major scheme in a different part of the Amazon Basin which also fits this mould is, of course, the Greater Carajás Programme (PGC) itself. What sets Calha Norte somewhat apart, however, is the central co-ordinating role of the National Security Council and the apparent exclusion of SEPLAN (Planning Secretariat of the Presidency of the Republic) from even minimal administrative involvement in the scheme, suggesting a loss of control over the planning process for a large portion of Amazonia as other State groups have manoeuvred for position. Nonetheless it is, perhaps, significant in terms of the general expansion of State influence in the region that Calha Norte and Carajás together embrace fully half of Brazilian Amazonia.

This chapter has outlined several major recent phases of policy-making and implementation for Brazil's Amazon Basin. A series of commercial, geopolitical and social reasons have been cited as the inspiration for this essentially *latifúndio*-biased model, which is based on strengthening corporate interests at the expense of small farmers, who are being pushed further and further into more distant frontier zones by a combination of market pressures and heightened land conflicts. In a more general sense also, however, the types of development strategy pursued in Amazonia are very much in keeping with Brazil's economic growth model of the past two decades. Throughout the 1960s and 1970s Brazilian economic policy has been characterised by a form of 'State capitalism' in which government has taken an increasingly interventionist stance, encouraging both import-substitution and export-based industrialisation via the attraction of domestic and foreign investment (Baer, 1975, 1986). This official role has been exercised and is reflected in a significant expansion of public activity and government spending which, as a proportion of Brazilian GNP, has risen from 17% in 1947 to one-third during the 1970s (Harris, 1987).

In Amazonia the State has played a crucial role in moulding the policies and strategies described in this chapter, culminating in the Greater Carajás Programme. It has achieved this through a series of direct measures, including investments in mining and infrastructure such as road and rail transport, as well as less direct incentives to agribusiness and land speculators by means of subsidised credit, fiscal incentives and other benefits. The agricultural development side of Brazil's import substitution and, latterly, more export-oriented growth model, has resulted in a growing polarisation of rural producers into two camps. On one hand is the heavily capitalised sector, oriented towards both speculative and productive activities, and in receipt of strong official support; on the other, in addition to the growing army of landless labourers, is the mass of smallholders, tenants and squatter farmers producing most of the nation's staple food supplies, but which receives almost no government backing. The pattern of large-scale commercial farming for export establishing for soybean, sugar and other products in southern Brazil is steadily being extended to Amazonia as a direct result of State encouragement. The Greater Carajás Programme is providing a substantial boost to this heavily biased strategy of agricultural development, exacerbating· already severe social and environmental problems. Chapter 2 will now examine the genesis of the PGC and the range of activities it embraces in eastern Amazonia as a prelude to detailed consideration of its wider consequences.

2

Developing Amazonia: the Greater Carajás Programme

The Greater Carajás Programme (PGC) is the largest 'integrated' development scheme ever undertaken in an area of tropical rain-forest, anywhere in the world. For better or worse, it will totally transform an area of what was until recently virgin forest, into an industrial and agro-livestock heartland. Officially inaugurated in 1980, thirteen years after its rich iron-ore deposits were discovered, the PGC is now spearheading the latest phase of Amazonian develop-ment based on export-oriented mineral exploitation and associated industrial activities. The sheer scale of the project is, to many ob-servers, simply awe-inspiring. Covering an area of almost 900,000 square kilometres, the size of Britain and France combined, or almost 11% of the country (see Fig. 1), investment in the PGC over a ten year period from 1981–90 was originally projected as US$62 billion, although the real figure over this period is expected to be substantially lower (CVRD, 1981b). At the core of the scheme are major investments in mineral extraction and processing, together with associated infrastructure, but the PGC also involves agricultural, livestock and forestry enterprises.

At a regional level the Carajás Programme has been instrumental in transforming the social and economic landscape, acting like a giant population magnet. It has attracted into eastern Amazonia thousands of construction workers in search of employment, gold panners in search of riches and small farmers in search of land as well as many other job-seekers. Urban areas, from the state capitals of São Luís and Belém to the provincial towns of Marabá, Açailândia and Imperatriz have seen their populations explode with the advent of the Carajás Programme and are expected to increase in size from 400% to 800% by the year 2,000. The potentially far-reaching con-

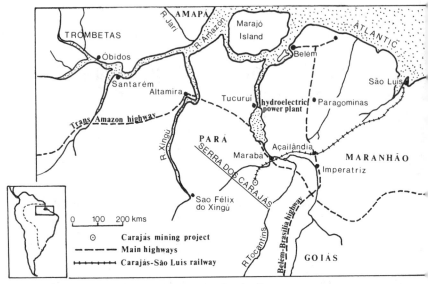

Fig. 1   Area covered by the Greater Carajás Programme
Source: *Journal of Development Studies*, 23(4), July 1987. Reproduced by
permission of Frank Cass of Co.

sequences of the PGC for the people and environment of this huge
section of the Amazon Basin have provoked much controversy. Its
strongest supporters see Carajás as the salvation not just of the
regional economy but of Brazil itself. Its detractors, on the other
hand, are sceptical about the scheme's contribution to balanced
regional growth and wary of its repercussions on longer-term, sustainable development possibilities in view of the wider costs involved.
One of the most controversial aspects of the Carajás Programme is its
relatively high level of foreign funding (US$1·8 billion by 1988) and
the extent to which this has undermined national sovereignty. Its
major industrial, agricultural and infrastructural activities will now
be described in the remainder of the chapter, before their broader
impact on the region is considered.

Origins and major components of the PGC

The backbone of the Carajás Programme is currently formed by four
major projects: an iron-ore mine, two aluminium plants at Barcarena,

near Belém, and in São Luís, and the Tucuruí hydroelectric scheme on the River Tocantins. Historically, however, the iron-ore complex, located in the Carajás Mountains, west of the town of Marabá in Pará state, was the first-born in the family of enterprises which now constitutes the Carajás Programme. The incident which led to the discovery of these rich deposits in 1967 has now become part of Carajás Programme folk-lore. Breno Augusto dos Santos, a geologist working for a subsidiary of US Steel, the *Companhia Meridional de Mineração* (CMM), recounts how he and his team virtually stumbled across the Carajás deposits when the company helicopter in which he was travelling landed in a clearing to refuel (dos Santos, 1986). Their significance was realised a month later when additional surveys revealed that Carajás had the largest known high-grade iron-ore reserves in the world (now put at eighteen billion tonnes with an average grade of 66% Fe). Excited by this prospect, US Steel placed a request with the Brazilian government for exploration rights over an area of 160,000 hectares. The Brazilian government was unwilling to place such power in the hands of a single foreign corporation and, after three years' intensive negotiations, a joint venture was formalised in 1970 through the creation of AMZA (*Amazônia Mineração SA*), with 51% of share capital in the hands of the CVRD and 49% with US Steel. In 1974 AMZA was granted exploration rights to the whole Carajás area (Cota, 1984; dos Santos, 1986).

As Chapter 1 noted, during the mid-1970s Brazilian governments were anxious to increase and diversify commercial enterprise in Amazonia. A series of factors, both domestic and international, combined to bring about a policy switch in favour of exploiting the region's mineral wealth and illustrate the sheer diversity of motives behind the scheme. These included the need to earn foreign exchange to service Brazil's growing foreign debt; frustration with the inability of Amazonian livestock production to generate export earnings; the State's decision to reject the 'social colonisation' model of small-farmer settlement on the frontier, in favour of agribusiness and mining; pressure from the CVRD to switch iron and steel production from the forest-depleted state of Minas Gerais to Amazonia; the move towards greater centralisation of planning in Brasília; and finally, pressure from transnational corporations and foreign governments for regional development in Brazil to be harnessed for serving the needs of their own enterprises and national economies. During the mid-1970s, while new directions for Amazonian development were thus being sought, the region's vast mineral potential was becoming evident with each discovery of fresh deposits, from iron-ore and manganese to bauxite and gold.

Accordingly, development of eastern Amazonia's mineral resources forms part of the Second National Development Plan, PND II (1975–79); this placed considerable emphasis on expanding the mineral sector, especially Carajás iron-ore and corresponding infrastructure, which were considered even then to be 'extremely important' for national development (SUDAM, 1976b, p. 55). The complementary POLAMAZONIA proposals, which were based on selective investment in fifteen major development poles throughout 'Legal Amazonia', also highlighted the importance of capitalising on the mineral riches of Carajás (SUDAM 1976a). Thus, six years before the advent of the Carajás Programme as such, the strategic importance of iron-ore, manganese and other deposits in eastern Amazonia was clearly recognised and stated. Plans were already in progress for AMZA to start iron-ore production in 1978 and a 900-kilometre railway link from the Carajás iron-ore mine to São Luís was projected even then. However, the joint venture collapsed in 1977 when the Amercian partner withdrew, selling its stake in AMZA to the CVRD for US $50 million (Cota, 1984). US Steel alleged that the project would be compromised by the 1973 oil price rise and its negative repercussions on world demand for iron-ore and that, in such circumstances, Brazilian production would merely compete with that from its other mines in Venezuela and Liberia.

However, the CVRD based its Carajás operations on rather more optimistic projections and, in 1978, construction of the iron-ore project and the Tucuruí hydroelectric scheme was finally started (Cota, 1984; dos Santos, 1986). Due to the CVRD's inability to attract all the foreign funding required for its US$4·5 billion iron-ore project in the depressed economic climate of the time, a scaled-down version was approved by the Geisel government in 1978 worth US$2·4 billion. At the same time, an initial eighty-kilometre section of the railway intended to link the mine to São Luís on the coast was built. Yet given the world steel crisis and the CVRD's consequent problems in securing markets for its produce, factors which had dissuaded US Steel from continuing with the venture, the Geisel administration was allegedly sceptical about the feasibility of Carajás and reluctant to commit funds to the project from the National Development Bank (BNDE). Also during the Geisel government, a joint venture between the CVRD and a Japanese consortium of primary aluminium producers to build the aluminium complex at Vila do Conde near Belém was cancelled in 1975 due to escalating costs and lack of funding (Neto, 1988).

This situation changed significantly with the coming to power of the Figueiredo government in 1980 which took a more positive stance in favour of proceeding with developing the region in an 'integrated' form, through the notion of a Carajás Programme. The role of official Japanese advisers appears to have been a critical factor at this stage in persuading the Brazilian government to act decisively. President Geisel had visited Japan in 1976 for exploratory talks and a mission came to Brazil three years later to advise the Figueiredo administration on developing the Carajás mineral province. Technicians from the Japan International Co-operation Agency (JICA), part of the Ministry of Foreign Affairs, were closely involved in preparing early studies by the State mining company (CVRD, 1979, 1980, 1981a) which subsequently formed the basis of regional development plans for the PGC area. JICA personnel retained this key advisory role until the mid-1980s, producing several influential reports of their own concerning industrial, agricultural, livestock and silvicultural development in Carajás, which left a clear mark on subsequent Brazilian proposals.

The PGC was thus formally established via Executive Act No. 1,183 of 24.11.80 which instituted the fundamental tax and financial incentive scheme for investors in the PGC's mineral, infrastructural and agroforestry projects. It was hoped that, once the basic mineral and infrastructural projects were set up, further industrial and agribusiness enterprises would be attracted to the area. Decree no. 85,387 of the same date created an Interministerial Council, which originally comprised eight ministers, since extended to eleven, as well as the head of the National Security Council. In 1985, with the advent of civilian rule, the state governors of Pará, Maranhão and Goiás were also included. The Council, which is directed by an Executive Secretariat, and is headed by the Minister of Planning and linked directly to the office of the President of the Republic, is responsible for appraising, approving and evaluating projects funded by the Carajás Programme (PGC, 1984a, 1985b).

From the outset, Japanese influece in determining the nature and direction of the Carajás Programme was marked, if not the only important factor. The CVRD commissioned a report from Japanese consultants (IDCJ, 1980) which concluded, although in rather general terms, that there was great potential in the Carajás region for investment into agricultural and mineral enterprises. These recommendations were very much in the mould of Japanese suggestions for large-scale, commercial soybean farming in the central Brazilian plateau (*cerrado*) made during the 1970s (San Martin and Pelegrini, 1984). The CVRD published its own report, 'Eastern Amazonia: A National Export Project' (CVRD, 1980), which argued along the same lines for priority to be given to export-oriented mineral and agricultural projects. The close similarity of the IDCJ and CVRD documents was noted, leading some observers to imply that national interests were being sacrificed to provide the Japanese with cheap commodities such as iron-ore and lumber; the region was allegedly undergoing an 'unarmed invasion' (Cota, 1984) and Brazil 'pawning its future' (IBASE, 1983). Further studies produced in the early 1980s by the Japanese official aid body, JICA, as well as the CVRD and the Ministry of Agriculture, deal mainly with non-industrial issues in the Carajás Programme. These are considered at greater length below in the discussion on agricultural components of the PGC.

The CVRD's 1980 document became the basic reference point for the both the company and the government in their respective strategies for eastern Amazonia. It systematically formalises for the first time the CVRD's interest in according top priority to large-scale, capital-intensive, export-oriented mineral and agricultural projects for the region. According to at least one study (Neto, 1988), the CVRD deliberately took a lead role in formulating a ready-made regional development policy for eastern Amazonia which the incoming Figueiredo government (1979–85) would enthustiastically embrace in view of its own search for a new and viable development strategy for Amazonia to assist with the growing problem of servicing Brazil's foreign debt. Yet the CVRD's self-interest was also evident in view of the serious difficulties it had encountered in securing adequate funding for the interdependent mineral (Carajás, ALBRAS and MRN) and infrastructural (Tucuruí, railway, Barcarena port and new town) projects in which it was involved and dependent upon to varying degrees. In the same publication the CVRD (1980, p. 3) thus emphasises the 'harmonious combination of State, private and foreign capital' as a prerequisite for the PGC's success.

More detailed plans for the PGC were soon published by the CVRD (1981a), which stressed the importance of completing the iron-ore, bauxite and other mineral projects outlined in the Second National Development Plan for 1975–79. Of the US$61·7 billion projected investment US$28 billion was earmarked for mineral-metallurgy projects, US$13 billion for agriculture, forestry and livestock, with US$22 billion for supporting infrastructure. By embracing a range of mineral developments, downstream activities such as pig-iron and steel-making as well as non-heavy industrial activities such as livestock, lumbering and commercial agriculture, it was hoped by both the CVRD and the Figueiredo administration to devise an 'integrated' regional development strategy for this vast area of eastern Amazonia. The previous Geisel administration had already declared its intention of developing Amazonia's mineral resources and the succeeding Figueiredo government had already commenced work on several subsequent PGC components, such as the iron-ore complex, the railway, Tucuruí, and the aluminium plants. However, the CVRD's plans and negotiations with government were instrumental in presenting a ready-made and attractive 'integrated' package which, on receipt of official approval, would undoubtedly attract overseas official and private capital and generate foreign exchange to service Brazil's foreign debt. Minister of Planning, Delfim Neto, later endorsed the programme as helping to 'eliminate the obstacles which hinder Brazil's growth', in view of the fact that, 'we are prisoners of the balance of payments...there is no alternative model' (*Folha de São Paulo*, 19.9.82).

The economic feasibility of the Carajás Programme is dependent upon heavy official subsidies to attract capital to an otherwise uninviting and inhospitable region for industrialists. A month after the government's announcement of the PGC a system of fiscal incentives was instituted (Decree-Law 1,825 of 22.12.80) which granted total exemption from payment of income tax to investors who channelled these funds into infrastructural or directly productive projects approved by the PGC Council. This provision embraced not just those companies making investments into industrial and manufacturing plant but also the powerful construction firms from the South undertaking building and infrastructural work. It is estimated, for example, that the Camargo Correia company saved US$100 million in this way (Treece, 1987). The period covered by these concessions ran initially only until 1985 but was later extended to 1990 (by

Decree-Law 2,152 of 18.7.84) and then to 1995. The concession to private investors into productive projects was reduced by the PGC Council's Resolution No. 11 of 30.12.85 from 100% to 50%, with the balance to be channelled into 'economic and social infrastructural undertakings that are part of the Programme'. This clause was later modified, in April 1986, to include small and medium-sized enterprises.

There are further potential benefits to encourage would-be investors in the Carajás Programme. These include exemptions from payment of the tax on manufactured goods and import duties on foreign machinery and equipment, priority in the allocation of bank credits, subsidised electricity prices, infrastructural improvements financed by the government and guaranteed supplies of minerals such as iron-ore at below world market prices. A number of other less official, but equally important, inducements for entrepreneurs within the PGC are lax controls on pollution and deforestation (particularly important for the planned pig-iron smelters, dependent as they are on large quantities of cheap charcoal), as well as the availability of cheap and weakly unionised labour (Caulfield, 1984; *Jornal do Brasil*, 29.7.84; PGC, 1985b). Furthermore, of course, the Carajás area of jurisdiction overlaps with that of SUDAM, which has its own fiscal incentive scheme. The major components of the PGC are now described in greater detail.

Iron-ore mining and processing
Literally at the heart of the Carajás Programme, both physically and economically, is the iron-ore mine. Although established as early as 1978, before the advent of the PGC itself, the CVRD'S enterprise only got under way after tax incentives were approved for it in August 1981 at the first meeting of the Interministerial Council. Its eighteen billion tonnes of high-grade iron-ore are the largest known reserves in the world and will provide 7·5% of global traded supplies. It was perceived as the corner-stone of the entire programme and strenuous efforts were made to bring the operations on stream as quickly as possible. Progress has, indeed, been rapid and today the Carajás mine is an impressive industrial – residential complex. The highly mechanised open-pit operations came on stream in January 1986 and in that year produced thirteen million tonnes of iron-ore (92% of which was exported, mainly to Japan, West Germany and Italy) rising to an expected twenty million tonnes by the end of 1987

1 Open-cast iron-ore mining at Carajás, which contains the largest known high-grade reserves in the world, discovered in 1967, estimated at eighteen billion tonnes. This mine and its associated infrastructure form the hub of the PGC.

(*Jornal do Comércio*, 14.10.86). This is well below projected levels, since by 1988 the mine had an annual capacity of thirty-five million tonnes. According to CVRD officials, current under-production is due to recent lack of world demand for iron-ore.

The Carajás mine is privileged in that, in addition to the high iron content of its surface deposits, the ore only requires straightforward crushing, screening and solid-recovery (dos Santos, 1986), after which the sinter feed and pellets are stockpiled or loaded directly from overhead silos into freight wagons. Consequently, Carajás ore reputedly enjoys the lowest production costs in the world (LAER, 31.10.86). In addition to iron-ore, the *Serra dos Carajás* also contains sixty-five million tonnes of manganese, the second largest reserve in the country, used in the production of iron alloys and batteries (CVRD, 1986). The list of other minerals in the Carajás deposits is lengthy and includes copper, chrome, nickel, cassiterite, tungsten and gold.

The 900-kilometre railway linking Carajás to Sao Luís, now also

2   Carajás iron ore is transported by rail to the coast for export, mainly to Japan, Europe and the USA, through a new deepwater port at São Luís, state capital of Maranhão.

used increasingly for passenger transport, was inaugurated by President Figueiredo in February 1985, a full year ahead of schedule. The new deep-water port at Ponta da Madeira in São Luis was officially opened in March 1986. Complementing industrial activities within the CVRD enclave at Carajás is an impressive company town for a population of up to 10,000 administrative staff and their families with most modern conveniences such as shops, hospital, sports and leisure club, comfortable hotel, public transport and airport, not to mention the zoological and botanical gardens. Manual workers commute by bus from the decidedly less comfortable twin-town of Parauapebas – Rio Verde situated outside the project perimeter. All forms of environmental destruction beyond the absolutely essential are strictly and effectively prohibited within this 411,000-hectare 'island', leading an air of unreality to the area given the unprecedented pace of deforestation which has reduced much of the surrounding tropical moist forest (TMF) to pitiful scrubland.

The CVRD's early problems in securing funding for the iron mine, railway and port complex soon disappeared when the PGC was

3 The new 900-kilometre railway which runs from Carajás (Parauapebas) to São Luís is also used increasingly for passenger transport, providing a valuable service which is much in demand, particularly during the rainy season when roads are often impassable.

finally approved in 1980. Of an initial investment of US$3·1 billion the CVRD was able to finance about half through selling debentures, reducing the government's ownership of the company from 70% to 56% by 1985 (Neto, 1989). The balance of funds required would be raised from domestic and foreign loans. In addition to US$1·1 billion from the BNDE, the then Minister of Planning, Delfim Neto, led several delegations abroad which resulted in loans forthcoming worth US$1·7 billion for Carajás, principally for the iron-ore mine at this stage; this included US$600 million from the EEC, US$500 million from Japan and US$305 million from the World Bank. PGC loans contracted later included US $250 million from US commercial banks and US$60 million from the USSR.

Repayment terms were generous, at a fixed interest rate of 10% over fifteen years. However, European and Japanese lenders had the long-term interests of their own steel industries very much in mind when granting these loads on such apparently attractive terms. The CVRD signed contracts with European and Japanese steel producers

Table 2.1 Pig-iron smelters and ferrous alloy plants projected for 1990
along the Carajás railway corridor

Company	Location	State of origin	Jobs created	Production [tonnes p.a.]
[*Pig-iron smelters*]				
Viana Siderúrgica do Maranhão	Acailândia	MG	180	54,000
Construtora Beter	Marabá	SP	148	50,000
Cia. Siderúrgica Vale do Pindaré [Construtora Brasil]	Acailândia	PN	147	55,000
Siderúrgica Servang Civilsan	Acailândia	MG	129	120,000
Companhia Siderúrgica do Maranhão [Itaminas Siderúrgica do Carajás–SICAR]	Acailândia	MG	490	350,000
Companhia Siderúrgica do Pará–COSIPAR [Itaminas Siderúrgica do Carajás]	Marabá	MG	490	350,000
Maranhão Gusa, SA–MARGUSA	Santa Inês	MA	367	54,000
Gusa Nordeste [Florice]	Acailândia	MG	148	53,000
Siderúrgica de Marabá–SIMARA	Acailândia	PA	320	12,000
Companhia Vale do Rio Pindaré–COVAP	Santa Inês	MA	257	50,000
Companhia Siderúrgica do Maranhão–COSIMA	Santa Inês	PE	–	15,000
SIDERSISA	Santa Inês	MG	–	84,000
Total				1,247,000 (+)
[*Ferrous alloy plants*]				
Irmãos Ayres	Rosário	MG	180	–
Metalman [Grupo Metalur]	Rosário	SP	321	17,000

Table 2.1 (continued)

Company	Location	State of origin	Jobs created	Production [tonnes p.a.]
Ferro-Ligas do Norte	Marabá	SP	320	49,000
PROMETAL	Parauapebas	SP	434	60,000
Cojan Engenharia	Parauapebas	MG	132	150,000
Total				276,000 (+)

Note: Data refer to projects approved by the PGC Interministerial Council at July 1987.
Sources: PGC, (1985, 1987); NATRON (1987); O Liberal (16.7.87)
Key: MG (Minas Gerais), SP (São Paulo), PE (Pernambuco), MA (Maranhão), PN (Paraná), PA (Pará).

for twenty-five million tonnes p.a. of iron-one (Neto, 1989). The EEC's loan, approved in 1982, was tied to a series of contracts signed by the CVRD with European firms for annual deliveries of thirteen million tonnes of iron-ore, which were officially admitted by the EEC's Vice President to contain 'favourable pricing conditions which will contribute to the competitiveness of the European steel industry' (quoted by Treece, 1987, p. 17). Contracts signed in the early 1980s stipulated that the iron-ore would be sold at current world market prices, which were expected (correctly) to fall by the middle of the decade when the mine came on stream.

A key element in the strategy to establish 'integrated' industrial development along the Carajás railway corridor is the setting up of some thirty pig-iron smelters and industrial plants processing iron-ore and manganese, grouped principally in the towns of Marabá, Acailândia and Santa Inês. As Table 2.1 shows, by 1987 plans were already well advanced, with twelve pig-iron and five iron-alloy projects approved by the PGC Council under the fiscal incentive scheme, with a total projected annual production of over 1·5 million tonnes. The first of these, the *Companhia Siderúrgica do Pará* (COSIPAR) in Marabá and the *Companhia Siderúrgica Vale do Pindaré* in Acailândia, came on stream in early 1988. By January 1988 a total of twenty pig-iron smelters had been approved and another fifteen were under consideration, with an estimated total annual production of 2·5 million tonnes. The potentially devastating ecological and social consequences of this industrial strategy, which will encourage wholesale destruction of vast areas of rainforest to supply these plants with cheap fuel, are dealt with at length in Chapter 4.

Contracts for future purchases have already been signed with several foreign companies. In April 1986 the Chinese State mining corporation, China Metallurgical Minimetals, signed an agreement to buy the entire pig-iron output of the Itaminas-owned smelter in Marabá, COSIPAR, in preparation for which the Brazilian firm was planning to double its capacity (*O Liberal*, 5.4.86). In June the CVRD signed a letter of intent with the USSR for the purchase of half the production form a new ferromanganese plant, over a twelve year period, a contract worth US$100 million; other agreements between Brazil and the Soviet Union call for co-operation over the minerals molybdenum and titanium as part of a bilateral trade package made in 1983 (*South*, December, 1986; LACR, 29.1.87). Russian, German and Brazilian investement is also involved in the $3·5 billion flat steel mill near São Luís, USIMAR (*Financial Times*, 28.4.88).

Aluminium and Tucuruí

Amazonia is believed to contain the world's largest bauxite reserves, estimated at 2·2 billion tonnes, in the Paragominas and Trombetas areas, which have been included within the Greater Carajás Programme. Two major integrated aluminium projects, the largest ventures in the region apart from the Carajás iron-ore mine itself, reflect the struggle between Japanese and US interests to gain control over the Amazon Basin's mineral resources. Thus the second major component of the Carajás Programme is the ALBRAS–ALUNORTE aluminium complex at Barcarena, near Belém, on the River Tocantins. Interest in bauxite mining and processing may be traced back to 1967 when the first commercially viable deposits were discovered in Trombetas, Pará, by ALCAN, the Canadian multinational. In view of the threat to its bauxite supplies posed by the independence of Guyana in 1966 and the subsequent nationalisation of all mining enterprises, a subsidiary, *Mineração do Rio Norte* (MRN) was created to exploit these Amazonian deposits. However, work was suspended after only one year due to a slump in world demand as well as renewed confidence in the stability of Guyanese supplies. MRN became a consortium led by the CVRD and ALCAN, with the participation of various other foreign companies such as Royal Dutch Shell–Billiton and Reynolds, and the enlarged US$400 million

Trombetas project eventually came on stream in 1979 (Neto, 1989).

As with the iron-ore mine, the ALBRAS-ALUNORTE aluminium complex has its origins well before the advent of the PGC itself. The Brazilian government had, in its PND II–POLAMAZÔNIA plans stated clearly that it wished to develop both iron-ore and bauxite mining in eastern Amazonia, and to encourage higher value-added production of alumina and aluminium at Trombetas (SUDAM, 1976a, 1976b). Following the 1973 petroleum price increases, which threatened the viability of Japan's oil-powered aluminium industry, the Japanese embarked on a global strategy of securing cheap, long-term supplies of primary aluminium in countries such as Brazil, Venezuela and Australia. Given the mutual interests of both parties in such an enterprise, the CVRD and a consortium of Japanese aluminium producers signed an agreement in 1974 to produce aluminium and alumina. However, implementation of the scheme was delayed by Japanese dissatisfaction with the high cost of infrastructure such as port installations and electricity supplies. Finally it was agreed that the scaled-down US$1·3 billion complex would comprise two distinct joint ventures between the Nippon Amazon Aluminium Company (NAAC) and the CVRD. *Alumínio do Brasil* (ALBRAS) would produce 320,000 tonnes of aluminium annually, while *Alúmina do Norte* (ALUNORTE) would supply 800,000 tonnes of alumina.

A period of uncertainty followed due to lack of funds to complete the essential Tucuruí project (in spite of US$230 million of tied French loans obtained in 1976 for the hydroelectric scheme), Brazil's growing foreign debt problem, fluctuating world aluminium prices and the 1979 oil price rise. Work on Tucuruí did not really start until 1981 and its inauguration was postponed until 1984. In order to gain Japanese co-operation and cheap loans, however, the Brazilian government agreed to provide basic infrastructure and heavily subsidised electricity prices over twenty years. ALBRAS pays the lowest tariff in Brazil, obtaining a 15% discount in addition to the already existing concessionary rates for aluminium smelting, and also enjoys a ceiling on its electricity costs of 25% of the world market price of aluminium. This arrangement was formalised in a 1981 contract with the North Brazil Electricity Board (ELETRONORTE), and has become a crucial factor in determining the economic feasibility of the project, paving the way for other moves (Neto, 1988, 1989). The electricity deal facilitated further Japanese loans, while the BNDE was also persuaded to support the project and the State-owned PORTOBRAS started to build the adjacent port of Vila do Conde.

Work on the US$1·9 billion complex finally got under way in 1982 and the first phase of ALBRAS, as well as the port at Vila do Conde (40,000 dwt), were inaugurated by President Figueiredo in 1985, the Tucuruí dam having already come on stream in late 1984. The plant produced 100,000 tonnes of aluminium in 1986, but implementation of the second phase of the scheme has been held up by Japanese attempts to transfer to the Brazilian government the entire US$62 million cost of building a second transmission line from Tucuruí designed for the exclusive use of ALBRAS. There have been further disagreements over concessionary price levels for aluminium purchased by the NAAC, while the government was contemplating reducing subsidies and raising the price of electricity charged to the company in an attempt to recover some of the capital costs of hydro-electric power generation (Neto, 1989; LACR, 30.10.86). Consequently, in mid-1986 the Japanese were threatening to make no further investments in ALBRAS and to withdraw from the venture, but in late 1987 the NAAC was still participating in the scheme, although plans to increase capacity to 320,000 tonnes p.a. had been delayed (*Província do Pará*, 18.7.86; LACR, 1.10.87).

The ALUNORTE half of this complex has experienced even more serious problems, its inauguration having been postponed from 1985 to 1989. During the intervening period it had been intended that the ALBRAS aluminium-smelting plant would import alumina from the Surinam Aluminium Company (SURALCO), owned jointly by the Aluminium Company of America (ALCOA) and Billiton Metals, a mining subsidiary of Royal Dutch-Shell, as well as from Venezuela. It has been noted that the cost of imported alumina was US$112 a tonne, while that produced by the Aluminium Company of Maranhão (ALUMAR) in São Luís and presumably, later, by ALUNORTE stood at US$200 a tonne (LACR, 30.10.86). This raised a serious question mark over the continued feasibility of ALUNORTE, but the Brazilian government was reluctant to cancel the project owing to the dependence that this would create on imports of alumina controlled by a major foreign multinational corporation. In 1987 the Japanese finally withdrew altogether from ALUNORTE, leaving the project at a standstill. It is suggested (Neto, 1989) that this move by the Japanese has effectively blocked the Brazilian government's attempts to create an integrated mining–metallurgical complex in

Carajás, since the ALUNORTE refinery is essential for transforming the Trombetas bauxite into alumina for smelting. The MRN bauxite, 80% of which must be exported, was sold either to ALCAN and its associate companies or to ALCOA's aluminium plant in São Luís, ALUMAR, enabling these to exert undue downward pressure on already low world prices of the raw material and leading to a serious dispute. Consequently, in 1986 the Brazilian government suspended MRN bauxite exports until the end of 1987 pending a decision by the International Chamber of Commerce in Paris.

A second alumina-aluminium complex, has been built on the Atlantic coast near São Luís, the state capital of Maranhão. Its US$1·3 billion investment makes it the largest privately-funded project ever undertaken in Brazil. Furthermore, ALUMAR is entirely owned by foreign multinationals: the American ALCOA, which holds 60% of the shares, and Billiton Metals, the mining subsidiary of Royal Dutch-Shell, with 40%. ALUMAR's annual capacity was planned at 500,000 tonnes of alumina and 110,000 tonnes of aluminium, using bauxite from Trombetas supplied under a ten-year contract. The Brazilian government saw great potential in the scheme for generating foreign exchange, while for ALOCA it formed part of a global strategy to relocate production in areas such as Brazil and Australia with cheap supplies of bauxite and electricity (Neto, 1988, 1989). In addition to benefiting from the urban infrastructural support offered in São Luís, ALUMAR was favoured by exceptionally strong official support, enabling it to come on stream in 1984, only four years after its inception and two years before the rival Japanese project, ALBRAS (LACR, 14.9.84). This support included rapid approval by the CONSIDER authority (*Conselho Siderúrgica Nacional*) to facilitate SUDAM fiscal incentives, heavily subsidised electricity supplies, like those granted to ALBRAS, and concessions from the Maranhão state government over access to land and water resources. Following the creation of the Carajás Programme in 1980 further benefits were forthcoming, such as PGC tax incentives and exemptions and, crucially for a plant so dependent on large supplies of electricity, a speeding up of the Tucuruí hydropower scheme and the transmission line to São Luís. The project also generated an estimated 10,000 jobs and US$800 million worth of orders for 500 national companies (LACR, 14.9.84).

In 1981 ALCOA expanded its influence by reaching an agreement with the Brazilian government to purchase large bauxite reserves at Trombetas, guaranteeing supplies for the ALUMAR plant and strengthening its competitive position in relation to the rival ALBRAS-ALUNORTE at Barcarena (Neto, 1989). ALCOA has consistenly tried to expand production against the wishes of its more cautious partner in ALUMAR, Billiton Metals, on the grounds that efficient, low-cost production methods in Brazil would place it in a favourable position in world markets. In fact, the ALUMAR complex was US$200 million below budget. The American company sold off 36% of its Brazilian subsidiary to Camargo Correa, using the US$240 million income, derived from tax incentives granted by the PGC to the construction company, to finance a second phase of ALUMAR, which was inaugurated by President Sarney in March, 1986. A third stage is planned and, by 1990, ALUMAR is expected to become the third largest aluminium smelter in the world (LACR, 14.9.84).

Industrial growth within Amazonia, particularly of the power-hungry mineral processing sector, is heavily dependent on abundant supplies of inexpensive electricity. Thus, the lynchpin in the whole Carajás Programme is the Tucuruí hydroelectric scheme on the River Tocantins, the largest ever built in a tropical rainforest area, and the fourth largest in the world. It will supply the aluminium complexes of ALBRAS – ALUNORTE and ALUMAR (which to-gether will consume over half of total output), as well as the iron-ore mine, pig-iron smelters and other plants along the Carajás–São Luís railway. Without Tucuruí it is doubtful whether any of these enter-prises would have been sufficiently attractive either to domestic or foreign investors. In addition, Tucuruí's heavily subsidised electri-city was designed to attract other development projects and to cater for the rapidly expanding urban needs of Belém, São Luís and other rapidly growing towns in the Carajás area. The dam, which cost US$4·6 billion, two-thirds funded by foreign loans, was inaugurated by President Figueiredo in November 1984 (*Veja*, 10.10.84; PGC, 1985c). Tucuruí generated an initial 330,000 kilowatts with the first of its twelve turbines, rising to 3·9 megawatts by 1990 and a possible maximum of 7·92 megawatts. It is merely the first in a series of twenty-seven dams along the Araguaia-Tocantins which will generate an estimated 22,000 megawatts (Barrow, 1986; Mougeot, 1987).

Given the potential repercussions of a project such as Tucuruí, particularly in an area of tropical rainforest, thorough social and environmental impact assessments should have been carried out.

However, such was the urgency in bringing Tucuruí on stream to service the other industrial components of Carajás within the project time-scale, that the authorities cast aside virtually all such considerations. These include, for example, the displacement with inadequate or no compensation of up to 35,000 people, as well as the potentially disastrous environmental consequences of flooding an area of almost 2,500 square kilometres of uncleared rainforest with all the associated problems of anaerobic decomposition, siltation, weed-clogging of the turbines, acidic water and others (see Chapter 4). Yet as early as 1977 a World Bank report had clearly warned of the potential dangers of failing to clear the flooded area (Goodland, 1977), as did a subsequent and more detailed INPA study. Yet both sets of findings were consistently ignored and INPA was even prohibited by ELETRONORTE from publishing its conclusions until Tucuruí was completed. The final preparations for the impoundment and flooding were carried out in great secrecy to minimise the risk of protests from environmental groups. An ELETRONORTE manager candidly admitted to one researcher (Neto, 1988) that, 'the environmental question was totally secondary to our main objective of completing the dam works on schedule, as the energy of Tucuruí is vital to the other great projects which are going to solve our foreign debt problem'.

The PGC's mineral extraction and processing activities are dependent not just upon Tucuruí's abundant electricity but also on the 900-kilometre railway, *Estrada de Ferro de Carajás* (EFC), which links the iron-ore mine to the port of Ponta da Madeira in São Luís (*Veja*, 9.11.83; *Railway Gazette International*, 1984; *Isto É*, 6.3.85). This enterprise has absorbed US$1·5 billion of the initial US$3·6 billion investment in the Carajás Programme. The first 213-kilometre stretch from São Luís to Santa Inês was inaugurated by President Figueiredo in November 1983, and the line finally opened in February 1985. The railway's strategic importance is illustrated by the fact that it was built in a record 780 days at a pace of one kilometre per day and completed a year and a half ahead of schedule, US$600 million under budget. As an engineering feat, the Carajás railway cannot fail to impress, with its sixty-one bridges and viaducts totalling over eleven kilometres; the largest, over the River Tocantins at Marabá, is 2,310 metres long. Groups of three diesel engines (manufactured by General Electric) each haul 160 freight wagons, reaching almost two kilometres in length and taking fifty-two hours for the round trip. It is estimated that if and when the iron-ore mine reaches its annual production target of thirty-five million tonnes, the EFC will require 2,876 wagons and sixty-eight locomotives. The existing single tracks can cope with up to fifty million tonnes annually. In addition to carrying freight, the EFC has proved increasingly valuable for passenger transport, particularly during the rainy season when local roads are often impassable. Due to the pressure of popular demand, the CVRD has expanded this role and, in little over a year after its official inauguration, the line carried 345,000 passengers (Pinto, 1987c).

Construction of the EFC has opened the way for the even more ambitious 'North – South' (*Norte – Sul*) railway project. This 1,600-kilometre line, originally projected for 1990, would connect the towns of Acailândia, on the Carajás – São Luís railway, and Anápolis, near Brasília, at an official estimated cost of US$2·6 billion. The idea for the scheme seems to have been thought up in 1982 by the CVRD which, believing that Japan would become a major grain importer, drew up agricultural development plans for the *cerrado* or central Brazilian plateau. Japan itself has plans to build a major new terminal capable of handling imports of thirty million tonnes of grain, iron-ore and coal. The two schemes, Cerrado and Carajás would thus enable a dual outlet for centre-west grain production and for Carajás minerals via both the deep-water Ponta da Madeira in São Luis and the port of Tubarão in Espírito Santo (Pinto, 1987a).

The 'North–South' railway idea was subsequently taken up by President Sarney and his Transport Minister, José Reinaldo Tavares, with strong backing from local politicians and landowners likely to benefit from the scheme, as well as the powerful lobby of construction companies. Conceived within the vaguely-defined 'Development Programme for Central Brazil' (*Programa de Desenvolvimento do Brasil Central*), the apparent rationale of the new railway became that of reducing transport costs by combining bulky, low-value iron-ore with high-value, low-density grain for export, primarily to Japan. Apart from any economic reasoning, the political attraction to President Sarney of another mega-project and the benefits it would bring to his home state of Maranhão made the scheme doubly appealing.

Thus, the 'North – South' railway was duly incorporated into the government's official goals (*Plano de Metas*) for agriculture for 1986–89, announced in August 1986. This would, according to official plans, involve increasing national production of basic food crops such as rice, beans, corn and manioc; the 935,000 square kilometres of *cerrado* traversed by the new railway would play a central role in this process, bringing under cultivation a further fifteen million hectares of arable land and producing 15·5 million tonnes of grain, or 20% of the total for Brazil (Momma, 1987; *O Senhor*, 12.5.87). According to the Ministry of Agriculture, the new project will 'link Amazonia by railway, particularly the Greater Carajás Programme area, to the markets of the Centre-South, at the same time stimulating the development of those regions under its influence' (Momma, 1987, p. 7).

Although this scheme became the pet project of President Sarney, as he himself put it (*O Senhor*, 12.5.87, p. 38), one of the 'two great projects of my government – the North – South railway and the bullet train (Rio–São Paulo)', it has been much-criticised on several grounds. Despite official assurances that the 'North–South' railway would bring untold benefits to the region and the country, initial engineering works were in fact started with no realistic assessment as to what these benefits might be, for no appraisal of economic or technical feasibility had been undertaken at that stage. Furthermore, it is an open secret that the powerful lobby of Brazilian construction companies, which was so influential in securing the rapid expansion of the road network into Amazonia during the 1970s, once again applied considerable pressure in favour of the scheme. The government, allegedly in debt to these same companies to the tune of US$5 billion, was also keen to generate the funds necessary to repay them. There is a strong suggestion, therefore, that the construction lobby has been instrumental in generating what may turn out to be an inappropriate venture. Parallels were drawn with Brazil's nuclear industry and the surface urban railway for the north-eastern city of Recife, built at a cost of US$400 million and subsequently operating at only 10% capacity due to a total miscalculation over future demand for its services (*Veja*, 20.5.87).

The 'hand-in-glove' relationship between government and company officials, their roles frequently overlapping, was amply illustrated by the scandal surrounding the submission of tenders for the first stage of the railway by some eighteen firms. In May 1987, just before the results were due to be officially announced, it was discovered that contracts had already been allocated in advance of the supposedly competitive tenders being submitted to VALEC, the

Ministry of Transport body in charge. An ex-Minister of Transport later revealed that it has always been common practice in Brazil for company representatives to meet with government officials beforehand to 'divide up to cake' rather than actively compete amongst themselves for public contracts (*Veja*, 20.5.87). In view of the public scandal which broke, President Sarney had little option but to cancel the tender; however, one month later an official enquiry 'identified irregularities but no cuplrits' (*Veja*, 10.6.87). Furthermore although the project was officially paralysed pending the results of a parliamentary commission of enquiry, VALEC continued to authorise survey work and negotiations with landowners over expropriations along northern sections of the railway in Maranhão and Goiás (*O Globo*, 26.7.87).

Doubts over the scheme's economic feasibility have not been in short supply. Arbitrarily budgeted at US$2·6 billion, with no funding sources clearly defined, its eventual cost has been variously put at between US$10 and US$30 billion (Pinto, 1987b; *O Senhor*, 12.5.87). Whatever the final outlay, such expenditure during a period when containment in public spending was being called for was not perceived as sound economic policy. In order to obtain initial funding for the railway and bypass resistance from the Finance Ministry to the project, Sarney sought to increase his control over the National Development Fund (FND) by appointing the then Planning Minister, Aníbal Teixeira, as vice-president of the board. However, since the FND can only approve projects when their economic feasibility has been demonstrated, this support will not be automatic (*Veja*, 10.6.87; *O Senhor*, 12.5.87). It is also alleged that, to justify the substantial capital investment involved the railway would have to export agricultural produce from the central plateau the whole year round, an impossible task without massive and unlikely irrigation works to stablise seasonally variable production levels.

Another commonly voiced concern surrounding the 'North – South' railway is that it has been given top government priority despite the doubts over its economic feasibility, while less grandiose projects have been ignored. These include the proposed railway link between Mato Grosso do Sul and the port of Paranaguá in Paraná state (known as the *Ferrovia de Produção*), which crosses already productive agricultural areas, and the 'East – West' railway between Rondônia and Cuiabá, in Mato Grosso, and Anápolis, in Goiás.

There has also been considerable interest by planners in improving the navigability of the Araguaia – Tocantins river system as a means of providing further production outlets, substituting the 'North – South' railway. A comprehensive integrated development package for the area was actually drawn up, with assistance from the Organisation of American States (OAS), under the Third National Development Plan (PND III, 1980–85), which included provisions for substantially improving fluvial transport as an outlet both for industrial and agricultural goods (PRODIAT, 1982–5). While many of the components of these Araguaia – Tocantins development plans were effectively absorbed by the Carajás Programme, however, it has been suggested that the fluvial transport system has become of merely secondary importance after the railway (Neto, 1988). Yet it is also alleged that improving the navigability of the Tocantins through the building of a lock at the Tucuruí dam by 1990, costing an estimated US$360 million, remains a top government priority (Pinto, 1987b).

Carajás plans for agricultural development

If mineral extraction and processing have formed the core of the Carajás Programme since its inception in the late 1970s, agriculture and forestry have also figured prominently in development plans for the region. The earliest studies, both by the CVRD itself (1979, 1980), as well its Japanese consultants (IDCJ, 1980), argued strongly in favour of utilising the expensive transport infrastructure, principally the Carajás railway, for expanding export-oriented capitalist farming and silvicultural activities. The Japanese document suggests, for example, that Carajás should become an 'export corridor' based on agriculture, ranching and forestry on huge estates covering some 8·5 million hectares (IDCJ, 1980). These vague proposals were later refined by the CVRD (1981a, 1981b), whose plan envisaged spending US$11 billion on rural schemes covering some ten million hectares of eastern Amazonia by 1990, yielding an annual income of over US$7 billion. One-third of the area would be divided into 300 cattle ranches of 10,000 hectares each, and a further four million hectares would be devoted to large-scale rice cultivation. Sugar and manioc plantations were planned for another 2·4 million hectares, and 800 distilleries would produce 5·4 billion litres of alcohol annually. Furthermore, areas totalling 1,800 square kilometres along the railway corridor would be set aside for eucalyptus plantations, designed to supply timber for charcoal production. The hopelessly ambitious targets were based on projected yields way above the national average and beyond those attainable under Amazonian conditions. In addition, the heavy inputs of fertilisers and pesticides, etc. would make most projects economically unsound (Baiardi, 1982). Subsequent studies by the CVRD (1984c; Falesi *et al*, 1985) re-emphasise the top priority given to highly capitalised, export-oriented farming, while ruling out low-capital units as unsuitable.

In February 1982 a technical co-operation agreement was signed between the Brazilian government and JICA, the Japan International Co-operation Agency (PGC, 1982). Japanese specialists were assigned to study the production and export potential of Carajás in the areas of mining, industry, transport, agriculture, cattle-raising and forestry, and their first report appeared the following year (JICA, 1983). A range of twenty-eight agricultural products was studied, in terms of both domestic and export demand, focusing on oilseeds, feedstuffs, ethyl alcohol, industrial crops, fibres, timber, cattle and tropical fruits. Significantly, food staples were omitted from the study, despite a declaration several months beforehand from the PGC's director, Nestor Jost, which implied that food crops were to be given a high priority (*Jornal do Brasil*, 7.9.82). The report's tentative conclusions suggest that there is export potential for certain 'mature' products which are well-established on international markets and for which demand is likely to expand; these include soybean, palm-oil and rubber, as well as hardwoods and by-products such as particle board and pulpwood. Others such as Brazil nuts, tropical fruits, cotton and animal feedstuffs merit more caution due to demand, production and marketing constraints. The consultants were clearly worried about the possible ecological consequences of blindly going ahead with such schemes, however, and recommend 'preservation of the environment with proper forest management' (JICA, 1983, p. S-30).

A further (Phase II) agreement was signed in June 1984 between JICA and the Brazilian government, in which a group of twenty-eight Japanese consultants was given three months, from July to September 1984, to formulate development projects for seven selected sub-regions of the Carajás Programme area in the fields of mining, metallurgy, agriculture and agroindustry (PGC, 1984b). Their subsequent report makes a commendable effort to strike a balance in its recommendations for agriculture, livestock and forestry expansion between the priority of commercial profitability and the need for environmental sustainability. A greater sensitivity to the needs of the small farm sector in Amazonia is illustrated by the fact that the report places basic food crop production, such as rice, maize, beans and cassava, for both domestic consumption and for sale, as the first priority, 'to improve the level of these farmers' living standards' (JICA, 1985, p. 26). Sedentarising farmers and discouraging shifting cultivation is stressed as a prerequisite for improving production levels and for minimising ecological damage. Increasing the competitiveness of certain commercial products is also highlighted; these include oil palm, a locally-adapted 'tropical' variety of soybean, pepper, Brazil nuts, beef and timber. Noting that two-thirds of the arable land in the Carajás area is still unused, the study proposes four farm models of five hectares (subsistence farm) and one hundred hectares (land rotation) for food crops, 200 hectares for perennial crops such as oil palm and 500 hectares for soybean.

Yet the Japanese consultants are under no illusions about potential political-institutional constraints, commenting on the need for official provision and co-ordination of supporting measures for farmers in the form of credit, price support, extension services, co-operatives, transport infrastructure, marketing channels and landownership regulation. In addition, they warn of the dangers of 'indiscriminate development', affirming that, 'Though development is essential, the most pressing issue in the area seems to be how to harmonise agricultural land development and environmental conservation' (JICA, 1985, p. 27). The report comments pointedly upon the 'remarkably poor' level of reforestation in Amazonia and calls for 'rational natural forest management for timber harvesting and the prevention of forest degradation', emphasising the need for careful controls and site selection for agricultural activities requiring further deforestation (JICA, 1985, pp. 59–61).

None of these direct Japanese recommendations for systematic agricultural development within the Carajás Programme area have so far been taken up. A number of reasons may be advanced for this apparently total waste of technical expertise; these include high project implementation costs, lack of an adequate institutional structure and inadequate farmer support mechanisms as well as an unstable landownership situation. A more convincing explanation would, however, be that mineral extraction and processing has always been the government's uppermost concern in the PGC, as reflected in the scale of investments into this sector during the 1980s, while agricultural development in Amazonia has a low priority due to its limited foreign exchange-earning capacity. The Japanese proposals were also severely attacked on social and environmental grounds, critics arguing (not altogether fairly) that such projects would encourage deforestation, land concentration and rural violence, and would discriminate against small farmers (Pinto, 1982; IBASE, 1983; SBPC, 1983).

However, even if Japanese proposals have not themselves been put into effect, they undoubtedly exerted a strong influence upon attempts by the Brazilian government to devise its own rural development strategy for the Carajás Programme. The most comprehensive plan for agricultural development and related activities in the Carajás region is undoubtedly the *Programa Grande Carajás Agrícola* (PGCA) prepared by the Ministry of Agriculture (Brazil, 1983). Budgeted at US$1·18 billion, it draws much of it inspiration from previous JICA reports with their emphasis on large-scale, commercial, export-oriented production using capital-intensive 'modern' (that is, non-indigenous) technology. Its broad aims were to increase and diversify production of food and industrial products within seven development 'poles' and in areas immediately surrouding the five largest towns and cities in the region. By sedentarising the traditionally itinerant agriculture of Amazonia and introducing modern inputs, the plan envisaged substantially increasing output not just of traditional food crops such as maize, beans rice and cassava but also of soybean, livestock, vegetables, ethanol (from sugar-cane) and charcoal, generating no fewer than 60,000 'direct' and 300,000 'indirect' jobs. In addition, by imposing controls on deforestation, making provisions for replanting, and creating a class of small-medium family farmers, the PGCA hoped to slow down environmental degradation and land concentration.

The plan made provisions for 238,000 hectares of mechanised soybean cultivation, 12,600 hectares of sugar-cane, and almost half a million hectares of pasture for beef cattle, which are judged to be 'well-suited' to Amazonia; a special 'sanitary pocket' of 225,000 hectares would be established where foot-and-mouth disease and undulant fever could be eliminated, thus opening up new markets for unprocessed beef in the USA, Japan and Europe (Fearnside, 1986b; Nation and Komer, 1987). In addition, 3·6 million hectares along the Carajás railway would be set aside for eucalyptus planta-tions to provide charcoal for the numerous pig-iron smelting plants. Nineteen farm models were drawn up for small (up to fifteen hectares), medium (sixty to eighty hectares) and large (80–500 hectares) producers. Capitalisation of some 16,000 farmers under the plan would, it was projected, increase the gross value of agricultural production almost eightfold, from US$42 million to US$317 million. Supplementary services were also to be provided to participants in the scheme, including extension services, co-operatives, market-ing facilities, improved transport, irrigation and resettlement where necessary.

As with previous proposals for the systematic development of the agricultural sector of Carajás, however, there are grave incon-sistencies between the laudable, if ambitious, overall objectives of the plan regarding production, environmental protection and social justice on the one hand, and the means suggested for achieving them on the other. The PGCA is consistent with previous agricultural development strategies for Amazonia in being, despite its professed concern for the plight of small producers, unashamedly *latifúndio*-biased. Only 17% of the land is in fact allocated to small farmers, while 83% is set aside for large and medium-sized producers. As will become evident from Chapter 3, such a distribution would not attack but mirror existing inequalities in a region where the pattern of landownership is highly skewed and becoming steadily more pola-rised, producing increasingly violent struggles over land access. The continued emphasis on ranching, which is expected under the PGCA to generate US$41 million p.a. in animal products, blatantly ignores the historical association of pasture formation with land concentra-tion, violent conflicts and environmental destruction. Furthermore, as is well known, little employment is created by large cattle ranches, yet small farms, which are accorded low priority in the plans, generate up to sixteen times as many jobs per hectare.

The plans have a heavy technocratic bias, which totally ignores the positive attributes of traditional indigenous and locally-adapted shifting cultivation (universally condemning these as 'primitive' and 'destructive'). They extol the virtues of mechanisation while being apparently blind to the wealth of accumulated evidence testifying to its negative ecological impact in terms of soil erosion and compaction. Low-capital farm management is considered unsuitable for the re-gion on the whole, with mechanised farming awarded high priority

(PGC, 1984c). However, the proposed farming systems with their optimistic projected yields and heavy reliance on expensive inputs, are high-risk and unlikely to appeal to smaller farmers with limited resources. While only 15% of the budget is allocated for 'social' projects such as co-operatives and colonisation, 70% is set aside for subsidies to large producers in the form of credit, transport and agroindustry (Brazil, 1983; Fearnside, 1986b).

The wisdom of establishing eucalyptus plantations has also been seriously called into question, due to the risks of pest invasion and soil degradation associated with reforestation by single species. However, the very notion of large scale re-planting in Amazonia for the commercial purposes of charcoal production is questionable since this will make investment unprofitable for the steel companies which are being so generously subsidised by the government as an incentive to draw capital into the Carajás region. Pig-iron smelting, as demonstrated by several studies (see Chapter 4), is only profitable in Amazonia if charcoal is supplied using the native rainforest; as soon as more expensive fuel produced in plantations is considered, the exercise becomes uneconomic.

As events turned out, the PGCA proposals got no further than the planning stage, with little likelihood that they will ever be implemented. The Ministry of Agriculture did entertain the idea that JICA would fund the scheme as part of the Japanese global strategy of increasing its food supplies from overseas (*Folha de Sao Paulo*, 7.10.84), but to no avail. There are several more obvious reasons for the shelving of this apparent attempt to balance industrial development with some form of agricultural modernisation. The cost of the scheme at US$1·2 billion, while far lower than that of previous plans, was still considered too high by the Brazilian government, which had industrial growth in Amazonia as its top priority. Nestor Jost, head of the PGC at the time, claimed that the outgoing government did not have the counterpart funds required by the Inter-American Development Bank (IDB), which had been approached for co-financing; the decision about the PGCA's future would be left to the incoming administration. The then Minister of Planning, Delfim Neto was, for both economic and political reasons, allegedly reluctant to guarantee the necessary cash; in addition to economic constraints, the proposed leading role for the Ministry of Agriculture in the Carajás region was not welcomed by the Planning Minister or by SUDENE and SUDAM, whose areas of jurisdication overlap with that of the PGC (MINAGRI, 1987a). Serious doubts were also raised about the technical and administrative feasibility of the scheme by Brazilian officials as well as by the IDB itself (Falesi, 1986).

It has also been suggested, however, that the time-consuming and expensive six-volume PGCA preliminary study was in fact no more than a cosmetic exercise. According to an official spokesman (MINAGRI, 1987b), it was conceived purely to present an image to foreign investors of the PGC as a well-integrated development plan for eastern Amazonia and thus to facilitate soft loans. The Brazilian government, it is suggested, never seriously intended implementing the PGCA, given the overriding concern with industrial investment and the need to complete projects such as the iron-ore mine, the railway, Tucuruí and improved port facilities in timely fashion in order to secure vital foreign loans and investments.

A series of proposals for developing the agricultural potential of the Carajás Programme area, advanced by both Brazilian and Japanese government organisations throughout the early 1980s has, for a variety of probably interrelated reasons, met with a similar fate. Yet even if these ambitious plans have themselves not been implemented, the Carajás Programme retains specific, if *ad hoc*, provisions for the development of agriculture and livestock. The major direct stimulus offered by the PGC in this field lies in the tax incentive scheme set up in 1980, discussed above. Although by far the major beneficiaries of fiscal incentives have been mineral extraction and processing enterprises, Brazilian as well as foreign, and the large construction companies, significant investments have been taking place into agriculture, livestock and lumbering. Table 2.2 shows that, by mid-1987, over twenty such projects had been approved by the PGC Interministerial Council, ranging from the Tucumã private colonisation scheme, oil palm plantations and processing facilities to ranching, meat plants, margarine, ethanol, poultry and charcoal production. In fact, many of the investors in these sectors are also major participants in industrial and infrastructural developments; these include, for example, Mêndes Júnior, Andrade Gutiérrez and Metaltec.

Although such schemes have absorbed only about 1% of total PGC funding, their impact is likely to severely exacerbate the symptoms of agrarian crisis observable in eastern Amazonia as a whole. On the basis of past experience in Amazonia, cattle ranching will certainly encourage land concentration, environmental degradation and land

Table 2.2 Agricultural, agroindustrial and livestock projects approved by the Carajás Programme

Project/Company	Products	Location
Dendê-Méndes Júnior Agricultura do Pará	Oil palm plantation (6000 ha), oil extraction (32,000 tons/a)	Acará-PA
Tucumã Colonisation Project, CONSAG.	Private colonisation scheme (400,000 ha)	Tucumã–PA
AGRIMA–Agrícola Industrial do Maranhão	Babaçú nut processing	Codó–MA
CIT–Cia. Ind. Técnica	Babaçú nut processing, charcoal, cellulose	São Luís–MA
METALTEC Ltda.	Charcoal (21,000 tons/a)	Itaquí–MA
Agropecuária Ceres, SA	Cattle, lumbering, babaçú nuts, charcoal	Rio Caxias–MA
Carajás SA	Meat processing (9,750 tons/a)	São Luís–MA
CIPASA–Castanha Industrial do Pará Ltda.	Lumbering, charcoal, Brazil nuts	Mojú–PA
MIAME–Madeira Itália Americana Com. Ind. Ltda	Lumbering, railway sleepers	Breves–PA
AGROPER– Agropecuária Rodominas Ltda.	Cattle (500 head)	Santa Luzia–MA
Pacajá–Queiróz Galvão do Carajás SA	Cattle (3,400 head)	Portel–PA
Cia de Terras da Meta Geral	Land parcelling (34,000 ha) cattle (16,500 head)	S.Félix do Xingú–PA
AGISA–A. O. Gaspar Indústria SA	Margarine (2,000 tons/a), soap, glycerine	São Luís–MA
Cia Agropecuária Santa Maria de Canarana	Ethanol (11,000m3/a)	S.João do Araguaia– PA

Table 2.2 (continued)

Project/Company	Products	Location
DENAM–Dendê da Amazonia SA	Brazil nuts (800 tons/a), cashew nuts (600 tons/a), charcoal (7,200 tons/a)	S.Domingos do Capim–PA
Meape Ltda.	Lumbering, charcoal	Turiaçú–MA
Agropecuária Rio Dezoito SA	Cattle (10,000 head)	S.Félix do Xingú–PA
A. O. Gaspar Indústria e Comércio SA	Oil extraction from babaçú (18,000 tons/a), soybean (300 tons/a)	São Luís–MA
Cia Avícola da Amazônia	Poultry (1,800 tons/a)	Paço do Lumiar–MA
Agropecuária Tratex do Marahão SA	Cattle (500 head), cereals	Riacho–MA
CODENPA–Cia. Dendê Norte Paraense	Dendê oil (7,200 tons/a) groundnut oil (1,400 tons/a)	S. António do Tauá–PA

Note: Data based on projects approved by the PGC Interministerial Council at July 1987.
Source: PGC (1987).

conflict by virtue of the large subsidies granted, subsequent land speculation and owners' total neglect of conservation. Ethanol production, if substantially expanded in Amazonia, will have a similarly adverse social impact to that experienced in the North-East, where small farmers have been evicted and food crops replaced by sugarcane. The most dramatic ecological consequences of fiscal incentives for agriculture and related activities will, however, be felt around the industrial foci such as Marabá and Acailândia along the Carajás–São Luís railway. As pig-iron smelting gets under way in 1988 and more of the proposed thirty plants come on stream, enterprises are being established, heavily subsidised by PGC incentives, to supply them with large quantities of charcoal. Indiscriminate rainforest destruction for charcoal production, already in evidence well before the commencement of pig-iron smelting itself, will eventually result in the removal of 29,000 hectares of forest every year (CVRD, 1987).

Chapter 3 and 4 deal with the likely social and environmental impact of these policies.

The PGC's area of jurisdiction for investment purposes overlaps with that of SUDAM, whose own fiscal incentive scheme (FINAM) also provides cheap funding for entrepreneurs within 'Legal Amazonia'. SUDAM's bias in its agricultural investment towards agroindustrial and livestock units is well known, with two-thirds of its approved projects falling into these categories. Their contribution toward developing the region has been called seriously into question by an official evaluation of ninety-three operational projects, which concluded that only 16% of proposed investments had been effected, and only three were commercially profitable (Gasques and Yokomizo, 1985; SUDAM, 1985). Most funds, it would appear, had been diverted into purely speculative, non-productive activities. Simultaneously, INCRA encourages deforestation and pasture-formation as proof of land 'improvement', a prerequisite for the granting of legal tenure (and, hence, subsidised funding). Thus, the combined impact of PGC and SUDAM incentives in liable to be doubly destructive and of dubious value in promoting sustainable or significantly productive development of any kind in eastern Amazonia.

Although there has so far been no implementation of systematically planned agricultural development in the Carajás region, this situation could change in the near future. The most ambitious enterprise in this connection is linked to the building of the 1,600-kilometre 'North–South' railway, discussed above, from Anápolis, near Brasília, to Acailândia, on the Carajás–São Luís line. Apart from creating an outlet for industrial products from the Carajás area, the 'North–South' railway is expected to stimulate agicultural development on thirty-two million hectares of the fertile *cerrado* or upland savanna region of central Brazil, expanding further still Japanese–Brazilian soybean and other projects in the area. It is also reminiscent of earlier plans formulated by EMBRAPA in its 'Grain Project' to deflect development from the rainforest itself to the central Brazilian plateau (EMBRAPA, 1982). The projected railway corridor area currently produces some 1·5 million tonnes of grain annually, but this figure could be increased to 100 million tonnes, according to official estimates, with 150 or even 180 million tonnes of rice, soybean, corn and wheat considered 'feasible' (Momma, 1987, p. 25). Most of this increased production would be transported by the new railway. However, as already mentioned, although the plan has been justified on economic grounds, much controversy surrounds the project which has been widely condemned as serving short-term political interests rather than broader developmental goals.

Whatever the economic feasibility of such agricultural plans for the *cerrado*, however, the constraints posed by soils, topography, climate and general environment are considerably fewer than are likely to be encountered further north in the heart of the Carajás Programme area itself. Although agricultural and livestock development has so far been *ad hoc*, with projects submitted and approved on an individual basis, attention has been given to promoting a more structured approach since the demise of the *Carajás Agrícola* plan. A year after the inauguration of Brazil's 'New Republic' in 1985, the Ministry of Planning announced its intention of setting up a series of agricultural schemes along 480 kilometres of the Carajás railway corridor, in addition to forestry projects already in existence (*Folha de São Paulo*, 31.5.86). Although it is still unclear whether these projects will form part of a more systematic, planned agricultural strategy for the region, thus departing from past practices, recent surveys of the area in question cast serious doubt over the feasibility of such an endeavour.

The CVRD and JICA have consistently expressed the desirability of developing agriculture, forestry and livestock along the Carajás–São Luís railway corridor in order to utilise more fully the rail transport facilities built primarily for industrial use. However, a study undertaken for the CVRD by EMBRAPA (Falesi *et al*, 1986) of the entire 900-kilometre line and its immediate area of influence drew some rather cautious conclusions in this respect. Over 90% of the soils in the region were classed as being of low fertility (acidic oxisols and ultisols). They impose severe limitations on the practice of continuous agriculture, that is, the 'modern', sedentary farm models envisaged by successive development plans for the region, requiring heavy inputs of fertilisers, selected seeds, insecticides and careful land management; these areas of poorer soils were recommended for perennial tree crops and managed pasture. A mere 3% of the soils was considered fertile enough for food crops, located in areas such as Santa Inês, the Pindaré Valley and Bacabal, which have for many years been centres of small farmer agriculture.

These soil characteristics should have come as no great surprise;

they mirror closely overall soil distribution within Amazonian *terra firme*, although the Carajás area has an even lower proportion of fertile soils (entisols) than the Amazon Basin's 10% (Furley, 1989). Generally speaking, then, agricultural expansion in the Carajás area is still conceived by planners in terms of high-cost, capital-intensive units, while the potential for making greater use of traditional technology and farming systems is, at best, extremely limited and confined to existing regions of more concentrated peasant occupation. Yet, as will be shown in the final chapter of this volume, although such an alternative has not received serious official consideration at the level of agrarian policy formulation, there is considerable potential for expanding agroforestry in Amazonia.

Aside from the grandiose schemes mentioned so far, something of a gesture towards peasant farmer development was made with the announcement in early 1986 of two so-called 'integrated rural development projects' in small communities along the railway corridor, chosen for their concentration of small settlers and degree of community organisation (PGC, 1986; Gistelninck, 1986, n.d.). Alto Alegre, near Santa Luzia in Maranhão, consists of some 1,500 families of *posseiros* and tenant farmers in one of the Carajás railway corridor's few pockets of really fertile soils. Despite the fact that it has been one of the most violent areas in Amazonia since the mid-1970s, small farmers have been reasonably successful in resisting incursions by land-grabbers. Alto Alegre thus has a history of community cohesiveness based on strong local political organisation. Sororó, near Marabá in Pará, was titled by GETAT in 1980 and consists of some 180 small plots of land covering an area of 13,000 hectares. As such, it is a recently established group of three communities and lacks such a politicised tradition (Falesi, 1986).

Plans for these two areas include improvements in agriculture, transport, health and educational facilities, as well as land-titling. In Sororó it is hoped to 'create' (sic) a stronger community organisation by obliging farmers from the communities to meet regularly. In addition, EMBRAPA will attempt to introduce a new crop system to supplement food crops with cash-earning perennials such as rubber, black pepper and citrus fruits (Falesi, 1986). When the project was officially announced in mid-1986 the sum of US$3,400,000 had supposedly been set aside for investments into this area (*O Liberal*, 2.6.86). It was hoped that, if they were successful, these schemes could be replicated at strategic points along the 900-kilometre railway, creating a stable class of small farmers (PGC, 1986). However, only a few months later these projects were effectively abandoned pending the November 1986 election and, by mid-1987, no further work had been undertaken on them. In any event, the limited scale of the exercise, should it be resumed at some later stage means that the vast majority of the 800,000 small farmers, landless labourers and their families within the PGC area will remain unaffected by such proposals.

Many different groups, both Brazilian and foreign, are being well-served by the Greater Carajás Programme. When the PGC first got under way it was justified by the Figueiredo administration, through Planning Minister, Delfim Neto, as primarily serving Brazil's national interest; in the short term the US$1·7 billion of loans would take pressure off the balance of payments, while in the longer run export earnings would help generate a trade surplus and assist in the servicing of the country's rapidly growing foreign debt. According to Delfim, the Carajás Programme was 'a great hope for Brazil' and export markets the only solution, declaring unequivocally that 'there is no alternative model' (*Folha de São Paulo*, 19.9.82; LARR, 17.9.82). The Geisel administration had laid out its plans for developing the mineral resources of Amazonia in its Second National Development Plan (1975–79), although it did not commit itself to an 'integrated' strategy as such. In addition, considerable internal pressure was exerted by the CVRD upon the administration to switch iron and steel production from the state of Minas Gerais, where natural forests were close to exhaustion and costs of production based on reforested timber were becoming excessive. Amazonia, with its vast stocks of lumber, presented an attractive alternative as long as adequate official subsidies were forthcoming.

At a time when the Brazilian government was seeking a more profitable, and possible less socially divisive strategy than cattle ranching for developing Amazonia, Japanese experts provided the technical gloss and the organisational framework within which a more systematic approach to exploiting the area's mineral resources could be justifiably undertaken. But however much such inputs were rationalised in terms of better regional planning, the fact is that Japan's involvement was motivated by its global stategy of diversifying supplies of strategic raw materials and processed minerals and it was able to negotiate generous concessions in exchange for soft loans; Carajás was to become a crucial source of iron-ore, pig-iron, aluminium, other minerals, lumber, and in future, agricultural produce. The Japanese are the largest bilateral donor in the scheme, with investments totalling over US$400 million in the iron-ore mine, railway and ALBRAS–ALUNORTE complex. The Carajás Programme is not ideologically one-sided however, since agreements have been reached not only with the US and EEC but also with the USSR and the People's Republic of China.

Brazilian nationalist fears over the possible foreign domination of Amazonia are as old as settlement of the region itself, epitomised perhaps in the condemnation by Reis two decades ago of 'international avarice' (*cobiça international*). Interestingly, the preface to a fifth edition of the book, published in 1982, spoke of the 'threats to the region which have been denounced...provoking the interest of foreign capital, which serve the political-economic interest of imperialism' (Reis, 1982, p. 11). The mantle has been taken up by more recent writings specifically on the PGC, an obvious target which has aroused considerably controversy. The programme has been criticised as an 'attack on the heart of Amazonia' and a 'Trojan horse' for US interests (Pinto, 1982). Another contemporary publication accused the government of 'mortgaging the country's future' and of 'internationalising Amazonia' at the expense of Brazilian sovereignty (IBASE, 1983) while a further critic branded the PGC 'an unarmed invasion' of Amazonia, by domestic as well as overseas alien interests which have no regard for the integrity of the region itself (Cota, 1984). A more recent analysis of the PGC concluded that foreign control over the programme has been so great that it totally distorted regional development planning for eastern Amazonia (Neto, 1988, 1989). These points of view are explored in the final chapter, which contends that it is too simple to see the PGC solely, or even primarily, as a vehicle for serving the interests of overseas end-users. It must also be viewed within the broader context of the Brazilian State's policy towards its multi-faceted use of the Amazonian frontier as a means of serving varied economic, political and social interests.

While previous strategies have perhaps achieved little in terms of declared commercial profit or export income, given the leakages and corruption endemic to the system, the Carajás Programme is, for the present, profitably oriented towards international markets, and its success will depend on maintenance of a satisfactory rate of return for investors. The one component which might have made some headway in the direction of serving peasant producers specifically, the *Programa Grande Carajás Agrícola* (PGC, 1983), was unceremoniously mothballed; furthermore, doubts persist whether it was ever taken seriously outside the Ministry of Agriculture in view of the Brazilian government's overriding concern with bringing the mining and industrial projects on stream in good time. Such relegation of small-farmer interests to the lowest of priorities is entirely consistent with development policy-making, not just in Amazonia but in every other region of Brazil.

In choosing, with foreign assistance, to modernise Amazonia through a policy of industrialisation and capital-intensive agriculture, however, planners have not only failed once more to cater for the interests of the vast majority of small rural producers. Policymakers in Brasília are not just guilty by omission. More than this, the various components of the Carajás Programme actively discriminate against peasant farmers. Already familiar adverse trends associated with Amazonian settlement processes during the 1960s and 1970s are being severely exacerbated by the PGC; these include land concentration, violent rural conflict and gradual loss of food security, as well as extensive environmental damage resulting primarily from growing deforestation. These worsening social and ecological impacts threaten further still the already tenuous grip of peasant farmers on land and resources in the region, aspects which will now be taken up in more detail.

3

Carajás and the agrarian crisis
I: violence, land and livelihood

Brazil's Amazon Basin is in a state of growing turmoil. Official development policies for the region in general, and the Carajás area in particular, have fostered a strongly *latifúndio*-biased development model which favours large-scale, individual and corporate landowners with generous subsidies of all kinds, while the interests of the vast majority of small cultivators have been almost totally neglected. The contradictory nature of Brazilian policies towards peasant cultivators is particularly evident in the Amazon Basin. Although land-hungry migrants from the North-East and South have been encouraged to colonise the tropical rainforest with, amongst other objectives, the aim of easing social conflicts in their regions of origin, the official support necessary to guarantee a stable existence in Amazonia has been denied them by the State which has, for a variety of reasons, concentrated its efforts on assisting commercial and speculative capital investment. As shown in the previous two chapters, this has taken the form principally of incentives to the livestock sector although, more recently, support has become increasingly diversified into other agricultural, industrial and mining enterprises, as in the Carajás Programme.

Such unbalanced development strategy has brought with it social and environmental disruption on a scale unprecedented in Brazilian history. This 'agrarian crisis' has made it increasingly difficult for small farmers to obtain a stable livelihood in Amazonia, generating a climate of widespread insecurity and instability which official action has done little to ameliorate and much to encourage. While integration and settlement policies during the 1970s certainly exacerbated these trends, the Carajás Programme represents a major new phase in this emerging crisis. Although, as Chapter 6 will argue, the State does have the technical ability to formulate and implement policies which could go some way towards a more sustainable and peasant-biased development strategy for Amazonia, it has chosen a very different path. Brazil's Carajás Programme is but the latest example of large-scale Amazonian development which has brought little progress to the majority of eastern Amazonia's rural populace but has, on the contrary, often been regressive in terms of the havoc and loss of livelihood created. Chapter 2 demonstrated the PGC's priorities in terms of capitalised, large-scale rural as well as industrial enterprises. Their contribution to Amazonia's mounting agrarian crisis will now be examined. The following sections deal with the issues of escalating rural violence associated with land conflict, land concentration and growing food insecurity, while Chapter 4 considers associated problems of environmental decay.

Rural violence

Perhaps the best-known feature of Amazonia's current predicament is escalating rural violence, a product of the struggle amongst competing social and economic groups over access to land, that most basic of commodities. Since the mid-1960s when, for the first time, Brazilian governments sought to integrate the region into the mainstream of national life in order to fulfil a multiplicity of goals, Amazonia has witnessed a rapid increase in land conflicts. Yet violent confrontation over access to land is certainly nothing new either to Brazil or to the Amazon Basin. The North-East, for example, has a violent history of land appropriation by powerful interests which still manifests itself in the form of land battles and deaths in the countryside (fifty-four in 1986). As many studies have shown (Goodman, 1978; Foweraker, 1981) land-grabbing or *grilagem* has followed the agricultural frontier in Brazil as it has moved westwards from the North-East and northwards from the South. In central Brazil land conflict may be traced back to the 1950s when the Centre-West replaced the southern state of Paraná as the principle destination of poor rural migrants from the North-East.

Clashes among poor peasant cultivators (*posseiros*), larger commercial farmers and indigenous groups have escalated dramatically in Amazonia as the frontier has been opened up to settlers. The federal roadbuilding programme and, in particular, SUDAM's policy from 1966 of granting large subsidies to agribusiness interests, were primarily responsible for speeding up both settlement and, with it, open conflicts of interest well beyond what would have otherwise been expected. Asselin (1982), for example, has described in great detail the penetration of land-grabbing in western Maranhão along the valley of the River Pindaré, which spread as a direct function of the federal and state road-building programmes and government subsidies to commercial farmers. This was facilitated by a lucrative industry which sprang up to supply would-be owners with false land titles, with the connivance of the State legal and administrative apparatus (Foweraker, 1981). So intense was this activity that one notorious politican, João Paraibano, 'was reputed to have sold the state of Maranhão twice over' (Asselin, 1982, p. 26). Even state governments were widely involved in the illegal 'sale' of lands. The state-backed Maranhão Colonisation Company (COMARCO), for example, defrauded many investors in the early 1970s, including large firms such as Volkswagen, by 'selling' false titles in the Pindaré sector, which covers almost three million hectares. The situation was complicated further still when, in 1971, the federal government decreed as government property subordinated to INCRA all land within one hundred kilometres along federal highways in Amazonia.

Two other measures have recently helped to increase the pace of land concentration and rural violence. The government's economic reform package of 1985–86, known as the 'Cruzado Plan', temporarily reduced the large speculative profits to be had on the money markets; property, both rural and urban, became the most profitable investment for those with funds to spare. In addition, the official announcement of Brazil's agrarian reform in 1985, which would expropriate targeted areas of under-utilised land, also encouraged peasant evictions and violent confrontation. Many landowners tried to expel occupants from estates in an attempt to plant pasture and persuade INCRA that the land was being put to 'productive' use, and thus ineligible for expropriation (see below). Peasant families themselves seized the opportunity and, overnight, occupied large estates in the hope of eventually acquiring titled land under the proposed reforms. There have been many such 'invasions', especially on the traditional Brazil nut estates in the *polígono dos castanhais*, the 'Brazil-nut polygon' near the town of Marabá, at the heart of the Carajás Programme; Chapter 5 details some of the better known peasant occupations and the bloody conflicts which have surrounded them.

Between the military takeover of 1964 and the end of 1986 some 1,500 people died in Brazilian land conflicts (MIRAD, 1986d, 1987; MST, 1987; Amnesty International, 1988). In recent years the annual death toll has been rising steadily. Latest available data show, for example, that over 1,000 such deaths occurred between 1980–86; there was a doubling of deaths from rural violence from 122 in 1984 to 261 in 1985, with a further 14% increase to 298 in 1986. Levels of rural conflict have been especially marked on the Amazon frontier. CONTAG has estimated that during the late 1970s, of a total peasant population of four million in Amazonia, about 30,000 families, or some 150,000 people, were evicted from the land each year, representing a rate of displacement of about 4% p.a. (Branford and Glock, 1985). By 1981 over half of all land conflicts in Brazil took place in the Amazon region. The latest and most comprehensive report on the subject, by the Ministry of Agrarian Reform, shows that by 1986 this fiugure had increased to 64%; the Centre-West in particular saw a jump of 148% from 1985 to 1986 (MIRAD, 1987). The Amazon frontier also shows the highest incidence of murders involving two or more victims, these being especially common on large estates of over 10,000 hectares. Within Amazonia itself, Pará has the highest death-rate from land conflicts, with ninety-three in 1986, or one-third of the national total. During 1986 no fewer than twenty-one violent deaths were registered on only four large properties in Pará.

Eastern Amazonia is a particularly strong focus of violent land conflict, notably in the 'parrot's beak' area, where the states of Pará, Maranhão and Goiás meet. Here, during 1986, six micro-regions (Araguaia Paraense, Marabá and Xingú in Pará, Mearim and Itapecurú in Maranhão, and Extremo Norte Goiano in Goiás) accounted for sixty-nine fatalities, almost two-thirds of the total deaths for those three states. This compares with 104 deaths in the same area the previous year (MIRAD, 1986d, 1987). In the first six months of 1985 no fewer than thirty-six peasant farmers from only three municipalities in the Carajás project area (Marabá, Sao João do Araguaia and Xinguara) died at the hands of gunmen in land conflicts, while sixteen such deaths occurred in a two-week period in May of 1986 (CEPASP, 1986; *The Sunday Times*, 1986).

It is no coincidence that the so-called 'parrot's beak', the most violent rural area in Brazil, also shows high and worsening indices of land concentration (see Table 3.6). In addition to the statistical evidence presented below, one particular example illustrates this point. In southern Pará, between 1978–81, eight enterprises expanded their properties by 4·5 million hectares to a total of six million hectares. This was equivalent to the entire area of public lands titled since 1963, or 40% of all farms with up to one hundred hectares (*Jornal do Brasil*, 16.6.87). Neither is it a coincidence that there exists this strong link between land concentration and rural violence at the heart of the Carajás Programme. Property accumulation in the area has to a large extent been a function of the degree of violence and intimidation employed by large landowners both to prevent smallholders from occupying their estates and to encroach upon peasants' lands, a process strongly encouraged by official subsidies.

As might be expected, the rising death toll comprises mainly peasant farmers and labourers. Individual murders of small farmers and rural union leaders are so common that they are hardly newsworthy and barely merit space in Brazilian newspapers. However, massacres occur periodically and are the focus of national attention for a while. In addition, the occasional deaths of lawyers and priests create a loud public outcry, at least temporarily, before these too are gradually forgotten. During 1985–87 two religious workers were murdered in the Carajás area: a nun, Adelaide Molinari (on 14.4.85) and a priest, Jósimo Tavares (on 10.5.86). Sister Adelaide was killed in error during an attempt on the life of a trade unionist in Marabá. Father Tavares was shot in the back on the steps of the Church Land Commission's Office in Imperatriz, of which he was the co-ordinator, his murder allegedly ordered by a local landowner. Three lawyers defending the interests of peasant farmers met a similar fate in this period, including Paulo Fontelles, in June 1987, on the outskirts of Belém, at the hands of an assassin reputed to have been paid by landowners resentful of his assistance to rural trades unions in land disputes (*Jornal do Brasil*, 12.6.87; *Folha de São Paulo*, 12.6.87).

Table 3.1 provides brief details of several major conflicts resulting in deaths within the Carajás area, particularly in southern Pará. Yet, as high as the above figures might seem, they represent to some extent the tip of an iceberg. Many fatalities go unregistered, the victims simply 'disappearing', perhaps into one of the numerous clandestine cemeteries on landowners' estates which are occasionally discovered, particularly in southern Pará (MIRAD, 1987). However,

Table 3.1 Major fatal incidents of rural violence in the Carajás Programme area, 1985–87

Date	Location	Details
January–April 1985	Fazenda Castanhal Pau Ferrado* [Xinguara–PA]	5 peasants shot by gunmen 5 gunmen also killed
May–July 1985	Fazenda Surubim [Xinguara–PA]	8 peasant farmers killed by gunmen
June 1985	Fazenda Castanhal Ubá* [S.João do Araguaia–PA]	8 peasants shot by gunmen
January–June 1985	Fazenda Fortaleza [Xinguara–PA]	12 peasant farmers killed by gunmen
August 1985	Santana do Araguaia–PA	6 gunmen killed by rural workers
September 1985	Fazenda Surubijú [Paragominas–PA]	5 rural workers shot by gunmen
September 1985	Fazenda Princesa* [Marabá–PA]	5 rural workers shot by gunmen
October 1985	Fazenda Capoema [Santa Luzia–MA]	2 peasant farmers shot by gunmen
October–Nov. 1985	Fazenda Canada [Xinguara-PA]	4 gunmen killed
April 1986	Fazenda Diadema [Xinguara–PA]	5 gunmen killed, and 1 rural worker
May 1986	Marabá–PA	Father Jósimo Tavares shot by hired gunman
June–October 1986	Fazenda Agropecus* (S.João do Araguaia–PA]	8 rural workers, 2 military police 2 gunmen killed
December 1986	Fazenda Forkilha* [S.João do Araguaia–PA]	Estate owner and driver killed
March 1987	Conceição do Araguaia–PA	2 policemen hired as gunmen by landowners ambushed by peasant farmers
April 1987	Marabá–PA	Sister Adelaide Molinari shot
April 1987	Fazenda Bela Vista [Conceição do Araguaia–PA]	Hired gunman killed by peasant farmers
May 1987	Fazenda Canaan [Xinguara–PA]	2 peasants killed

Table 3.1   (continued)

Date	Location	Details
June 1987	near Belém–PA	Paulo Fontelles, lawyer, shot by hired gunmen
October 1987	Goianésia–PA	Community leader and three-year-old son shot by gunmen

* See chapter 5 for details of these cases.
Sources: MIRAD (1986, 1987), *O Liberal* (19.8.87), *O Globo* (28.5.87), Amnesty
     International (1988).
Key: PA (Pará), MA (Maranhão).

the vigilance of the Catholic church and rural trades unions makes it increasingly difficult for such murders to pass unnoticed. Chapter 5 cites a number of the more infamous cases of conflicts resulting in multiple deaths, in which peasant farmers put up strong resistance to land-grabbers and their hired gunmen.

The escalating violence in the 'parrot's beak' region, which culminated in the death of Father Tavares, sparked off a wave of national and international protest at the 'imminent state of civil war between peasant farmers and landowners', and led to a largely ineffective government campaign to disarm peasants and landowners in the region (Mattos and Guanziroli, 1985; *The Sunday Times*, 1986; CNBB, 13.5.86; *Jornal do Brasil*, 10.6.86; *The Guardian*, 16.6.86). Another such intervention in February 1987 provoked the bishops of four major dioceses in southern Pará to issue a public statement protesting at police tactics used against peasant families, while leaving landowners untouched. They denounced the use of the Bamerindus estate as the headquarters for one hundred policemen and gunmen who rampaged through local villages, illegally detaining fifty people. Their words are all the more poignant, coming as they do from Catholic churchmen:

> Women were raped, children bound and hung up by their hair, forced to act as bait for their parents; men tied up and beaten with rifle butts, kicked and trampled, forced to eat animal excrement, swallow cigarettes and spiny leaves...tear gas thrown into the local church...con-

tinuous threats of sexual violence... forced interrogations at the Fazenda Bamerindus farmhouse... (Rossato *et al*, 1987).

Evidence gathered by Amnesty International (1988) corroborates this account, and speaks of gross physical and sexual abuse committed by the military police against the peasant families, including several minors.

Over a third of deaths over land disputes in 1986 were at the hands of gunmen 'hired by landowners, mining companies, property companies and agro-livestock enterprises' to remove small farmers from the land or to liquidate activist peasants who decided to offer resistance to land-grabbers (MIRAD, 1987, p. 61). The rising number of fatalities is to some extent due to a decision taken by peasant farmers to resist *grileiros* rather than passively let themselves be evicted. Significantly, twenty-eight of up to 200 gunmen hired by landowners in 1986 were themselves killed in land disputes by their own intended victims (MIRAD, 1987). Many bodyguards and killers recruited by estate owners are, in fact, policemen in civilian clothes. Such a case came to light in March 1987 when two members of the Brasília police force working with clandestine paramilitary organisations in southern Pará, for the purpose of evicting peasant farmers and guarding shipments of contraband gold, were killed in an ambush (*O Globo*, 28.5.87).

Yet the number of deaths in the countryside is but one yardstick against which violence may be measured. Even though the number of deaths may be decreasing in certain areas, this does not necessarily signify a reduction in violence. The nature of rural violence in Brazil is changing, with more emphasis being given by oppressors to non-fatal aggression. As the official MIRAD documents quoted above and countless press reports make very clear, land-grabbers are relying more and more on threats, intimidation, evictions, kidnappings, beatings and use of slave labour. The number of peasant farmers arrested in Pará for example, in the main illegally by police in the pay of landowners, rose from forty-seven in 1985 to over 700 in 1986 (CPT Norte II, 1987). Data collected by MIRAD (1987) for the states of Maranhão, Goiás and Amazonas show that, in 1986, fewer rural deaths were registered but other forms of violence escalated, as if in compensation.

Denunciations of slave labour on forty-six estates in Pará during the first six months of 1987 alone were received by the Church Land

Commission (CPT). The announcement of agrarian reform plans in 1985 (National) and 1986 (Regional) produced a flurry of activity by landowners with idle estates, acquired essentially as speculative investments, anxious to persuade INCRA that their lands were 'productive' and thus ineligible for expropriation. Intermediaries or *gatos* busied themselves on behalf of landowners hiring rural labourers who were subsequently forced to work in conditions of outright or semislavery (MIRAD, 1987; *Folha de São Paulo*, 14.6.87).

Evictions of peasant farmers have always taken place on a large scale, but have gone mainly unrecorded. This form of intimidation is still rife; MIRAD (1987), for example, has documented cases of illegal expulsions involving 250 families in Marabá (Fazendas Pedra Furada and Agua Fria) and Santana do Araguaia (Fazenda Campo Alegre) and a further 400 in Maranhão in only two months, from December 1986 to January 1987. Of course, many more cases, usually on a much smaller scale, never come to light by virtue of the isolated circumstances in which they take place, combined with the frequent disinterest of police and judicial authorities. Peasant cultivators have often seen their lands taken over not just by cattle ranches but also by lumbering companies, whose predatory activities are virtually uncontrollable. One case which came to light in August 1987 concerns three such enterprises: IMPAR from São Geraldo do Araguaia in Pará, MADESCAN and SUNIL from Açailândia in Maranhão. They started illegally clearing the rainforst in a 150,000-hectare region of government land at Tueré, near Tucuruí, which had been set aside by INCRA for resettling 3,000 small farmers. It was reported that 500 workers using 150 motorised saws were 'devastating' the area and transporting the timber to sawmills at Tucuruí and Marabá, leading the would-be colonists to sequestor a lorry-load of illicit timber and denounce the operations to state authorities (*O Liberal*, 12–16.8.87).

Another distinctive trend is the move away from sporadic, largely unorganised acts of violence by individual land-grabbers themselves towards a more systematic strategy. As rural killings have increased the victims have been more carefully selected from the ranks of peasant community leaders, union activists and others involved in defending peasants' interests in land disputes. Furthermore, such leaders are targeted precisely to weaken their resistance when it has been successful in pursuit of justice through the courts. Those church and lay workers who devote their time to defending the interests of peasant farmers are also under constant pressure. In 1987 the Church Land Commission released a list it had compiled of 125 bishops, priests, politicians, trades unionists and other professionals whose lives had been threatened as a result of their involvement in the land conflict issue (*Folha de São Paulo*, 14.6.87). As the deaths of Jósimo Tavares and Paulo Fontelles make only too clear, these threats are increasingly likely to be carried out. However, as Chapter 5 shows, the Church's role continues to be a crucial one in helping to articulate popular protest in defence of small farmer interests in the region.

The rapid increase in organisation amongst large landowners was epitomised in 1985 by the setting up of a nation-wide landowners' lobby, the *União Democrática Ruralista* (UDR) which, by 1987, already boasted some 270,000 members with branches in all the country's major towns and cities. It was established primarily to contest the government's agrarian reform proposals, to which it is vehemently opposed, but is suspected of propagating wider acts of violence for the purpose of land-grabbing. The UDR is thought to have been behind several of the most infamous assassinations, including those mentioned above of Father Tavares, in May 1986, and that of the lawyer and ex-state deputy, Paulo Fontelles, in June 1987, both in southern Pará. In order to raise funds the UDR has organised cattle auctions in Pará and Maranhão of livestock donated by its members to their self-confessed cause of arming themselves to defend their large estates (*Veja*, 21.5.86, 18.6.86). In 1986 another organisation came to light, the *Empresa Solução-Empreendimentos e Serviços de Imóveis Ltda.*, which translates roughly as The Solution Company-Property Ventures and Services Ltd, (MIRAD, 1987). It was also suspected of involvement in land conflicts and was duly denounced to the Ministry of Justice, although to what effect is uncertain given the relative freedom to operate which such groups enjoy regardless of whether their activities fall within or outside the law.

While government toleration of and even active connivance with land-grabbing has been well-documented in the past, it has now reached such dimensions that a major report from Amnesty International declared its serious concern over the failure of the judicial system and the police to enforce the law. Amnesty documents case after case in the Carajás region in which small farmers' pursuit of justice is constantly frustrated by severe irregularities in judicial and police procedures which favour the very perpetrators of these offences. The litany of malpractices is a long one: arbitrary arrests, detentions and torture of peasants, police failure to record crimes reported to them or arrest criminal suspects, the premature closure of investigations, the 'escape' of gunmen and flight of key witnesses, the 'disappearance' of inquiry records and the failure of the courts to respond promptly or, indeed, even at all. According to Amnesty International (1988, p. 62), 'their sheer number and persistence suggest very strongly that such obstruction is systematic rather than incidental and is deliberately intended to impede the effective and equal application of the law'.

While the slow and corrupt local or state judiciary and police are frequently blamed for such procrastination, there is often strong evidence of reluctance on the part of central authorities to intervene. The Ministry of Justice, for example, in at least three documented instances, refused requests by Pará judges for federal police assistance to arrest gunmen who had crossed state boundaries. There is, according to Amnesty:

> evidence of inadequate State response or even State acquiescence in these crimes...a pattern of gross omission over so many years (which) cannot be ascribed simply to inefficiency, lack of resources or genuine problems in making investigations. (1988, p. 1).

The organisation concluded that it was:

> not aware of a single instance involving the assassination of rural workers, when federal courts – because of prevarication by state judges – have exercised their rights to hear such cases. Amnesty International is concerned by the Federal Government's failure to use its full powers to ensure that the rule of law is respected in all parts of the Union. (1988, pp. 69–70).

From the point of view of designing and executing more appropriate development policies for Brazilian Amazonia, which would help diminish the degree of land concentration to accommodate a larger small farmer population, the question of official inertia in the face of mounting rural violence is a critical issue which must at some point be faced up to by the State.

Carajás and the indigenous question

It is estimated that there are up to a million small farmers and their families eking out a living in the Carajás Programme area and, thus, liable to be involved in the struggle for land at some stage in their lives. In addition, there are some fifteen distinct indigenous groups totalling 13,000 indians, located in twenty-seven tribal territories within the direct area of influence of the Carajás iron-ore project; that is, within a 100-kilometre radius of the mine and railway (Treece, 1987). An agreement worth US$13·6 million, backed by the World Bank, was signed by the CVRD and FUNAI in 1982 to provide twenty-three of these groups with support for land demarcations and longer-term development. Thirteen areas were included in the original Accord, followed by another ten in 1984 and 1985 (Ferraz, 1986; Ferraz and Ladeira, 1988). A further eleven groups of the total of thirty-four within the Greater Carajás area, as opposed to the railway corridor itself (including the Koatinemo, Arawaeté-Igarapé Ixuna, Xingú-Bacajá, Bacajá, Kayapó, Kraolândia and Xamboia), remain unrecognised by the PGC's Interministerial Council and have been omitted from the official agreement.

Officials reluctance to acknowledge the indians' presence is reflected in the statement by the then chairman of the Greater Carajás Council and former Planning Minister, João Sayad, when he declared in Washington that, 'Unless I am mistaken there are no indians in the Greater Carajás region' (Treece, 1987, p. 46). The authorities' slowness in meeting the indians' demands for territorial protection is perhaps shown by the fact that, five years later at the end of the Accord period, in 1987, of the twenty-one indigenous areas included in the 1982 agreement, only twelve had been fully legalised. Nine demarcations had not been ratified and there were irregularities in the borders established for a further three (Ferraz and Ladeira, 1988; Vidal, 1988). It was hoped that the US$3·6 million Accord budget surplus would be used to settle these issues, amongst others.

Such procrastination is understandable in terms of the priorities evident in past and present policies towards Amazonian development. According to many observers the decimation of the indigenous population 'is a direct result of the economic development policies of the military government of Brazil' (Davis, 1977, p. xi). This has been no less true during the civilian administrations in power after 1985. Agricultural, mining and lumbering enterprises have set their sights on indian land in the Carajás region, as elsewhere, for the valuable natural resources they harbour. Treece (1987, pp. 44–57) catalogues a series of recent violations of indian lands in the PGC region: these include invasion by cattle ranchers (Cateté reserve, Xicrín-Kayapó tribes, and the Alto Rio Guama reserve, Tembé, Guajá and Urubú tribes); official colonisation by GETAT (Mãe Maria reserve, Gaviões tribe); incursions by landless farmers evicted by estate owners or manipulated by local politicians (Apinayé reserve); bisection of territories by the PA 156 road, by the BR 222 highway from Açailândia to São Luís, the Carajás railway line and power transmission lines (Guajajara of Rio Pindaré and the Gaviões of Mãe Maria); and trespass by logging companies and mining enterprise (Suruí and Guajá). The pressure from mining companies was boosted by Decree No. 88,985 of 1983 which authorised mechanised mineral extraction on all indian lands, demarcated or not, as a result of which applications from State, private, Brazilian and multinational companies, including the CVRD, flooded in to work in eight Carajás reserves. Even legal demarcation is therefore no guarantee that indian territories will be respected.

The contradictory nature of Amazonian development policy is amply illustrated by the example of this official agreement. The CVRD is signatory to an Accord whose ostensible aim is to protect indian groups in the Carajás project area. On the one hand the company is overseeing the Indian Support Programme yet, on the other, it has joined others in encroaching upon indigenous lands in search of minerals. The CVRD has made several applications to prospect in the Cateté and Alto Rio Guama reserves and 'is one of several companies which have already invaded the territory of the Guajá, in the still undemarcated Awa-Gurupí reserve...(and)...has actually obstructed the demarcation process in an attempt to guarantee access to valuable bauxite deposits' (Treece, 1987, p. 47).

Other anomalies abound. Demarcation may actually take place to the detriment of indigenous groups, as in the case of the Xicrín, whose southern boundary left an eight kilometre-wide strip that was subsequently occupied by sawmills and a GETAT colonisation project, which resulted in further invasions of the reserve by small farmers and timber extractors. Other tribes such as the Sororó and Tembé have seen their lands reduced to a fraction of their traditional size by demarcations which institutionalised illegal encroachment. Yet further groups, such as the Apinayé, have lost traditional burial and hunting grounds. Malevolence has also been compounded by inefficient planning. The Parakanã indians had been resettled once by the government in 1971 when they were again forcibly removed to make way for the Tucuruí reservoir in 1982, the population decimated by disease, their lands deforested by CAPEMI (the Military Pension Fund) (see Chapter 4) and invaded by cassiterite miners.

Despite the 1982 CVRD/FUNAI/World Bank agreement, fears about the future and the territorial integrity of indigenous groups in the Carajás region continue. In line with its new policy on indigenous issues (World Bank, 1982), the Bank made a commitment to the prior consultation of indian groups and the demarcation of indian lands during project preparation. This seemed natural since the Bank is a major funder of the iron-ore component of Carajás. Yet the importance attached to land guarantees is not matched by budgetary allocations, with a mere 0·06% for demarcating of reserves, compared with 21% for agricultural projects and 14% for administration. After much protest by anthropologists hired by FUNAI to implement the scheme, the 0·06% was increased to 10·5%, but very late in the day with less than a year to go before the end of the Accord. Several major reasons have been suggested to account for the discrepancy between the rhetoric and the reality of indigenist policy.

Firstly, the Bank was happy to hand over to FUNAI the responsibility for allocating a specific budget for land demarcation. Yet the agency is renowned for not fulfilling its statutory obligations, for getting rid of staff sensitive to indian interests, for putting all sorts of bureaucratic and administrative obstacles in the way of committed individuals, employees and outside consultants, and for submitting to pressure from military, government and commercial interests. This disinterest and lack of central government funding is reflected in the fact that, 'Resources provided by the Agreement have thus been used by FUNAI to meet its own budgetary deficiencies and to maintain and develop its own infrastructure...(It) is little more than a cost sheet for the immense economic infrastructure which FUNAI has designed in order to incorporate the indian population into the Carajás project' (Treece, 1987, pp. 36–7).

Secondly, the indian groups have not been consulted prior to project implementation, as laid down by World Bank guidelines, and have thus not been able to lobby effectively for their financial due. Finally, the familiar and depressingly obvious must be restated; namely, that the ultimate objective of official indian policy seems to be not to give them a degree of self-determination and control over their own future, but rather to fully assimilate them into Brazil's mainstream culture. Nestor Jost, then head of the Carajás Inter-ministerial Council, expressed this fittingly when he said that, 'The indians will reach a degree of acculturation sufficient for them to be assimilated as workers on the project' (quoted by Treece, 1987, p. 34). As one anthropologist's report noted (Gomes, 1984), even if funds do reach the communities in question, unless they are pro-perly administered they could introduce distortions and internally destructive conflicts which will lead to their eventual demise. The lack of commitment to indian rights in Carajás is merely a micro-cosm of what is happening at national level in Brazil. In 1973 the Statute of the Indian required all tribal lands to be demarcated by 1978, but the deadline passed with only one-third of the target having been reached.

The lack of progress within the Carajás Programme on tribal issues has prompted many clashes between FUNAI/CVRD and defenders of indian rights. Anthropologists hired by FUNAI to put the Accord into practice have, on several occasions, protested about the lack of progress (Magalhães *et al*, 1985; GTPI, 1985). Tribal support groups such as the Indian Missionary Council (CIMI), as well as international pro-indian lobbyists, have also voiced strong criticisms of official policy. In March 1986, as a result of these mount-ing pressures, the CVRD temporaily suspended payments to FUNAI under the agreement, accusing the agency of diverting US$8 million for its own bureaucratic uses (*Estado do Maranhão*, 23.7.86). How-ever, such action is likely to have a limited impact. In the first place, as Ferraz (1986) points out, the CVRD does not have the necessary legal powers to decide on many of the crucial issues upon which implementation of the Accord depends, such as controlling popula-tion movements and undertaking demarcations. Secondly, and perhaps more importantly, those individuals within the CVRD concerned with improving the indian Support Programme have very little influence and no significant decision-making powers to oppose company policy which is, after all, in line with government priorities.

The rising and seemingly irreversible tide of violence and land-grabbing practised against peasants and indians in Amazonia, as exemplified most recently by the Carajás Programme, has gathered pace as a result of government policy towards settling and 'devel-oping' the region. The PGC has given a new and strong impetus to such violence by generating further opportunities for both pro-

ductive industrial and agricultural investment as well as land speculation. The realisation of these economic gains and short-term profits
by Brazilian and foreign interests is endangered by the inconvenient
presence of small farmers and tribal groups, which may prevent
immediate access to valuable natural resources such as land and
minerals. The removal, or at least the suppression of these groups,
with the apparent connivance of officialdom, seems to have become
a *sine qua non* of 'progress' in the Amazon Basin. Yet it should not
be thought that the victims of such strategies are content to passively
accept their fate. Resistance is growing and takes many forms, both
individual and collective, spontaneous and more organised; this
theme is taken up in Chapter 5.

The land problem

Directly associated with increased rural violence is the phenomenon
of land concentration. Polarisation in the ownership of, and access
to, land is a second major feature of the agrarian crisis in Amazonia,
being at once both a cause and a product of conflict in the countryside. It goes without saying that, for farmers everywhere, access to
land is the single most important factor in securing a livelihood. In
Brazil, as in many parts of the world, small cultivators have been
struggling with increasing determination to maintain such access in
the face of adversity. What might justly be termed a fight for survival
by Brazilian peasants has been reflected in the increasingly rapid
occupation of Amazonia during the past two decades.

Successive governments have consciously used the region as a
'safety valve' to diffuse pressures in other areas of growing tension
and misery. Over a century ago shiploads of emaciated drought
victims were transported from the North-East to work as rubber
tappers in the rainforest. During the early 1970s the Médici administration, rather than undertake structural reforms, hoped to
syphon off the so-called 'excess' rural population of the North-East
in order to colonise the Trans-Amazon and other highways as a
complementary part of its geopolitically and commercially-inspired
programme of Amazonian development. More recently, officially
sponsored resettlement projects in Rondônia and Acre, as well as
private colonisation schemes in various parts of eastern Amazonia,
have sought to attract migrants with capital and expertise both from
within the region and, via recruitment drives, from among the

better-off small farmers of southern Brazil. However, although official schemes such as the *Transamazônica* have received much publicity, it should not be forgotten that the vast majority of settlers in Amazonia receive no government support. They leave their old homes, migrate thousands of miles overland, stake their claims, build their houses, clear the forest by hand, cultivate and sell their crops and cure their sick, struggling constantly against both a harsh physical and human environment, most of them with little or no official assistance.

Such human endeavour has inspired a recurring cycle of occupation and usurpation as the Amazonian frontier has been pushed further and further back; no sooner have small farmers completed the labour-intensive task of clearing the forest, so larger commercial interests have, in their wake, dispossessed them by fair means or foul in order to establish cattle ranches and other enterprises. The occupation of vast tracts in the form of estates has, as was demonstrated in Chapter 1, been facilitated by heavy government subsidies while, at the same time, peasants have been denied official support within the overwhelmingly *latifúndio*-biased agrarian development policies of successive Brazilian adminstrations.

Without State support, fighting the active hostility of political–juridical structures, and with few class-based organisations to represent their interests, small settlers in Amazonia have, generally speaking, been unable to resist the land-grabbers or *grileiros* for any significant period. Having cleared the rainforest and planted their few subsistence crops, peasant farmers are obliged to vacate the land under duress or themselves become 'mini speculators', selling their tracts for a (by commercial standards) modest profit in order to provide capital for the next stage. The displaced farmers then seek new areas of virgin rainforest where, sooner or later, the whole process will be repeated. As frontier zones become monopolised or 'pre-emptively occupied' by commercial interests, so small farmers are gradually squeezed out to seek newer areas and some breathing space before the cycle recurs. The Amazonian 'frontier' has moved steadily northwards from Goiás and Mato Grosso, as well as westwards from Maranhão and eastern Pará. The frontline of this struggle over land, so far centred on eastern Amazonia around the Carajás region, is perceptibly shifting, as the highway network expands, to the newer frontier zones of Rondônia, Acre and, most recently, Roraima.

The rapid escalation of rural violence in Amazonia described above is the product of a continuing struggle over access to land between small settlers and indians on the one hand, and heavily subsidised commercial and speculative interests on the other. Associated with this confrontation is the phenomenon of land concentration which, as in other regions of the country, is resulting in the gradual monopolisation of agricultural land by larger groups at the expense of peasant cultivators. Such land concentration, along with periodic droughts and demographic pressures, has been a major factor in displacing subsistence producers from longer-settled regions to the Amazonian frontier. In the North-East subsidised credit for cattle ranching (*pecuarização*), as well as support under the PROALCOOL programme for alcohol production from sugar-cane, has forced many small farmers off the land and produced a more skewed distribution (Hall, 1978a; Saint, 1982; World Bank, 1983; Pereira, 1986). In southern Brazil the modernisation of agriculture as reflected in the expansion of soybean, wheat and other commercial crops has had a similar effect (Graziano da Silva, 1981, 1984; IBASE, 1984a; Guanziroli, 1984a, 1984b).

In order to understand Brazil's current highly inegalitarian structure of land ownership and occupation, its roots in Portuguese colonial policy need to be briefly examined. Land grants (*sesmarias*) were made by the Portuguese Crown to colonisers either as a direct reward for services rendered or because they promised to put the land into productive use by establishing sugar plantations, coffee estates and cattle ranches. Legal limits on the maximum size of land grants were ignored and several members of the same family often received tracts. At the same time, 'it never occurred to the Portuguese Crown to distribute land to ordinary people' (Guimarães, 1968, p. 53). Brazil's extremely skewed landownership structure thus developed as a function of Portugal's desire to maintain its dominant position within the European system of mercantile capitalism. This contrasted strongly, for example, with the homesteading tradition of the small pioneer farmer in the USA. The monopoly of the *latifúndio* was reinforced by the Land Law (*Lei de Terras*) of 1850, which attempted to reserve land for the plantation system by prohibiting squatting and raising land prices (Guimarães, 1968; Graziano da Silva *et al*, 1980). Although such legislation may have been effective in the coastal sugar-cane growing areas, the agricultural frontiers of southern, central and northern Brazil remained effectively open, to be settled by waves of migrants throughout the twentieth century, although with varying degrees of permanence.

The distribution of landownership in Brazil is one of the most unequal in the world. The 1985 agricultural census revealed that, nationwide, 53% of establishments are under ten hectares but occupy only 2·6% of the agricultural land; at the other extreme, the 0·8% of establishments with over 1,000 hectares take up 44% of productive land (IBGE, 1987). However, census data in Brazil tend to understate the degree of land concentration since they are based on 'establishments' which are administrative units and do not reflect total ownership of property by any one person. INCRA data, on the other hand, are more accurate since they use 'rural property', a juridical category which takes ownership of contiguous properties into account even when administered by third parties.

INCRA's most recent survey, carried out in 1985, showed that 30% of rural properties in Brazil were under ten hectares but occupied a mere 0·1% of the farmland; conversely, the 1·9% of properties with over 1,000 hectares cover 57% of the agricultural land (INCRA, 1986). Yet the true extent of land concentration in Brazil may never be known since neither the census nor INCRA survey shows the distribution of total areas owned by the same person, regardless of geographical distribution (Hall, 1978a). However, be that as it may, INCRA's 1985 survey confirms in no uncertain terms the degree of inequality, with 69% of agricultural land in Brazil occupied by *latifúndia* (see Table 3.2), half of which is totally unproductive; less than one-third of the land is being put to productive use either by smallholders or by rural enterprises.

Brazil's historically skewed landownership patterns have been faithfully reproduced as the agricultural frontier has advanced from

Table 3.2   Distribution of landownership, Brazil, 1967–85(%)

	1967	1972	1978	1985
Minifúndio	12·2	12·5	8·8	8·2
Rural Enterprise	4·6	9·7	5·6	22·6
Latifúndia (land-use)[a]	76·4	72·9	77·7	62·0
Latifúndia (size)[b]	6·4	4·9	7·8	6·7

Notes:
a Defined by the Land Statue of 1964 as those properties within 600 times the INCRA module limit but as unproductive.
b Defined as those properties over the limit of 600 times the INCRA module, whether productive or not.
Source: Guanziroli (1984b), INCRA (1986)

the North-East and Centre-South of the country towards Amazonia. Despite its imperfections, the latest census data for 1985 clearly illustrate the advanced nature of land concentration in states either totally or partially within the Amazon Basin (see Table 3.3). In Amazonia as a whole some 91% of lands colonised between 1970 and 1980 were occupied by farms of over one hundred hectares; over the same period the area occupied by farms of over 1,000 hectares rose from 48% to 58·5% (Souza Martins, 1984; IBASE, 1984b). There are at least eight estates of over one million hectares while the largest, the Manasa Madeira Nacional SA, in Amazonas state, occupies an astounding 4·3 million hectares (approximately the same size as the Irish Republic). The largest 152 Amazonian estates occupy forty million hectares, or the equivalent of the total area of cultivated land in Brazil. As Table 3.3 shows, in the states of Mato Grosso, Pará, Maranhão and Goiás smallholdings of less than one hundred hectares account for between 55% and 85% of properties but a mere 3% to 21% of agricultural land. Conversely, large estates of over 1,000 hectares form about 0·5% to 7·0% of units but cover between 41% and 84% of farmland. The most extreme case is that of Mato Grosso, where small farmers with under one hundred hectares account for 70% of farmers but farm only 3% of the land, while 7% of landowners with over 1,000 hectares own 84% of the area cultivated. In Pará a similar situation prevails, with the state's 1% of *latifúndia* covering over half of the farmland.

In eastern Amazonia, the specific area covered by the Carajás Programme, polarisation of landownership had reached an advanced stage well before the birth of the PGC. However, since 1980 when

Table 3.3 Distribution of landownership in key Amazonian states, 1985

Property size (ha)	Mato Grosso		Pará		Maranhão		Goiás	
	N	A	N	A	N	A	N	A
0-9	33·3	0·3	33·0	1·3	46·0	4·4	16·4	0·03
10-99	37·6	2·9	51·7	19·4	10·7	15·3	42.4	7·2
100-999	22·1	13·3	14·3	26·6	42·9	38·8	36·0	41·5
1000-9999	6·2	37·1	0·9	23·0	0·4	32·4	5·1	43·0
10000+	0·8	46·4	0·1	29·7	0·01	9·1	0·1	8·3

Source: IBGE (1987)

the scheme was officially launched, it has encouraged this process in a number of ways, both directly, through its generous subsides to large farmers, as well as indirectly, through the general appreciation in land values brought about by the scheme and associated infrastructural development. In this region as a whole, 0·1% of properties with over 10,000 hectares occupy 30% of the land, but small farms of under one hundred hectares, which account for 70% of establishments, control only 11% of the agricultural area (Hecht, 1983). Taking an even closer look at landownership by 'microregion' (the intermediate geographical division used by the census between state and municipality levels), key areas of the Carajás Programme close to the iron-ore mining complex reveal a particularly advanced degree of land concentration. Table 3.6 below demonstrates that, in the Marabá area, small cultivators (with less than one hundred hectares) make up 70% of farmers but occupy 19% of the land while the 2% of estate owners (with over 1,000 hectares) own half the farmland. In the region of Imperatriz the figures are similarly skewed: 89% of farmers are smallholders with access to only 17% of the land, while 1% are *latifundistas*, occupying 37% of farmland.

An even closer look at key municipalities along the Carajás railway corridor reveals just how advanced the process of land concentration has become. Açailândia, for example, is the site of several major pig-iron smelters expected to come on stream by 1990 (see Chapter 2). Violent competition over access to land will probably increase in such 'industrialised' areas as commercial producers of charcoal fuel, which will be obtained by indiscriminately stripping the rainforest, attempt to expand their control over the region during this predatory exercise. According to the latest census of 1985, fully 73% of farms are under ten hectares but occupy only 2% of agricultural land. At the other end of the scale, a mere 2·3% of establishments are over 1,000 hectares but these estates account of 55% of agricultural land (IBGE, 1987).

Statistics for Brazil as a whole clearly show an exacerbation of this situation over time. A greater percentage of the land is being concentrated into larger units, while peasant farms are becoming more fragmented and small cultivators squeezed out. This has been particularly evidence since the mid-1960s when aggressive policies of agricultural modernisation and frontier occupation have been pursued. The Gini coefficient of landownership in Brazil has risen from 0·820 in 1960 to 0·850 in 1970 and 0·854 in 1985 (Graziano da Silva,

1981; Mueller, 1987). Table 3.2 above shows how, in Brazil as a whole, from 1967 to 1985 the proportion of agricultural land occupied by smallholders has dropped significantly from 12·6% to 8·2%; from 1967–78 large properties expanded from 82·8% to 85·5%. The unexpected quadrupling (from 5% to 22%) between 1978–85 in the area occupied by rural enterprises is a statistical quirk, due largely to the reclassification of lands which have been rapidly brought into nominally 'productive' use by their owners in order to make them ineligible for expropriation under the agrarian reform plans announced in May 1985 (the INCRA survey having been carried out in December 1985).

Again illustrating the continued squeeze on peasant farmers in Brazil, from 1960–80 the average size of smallholding under ten hectares fell from 4·0 to 3·4 hectares, but larger estates increased their size from 24,354 to 26,367 hectares (Guanziroli, 1984a). In Brazil as a whole and in Amazonia itself, smallholdings are occupying a relatively smaller proportion of cultivable land than ever before. Table 3.4 shows that, in terms of numbers of units also, small farms of under ten hectares have, since the early 1960s, been growing at a much slower rate than large estates. Establishments of under ten hectares increased in number by 5·4% p.a. from 1960–70 but at a rate of only 0·6% p.a. in 1970–75. At the other extreme, farms of over 10,000 hectares leapt from −1·0% p.a. to 4·7% p.a. over the same period.

Table 3.4 Expansion and contraction of rural properties and establishments in Brazil (% p.a.)

Size (ha)	Properties (INCRA)			Establishments (IBGE)	
	1965–7	1967–72	1972–6	1960–70	1970–75
Under 10	4·1	−4·5	−0·9	5·4	0·6
10–100	3·1	0·0	1·0	2·6	−0·4
100–1000	3·8	1·0	2·1	2·8	1·5
1000–10,000	7·1	0·8	3·2	1·4	2·3
Over 10,000	6·5	4·4	5·3	−1·0	4·7
Total units	3·6	−1·4	0·5	4·0	0·3
Area occupied	6·7	0·6	2·6	1·6	1·9

Source: Graziano da Silva (1981), p. 5.

The heavily skewed distribution of land in Brazil revealed by these aggregate figures has been reproduced in every occupied region of the country, including the Amazonian frontier(s). The notion of Amazonia as a vast, fertile empty space ready to permanently absorb the land-hungry masses from north-eastern and southern Brazil has, within the current agrarian policy environment, been exposed as a myth. The first waves of pioneer migrants in the 1950s and 1960s were soon followed by large landowners and commercial interests anxious to take advantage of generous government financial inducements to establish cattle ranches, lumbering and other activities as well as simply leaving the land idle as a speculative hedge against inflation. Although in the initial phases of colonisation there is ample scope for peasant farmers to establish a livelihood in Amazonia, the subsequent influx of commercial and speculative capital means that the honeymoon is shortlived and they come under increasing pressure to vacate their plots, to be absorbed by larger enterprises. This pattern is clearly reflected in landownership statistics for the older frontier zones, where land is becoming as concentrated as anywhere in Brazil.

In the state of Pará, for example, the Gini coefficient of landownership worsened steadily from 0·82 in 1960 to 0·88 by 1972 (Hebette and Acevedo Marin, 1979). Table 3.5 further demonstrates that in the same state from 1960–85 smallholders, with less than one hundred hectares, tripled in number, as did their share of agricultural land. Yet while the number of estate owners with over 1,000 hectares quadrupled, their area of farmland grew by five times. The gradual erosion of peasants' landrights is illustrated by the fact that smallholders saw their share of cultivated land fall from 26% to 20% over this period, but *latifundistas* property grew from 47% to 53%. Given the tendency of census data in Brazil to significantly understate the extent of land concentration, these figures are probably rather conservative.

The rapid pace of land concentration in Brazil is no better illustrated than by data from the more recent frontier zones colonised since the mid-1970s. In Rondônia, in spite of a massive programme of directed small farmer colonisation which, by 1983, had settled some 25,000 farmers, two-thirds of the land is already occupied by farms of over 1,000 hectares (which account for only 2·3% of the total number), whereas peasant farmers with up to one hundred hectares (two-thirds of the total number) control only 7% of the

Table 3.5 Changes in farm ownership in Pará, 1960–85

Property size (ha)	Number of properties				Land area covered			
	1960	1970	1980	1985	1960	1970	1980	1985
0–9	41·8	48·05	36·2	32·7	2·5	2·1	1·5	1·3
10–99	46·9	45·2	51·3	51·8	23·0	19·7	19·1	19·4
100–999	6·9	4·7	11·5	14·3	28·0	15·3	22·0	26·7
1000–9999	0·6	0·8	0·7	0·9	28·0	30·3	22·0	23·0
10000+	0·03	0·05	0·1	0·1	18·5	32·6	35·4	29·6

Source: IBGE (1975, 1984, 1987)

agricultural land (World Bank, 1981a, pp. 71–2; IBASE, 1984b). In fact, the Gini coefficient of farm size in Rondônia has risen steadily from 0·619 in 1975 during the earlier settlement phase, to 0·647 in 1985, by which time occupation was well advanced (Mueller, 1987). Bakx (1987) has described a similar process of concentration in the even newer frontier zone of Acre, where INCRA has so far absorbed relatively few landless migrants on its colonisation schemes but where the advance of the SUDAM-funded 'ranching front' has resulted in a doubling in the number of *latifúndia* between 1978 and 1984. In Acre the Gini coefficient rose from 0·619 to 0·679 in the five years to 1980 (Mueller, 1987). No doubt a similar fate awaits the state of Roraima, which has not yet received settlers on such a large scale.

The tendency towards greater concentration of property ownership at national and regional levels is mirrored in eastern Amazonia. Despite the imperfections of census data which, as has been mentioned, understate the degree of land concentration, figures from microregions covered by the Carajás Programme clearly illustrate a similar trend. According to Table 3.6, between 1970–80 there was a dramatic fall in the percentage of rural establishments under ten hectares; in Marabá from 71% to 2.7% and in Xingú from 42% to just over 1%. The proportion of farmland cultivated by these smallholders also fell significantly from, for example, 0·9% to 0·03% in Marabá, from 0·9% to 0·02% in Xingú and from 77% to 59% in Imperatriz. Over the same period larger estates expanded their control over agricultural land; in the 100–1,000 hectare category, for example, the share of land rose from 3% to 27% in Marabá and from

5% to 14% in Araguaia Paraense. In other regions larger units of over 1,000 hectares tended to predominate, advancing their share of farmland from 49% to 70% in Xingú, from 10% to 47% in Pindaré and from 38% to 60% in Extremo Norte Goiano.

It has been claimed that these polarising trends in the Brazilian countryside, observed over the past three decades, may have abated during the period 1980–85. Studies based on the 1985 census note that, in the country as a whole, the rate of increase in land concentration, livestock-rearing (*pecuarização*) and the use of rural wage-labour has slowed down. This is attributed to a combination of factors such as the general economic crisis, reduction in availability of subsidised credit to commercial farmers, consequent lower profitability of soybean and beefcattle, especially in the South, a relative decline in land prices during 1980–83 which discouraged property sales by small farmers, and the inability of the urban economy to absorb rural migrants (Martine, 1987; Resende, 1988).

These trends have been interpreted at national level as leading to a long-term strengthening of the small farmer class and of the 'rural informal sector' of unpaid family labour, especially in the North and North-East, where units of under one hundred hectares have slightly increased their share of the rural labour force from 78% to 79%. In Brazil average property size rose from sixty to seventy-one hectares from 1970–80, but dropped to sixty-four hectares by 1985. In the northern region average farm size rose from eighty-nine to 102 hectares over 1970–80 but fell back to ninety hectares five years later. The Gini coefficient of land concentration has also been falling in the North from 0·865 in 1975 to 0·830 in 1980 to 0·795 in 1985 (Mueller, 1987). This apparent increase in relative importance of the small family farm or *minifundização* may have created 'a certain space for the small producer and perhaps for subsistence agriculture ...(and is)...quite important for the survival of a significant number of small farmers and rural labourers' (Martine, 1987, p. 69).

In the same analysis, Martine suggests that this slowing down in the pace of agricultural modernisation in Brazil generally has also been felt in Amazonia. The reduction in official SUDAM subsidies for cattle-raising (in 1979), it is suggested, has made the region less attractive to investors and has led to a diminished rate of frontier incorporation with the result, it is claimed, that there has been a 'virtual abandonment' of attempts to occupy Amazonia via large commercial or speculative enterprises, thus creating more opport-

Table 3.6 Changes in landownership patterns in key areas of the Carajás Programme, 1970–85

Property size (ha)	Xingú						Marabá						Araguaia Paraense					
	1970		1980		1985		1970		1980		1985		1970		1980		1985	
	N	A	N	A	N	A	N	A	N	A	N	A	N	A	N	A	N	A
0–9	42.3	0.9	1.3	0.02	3.4	0.1	71.0	0.9	2.7	0.03	10.0	0.3	33.2	0.4	9.3	0.01	8.9	0.2
10–99	41.0	21.0	48.7	6.7	52.5	18.6	21.4	3.7	37.9	6.3	60.4	18.6	57.1	11.3	68.7	16.0	68.2	11.6
100–999	16.6	28.4	48.5	23.2	42.2	35.4	2.8	3.4	50.0	27.2	27.6	31.6	6.8	4.9	19.3	14.7	20.4	16.4
1000–9999	0.8	49.5	1.2	12.3	0.7	14.0	4.5	83.7	5.4	40.7	1.9	35.2	2.4	31.0	2.1	21.2	2.2	17.9
10000+	–	–	0.3	57.8	1.2	31.9	0.1	8.3	4.0	25.8	0.09	14.3	0.5	52.4	0.6	48.0	0.3	53.9

Property size (ha)	Pindaré						Imperatriz						Extremo Norte Goiano					
	1970		1980		1985		1970		1980		1985		1970		1980		1985	
	N	A	N	A	N	A	N	A	N	A	N	A	N	A	N	A	N	A
0–9	85.3	15.5	78.4	0.08	75.3	4.3	76.6	3.9	59.1	2.0	70.6	2.9	16.3	0.7	21.2	0.3	15.4	0.2
10–99	14.0	33.8	16.5	19.6	18.6	22.4	14.0	8.2	25.6	14.6	18.3	14.5	59.5	16.4	42.2	3.6	48.0	7.8
100–999	2.4	40.7	5.0	33.1	5.8	36.0	8.3	45.9	14.0	46.3	10.2	46.1	22.5	44.8	32.0	36.3	31.7	33.6
1000–9999	0.6	10.0	0.1	16.0	0.3	20.8	1.1	38.6	1.0	31.0	0.9	33.9	1.6	26.1	4.0	42.8	4.2	42.7
10000+	–	–	0.04	31.2	0.02	16.5	0.01	3.4	0.3	6.1	0.05	2.6	0.06	12.0	0.6	17.3	0.7	15.7

Source: IBGE (1975, 1984, 1987)

unities for smallholders. At the same time, the Centre-West region
has become more profitable for larger investors and has witnessed
substantial increases in mechanised, capital-intensive soybean farming (due to the development of appropriate, hardier strains as well as
favourable minimum prices from 1984 under the then Minister of
Agriculture, Nestor Jost) and in the size of its cattle herds. From
1980–85 the rural labour force in the Centre-West grew by 32,000
but the number of tractors rose by 8,100; its livestock population
expanded rapidly from half of Brazil's total in 1980 to two-thirds
by 1985.

   This should not, however, be seen as the start of a new, long-term
trend but, rather, as yet another cyclical variation in the rate of agricultural modernisation in Brazil. The slight amelioration in land
concentration from 1980–85 was also observed during the early
1970s; between 1960–70, for example, there was a general growth in
smallholdings. However, this reflected not a 'peasantisation' of the
rural economy but a desire of larger estate-owners (such as coffee)
to hand back land temporarily to tenant farmers during a period of
relative economic depression in order to relieve themselves of overhead costs (Graziano da Silva, 1981). In the case of Amazonia, the
figures also reflect the role of the peasantry in pushing forward the
agricultural frontier, principally via 'spontaneous' forms of colonisation. Small squatter farmers were not only crucial in clearing the
rainforest for eventual pasture formation but they also provided a
pool of temporary labour for future commercial enterprises as well
as food supplies for burgeoning local and regional urban centres,
which have grown up at spectacular rates. Thus, it is difficult to
avoid concluding, along with Graziano da Silva, that 'the multipli-
cation of small properties only occurs with frontier expansion, to be
swallowed up as the agrarian structure consolidates itself in these
regions during times of cyclical economic expansion' (1981, p. 54).

   To conclude from these census data that we are witnessing a 're-
opening' of Amazonia's frontier to small farmers, even on a purely
temporary basis, is thus rather premature. Certainly in eastern
Amazonia, home of the Carajás Programme, this does not appear to
be the case. The national trend towards a lower average farm size
is not mirrored in the state of Pará where it rose from 76·3 hectares
in 1970, to 91·4 in 1980 and 92·5 in 1985 (Martine, 1987). The *de
facto* continuation of SUDAM tax incentives, in addition to the new
subsidies given by the Carajás Programme within its 900,000 square

kilometre (over 10% of Brazil's national territory) area of jurisdiction have led, if anything, to an exacerbation of land concentration and its attendant pressures on peasant cultivators. A more detailed examination of census data at sub-regional level contradicts the hypothesis that, in this part of Amazonia at least, smallholders have so far gained a significantly stronger foothold.

Land concentration and Carajás

Evidence provided by the latest agricultural census (1985) allows examination of trends in landownership and other indicators at regional and municipal levels during the period since 1980, when the Carajás Programme was inaugurated. At the lower end of the scale, farms with less than one hundred hectares have actually increased their share of agricultural land in some areas such as Xingú and Marabá (from 6% to 18%). However, medium and large estates of 100–10,000 hectares have also increased their land areas (from 35% to 49% in Xingú, 49% to 57% in Pindaré). Furthermore, as mentioned previously, these data do not take account of the artificial legal division of property ownership which undoubtedly takes place for land-tax avoidance purposes, thus understating the true extent of polarisation in ownership. This factor would also explain the apparent decrease in percentage of farmland occupied by the largest estates of over 10,000 hectares.

In areas marked by intense land conflict the pace of peasant farmer explusion had quickened unmistakably. In the municipality of Santa Luzia, for example, in the heart of the Carajás programme area, which has a long and violent history of land-grabbing, the number of peasant squatter farmers or *ocupantes* fell by 20% from 1975–80 but the total area occupied by these farms fell by 74%, indicating a strong polarisation of landownership (Wagner, 1985). The 1985 census shows that this trend continued unabated between 1980–85; the number of smallholdings under ten hectares, as well as the area occupied, fell during this period, while the proportion of farmland covered by units of 100–1,000 hectares increased from 36% to 49%, quite a substantial change in the relatively short time-span of five years. Similarly, in Santa Inês, the site of at least four mineral processing plants within the Carajás Programme, smallholders with less than one hundred hectares have seen their share of farmland fall from 33% to 21%, while the area controlled by *latifúndia* of between 1,000 and 10,000 hectares has leapt dramatically from 23% to 49%

4 Land concentration in the Carajás Programme area has resulted in a rural exodus as peasant farmers are expelled from their plots, either under duress or as a result of their inability to survive under current, pro-*latifúndio* agrarian policies. Given the already advanced stage of polarisation in landownership in eastern Amazonia many farmers, such as those in the photo, have been forced into a precarious and illegal occupation of federal property bordering the inter-state highways.

over the same short period. The available evidence from these two examples strongly suggests that the advent of the Carajás Programme has had a significant impact on landownership patterns by encouraging further concentration and expulsion of small farmers. A direct cause is the subsidies provided to large-scale agricultural and industrial commercial enterprises, but perhaps even more important is the indirect stimulus given by such 'development poles' to land values and the increasing attractiveness of the area as a source of purely speculative, as opposed to productive, investment in land as a long-term hedge against Brazil's rampant inflation.

Historically there has been a close association between land concentration and the spread of livestock production in Brazil. Census data reveal that, in those Amazonian frontier states where landownership polarisation is proceeding at a rapid pace, cattle herds

5   The Carajás Programme has attracted many thousands in search of employment in the construction industry and associated activities, generating rapid urban growth in towns such as Parauapebas–Rio Verde, where 90% of the houses are crude, poor dwellings typical of shanty towns elsewhere in the country.

have also expanded considerably. From 1960–75 numbers of beef cattle increased by 1,500% in Rondônia, by 364% in Acre and by 260% in Goiás, compared with a national average figure of 80% (IBASE, 1984b). Despite the proven negative economic, social and environmental consequences of ranching in Amazonia, the Carajás Programme and SUDAM have both continued to finance livestock production through their fiscal incentive schemes. The northern region, which includes a large part of the Carajás Programme area, accounted for 14% of Brazil's increase in beef cattle from 1980–85, although this state only has 4% of the national total (Martine, 1987). Data from key areas of the PGC show that from 1980, when the Carajás Programme was officially inaugurated, until 1985, cattle herds in the area grew by figures ranging from 10% in the microregion of Marabá, to 50% in Xingú and as much as 240% in Araguaia Paraense (IBGE, 1987).

As landownership in Brazil has become more concentrated, so the reserve army of landless and temporary wage labourers has grown larger. Many dispossessed smallholders migrate to urban areas in search of a livelihood but, given the increasing difficulties of ful-filling such ambitions within the swollen 'informal sectors', a large proportion chooses to stay in the countryside. As such, the migrant labourer or *volante* of the North-East and the *boias frias* of the Centre-South have become increasingly familiar sights during the cane-cutting season as well as the coffee and fruit harvests. Although the exact number of landless rural labourers is difficult to ascertain because many work seasonally on estates or as small-scale mineral prospectors or *garimpeiros* (Cleary, 1986) while maintaining their own plots of land back home, it is possible to arrive at a rough estimate.

The 1980 census shows a significant fall in both the absolute number and the proportion of landowners and their family members in Brazil, from 80·5% (16·3 million) in 1975 to 74% (15·6 million) in 1980. This coincides with trends indicated in Table 3.3 above, which show the decreasing importance of smallholdings overall. There was a corresponding increase in the numbers and proportion of temporary wage labourers over the same period from 8·3% (1·7 million) to 13·1% (2·8 million) and in permanent wage workers from 7·6% (1·6 million) to 10·3% (2·2 million). While out-migration accounts for part of the diminution of the smallholder class, a signi-ficant portion of former occupiers would have become transformed into landless rural workers, accounting for the changing occupational structure in the countryside (Guanziroli, 1984b).

In Amazonia a commercial and speculative monopoly over land, reinforced by land-grabbing, inflationary market pressures and an official policy bias against small farmer agriculture, has prevented the region from permanently absorbing landowning peasant farmers on a significant scale. INCRA data during the period 1972–86 (see Table 3.7) show that in northern Brazil, which covers Amazonia, temporary wage-labour has expanded by 120% from 1972–78 and by 55% from 1978–86. This has been concentrated in smaller (10–100 hectares) and medium-sized (100–1,000 hectares) farms, which together employ two-thirds of all temporary farmhands. Data for the 1972–78 period only show that, in terms of absolute numbers employed, most of this increase is in the 50–200 hectare category, which almost tripled from 24,000 to 65,000 (preliminary INCRA statistics for 1986 do not allow such disaggregation). The increase in

Table 3.7 Growth and change in Amazonia's rural labour force, according
to property size, 1972–86

	% change 1972–78	% change 1978–85	% of total labour force 1986
Temporary wage labour/ property (ha)			
0–9	−58	+52	1
10–99	+24	+70	30
100–999	+170	+52	37
1000+	+323	+47	32
Total	+120	+55	100
Permanent wage labour/ property (ha)			
0–9	+2	+15	1
10–99	+24	+59	18
100–999	+26	+89	25
1000+	+38	+75	56
Total	+32	+75	100
Family labour/ property (ha)			
0–9	−30	+71	5
10–99	+8	+133	52
100–999	+100	+83	37
1000+	−20	+87	6
Total	+26	+106	100

Source: INCRA (1974, 1985, 1986)

use of permanent wage labour has also been significant at 75% from
1978–86, with large estates of over 1,000 hectares employing over
half. Temporary labourers, however, outnumber permanent farmhands by five to one in Amazonia.

The figures in Table 3.7 might suggest at first sight that large
estates are prodigious employers of rural labour in Amazonia, yet
this is not the case. In relation to the area actually cultivated, smaller
properties provide many more jobs than *latifúndia*, particularly in
terms of family labour. Units of over 1,000 hectares in Amazonia
have been responsible for providing an increasing number of temporary jobs in order to clear land for pasture formation, but this
is a function of their increasing monopoly over land. No only do
smaller farms employ more outside labour in relation to the land

owned than larger units, but they also absorb family labour far more intensively. Farms in the 0–100 hectare category in Amazonia occupy a mere 13% of the agricultural land but employ 31% of temporary labourers, 19% of permanent wage workers and 57% of family labour in the region (INCRA, 1986). Census data confirm these trends identified on the basis of INCRA surveys. In the northern region, according to the 1985 census, 80% of all those employed in the countryside work on farms of less than one hundred hectares although these units occupy only 21% of total agricultural land. In the state of Pará three-quarters of all temporary wage labourers are employed on farms of less than one hundred hectares which, although they make up 87% of all rural establishments, occupy only 20% of agricultural land according to IBGE criteria.

Yet the agrarian crisis in Amazonia is not so much a result of the region's evolving landownership and occupational structure *per se* as of the specific direction in which these have changed. Land concentration and the growth of temporary wage labour have simply not been accompanied by an appropriate increase in employment opportunities in the countryside. Cattle ranching and lumbering, the two most common commercial enterprises in Amazonia, create fewer jobs than virtually any other conceivable rural activity. The larger the property the smaller the number of jobs created, in relation to total area and resources invested. Cattle estates, for example, generate on average one job per 2,000 cattle or per twelve square miles, compared with the much larger number which can be supported by peasant agriculture in the rainforest, estimates of which vary from ten people per square kilometre (Goodland, 1980) to one hundred people per square mile (Caulfield, 1986). In the municipality of São Félix in eastern Amazonia, twenty-nine cattle ranches with 1·5 million hectares of pasture generated only 200 permanent and 750 temporary jobs (Wagner, 1985). Those few permanent jobs created cost an average of US$63,000 each or double that of a job in the industrial sector (Skillings and Tcheyan, 1979). Given the fact that cattle ranches have often, even so, been found to be underproductive and hoarding land for speculative purposes, their potential for job-creation is reduced further still. Lumbering seems to generate even less employment than livestock; the ten largest Amazonian property owners, whose 152 estates occupy 11·8 million hectares, are mainly timber enterprises and have no cattle at all; they employ a mere 313 people (IBASE, 1985).

Land titling and colonisation by GETAT

As already mentioned in Chapter 1, the Executive Group for the Araguaia-Tocantins region (GETAT), with jurisdiction over half of the area covered by the Carajás Programme, was set up in 1980 to try and defuse the volatile land conflict situation centred around the 'parrot's beak' region. Attached directly to the National Security Council, GETAT was granted special powers to expropriate land, resettle the landless, grant titles and initiate colonisation schemes. GETAT was finally abolished in May 1987, its responsibility taken over by INCRA, amid accusations that the organisation had totally failed to achieve its stated aim of reducing rural conflicts by 'justly redistributing land... setting up physical – social infrastructure... and fixing man to the land' (GETAT, 1986a, p. 1).

At first sight GETAT's achievements during its seven years seem quite impressive, with some 60,000 land titles granted covering over seven million hectares, almost one-sixth of the agency's total forty-five million hectare programme area. Yet closer examination of the figures reveals that this 'redistribution' has, in no uncertain manner, largely consolidated the pre-existing inegalitarian structure rather than improved it in the interests of peasant farmers. During the period under military administration, from 1980–85, over five million hectares were demarcated by GETAT, but most of this was in the hands of larger owners. Some 70% of titles were for farms under one hundred hectares but these accounted for only 21% of the total area legalised, while the 8% of properties over 300 hectares took up 51% of the titled land. GETAT's actions were seen (Wagner, 1988, p. 5) as 'assuring a certain kind of capitalist development... legalisation attending to those groups which maintain a mercantilist relation to the land', in opposition to the interests of peasant farmers.

Neither did the situation improve under the civilian 'New Republic'. From 1985–86 the 384 (3%) properties with over 1,000 hectares titled by GETAT occupied 45% of the area, whereas the 3,600 (33%) of under fifty hectares had to be content with a mere 7%. One estate of 400,000 hectares occupied 6% of the entire area distributed (Wagner, 1985; MIRAD/SEPLAN, 1987a, 1987b). Furthermore, many smallholders were put at a disadvantage by being granted plots much smaller than the one hundred hectare minimum recommended for Amazonia by INCRA (GETAT, 1986b), while resettlement was undertaken with scant regard for maintaining family or community cohesiveness. As Wagner (1985) reports, the arbitrary relocation of *posseiros* destroys many traditional collective customs which offer mutual support essential for agricultural practices, as well as denying them access to communal areas for the practice of shifting cultivation. Another consideration is the fact that small farmers, even if granted land titles, were given no additional support in the form of extension services, credit, marketing facilties, etc., necessary to strengthen their economic position. Other criticisms of GETAT relate to its failure to tackle the issue of expropriation in the 'social interest' (resurrected under the 1985 agrarian reform plans discussed below), to corruption and to numerous obstacles of a bureaucratic nature which hampered the organisation in the performance of its duties.

Although GETAT demarcated over seven million hectares it actually expropriated 'in the social interest' (as defined by the 1964 Land Statute and the 1985 Agrarian Reform Plan) a mere six properties, totalling 397,000 hectares but initiated no resettlement on these estates. The government's initial commitment to expropriation and land redistribution thus appeared largely rhetorical. GETAT was slow to set this process in motion, initiating only 109 expropriations, although such intervention was considered urgent on a further ninety-eight estates. To avoid confrontation between large landowners and the government, small farmers were encouraged to leave areas of conflict with the promise of resettlement elsewhere, such as the Xingú Valley, allowing estate-owners to consolidate their position (Wagner, 1988).

The processing of these measures was notoriously slow and disorganised, sometimes due to GETAT's inefficiency but also to circumstances beyond its control. For example, expropriation of the Fazenda Agropecus (see Table 3.1), scene of a dozen deaths in land conflicts, was started in March 1986 but had, one year later, not been considered by Pará's Agrarian Commission under the PNRA because of political changes at state level. Also caught up in the administrative machine were thirty-two expropriations under consideration for over one year by the Working Group on the Brazil-nut polygon (*Grupo de Trabalho do Polígono dos Castanhais*). Being heavily dependent upon INCRA for executing key stages in this whole process, such as emitting agrarian bonds (TDAs) and carrying out property surveys, GETAT's hands were to a large degree tied.

The fact that GETAT had no legal powers of its own, but was obliged to work through the General Procurator of the Republic, was also a crucial limiting factor (MIRAD/SEPLAN, 1987b, 1987c).

Bureaucratic inefficiency and procrastination, difficult to distinguish at times, were compounded by blatant corruption; the documents relating to twenty-four expropriations, for example, covering an area of 342,000 hectares, inexplicably 'disappeared' from GETAT's files during the transfer to INCRA's jurisdiction (MIRAD/SEPLAN, 1987b; *Jornal to Brasil*, 2.6.87). During 1987 the Agrarian Commission for Pará, in what was widely held to be a deliberate ploy to slow down the reforms, met only once. GETAT's credibilty and commitment to land reform were further undermined when an ex-employee revealed that the organisation's local director in Imperatriz had taken advantage of his position to title for himself lands in the Pindaré region, traditionally one of eastern Amazonia's most violent and hotly contested areas (*Jornal do Brasil*, 2.6.87). MIRAD appeared increasingly reluctant to exercise its emergency powers in conflict areas, intervening only twice between August 1986 and May 1987, on the Aymoré and Araras estates in Mato Grosso and Pará respectively (Wagner, 1988).

Apart from land titling, GETAT's other major activity was directed resettlement on a number of colonisation projects. The original three schemes, Carajas I, II and III are located near the iron-ore complex and cover an area of 636,000 hectares. Inaugurated in 1983, by late 1988 only the latter two were operational, with 1,551 families in Carajas II and 585 in Carajas III, in receipt of fifty-hectare plots. It is expected that Carajas I will accommodate another 4,000 families, while a further eight projects such as Tueré (Tucuruí), Rio Preto (Marabá) and Colónia Verde Brasileira (Conceição do Araguaia), will absorb an additional 5,000 (GETAT, 1986b; INCRA, 1987). Candidates are taken from areas of land conflict and officially put through a rigorous selection process involving social, economic and psychological criteria, which eliminate many on minor grounds and place a high priority on conformity to the fairly authoritarian management structure (CPT, 1986).

GETAT's colonisation schemes also have had a very mixed record. They have provided temporary respite to several thousand small farmers and their families but have not generated the stability for peasant cultivators that was envisaged when the projects were drawn up. Common complaints from colonists include lack of inputs

such as credit, seeds, suitable extension advice and marketing channels, as well as the totally inadequate health-care and educational
infrastructure (CPT, 1986; *Correio do Tocantins*, 8–13.8.87). This
has contributed to a turnover rate of up to 90% among the farmers,
many of whom have sold their plots to incoming colonists (Miranda,
1988). The 1985 'Cruzado Plan' encouraged this process by driving
up land values substantially to the extent that, in mid-1987 according to INCRA officials in Marabá, a fifty-hectare plot was worth
£4,000–£8,000 (INCRA, 1987). In response, GETAT changed its
policy in July 1985 to issue usufruct rights (*concessão de uso*) to
colonists rather than definitive land titles, although this has not prevented illicit sales.

INCRA has condemned these land transfers as an 'irrational'
submission to so-called 'nomadic instincts' (GETAT, 1986b), but
they are simply a logical response by small farmers to the market
situation and the defects inherent in this type of colonisation model,
as they attempt to acquire a minimum of capital. A further catalyst
to small farmer expulsion is the nearby presence of estate owners
who have, ironically, bought up large areas of colonisation schemes
intended for peasant farmers. On the Carajás II project, for example,
over forty plots have been thus repossessed by a rancher from Balsas
in Maranhão; on these 2,000 hectares he hopes to expand his cattle
herd from 10,000 to 50,000 head. This has been made possible by
several factors: the poor economic returns achieved by farmers on
the project and the reasonably good price offered, together with a
little additional 'pressure' from the landowner, who sowed his land
(and the adjacent colonists land) with grass seed from the air. As
with its land titling activities, colonisation under GETAT has led
inexorably to a strengthening of land concentration rather than its
amelioration. In April 1987 an official evaluation of GETAT's reign
condemned the institution as 'concentrationist', concluding that,
'This region retains a climate of generalised insecurity: the murder of peasants, gunmen and estate owners, the massacre of rural
workers' families, illegal imprisonment and evictions, the existence
of armed groups defending private properties…private militias
which operate freely in the area' (MIRAD/SEPLAN, 1987b, pp.
4–5). The lack of official support for these colonisation projects
along the Carajás railway corridor further testifies to the current bias
in agrarian policy for eastern Amazonia and is reminiscent of the
situation along the Trans-Amazon highway.

The Agrarian Reform Plan

During the 1970s solutions to the growing problem of land conflict were seen primarily in terms of non-confrontational policies. 'Excess' peasant populations from the North-East and South could be resettled on Amazonia's frontier zones via directed public and private colonisation schemes, as well as being encouraged, as was more often the case, to migrate in a more 'spontaneous' manner without official support. In addition, regulation of land titles, it was thought, would defuse rural violence by providing stable tenure. By the end of 1984, for example, 115 million hectares in Amazonia had been thus titled (Wagner, 1988). However, this has done little or nothing to guarantee more permanent access for smaller farmers. The GETAT experience offers a salutory lesson of the limitations of this policy for resolving the problem of rural violence surrounding land disputes.

Growing discontent with this situation led to more radical plans being formulated by the new civilian government in 1985, which would seek more active intervention to expropriate under-utilised properties for redistribution to landless farmers 'in the social interest'. The National Agrarian Reform Plan (PNRA), was published in May 1985, only two months after the change of regime, by the newly-formed Ministry of Agrarian Reform and Development (MIRAD), headed by Nelson Ribeiro. However, the PNRA did not survive for long in its original form and, as result of pressure from large landowning interests, the plan was redrafted no fewer than twelve times during the ensuing months, before becoming law on 10 October. It planned ostensibly to redistribute a total of some forty-three million hectares of under-utilised public and private property to some 1·4 million landless peasant families by 1989 and seven million by the year 2000. In Amazonia (the northern region), a total of ten million hectares was to be redistributed by 1989 to resettle 630,000 landless families (MIRAD, 1985b). Regional reform plans were finally approved by the federal government on 2 May 1986 with the signing of Decree No. 92,623, after much heated debate and subsequent modification as a result of protests from politically powerful landowners.

The announcement was made following a sudden intensification of rural violence in the Carajás area which resulted in the deaths of a number of rural union leaders, culminating in the above-mentioned murder, near Marabá, of Father Jósimo Tavares. It was hoped that the long-awaited announcement of these regional plans under the new Minister, Dante de Oliveira (Nelson Ribeiro having already resigned in protest at government concessions to landowners and procrastination in implementing the reform), would diffuse 'social tension' in the region, which had built up as a product of people's efforts to defend their livelihoods from land-grabbers. The first stated goal of the PNRA for Pará is to 'reduce the major centres of conflict over the occupation and use of land' (MIRAD, 1986a, p. 9). The military governments' poor record on land issues was condemned and official statements spoke in radical terms of the need for 'expropriations in the social interest' (as laid down by the 1964 Land Statute) rather than amicable land purchases, taxation or re-settlement schemes. In Amazonia alone 154 properties occupying over three million hectares were identified as areas of social tension ripe for expropriation and redistribution (Wagner, 1988).

Figures relating to the first stage of the agrarian reform from 1985–89 were ostensibly quite impressive (MIRAD, 1985b, 1986a). From 1985–89 in the state of Pará 75,200 families would be reset-tled, involving 5·4 million hectares of land, with 8,000 families to be catered for during 1986. Initial plans prepared at state level identify nine estates to be expropriated in the first wave, involving 114,000 hectares and 1,490 families. (INCRA-Belém, 1986). In Maranhão, 118,000 families will be resettled from 1986–89, with 12,700 in the first year alone on 422,000 hectares of expropriated land (MIRAD, 1986b). In Goiás during 1986–89 some 125,500 families will be catered for; in 1986 alone 13,5000 families would be resettled, redistributing almost 900,000 hectares (MIRAD, 1986c). Yet although these goals could be interpreted as an indication of goodwill on the part of the Brazilian State to benefit the rural poor, serious doubts exist whether these targets will ever be reached and, even if they are, whether they will ameliorate the problems to which they are addressed.

Firstly the agrarian reform proposals are, even if modest in prin-ciple, hopelessly ambitious in practice. Regional targets for 1985–89 contained in the main plan greatly exceed initial priority goals drawn up at state level. In Pará, for example, of 75,200 families to be re-settled in four years, by 1988 barely 16,000 had been included in specific proposals. A second objection arises from the fact that the PNRA will not expropriate properties of whatever size, no matter how large, as long as they are considered to be on-going, 'productive' farms or are offically classified as 'rural enterprises'. This is a major departure from the 1964 Land Statute (which provided for the expropriation of all *latifúndia* beyond a given dimension, 'productive' or not) and was subsequently written into the new Brazilian constitution following intense pressure during 1987–88 in the Constituent Assembly. The original land reform proposals (MIRAD, 1985a) did in fact make such a provision but the government was forced to make concessions in the face of severe political opposition. Also excluded are properties of less than three times the INCRA 'module' size for a particular region (MIRAD, 1985b). Thus, huge estates which are in theory productive but, in practice, all but idle will remain untouched and the degree of land concentration basically unchanged.

The agrarian reform suffered its *coup de grâce* in May 1988, when the 559-member Constituent Assembly voted out a proposal which would have approved the compulsory appropriation of property for land reform if it was not fulfilling its 'social function'. This was heralded as a historic victory by the landowners' lobby, and reduced 'land reform' to voluntary property sales. That same month the Minister of Agrarian Reform signed land purchase agreements in Pará for the acquisition of fifty-seven properties in the volatile 'Brazil-nut polygon', discussed above, occupying some 230,000 hectares and with 2,670 peasant families. The Pará state land agency, ITERPA, was then charged with redistributing the land. However, although apparently a progressive step, the purchases were effected as the result of pressure from the owners who wished to profitably rid themselves of the properties in question, while other more critical areas were ignored by MIRAD. One observer (Wagner, 1988, p. 16) commented that MIRAD ran the risk of becoming a glorified 'real estate agent'.

A third criticism concerns the implied assumption that, with the resettlement of 7·1 million rural labourers and their families by the year 2000, the problem of landlessness would be eliminated for good. The PNRA's projections do not take into account the fact that, throughout the intervening fifteen years, more and more landless workers will enter the job market, taking the total number to be accommodated well beyond the original target of 7·1 million (Graziano da Silva, 1985). Another area of doubt surrounds the assertion that, under the new National Policy for Rural Development

(PNDR), of which the PNRA forms part, new smallholders would receive government support in terms of credit, extension and other services essential to strengthen the position of the small cultivator (MIRAD, 1985b). This flies in the face of current official policy and would require a major redistribution of federal and state funds away from the traditionally favoured large-scale commercial farmers and land speculators towards the mainly food-producing small farm sector. Financial and logistical assistance of the type implied is unlikely to be forthcoming without more fundamental changes in property ownership than those currently proposed, and without concomitant political action by the government in support of small farmer interests.

This touches upon the crux of the matter. The agrarian reform plans do not alter in any way the basic forces which continue to exacerbate the agrarian crisis in Amazonia. They may even make matters worse in some cases, where landowners are hurrying to clear their properties of forest to establish projects with federal money as proof that they are economically 'productive' and therefore not eligible for expropriation. INCRA already insists on landowners devoting a proportion of their properties to pasture as an indication of long-term occupation and proof of ownership. Such a spur to unnecessary pasture formation will merely aggravate growing environmental problems arising from deforestation.It has also been widely alleged that most expropriations have so far been voluntary, from usually absentee landowners, most of whom are only too pleased to sell off their poorer quality land at profitable prices in so-called 'friendly expropriations' (EMATER, 1986; Wagner, 1988).

This fact is compatible with the widespread opposition to the plan from estate owners anxious to make sure that any expropriations remain 'friendly'. As mentioned earlier, the landowners' lobby has, via the *União Democrática Ruralista* (UDR), active since 1985 in response to the reform plans, but officially set up in April 1986, mounted an intense campaign against the PNRA. According to its president, Ronaldo Caiado, the UDR had more than 150 regional offices and over 230,000 members throughout the country by the end of 1987. The UDR used any means at its disposal to frustrate attempts at either implementing existing legislation or moves being drafted at the time by 'progressive' politicians to include a government commitment to agrarian reform within the new constitution. As was shown above, the UDR made extensive use of violence and intimidation against peasant farmers as well as church and lay agents working with poor groups in support of the government's proposals. These extra-legal means were complemented by an extensive and well-organised publicity campaign through public demonstrations and via the media.

Intensive political lobbying by the UDR had already resulted in the original reform proposals of May 1985 being significantly diluted. In line with the 1964 Land Statute, these had allowed for the expropriation of any large estates beyond a given maximum size. The final PNRA however, published in October 1985, exempted all 'productive' rural enterprises and properties smaller than three times the INCRA 'module' for the region. Publication of the detailed regional reform plans was also delayed by the landowners' lobby until April 1986. In July 1987 the UDR organised a demonstration of 30,000 landowners and supporters in Brasília, at an estimated cost of thirty million *cruzados* (about US$600,000), to put pressure on the Constituent Assembly, then in the process of drafting a new Brazilian constitution, which would include longer-term provisions for agrarian reform. Eighty hired buses as well as thirty private planes brought the demonstrators to the capital.

The UDR had two major concerns: firstly, the general long-term provision for agrarian reform within the new constitution and, secondly, a particular new clause which was being introduced to speed up the implementation of the existing PNRA. Eleven of the twenty-four members of the Sub-Commission for Agrarian Reform in the Constitutent Assembly were 'recognised representatives' of the UDR, federal deputies who were all 'large and powerful landowners', including an ex-Minister of Agriculture, Alysson Paulinelli (*Correio Brasiliense*, 15.5.87). They set themselves the task of opposing the attempt by reformist members of the Sub-Commission to include radical reformist clauses in Brazil's new constitution. This move reflected widespread opposition by conservative landowning interests who saw the PNRA, and all similar legislation, as 'incompatible with the basic right to private property' (*Visão*, 19.8.87) and, therefore, to be opposed at all costs and regardless of whatever guise such reform plans may be under. The demonstrators were anxious to make sure that, at best, the new constitution would make no mention of agrarian reform or, at worst, that any provisons for the long term should be as benign as possible.

In addition to this general concern, however, a more specific worry concerned a particular clause in the draft constitution which would allow INCRA to grant titles for expropriated lands to beneficiaries of the programme immediately after expropriation by INCRA (known as *imissão imediata de posse*) without allowing landowners the right of appeal. Such a right had been one of the major obstacles to the implementation of land reform to date; through the courts, dissatisfied owners could prevent their land being handed over for a more or less indefinite period, an obstacle which MIRAD was attempting to remove (*Veja*, 15.7.87; *Jornal do Brasil*, 20.8.87). Many cases came to light of particular areas which had been expropriated by INCRA under the plan but which had already been held up for one year as a result of the appeal procedure.

The Brazilian government could not indefinitely resist such pressures from this powerful economic and political lobby. A matter of weeks later, the then Minister for Agrarian Reform, Marcos Freire, announced in a nationwide radio and TV broadcast (only a week before his death in a plane crash on departure from the Carajás project) that, as a major concession, the government would decree ineligible for expropriation any land 'effectively exploited' by the landowner (*Folha de São Paulo*, 3.9.87). On 21 October 1987 Decree-Law 2,363 was passed which effectively exempted from expropriation 97·4% of all landowners and 53% of the country's agricultural area. Firstly, it made ineligible for expropriation all 'small' and 'medium-sized' properties. In Amazonia this meant any holding with less than 1,500 hectares (compared 1,000 hectares in the Centre-West, 250 hectares for the South and 500 hectares in the North-East). Secondly, it exempted all farmowners of whatever size as long as they were 'productive', although what this meant was not clearly defined. Any expropriation would be limited to 75% of the property in question, with the owner retaining the right to choose which 25% (up to a maximum 2,500 hectares) should be exempt. Large agro-livestock projects in Amazonia were to be encouraged, as long as they set aside 10% of their land for small farmer resettlement.

As a further concession, agrarian debt bonds were transformed into highly liquid assets; a decree passed in February 1988 allowed TDAs (which were indexed to inflation and carried a 6% annual interest rate) to be cashed in after only one year. They could also in future be used as capital in financial transactions, for payment of land taxes and for the purchase of public lands, amongst other things (Tavares dos Santos, 1988). A series of advertisements in the Brazilian media posed the somewhat rhetorical question, 'Who is afraid of agrarian reform?' attempting to placate the majority by clearly identifying as targets the 2·6% minority of owners who held 'unproductive *latifúndia*', which cover no less than 47% of Brazil's agricultural land. The govenment's message was that 'those who produce have nothing to fear' (*Veja*, 18.11.87), in line with the watered down, redrafted agrarian reform plan of October 1985 which, under intense pressure from the UDR, had replaced the more radical proposals published in May the same year.

These measures, together with the later rejection by the Constituent Assembly of compulsory expropriations, made the PNRA an almost completely ineffectual tool for land redistribution. This is clearly reflected in the limited progress towards the PNRA's relatively modest goals. Although 30% of the expropriation target for 1986 to 4·6 million hectares was reached, INCRA took possession of only 10%, or 463,000 hectares, and just 2,000 of the 150,000 families (1·3%) to be resettled in this year were acommodated (Pereira, 1987; LACR, 9.4.87). One observer (Pereira, 1987) calculated that, at this rate, it would take 1,026 years to settle all the 1·4 million targeted families. Circumstances for 1987 were no better, since the federal government allocated to INCRA only 30% of the funds necessary for meeting its official targets for the year. In tacit recognition of its failure, the Brazilian government announced in June 1987 that it had cut its resettlement goal for the year by 70% from 300,000 to 80,000, while the new Planning Minister, Aníbal Teixeira, declared in October that the target for 1988 had been reduced from 450,000 to 200,000 families (*Jornal do Brasil*, 24.6.87; LARR, 22.10.87). By February 1988, according to MIRAD figures (Tavares dos Santos, 1988), 11,526 families or 4% of the original target had been resettled on just over two million hectares. Despite the intensity of land conflicts in Amazonia, a mere 836 families were resettled in the North.

It was hardly surprising that the initially cautious optimism which some reform-minded planners had allowed themselves should rapidly be transformed into familiar pessimism. Hopes that a small, albeit promising restructuring of land tenure would bring greater security to a significant portion of Brazil's landless peasantry, as well as improve their livelihoods and increase the production of staple foodstuffs, were soon dashed. The legal system was seen as an 'agent of counter-reform', while the government was accused of 'having no political will to undertake an agrarian reform in Brazil, even a capitalist-type reform (Pereira, 1987, pp. 6–8). The appointment in October 1987 of Jader Barbalho, ex-governor of Pará, as the new head of MIRAD, did nothing to quell such fears. Disillusionment with the abject failure of the Brazilian government to implement an effective agrarian reform has led to speculation by observers (Tavares dos Santos, 1988) that a new wave of public and private colonisation in Amazonia is likely to be instituted, linked to economically and strategically important projects such as the North – South railway and *Calha Norte*.

Carajás and food security

Rural violence, land conflict and concentration in Amazonia are the most sensational and widely publicised features of the growing agrarian crisis in the region. Yet another closely related and no less important consideration is the impact which such development patterns have had on people's food security in the area and, consequently, on nutritional levels. Food 'entitlement' (Sen, 1981), measured in terms of the local availability of basic foodstuffs and the ability of peasant farmers and their families to acquire sufficient food, is likely to be severely compromised by the particular development path taken by the Brazilian government and private business interests in eastern Amazonia. This is so for two major reasons.

Firstly, the general squeeze on peasant agriculture by larger commercial and speculative interests has had the dual effect of simultaneously eroding small farmers' ability to provide for their own subsistence needs and, in all probability, reducing farm income and purchasing power in the market-place, thus increasing levels of poverty and insecurity. Temporary wage-labour on larger estates has, as was demonstrated above, become far more common in Amazonia in response to the growing difficulties experienced by migrant farmers in earning a stable livelihood as independent smallholders; difficulties which are partly environmental but primarily political in nature. A second major aspect of the food security question in Amazonia concerns decreasing production of basic foodstuffs as lands are taken over for commercial (cattle and industrial crops) use and as the traditional class of smallholders, Brazil's major producers of staple food crops, is gradually eroded by a continual process of expulsion from frontier to frontier and denied the right to settle permanently. In short, not only is the production of staple food crops declining relative to non-food crops, but peasant families are less able to grow or buy their own supplies.

This latter issue, that of declining food production as a source of food insecurity, will be considered first. The 'myth' of global food shortages as a major cause of hunger and malnutrition has been exploded by a growing body of literature (Lappé and Collins, 1977; Tudge, 1977; Dumont, and Cohen, 1980; George, 1984; World Bank, 1986). Critics of neo-Malthusian pessimism point to the fact that global food production per capita has expanded faster than total population. Absolute shortages of food are not the problem, it is argued but, rather, its maldistribution in the world combined with acute and worsening mass poverty. Politically-dictated agricultural policy in the West has created vast food surpluses while large populations in the Third World, quite literally, starve to death. The EEC's Common Agricultural Policy (CAP) has, for example, generated huge, unused stocks of grain, dairy produce and wine in order to protect European farmers. In the USA similar protectionist measures have generated the infamous 'grain' mountains which are then offloaded under the PL480 scheme to developing countries in the form of food aid. In many Third World countried themselves there is frequently a food surplus, nations such as India, Thailand and Indonesia having become self-sufficient in rice as the result of Green Revolution technology, while the majority of the population still suffers from malnutrition. Except for sub-Saharan Africa, production per capita of food staples has risen steadily and is expected to increase annually up to the year 2000 in the developing world, including Latin America (WRI/IIED, 1987). The general rule is that food shortages are not a major cause of hunger, which is due, rather, to people's inability to meet their food requirements through sheer poverty.

In Brazil's case, however, declining food production does seem to have played a key role in exposing larger sections of the population, both rural and urban, to hunger and deprivation. A fundamental component of Brazil's development model over the past twenty-five years, particularly since the mid-1970s, has been the importance accorded by agricultural policy-makers to the production of cash crops for export, which has taken place to a large degree at the expense of food staples. Of course, Brazil was colonised and settled on the basis of plantation agriculture for export of valuable crops such as sugar and cocoa. Throughout the industialisation process, this bias has remained and been reinforced by several factors.

Agricultural 'modernisation' has been facilitated by subsidised official credit since 1965 for large-scale producers of export crops. From 1968 exchange rates pegged to inflation, together with technological innovations funded by heavily subsidised government credit, have encouraged export production. In addition, favourable world prices for key products such as soybean in 1969–70 and 1975–76 encouraged the spread of such crops, substituting food staples for internal consumption (Homem de Mello, 1985). Fuelled by the need to service an ever-growing external debt (of $115 billion by 1988), agricultural policy in the post 'miracle' years has been increasingly concerned with generating foreign exchange, regardless of the social and environmental costs. Brazil is not unique in this policy choice and the expansion of cash-cropping for export, to the detriment of staple food production, has been typical of several other developing countries such as Ghana, Kenya, Burkina Faso, Senegal and Mexico (World Bank, 1981b; Timberlake, 1985; WRI/IIED, 1987). The exigencies of structural adjustment programmes in the 1980s, with their emphasis on the generation of foreign exchange for debt-servicing, is further likely to hinder the expansion of staple food crops.

Strong official support has allowed Brazil's production of soybean, for example, to increase almost fourfold from 1971–81. During 1984–85, production of coffee rose by 40%, oranges by 10% and soybean by 18%. The area planted to sugar-cane more than doubled (under the PROALCOOL programme) from 1·5 million hectares in 1972 to 3·8 million hectares in 1985, allowing Brazil to produce 15 billion litres of alcohol in 1988, largely as a petrol substitute. On the other hand, over the same period, output of beans and cassava, the two most important basic foods in Brazil, fell by 8% and 14% respectively; by 1983 food production per capita had fallen to three-quarters of the figure for 1977 (IBASE, 1984a; Guanziroli, 1984a; Carneiro, 1986; Rosillo-Calle and Hall, 1988). By 1983 production levels of basic foodstuffs had fallen significantly in relation to 1975; rice dropped by 19%, beans by 43%, and cassava by 31%, while soybean production grew by 20% per capita over the same period (Jaguaribe *et al*, 1986). Excluding soybean, which is largerly an export crop used primarily for animal feed, the supply of foodstuffs per urban inhabitant in Brazil between 1970–80 declined by around

35% (LARR, 7.8.81). Brazil has had to import an increasing proportion of its food requirements, amounting to $1·5 billion in 1981, for example (Neto, 1982). Largely as a result of falling domestic production, food prices in Brazil have risen faster than services, housing, household goods or clothing. A recent major study of Brazil's social situation recommended that, by the year 2000, Brazil's food production should be increased by 40% of its 1983 level. This would help to keep food prices down and 'have a powerful impact on labour productivity and income distribution...in view of the deteriorating nutritional levels among Brazil's low-income population' (Jaguaribe *et al*, 1986, p. 156).

The increasingly precarious position of peasant farmers in Brazil has to be seen within the context of Brazilian government agricultural policy, which has blatantly discriminated against the mass of smallholders in favour of large-scale, commercial farming for export. At a regional level this bias has been clearly reflected in development plans for Amazonia since the setting up of SUDAM in 1966 to the present day, dealt with at length in Chapter 1. Although the promotion of capitalist agriculture in Amazonia has always been an explicit official objective, an equally important goal has been the diffusion of 'social tensions' elsewhere through the resettlement of peasant families expelled by agarian crises in the South and North-East, the product of land concentration and agricultural mechanisation, exacerbated by periodic drought and famine. Yet, paradoxically, peasant farmers have been prevented from settling permanently because of pressures from land-grabbers and hostile official policies which offer small farmers no logistical or legal support. This lack of government assistance is apparent in many crucial fields such as land titling, rural extension and marketing but it is particularly evident in the failure to provide agricultural credit to small farmers during a period when such finance has seen a tremendous expansion in Brazil.

Institutional or formal credit for agriculture was created in 1937 with the National System of Rural Credit (SNCR) but expanded rapidly after the military takeover in 1964. In the 1970s agricultural credit saw a fivefold increase in real terms, including a subsidy element of some 30% during this period of rising inflation, when the SNCR interest rate was fixed at around 15%. At the same time, however, this expanding credit was highly selective and concentrated by type of producer, by crop and by region. By 1979 about 3·7 million of Brazil's 4·9 million farmers had never received an SNCR loan; namely, the vast majority of staple food producers whose relative output has declined so dramatically. Of those farmers in receipt of formal loans the top 1% (12,000 large landowners) received 38·5% of total credit, the top 10% received 73% and the bottom 50% a mere 5% (LARR, 3.7.81). Small contracts received only 5% of the huge increase in rural credit which became available from 1969–76, while large loans absorbed over 60% and doubled their share of total credit (Goodman, 1986). INCRA survey data for 1978 show that, in Amazonia, only 0·5% of total loan disbursements went to farms of less than ten hectares, while 58% of rural credit went to those with over 1,000 hectares (INCRA, 1986).

As well as being highly discriminatory in terms of farm size, rural credit has been heavily concentrated by crop, with a pronounced bias in the allocation of operating credit towards export commodities, industrial raw materials and wheat production (the latter promoted for import-substitution purposes). Coffee, sugar, cotton, peanuts, soybean and wheat together accounted for 50% of operating credit in 1980, while rice, cassava, corn and beans absorbed 31% (Goodman, 1986). The expansion of wheat production in Brazil (at the expense of cassava) has been facilitated by huge official subsidies, which in 1986 alone amounted to US$1·5 billion (Rosillo-Calle and Hall, 1988). The reallocation of resources to large-scale, capital-intensive agriculture in Brazil through SNCR credit has served to promote agroindustrial investments and export corridors, as well as import-substitution programmes in agricultural machinery and materials. This has been concentrated in the South-East, South and Centre-West of Brazil, while the participation of the North and North-East is far smaller. In addition to SNCR credit, a whole range of fiscal incentive schemes exists to promote agroindustrial enterprises. The small but growing list of agricultural, lumbering and livestock projects subsidised through the PGC scheme (see Table 2.2) bears ample testimony to this direct integration of agriculture into the industralisation process.

The discrimination against small, staple food producers so evident in agricultural policy and, in particular, formal credit disbursements, has undoubtedly contributed to the weakening of the Brazilian peasantry and encouraged the contraction of this class of farmer. Further associated pressures such as land polarisation, landlessness and rural violence have also made small-scale farming increasingly unattractive and non-sustainable under current economic and political circumstances. The gradual diminution in the relative importance of independent smallholders in the countryside must, in the long run, be a key reason behind growing food deficits in Brazil since they account for 70% of corn, 81% of beans and 90% of cassava production (IBASE, 1984a). Within the specific Carajás Programme area of eastern Amazonia small farmers, while occupying only 20% of agricultural land, nevertheless produce 80% of the region's basic food crops, and generate 82% of jobs in the country-side (Burger and Kitamura, 1987). Clearly, to destroy this class is to destroy the major source of staple foodstuffs and rural employment.

Furthermore, Carajás agricultural policy has done little or nothing to encourage increased food production to meet rapidly increasing local demand. Given the region's burgeoning immigrant population, attracted to foci of industrial and commercial employment, it would have made sense to stimulate small farmers to grow the staple food required by the region's urban centres such as Marabá, Acailândia and Imperatriz which have, in a few years, grown from large villages to bustling towns. Somewhat irrationally, however, the traditional pro-*latifúndio* bias of official policy has been faithfully reproduced in the Carajás Programme, with its emphasis on livestock, lumbering and cash crops for export. These priorities not only ignore staple food requirements but, as we have seen, actually displace existing semi-subsistence cultivators, threatening to generate a severe long-term deficit in locally-produced basic food commodities.

Yet the roots of hunger in Amazonia do not lie simply in the declining importance in the regional economy of food staples. Changing crop production patterns have not only created shortages but have, through the associated phenomena of rural violence, land concentration, and worsening landlesness, made peasants farmers poorer. Such lack of effective demand, rooted in basic poverty, argues Sen (1981), is the fundamental cause of people's lack of food 'entitlement'. As far as Brazil and Amazonia are concerned food entitlement in the countryside has undoubtedly been adversely affected as peasant farmers have been squeezed by the advance of large-scale commercial and speculative enterprises. Although no direct evidence exists on rural income distribution in Amazonia and, specifically, its relationship with changes in the rural structure, the evidence strongly suggests that smallholders are finding it increasingly difficult to establish a stable livelihood. Certainly at national level it seems that land concentration has been accompanied by a marked polarisation of incomes in the countryside. Using INCRA survey data Coelho (1985) calculated that, from 1970–80, the poorest 50% of the rural poulation saw its share of total income fall from 22·4% to 14·9%, while the wealthiest 5% enjoyed an increase from 23·7% to 44·9%. In all probability the same tendency is present in Amazonia, even allowing for off-farm sources of income.

The food deficits noted for Brazil as a whole have become apparent regionally. In eastern Amazonia, for example, the dispossession of peasant farmers by livestock enterprises and land speculators has created problems in maintaining supplies of foodstuffs to major cities such as Belém, which must now expensively import much of its supplies from the South of the country, over two thousand miles away (Hecht, 1983). A national survey carried out during the mid-1970s showed that Belém and other urban area in Amazonia boast the nation's highest prices for staple foods such as root vegetables, green vegetables, beans and fruits, surpassing levels in other major cities by a substantial margin (Thomas, 1982). This must be seen, in large measure, as a consequence of changing crop production patterns in the region. Since the early 1970s agricultural and livestock production have expanded rapidly as the Amazon basin has become settled by both peasant farmers and larger-scale commercial producers. As Chapter 1 demonstrated, the nature of this occupation and production process has been profoundly influenced by official agricultural policy in support of the latter, and largely at the expense of the former. Thus, while the area farmed under both permanent and temporary crops has expanded very quickly, staple foods which form the mainstay of the regional diet have gradually lost ground to industrial and higher-value crops for domestic use as well as for export. This bias has been extended to resettlement schemes, both public and private, in Rondônia, Mato Grosso and Pará (World Bank, 1981a; Butler, 1985; Kinzo, 1986). In these schemes a privileged elite of small farmers (usually from the South), backed by an alliance of State subsidies and agroindustrial capital, profit from the production of permanent cash crops such as coffee, cocoa and guaraná, while the needs of the majority of peasant farmers in the region are ignored.

Taking the state of Pará as an example, these longer-term trends can be clearly discerned. The area planted to long-cycle or permanent crops (coffee, cocoa, bananas, black pepper, rubber, etc.) grew by 190% from 1970–80 and by 25% from 1980–85. However, while expansion of short-cycle or temporary crops (rice, corn, manioc, vegetables, etc.) was almost as fast during the 1970s at 140%, during the subsequent five years they grew by only 12%. In this same period, from 1980–85, the beef cattle population of Pará rose by 34% from four million to five and a half million head (IBGE, 1984, 1987). It seems clear, then, that there has been a significant slowing down of the rate at which land in eastern Amazonia is being used to produce staple foods, while other more commercially valuable products expand their influence disproportionately. This evolving pattern contributes towards long-term food price increases in the region and helps to explain the supply problems experienced by Belém.

The gradual switch from food to livestock and cash crops for export, together with the monopoly over agricultural lands of unproductive estates, is also bound to have serious repercussions on nutritional levels, particularly among the growing army of landless rural workers, both in Brazil as a whole and within Amazonia itself. There are no disaggregated data for Amazonia which would allow a close examination of the spatial distribution of malnutrition within the region's rural areas (Batista Filho, 1985). Yet this 'frontier' zone has, according to the results of a national survey published in 1980, a calorie deficit of 15%, the highest in Brazil (Thomas, 1982). Although rural areas were excluded from the survey in Amazonia, it is nevertheless significant since these results must reflect general nutritional levels in the region as a whole (although nationally rural dwellers fared better than urban residents in this respect).

In addition to direct Brazilian experience, research conducted in other 'modernising' Third World countries also suggests a strong association between expanding commercial production in agriculture and growing malnutrition. A close link between commercial crop production and worsening rural poverty and malnutrition has also been recorded in parts of Africa (Ghai and Radwan, 1983) and Asia (ILO, 1977). It is worth quoting what at first sight appears to be an unlikely Indian analogy to the Brazilian situation where,

what has actually happened is that there has apparently been a shift towards the production of agroindustrial and expensive food crops with high income elasticities of demand...and...the production structure has moved against the consumption requirements of the masses...associated with falling rates of growth in per capita incomes as well as increases in the relative poverty of at least half of the population (Pacey and Payne, 1985, p. 161).

Multi-cropping production strategies for subsistence agriculture, such as the slash-and-burn techniques practised in Amazonia, are risk-minimising and use the limited technology available to stabilise food supply as much as possible (Moran, 1981; Lipton, 1982; Posey, 1983, 1985; Fearnside, 1985b). In most case studies the deleterious effects of cash-cropping on the nutritional status of small farmers and their families are due to the replacement of subsistence crops by cash crops such as cocoa, coffee or sisal. In such instances, the peasantry is obliged to concentrate on a commercial cultigen, inducing a decline in crop diversity. This means that less food is available to feed the family overall and this also makes it more difficult to withstand seasonal variations in food availability. In addition, the traditionally balanced diet may be upset as new, exogenous staples such as wheat are introduced (Fleuret and Fleuret, 1980).

These conclusions, reached on the basis of studies in Asia, Africa and Latin America, are corroborated by research undertaken in Brazil. Gross and Underwood (1971), for example, carried out a detailed examination of the nutritional impact of the introduction of commercial sisal production in the north-eastern states of Paraíba and Bahia, and reached two important conclusions. Firstly, the distribution of wealth and income became more skewed as the owners of the means of production (the decortication units) became richer at the expense of their labourers. Secondly, as a consequence of low wages, workers were unable to meet the subsistence needs of their families and the young suffered significantly higher levels of malnutrition. As the authors put it (p. 736), 'Some sisal workers in northeastern Brazil appear to be forced systematically to deprive their dependents of an adequate diet...if they did not they could not function as wage-earners'.

Similar results were obtained by Victoria and Vaughan (1985) in their study of the links between land tenure patterns and child health in the state of Rio Grande do Sul. They found that children in areas with large landholdings devoted to cattle-raising and cash crops (mainly soybean), with a high proportion of agricultural wage-labourers, had a significantly poorer nutritional status and higher rates of infant mortality than children from areas with small farms, diversified food crops and self-employed family labour. Evidence suggested, not surprisingly, a casual relationship between, on the one hand, lack of access to land with its resulting low incomes, inadequate diet, poor housing and lack of adequate water and sanitation and, on the other, childhood malnutrition and mortality. Furthermore, the nutritional status of small farmers was thought to have worsened as land had become more concentrated and there had been a shift from basic food staples such as beans, corn and potatoes to commercial soybean production.

Although no such case studies exist for Amazonia itself, these results from other parts of Brazil undoubtedly indicate likely trends in the Carajás area. All the characteristics which, in other parts of Brazil, have been found to generate hunger and poor health, are presently encountered in the Carajás zone as well as other parts of the Amazon Basin. As the above analysis has shown, these variables include growing land concentration (associated with acute rural violence), increased landlessness and a gradual switch from food staples to commercial and industrial crop production. However, in Amazonia generally, and in the Carajás area in particular, the vast majority of peasant farmers are excluded not only from cash crop production but, increasingly, from any form of stable subsistence agriculture as well. This will make family food-supply more unstable and subject to the vagaries of market prices, which tend to rise faster than those of other commodities because of localised shortages. Even quite small variations in rural income can have quite profound effects on nutrition. Studies in Costa Rica and Guatemala show a strong link between small, inadequate landholdings and malnutrition, especially among young children, where the need to undertake poorly paid, unstable off-farm employment both disrupted subsistence production and also failed to supplement family resources sufficiently well to guarantee an adequate diet (Victoria and Vaughan, 1985). The evidence analysed above, on land concentration, landlessness and the spread of temporary wage labour in Amazonia and the Carajás programme area suggest that nutritional studies carried out in this part of the world would yield similar results.

Official development interventions in Amazonia have quite explicitly and deliberately, in line with national priorities, sought to perpetuate an anti-peasant bias. Other chapters in this book have detailed the rapid spread of cattle ranching in Amazonia since the mid-1960s under the auspices of SUDAM, with all its 'leakages' and inherent social–environmental contradictions. The increasing emphasis in Brazil on non-staple cash-crops for export is evidence on Amazonia's borders and involves developing the Centre-West

savanna grasslands or *cerrado* for grain production. Like the Carajás
Programme, this scheme was conceived largely by Japanese technicians to guarantee future supplies of essential goods and raw
materials, in this case foodgrains, for Japan's growing internal
market (IBASE, 1984c). From its inauguration in 1979, with technical assistance and loans totalling over $400 million from JICA, the
project, which straddles the borders of Minas Gerais and Goiás to the
west of Brasília, has brought over 60,000 hectares into production. A
further 500,000 hectares are planned and eventually it is hoped to
cultivate a total of 4·2 million hectares. During 1984 over 100,000
tonnes of soybean were harvested, rising to 180,000 tonnes, p.a., as
well as 35,000 tonnes of maize, 18,000 tonnes of wheat and 21,000
tonnes of coffee annually (LARR, 8.2.85).

Since the scheme's inception widespread nationalist fears have
been registered in Brazil about its potential impact on the nation's
ability to control its own affairs, as well as the social effects in the
countryside of JICA's interventions. The *cerrados* project is run by
the Agricultural Promotion Company (CPA); this is a partnership
between twenty-four Brazilian enterprises (including the CVRD)
under the name of BRASAGRO, owning 51% of the CPA's shares,
and a Japanese holding company, JADECO, comprising forty-eight
firms and JICA, which owns 50% of the Japanese side's shares and
thus has a controlling interest (San Martin and Pelegrini, 1984).
While the *cerrado* is more suited to intensive agricultural development than the relatively poor soils of Amazonia proper, fears have
been expressed about the scheme's negative social impact. Large-
scale mechanised farming of the sort envisaged here will exacerbate
land concentration as values increase, forcing out small farmers,
paralleling trends in Brazil generally and in Amazonia. Rural trades
unions protested in 1981 that, 'The JICA project and others in the
cerrado are forcing small farmers...to sell their land...increasing
the number of temporary rural labourers in the region, and depres-
sing wage rates' (San Martin and Pelegrini, 1984, p. 32), while
the Church Land Commission sought to make peasant farmers
aware of the threat to their livelihoods posed by the capitalisation
of agriculture.

Development of the central plateau will be facilitated by the
building of the 1,300-kilometre North–South railway, announced
in late 1986, linking Anápolis (one hundred kilometres west of
Brasília) with Açailândia (Pequiá) on the Carajás railway. *Cerrado*

grain production would then have direct outlets through ports at São Luís and, via the River Tocantins, through Belém (*Financial Times*, 29.12.86). A major stated concern in developing the central savannah is to increase food production to meet serious national foodgrain deficits and control rising prices. The application of fertilisers to correct soil acidity would allow production of soybean, sorghum, wheat, rice, coffee and livestock, as well as fruits and beans (Momma, 1987). Yet it remains to be seen how far such modernisation actually benefits small farmers, or to what extent it will hasten their demise.

Agricultural development plans associated specifically with the Carajás Programme will, on the evidence to date, only serve to exacerbate the trend towards worsening food security described above for Amazonia as a whole. As Chapter 2 made quite clear, from the very first proposals submitted by Japanese government consultants (ICDJ, 1980) to the latest plans prepared by the Ministry of Agriculture (Brazil, 1983), there has been a consistent emphasis on large-scale, commercial and export-oriented agricultural enterprise. Even small, 'modern' producers of the type recruited on private resettlement schemes in Amazonia have been accorded a very low priority while non-capitalised peasant cultivators, which form the vast majority of the farming population, are totally ignored. The crop production patterns envisaged by these successive plans for the Carajás region are significant in their implications for food security in the region. They would, if implemented, certainly strengthen the marked national and regional tendency, documented above, to substitute basic foodstuffs with non-staples. The priorities expressed in these planning documents have a depressingly familiar ring to them: livestock, sugar and cassava plantations, alcohol distilleries, soybean, charcoal production and lumbering. There are also several ecologically-sound components such as palm oil, rubber and tropical fruit production but, once again, the emphasis is on larger units, non-staples and catering for export markets. Meeting local basic needs does not appear to be a primary or even a secondary objective of agricultural development plans for Carajás.

For a variety of reasons, as explained in Chapter 2, none of the series of proposals for exploiting the agricultural potential of the vast Carajás region has got beyond the planning stage. Those projects implemented so far have been approved on a largely *ad hoc* basis through the tax incentive scheme instituted for the PGC in order to stimulate investiment in the programme, much as the SUDAM subsidies were intended to do. Most of the funds so far approved have been absorbed by mining, mineral processing and infrastructural projects such as the iron-ore complex, pig-iron smelters and the Carajás railway. However, the few agricultural or agroindustrial investments made with PGC fiscal incentives clearly reflect the low priority given by planners to the interests of small farmers or to local consumption needs.

This is evident from Table 2.2, which lists all agricultural, agroindustrial and livestock projects approved by the Carajás programme's Executive Secretariat to July 1987. These are based on livestock, lumbering, charcoal production, ethanol distilling, poultry, and oil extraction from *babaçú, dendé* palm and groundnuts. Only one of the twenty-one schemes approved involves small farmers, the Tucumã private colonisation scheme set up by the Andrade Gutiérrez construction company in 1980. As detailed in Chapter 1, even this has been plagued by mounting problems of land invasions, rural violence and abandonment of the project by the original colonists. By mid-1987 the company had given up trying to manage it and was negotiating its sale to the Ministry of Agrarian Reform. The *Dendê do Pará SA* (DENPASA) palm oil processing plant, which receives support from the Carajás fiscal incentive scheme, has been denounced for encouraging, the use of child labour. According to the Church Land Commission (CPT Norte II, 1987) up to 300 children, from the age of six upwards, are used for collecting the kernels for wages of £5 per month.

These enterprises are so far relatively small-scale in terms of funding for the PGC to date, accounting for less than 1% of the total. However, despite their small share of investments compared with mineral and infrastructural projects, they are significant in that they clearly reinforce the agroindustrial bias of government policy in Amazonia and its corresponding neglect of small farmer interests. These projects are growing in number and importance, encouraging pasture formation, land concentration and environmental destruction, with attendant consequences for worsening food security. Investment patterns in the rural sector encouraged by the Carajás Programme will, therefore, be very much in the mould of past experience in Amazonia.

4

Carajás and the agrarian crisis
II: the disappearing rainforest

Environmental degradation is a major feature of the worsening agrarian crisis associated with Amazonian development. The side effects of increasingly rapid deforestation present a formidable list of negative impacts: soil erosion; siltation of rivers, dams and reservoirs; soil compacting and leaching; flooding; climatic changes including diminution of rainfall and localised desertification; reduction of fish catches through siltation of rivers as well as pollution from agricultural pesticides and herbicides; and the permanent loss of plant and animal species. The tropical rainforest is a particularly fragile ecosystem which fulfils a number of linked environmental and socio-economic roles that are vital to the well-being not simply of the populations immediately affected but also the inhabitants of more distant regions and even other countries. Eastern Amazonia and the Carajás Programme are passing through a phase of heightened ecological destruction. Policy-makers have not only ignored the broader role of the environment in future growth but see its destruction as an inevitable cost of 'progress' and 'national development'. The importance of gradual and controlled harnessing of the rainforest ecosystem in the interests of longer-term stability is an issue which has escaped the attention of Brazilian planners. Although the increasingly large body of literature on environmental destruction stresses the crucial role of the tropical forest in fulfilling a number of vital linked environmental and socio-economic functions, current development strategy in Amazonia clearly has no regard for him. For this reason they are worth briefly re-emphasising.

Rainforest and environment

The tropical moist forest (TMF) provides a number of key wood and forest products to indigenous and migrant populations of hunter-gatherers and small cultivators. Food is supplied in the form of fruits, nuts, honey, fish, wild animals (as well as food staples such as rice, beans and cassava) to some 200 million people living in or around the world's rainforests (Ledec, 1985; Myers, 1985; Brundtland Report, 1987). As an example of the interdependence of rainforest species, Amazonian rivers are a rich source of fish but their survival is threatened by loss of the fruits and nuts upon which the fish depend for food; at the same time, the fish help to prepare nuts for germination through this feeding process. At least 200 fish and tree species in Amazonia depend upon each other in this way, comprising three-quarters of the total Amazonian catch. In addition to subsistence food, the TMF supplies a range of building materials as well as commercial and industrial crops from hardwoods to black pepper. Indigenous and adapted populations have evolved systems for managing agroforestry resources in a relatively sustainable fashion, upon which western research has so far failed to capitalise.

Biologically, the tropical rainforest is the richest ecosystem on Earth. Although it covers only 6% of the world's land area, the rainforest contains at least half of all known plant and animal species, of which there are estimated to be between five to thirty million, and possibly as many as 90% (Brundtland Report, 1987). While a hectare of temperate forest may contain ten to fifteen species, a hectare of TMF may hold 200 (Ledec, 1985; WRI/IIED, 1986). The Amazonian rainforest is the richest single region, containing an estimated 20% of all higher plant species on Earth, possibly 3,000 varieties of fish and 20% of all bird species (Wetterberg, 1981; Myers, 1985). Tropical forests are also an invaluable source of medications, and over 40% of all modern prescriptions contain drugs of natural origin; its destruction could even hinder efforts to find a cure for cancer. The emergence of chloroquinine-resistant strains of malaria has led scientists to tap sources of natural quinine in the jungle. As one author has noted, 'TMFs are the earth's principal depository of drug-yielding plants' (Ledec, 1985, p. 185).

Animal and plant species also provide a wide range of industrially useful compounds such as dyes, resins, fibres, oils and tannins. Yet less than 20% of rainforest species have so far been catalogued by scientists and the obvious danger is that many will be permanently lost to humanity through uncontrolled deforestation before they can be discovered and assessed for their commercial potential. It has been estimated by the US Council on Environmental Quality, for example that, at current rates, some 20% of all animal and plant species, two-thirds of which originate in the TMF, will have disappeared by the year 2000; without corrective measures, a century later this figure could rise to 50% (Ledec, 1985). *Hevea brasiliensis,* or natural rubber, was itself of course such an 'unknown' species until the last century. Another poignant example comes from Brazil; when its coffee crop was failing, the remaining forest of Ethiopia provided the material to develop a new strain which was resistant to the leaf rust that had decimated harvests in Central and South America throughout the 1970s (Oldfield, 1981; *The Economist,* 4.9.82). The ability of TMF plants to make efficient use of scarce nutrients is a quality that could be harnessed to develop strains which would be naturally capable of fixing nitrogen and controlling pests. Deforestation of Amazonia at the exponential rates currently witnessed could result in the irreparable loss of much valuable genetic material before its potential has been fully explored.

Apologists of tropical deforestation as a prerequisite for regional and national 'progress' often point to the 'island' theory as a justification for this policy of indiscriminate destruction. Based on an analysis of the geographical distribution of Amazonia's plant and animal groups, this hypothesis maintains that, during glacial periods when the climate was cooler and drier, these species took 'refuge' in forest islands surrounded by a sea of grassland or *cerrado,* where genetic diversity was preserved; maps have even been produced showing such 'islands'. The implication of this theory for some government planners and private entrepreneurs is that, by preserving key areas, amounting to only 10% of the total forest, these species could be saved. However, this hypothesis is open to criticism on many grounds and has never been validated. Sioli highlights several weaknesses, including the fact that there is no evidence to suggest that central Amazonia was ever covered by savanna grassland. Furthermore, if the maps produced by the diverse proponents of this hyothesis were superimposed, 'it could be seen that practically the whole of Amazonia would then have been covered by forest' (Sioli, 1985, p. 47). Unfortunately, the theory has in the past been used by government planners to justify a policy of widespread deforestation on the grounds that the creation of key 'islands' merely represents a return to Amazonia's original state. Hence, ecologists warn, it must be treated with extreme caution and scepticism.

Widespread deforestation leads not only to the loss of valuable resources but also to significant environmental disruption. The TMF naturally provides what ecologists call 'environmental services', which include watershed protection, soil stabilisation and the maintenance of regional (and even global) climatic stability. Rainforests cover 6% of the Earth's surface yet receive almost 50% of its rainfall (Myers, 1985). In effect, the TMF acts as giant 'sponge', absorbing vast quantities of water and releasing it gradually. This service is bound to be even more critical in Brazil, where the rainforest covers 40% of the country; the largest rainforest in the world in the fifth largest country. Trees are vital because they fix the usually thin layer of tropical rainforest soil to the ground, avoiding erosion and associated problems of river and reservoir siltation. The thick canopy protects the earth from the violent impact of heavy showers. Increased rainwater run-off through exposure to heavy rains as this canopy and tree roots are removed may also result in worse flooding during the rainy season and reduced flow in the dry period, thus disrupting transport, fishing and floodplain-based farming systems. Some of the detrimental effects of deforestation on dams and reservoirs, on canal and river transport and on agriculture are discussed in greater detail below with reference to Brazilian Amazonia and other regions of TMF where environmental degradation has reached a more advanced stage.

Apart from these localised phenomena, large-scale deforestation could, in the opinion of many scientists, cause major regional and even wider climatic instability. The Amazonian rainforest generates about half of its own rainfall through the process of evapotranspiration, by which rainclouds form through the vaporisation of water by means of evaporation and transpiration from plants. As this process takes place prevailing winds in the Amazon Basin carry the clouds from east to west, and rainfall gradually increases in the same direction towards the Andes (Sioli, 1985). The widespread removal of plant life essential to evapo-transpiration could effectively create drier conditions not only within the Basin itself but also in other regions of the country. TMF deforestation has already been linked to the increased incidence of such climatic changes in Mexico, Costa Rica, India and Malaysia (Myers, 1985; Ledec, 1985). In Brazil, drier conditions and frost-induced crop damage in the south of the country have been attributed to deforestation in Amazonia (Salati and Voge, 1984), while the dangers to Amazonia's own rainfall pattern of large-scale tree-felling have been noted (Sioli, 1985). Localised drought in Manaus, for example, has recently been seen as the first sign of a gradual climatic change, associated with surrounding deforestation. Furthermore, even if as much as half of the Amazonian rainforest were to be protected from deforestation (which is unlikely given present policies), there still might not be enough moisture in the ecosystem to sustain the rainfall needed to maintain the required humidity in the remaining forest; even with belated safeguards, therefore, the damage could be irreversible.

At a global level, tropical deforestation is one major human activity which is contributing to climatic changes. Although the issues are still controversial, there is agreement among many scientists that the burning of fossil fuels and biomass such as tropical vegetation is closely associated with an accumulation in the atmosphere of carbon-dioxide, whose concentration has increased by 25% in the last one hundred years, from 275 parts per million in the late nineteenth century to 343 parts per million in 1983 (WRI/IIED, 1986). In addition to carbon-dioxide, increases have also been noted in methane, chlorofluorocarbons (from aerosol sprays) and nitrous-oxide, said to have depleted the Earth's ozone layer, whose major function is to filter the Sun's harmful ultra-violet rays before they reach the surface of our planet. The accumulation of man-made gases, together with destruction of the ozone band, is now widely acknowledged to be responsible for producing a 'greenhouse effect', leading to a global temperature rise. Evidence for this lies in the close relationship between the observed increase in carbon-dioxide and other gases generated by economic development, and an average increase in the world's temperature of between 0·3 to 0·7 degrees C over the past century. This could, in the opinion of some experts, eventually produce a rise of two degrees F at the Equator, five degrees F at temperate latitudes and eight to twelve degrees F at the Poles (WRI/IIED, 1986; Myers, 1985).

Data from recent US satellite surveys have led scientists to speculate on a direct link between extensive Amazonian deforestation and depletion of the ozone layer above Antarctica (*The Guardian*, 20.4.88). In August 1987 the NOAA satellite discovered a dry season peak of 8,000 forest burnings in Brazilian Amazonia of over one square kilometre each. Prevailing south winds are thought to have subsequently carried the smoke to Antarctica and caused a sudden 10% decrease in the region's protective ozone band. Rainfall patterns would be modified and food production, particularly on marginal lands, such as those in areas of deforested TMF like Amazonia, would be adversely affected, leading to reduced crop yields. However, there may be some cause for optimism following an international agreement to limit the production of chlorofluorocarbons and halons, signed in New York in September 1987 by the USA, the EEC and twenty-three other countries, brought together by the United Nations Environment Programme (*The Times*, 18.9.87). Yet the major problem of TMF deforestation and its impact on the Earth remains untackled.

In addition to the broader impact of rainforest destruction on species loss and climatic change, the most immediate consequence for the region's small farmer and indigenous population is soil erosion and its side effects. Over 90% of Amazonian soils are already of poor quality, nutrients being contained in the biomass itself. While destruction of the vegetation removes most of the earth's nutrients at a stroke, further soil erosion carries this process further still. Increased rainwater run-off leads to compaction, sheet erosion, gulleying and surface-lowering on bare lands and in all areas, whether planted to annual crops such as corn and rice, perennial crops such as coffee and black pepper, or in silvicultural plantations (Fearnside, 1989). As will be discussed below, the problem is particularly acute in areas converted to pasture for cattle-raising. Although fertilisers can compensate for the loss of soil nutrients, the huge areas involved, the lack of phosphate deposits and expense of importing additives makes this highly impractical and cost-prohibitive. Siltation of reservoirs and reduction of water-flows have also been found to severely affect the operation of hydroelectric schemes and the flood cycle for *várzea* (riverine) agriculture.

The scale of rainforest destruction

In discussing the phenomenon of tropical deforestation, whether we use the broad term 'conversion' adopted by Myers (1985) or the narrower definition of 'outright elimination of the TMF' used by other ecologists such as Ledec (1985, p. 182), there is no doubt that profound modifications to the rainforest ecosystem have been taking place globally. Accurate figures on rates of tropical deforestation are notoriously difficult to obtain, because of both the criteria used to define this process as well as the practical problems of data gathering. Some studies such as those by the US Council on Environmental Quality and the US National Academy of Sciences paint a grim picture, indicating an annual global rainforest destruction rate of 2% per annum, and suggesting that half of the world's remaining TMF will have vanished by the year 2000. Others such as the United Nations Environment Programme (UNEP) are more optimistic, putting the annual loss at the much lower figure of 0·6% (Myers, 1985; Ledec, 1985). The Brundtland Report (1987) suggests that as much as 60% of the world's original 1·5 billion hectares of TMF has already been destroyed. Myers (1980) calculates that around twenty million hectares of TMF are converted annually while Lanly (1983) puts the figure at 11·3 million. However, although such estimates of the rate of deforestation vary somewhat, there is broad agreement that the world's forested area is diminishing both in absolute terms and particularly in relation to population: from an estimated two hectares p.c. in the 1930s to less than one hectare p.c. today and possibly 0·5 hectare p.c. by the end of the century (Mather, 1987).

National rates of deforestation vary considerably (Ledec, 1985; WRI/IIED, 1986). In many developing nations large areas have already been deforested; West Africa has already lost 72% of its rainforest and southern Asia 63%. High annual rates of forest removal are being maintained in many countries; they include the Ivory Coast (5·9%) which has the dubious distinction of enjoying the world's highest rate of forest destruction, Paraguay (4·6%), Nigeria (4·0%) and Costa Rica (3·9%), the last of which was already two-thirds deforested by 1980. In other countries low overall rates of deforestation conceal much higher concentrations in particular frontier zones; examples are Indonesia (0·5%), Peru (0·4%), Bolivia (0·2%), Burma (0·3%), Zaire (0·4%), and Brazil itself (0·4%). In another group of nations depredation has been so great that there is little forest left at all; these include Jamaica, El Salvador, Kenya, Mozambique, Brunei and Haiti, the last having lost 90% of its original cover. Mexico disposed of half of its TMF during only twenty years from 1950–70 (Redclift, 1984). Nations with small areas of rainforest, such as Thailand and the Philippines, are in the greatest immediate danger as their timber exports increase. There are only a few nations where little forest has been lost and where pressures are not increasing visibly, including Guyana, Congo, Brunei, Zaire and Gabon.

Brazil's Amazonian rainforest has, by comparison with most countries, remained reasonably intact so far, but this is certainly no justification for complacency. Deforestation in the region is still relatively small-scale when set against the experience of Central America, West Africa or South-East Asia, but it is increasing at rates which are close to exponential as the speed of frontier development has gathered pace over the past two decades. In Amazonia the area deforested leapt by 150% between 1975 and 1978 to 7·3 million hectares (WRI/IIED, 1986), induced by settlement policies for the region throughout the 1960s and 1970s, and severely exacerbated by the Carajás Programme in eastern Amazonia. Official estimates by the Ministry of Agriculture based on LANDSAT data show that deforestation in the Amazon region overall has increased from 0·9% in 1975 to 2·4% in 1978 to 4·0% in 1980, more than quadrupling in the space of fifteen years. Possibly three million hectares of Amazonian rainforest are destroyed annually in Brazil (Salati, 1987). Rates of deforestation for Amazonian states in the 1980s were: Pará 2·7%, Maranhão 4·1%, Goiás 4·0%, Acre 3·0%, Rondônia 3·1%, Mato Grosso 6·0% and Amazonas (for 1978) 0·1% (Fearnside, 1984b, 1986c). Latest data indicate that an area of 27,000 square kilometres (the size of Belgium) of Amazonian rainforest is cleared annually, and that by 1988 roughly 7% of the total Brazilian TMF had been cleared (Fearnside, 1989). Other observers put the figure even higher at around 10% (Pearce and Myers, 1989).

Due to the methods of data collection and interpretation employed, these figures probably underestimate the true extent of forest clearance and its impact on the ecosystem. Much of the LANDSAT data is outdated and sensors are frequently unable to provide crucial information such as the difference between primary and secondary forest, the occurrence of small clearings and removal of timber less than total clear-felling (Fearnside, 1984b, 1989). The gravity of the situation is, however, corroborated by many independent studies. In the western frontier state of Rondônia evidence gathered by the American satellite NASA-7 further illustrates the tremendous speed of rainforest destruction in particular areas of Amazonian settlement. In the space of only three years from 1982–85 the area deforested increased from 10,000 square kilometres (4% of Rondônia) to 27,000 square kilometres (11%), and was confidently expected to reach 54,000 square kilometres (22%) by the end of 1987. NASA estimated that by 1992 Rondônia could be 'totally deforested' (*Jornal do Brasil*, 19.7.87).

A major problem with aggregate regional figures on deforestation in Amazonia is that they hide the localised impact of particular development patterns. The states of Rondônia, Acre and Mato Grosso show an exponential increase while Pará, Maranhão and Goiás exhibit a linear growth in deforestation. Deforestation is in fact heavily concentrated in areas of especially rapid settlement opened up by the building of new highways and spurred on by the availability of subsidised government funding under fiscal incentive schemes such as those offered by SUDAM and the Carajás Programme. Strong foci with exponential clearing patterns occur along the BR 364 highway in Rondônia and Acre, built to link the cities of Cuiabá, Porto Velho and Rio Branco. The same phenomenon occurs along the Belém–Brasília highway (BR 010) and in southern Pará at the heart of the Carajás Programme (Fearnside, 1986a, 1987a).

LANDSAT surveys show that, from only 1979 to 1983 in southern Pará (equivalent to 10% of Amazonia), heart of the Carajás Programme, the area deforested rose dramatically from 7·4% to 14%, an annual rate of increase of 22·5%. In the municipality of Conceição do Araguaia 32% of the rainforest had been destroyed, while a similar state has been reached in a 1·3 million-hectare region centred around Marabá and the Carajás Programme (Pinto, 1986a). INPA scrutiny of satellite photos (LARR, 23.10.86) has confirmed the dramatic rise in the pace of rainforest destruction in the Carajás area; in southern Pará the area deforested annually has risen from a mere 700 hectares in 1977, before the advent of the PGC, to over 47,000 hectares by 1985, an increase of almost 7,000%.

Many estates flout laws which limit deforestation to a maximum 50% of farm area; this is done either openly with total disregard for regulations laid down by the Brazilian Institute for Forestry Development (IBDF), or by tactics such as splitting up properties among members of the same family in order to increase the area eligible for deforestation. Furthermore, although Brazil has several kinds of protected areas (research, ecological, biological, national parks, indian reserves and forest reserves), 'they are small in relation to the size and diversity of forest types. . . and are rarely adequately protected against squatters'. In addition, they are prone to being violated 'whenever land is desired for development purposes. . .

(and)... violations of reserves are liable to be even more frequent in future as highway construction proceeds' (Fearnside, 1986c, p. 7).

The roots of environmental decay in Amazonia and Carajás

Explanations for growing problems of environmental degradation such as tropical deforestation are frequently sought in the Malthusian logic of demographic pressures on finite resources. As Mather noted (1987, p. 5), 'the statistical correlation between countries' forest area change and population growth is moderately close'. Yet reality is, of course, far more complex than a simple numbers game of population growth. Nowhere is this revealed more clearly than in Brazilian Amazonia where it is precisely those forms of *least intensive* human settlement, such as livestock production and lumbering, which have had, directly or indirectly, the gravest and most lasting ecological impact. The concentration of more and more resources (land and capital) into relatively fewer and fewer hands is not only producing environmentally damaging practices on large estates themselves through deforestation and pasture formation followed by soil erosion and all the associated ills. The same interests and forces are also expelling small farmers from the frontier zones which they have pioneered and pushing them further afield, confining them to more distant and marginal areas with locally concentrated populations whose farming practices become incompatible with the rainforest ecosystem as their numbers increase beyond a certain limit, exceeding the 'human carrying capacity' of the land.

The nature and pace of environmental destruction, then, becomes essentially a product of political economy, of a particular set of development policies and practices pursued by commercial interests with State backing. The opening up and integration of Amazonia into the Brazilian national economy since the mid-1960s has, as became apparent in Chapter 1, been pursued through a number of private and government-sponsored initiatives. These include highway construction, cattle-ranching, lumbering, some large-scale commercial farming, directed as well as 'spontaneous' small farmer colonisation and, more recently, mining along with associated infrastructural projects such as hydroelectric power.

Livestock and pasture formation
It is difficult to quantify or isolate one factor from another as the major stimulus to rainforest destruction, and its root causes will vary

from one part of Amazonia to another. Yet, generally speaking, there is a consensus amongst environmentalists that pasture formation for cattle ranching appears to be the most important single source of deforestation in the region. According to figures published by the IBDF, livestock production was responsible for some 38% of the region's loss of forest cover from 1966–75, 90% of which was subsidised by SUDAM. This was followed by peasant settler farming at 31%, highway-building at 27% and forestry at 4% (cited by Davis, 1977, p. 148). More recent studies, however, suggest that the contribution of pasture formation to Amazonian deforestation may be much higher than these official figures suggest. In Brazilian Amazonia between 1966 and 1983 over 100,000 square kilometres were converted to cattle pasture, creating 350 major and 20,000 smaller ranches with a total cattle population of ten million head. The cattle population of Pará alone grew by almost 500%, to 4·9 million head, between 1970–85 (Hecht *et al*, 1988b). Details of specific large ranching enterprises, both national and foreign-owned, are given in Chapter 1 above but, generally speaking, 'A good-sized ranch covers more than 2,000 square kilometres, supporting 15,000 head of cattle or more' (Myers, 1985, p. 137).

The means through which property for cattle ranching is obtained are various. The normal pattern is for cattle-breeders to follow in the wake of small pioneer farmer settlers, taking over land either through agreed purchase or, as is commonly the case, through violence and coercion in situations where genuine land-titles are the exception rather than the rule and a whole corrupt industry exists to fabricate such documents. Often small farmers trade a year's use of the land for pasture formation and exit from the area, a practice known as *troca pela forma*. Frequently also, logging companies will in the first instance open up crude trails through the forest, or official highway construction will be commenced, facilitating subsequent penetration. The original vegetation will be removed usually by the small settlers so that they may practise slash-and-burn agriculture for a few years until moving on. Alternatively, huge areas of virgin forest can be quickly flattened by means of a large one hundred-metre chain (*correntão*) drawn by a pair of bulldozers, combined with burning and the application of chemical defoliants such as Agent Orange, used in the Vietnam War (Branford and Glock, 1985; Ledec, 1985). This method is said to be cheaper and faster than relying on large gangs of manual labourers laboriously sawing and hacking away at the huge tree trunks.

6 The impact of government subsides on pasture formation and livestock production is graphically illustrated by this cattle ranch in the Carajás area, where the original tropical moist forest has been totally removed, creating a virtual scrubland which will become permanently degraded in only a few years.

An examination of the reasons behind Amazonia's growing cattle herds illustrates how politically-motivated policy-making for the region has distorted development, with its attendant social and environmental ills. Starting with the purely commercial motive of beef production for profit, it is immediately obvious that contradictions are apparent. Beef yields in the region are small because of the rapid decline in pasture productivity as the soil is compacted, eroded and nutrients lost to torrential rainfall. Stocking rates are already low at one animal per hectare for new pasture; this decreases rapidly to one head per five hectares after five years, due to loss of soil fertility and nutritional grasses. The most widely-planted forage grass, *panicum maximum* or guinea grass, originates from areas of rich volcanic soils in Africa. Imported successfully to cattle regions in southern Brazil, it was transferred wholesale to the tropics but has been found, perhaps not unsurprisingly, to fare rather badly on the poorer and impoverished Amazonian soils (Hecht, 1983).

Soil erosion and leaching quickly take place as the heavy tropical rains strip the earth, unprotected by its natural vegetation. Soil compaction by cattle hooves results and, without heavy applications of expensive fertilisers and herbicides, soils quickly become exhausted and subject to invasion by weeds, many of which are poisonous to the cattle. The economic viability of cattle ranching is further undermined by the difficulties of administering such large properties without the necessary expertise. As a result of these and other problems, cattle yields in Amazonia were found by independent observers to have fallen well below expectations, contradicting official predictions, by EMBRAPA for example (Falesi, 1976), that pasture would actually improve soil quality. A detailed study by Fearnside found that loss of soil fertility and weed invasion cast serious doubt on 'the potential of pasture to provide the sustained yields which Brazilian planners currently anticipate' (1979, p. 225). Hecht (1983) has also described a severe drop in Amazonian pasture productivity, noting that about half of Amazonia's pastureland has already become degraded. Furthermore, in the Paragominas region, where cattle ranching has been longest established, about 85% of such enterprises had failed by 1978.

Although domestic demand is more buoyant, Brazil is excluded from world markets in unprocessed beef due to the presence of foot-and-mouth disease (afthosis). Furthermore, the FAO has concluded that world beef markets will be depressed for the forseeable future due to demand saturation in industrialised countries, and that there is little prospect of expanding Third World meat exports (LACR, 26.2.87). This fundamental economic weakness was underlined by an official survey undertaken in 1976 of thirty-one operational ranches, reported by Branford and Glock (1985), which concluded that they were supporting only 36% of the cattle stated in the investment proposals submitted to SUDAM for subsidised funding. An official and more recent evaluation discovered that only 10–30% of the subisided funds granted had actually been invested. Furthermore, cattle ranches reached a mere 16% of their officially-projected production and sales targets, indicating unequivocally that funds had been diverted to non-productive activities (Gasques and Yokomizo, 1985). This overall pattern of officially subsidised livestock production as the major single force behind rainforest destruction is one that is repeated throughout tropical Central and South America, often, as shown in Chapter 1, with financial backing from multilateral development banks. Aside from the many other criticisms levelled against beef production in areas of TMF, it is classed as being an extremely inefficient means of manufacturing protein compared with cereals, legumes and leafy vegetables. Its environmental value lies in the recycling of agricultural waste such as crop residues and the production of dung as a fertiliser, fuel and building material (Goodland *et al*, 1984). But in Amazonia such as association is rare, cattle ranching and crop production tending to be mutually exclusive activities.

An observer could be forgiven for wondering why, in the face of such apparently disastrous ecological, economic and social consequences, cattle ranching has continued to expand relatively unabated. Clearly, other motives must be sought for the regular conversion to pasture of large Amazonian tracts. In Brazil's highly inflationary economy, land is seen as a profitable investment which increases in value faster than the rate of inflation itself and yields generous institutional rents to those that can hoard and resell property. Tax incentives, such as those offered by SUDAM and the Carajás Programme, as well as subsidised credit at negative interest rates, make such activities doubly attractive. It was found that 80% of ranches in eastern Amazonia availed themselves of such facilities (Hecht *et al*, 1988b). Values are increased further still by the government's provision of access roads and other infrastructure, or the acquisition of a 'legal' land title. Furthermore, Brazilian law encourages non-productive pasture formation by making the acquisition of land titles dependent upon the sowing to grass of some 50% of the area in question as a sign that the land is being put to 'effective' use. INCRA, for example, will recognise a holding five times the area cleared, while for ITERPA, Pará's land authority, the ratio is even greater at 1:12 (Hecht, 1988). A similar scenario applies to landowners wishing to protect themselves from expropriation under the agrarian reform laws. Paradoxically, however, this process merely fuels inflation further still, leading to more deforestation and pasture formation, in a seemingly never-ending vicious circle.

A slightly more cautious official attitude to livestock expansion has ostensibly prevailed since 1979, when SUDAM announced that new incentives would only be granted to transition forest areas in southern Amazonia as well as maintaining the existing 300 projects in high forest zones. However, these transition areas are in practice a mixture of dense forest and scrubland, and cattle ranchers prefer to convert the tree-covered portion to pasture (Fearnside, 1989). Thus, the 1979 measures have probably had little or no effect and cattle ranching continues to receive generous official subsidies in the form of SUDAM and PGC fiscal and other incentives, which speed up the process of deforestation. Even without government subsidies, clearing continues due to the handsome profits to be made from pure land speculation. With or without official assistance, most large landowners prefer to clear larger areas, as a means of establishing a claim to the land, rather than improving their existing pastures. Pasture formation is the easiest way to occupy an area and prevent it reverting back to secondary forest once it has been cleared (Fearnside, 1985b). From 1966–75 Amazonian land prices rose in real terms by 100% p.a., far outweighing the returns that could be expected from agricultural production (Hecht, 1985; Fearnside, 1985b). As Hecht states in relation to eastern Amazonia, 'The productivity of the land became secondary because the land itself was the commodity. . .If the productivity of the land itself had little importance, cautious land management becomes irrelevant, and environmental degradation is the inevitable result' (1985, p. 680).

Although, as will be argued below, slash-and-burn agriculture is partly accountable for environmental damage in Amazonia, it is worth re-emphasising the point that, 'The establishment of cattle pasture to secure speculative claims greatly magnifies the impact a small population can have on the forest' (Fearnside, 1979, p. 81). By either 'pre-emptively occupying' virgin rainforest or by converting swidden agricultural lands to pasture, expelling the pioneer colonists, cattle farms prevent these areas from ever being used for permanent agriculture. The advanced stage reached by this process may be gauged from data on land concentration in eastern Amazonia, comparing agricultural with cattle-raising areas (Hecht, 1983). In predominantly ranching areas, estates of over 1,000 hectares control 85% of the land; small farms, of less than one hundred hectares, account for 70% of establishments but only 6% of the land, compared with a regional average of 11%. In mainly agricultural areas, near the city of Belém, small farmers with less than one hundred hectares account for 95% of holdings and occupy 62% of the land. The penetration of the cattle economy has polarised landownership, created severe environmental problems in areas such as Paragominas on the Belém–Brasília highway, and is already causing significant localised food deficits, an issue discussed in Chapter 3.

Slash-and-burn agriculture
In Brazilian Amazonia the second most important cause of deforestation after cattle raising is small-scale peasant agriculture and fuelwood gathering; according to official IBDF estimates, from 1966–75 State-directed colonisation accounted for 17% of forest destruction, while other forms of 'spontaneous' occupation were responsible for 13% (Davis, 1977). In the Carajás Programme area this figure may well be lower, given the unduly heavy concentration of livestock enterprises and advanced polarisation in the ownership and control of land. Nonetheless, the significance of uncontrolled and inappropriate forms of small farmer settlement and cultivation should not be underestimated. Apart from a still relatively insigificant minority of small-scale commercial farmers on private colonisation schemes in Amazonia who use modern techniques, the main form of agricultural production practised by migrant farmers is 'slash-and-burn'.

This is a form of shifting cultivation in which producers clear small areas of forest, burn the vegetation (perhaps selling off some timber), grow two or three harvests of food crops and then abandon the depleted soil to repeat the same process elsewhere. Such mobility is necessary because TMF soils are unable to sustain permanent agriculture, especially of annual crops, without careful management and the application of inputs. The reason for this is that, as many authors have by now pointed out, in the rainforest, unlike in temperate zones, the nutrients are contained in the biomass (trees and plants) rather than the soil. If deforestation is limited in scope, as undertaken by 'slash-and-burn' indigenous, forest-dwelling cultivators such as Amerindians and *caboclos*, the system is sustainable and little impact will be felt on the environment. Traditional burning techniques are normally far less destructive of the rainforest and more conducive to higher crop yields than mechanised clearing with bulldozers (Goodland *et al*, 1984). Major problems arise, however, when this balance is disrupted by large influxes of land-hungry peasants from other areas and crop rotations shorten, with the result that the forest is unable to recover and the hitherto 'sustainable' system breaks down.

On environmental grounds, the chief objection to occupation of the rainforest by migrant peasant farmers lies in the fact that, given the generally poor quality of soils in such areas, traditional forms of 'slash-and-burn' agriculture are not sustainable beyond a certain population density. Such techniques are successful on a small-scale, but this demands that the same plots can be recultivated only after many years, a fallow period long enough for the soil to recoup its fertility, as long as the areas thus cleared are small in relation to the intact TMF (Goodland and Irwin, 1975). The essential mobility and high rotation required by this traditional system has broken down in many areas of Amazonia with the migration of large numbers of poor farmers accustomed to different practices. As one researcher notes, 'true shifting cultivation with small isolated clearings and long fallows is becoming a rarity in the region...(and)...can be expected to disappear' (Fearnside, 1985b, p. 395). As population densities increase and rotations shorten, so the land is unable to recover, as it had done in the past.

Furthermore, incoming colonists often do not have the skills of indigenous farmers and find it extremely difficult to adapt to the harsh environment. Colonists bring with them farming systems which are usually inappropriate to Amazonian conditions; they do not cultivate the wide variety of crops planted by indigenous shifting cultivators, and their short-cycle subsistence crops rapidly exhaust the already poor Amazonian soil. Their larger and more homogenous fields are thus more vulnerable to pest and disease problems, as witnessed for example on the Trans-Amazon highway colonisation schemes. Decreased yields, leaching, laterisation, weed invasion, soil erosion and permanent nutrient loss are the unavoidable results. The increasingly intensive pattern of 'slash-and-burn' farming by small producers desperately searching for a livelihood has thus helped to degrade large areas of Amazonia (Goodland and Irwin, 1975; Caulfield, 1982a, 1986; Myers, 1985. This has often led to appeals by Brazilian policy-makers that 'slash-and-burn' agriculture should be eradicated altogether in favour of cash-crop farming with modern inputs, as witnessed following the somewhat abortive *Transamazônica* colonisation schemes (Fearnside, 1986c). Yet such suggestions are only partly motivated by environmental concern, for the same people often advocate cattle ranching in its place.

An increasingly significant characteristic of many countries with substantial remaining areas of TMF is the speed with which they are being occupied by peasant farmers practising shifting cultivation. This is frequently explained in terms of growing demographic pressure, and of the need to utilise empty spaces to absorb 'excess' rural populations. This may help to justify schemes such as Indonesia's Transmigration programme, which aims to resettle two million peasants and their families from Java, Bali, Madura and Lombok to the outer islands of Sumatra and Kalimantan (Plumwood and Routley, 1982; Ledec, 1985). However, such Malthusian reasoning, while questioned even in the case of Indonesia, is clearly irrelevant to Brazil. Migratory movements from traditional agricultural areas in the North-East and South of the country are due not to population pressure *per se* but to a series of climatic and structural factors which have squeezed out small cultivators. Landless peasants destroy the rainforest for shifting cultivation not for biological reasons but because they are increasingly excluded from existing agricultural areas by the *latifúndio*-biased agrarian development policies of the Brazilian government, which are largely inimical to peasant farmer interests.

In the North-East land concentration, aided by the spread of officially-subsidised cattle-raising, and the government's failure to support small farmer agriculture, exacerbated by climatic vicissitudes such as drought, have combined to produce a massive rural exodus to urban areas as well as to the Amazonian frontier (Hall, 1978a). In southern Brazil, the original pioneer frontier, smallholders have been driven out by landownership polarisation associated with the State-aided spread of export crops such as soybean, sugar-cane, oranges, coffee and cocoa (Sorj, 1980; Graziano da Silva, 1981, 1984; IBASE, 1984a). In fact, southerners have tended to form the majority of successful pioneer squatters, particularly in private colonisation schemes, because of the capital and skills they bring with them. In theory, the land in both of these long-established agricultural zones could absorb far more labour than it does at present. Yet trends are in the opposite direction, for smallholders and resident tenant farmers to be expelled to make way for mechanised production. A prerequisite for increasing the land's capacity to absorb manpower would, however, be the imposition of sweeping land reforms far greater than even those proposed by the Sarney administration. By failing to tackle the issue of land redistribution, successive Brazilian governments since 1964 can be said literally to have used Amazonia as a 'safety valve' for diffusing social pressure in the South and North-East by fuelling frontier settlement, along with the 'slash-and-burn' agricultural techniques that have accompanied it and the environmental damage which has resulted.

It may be an exaggeration to claim, as Myers does, that 'the forest farmer deserves to be regarded as an unwitting instrument, rather than a deliberate agent, of forest destruction', on the grounds that 'he finds himself pushed into the forest by circumstances beyond his control' (1985, p. 150). There is no reason to suppose that small farmers, as well as larger producers, will not utilise the system to their advantage wherever possible; for example, by engaging in their own form of modest but speculative ventures, selling off cleared land to incoming settlers for a profit which, in their terms, may be quite handsome (Fearnside, 1985b). Yet in general there seems to be little opportunity for small pioneer settlers to realise such quick gains and they are, typically, victims of the system rather than its manipulators. The generosity of official development policy towards large commercial producers has encouraged pasture formation and environmental decay.

Conversely, rigid institutional constraints on smallholders frequently oblige them, largely against their best instincts, to over-exploit the land. The linking of small farmer credit to rice production in Amazonia, for example, has obliged many such producers to respond to declining yields and increased indebtedness by intensifying or expanding cultivation. Techniques employed include predatory burning, shortening of the fallow period, deforestation and moving in the direction of monoculture in order to maximise short-term gains and be able to repay debts. This is the only way in which they are able to hold onto their property and avoid appropriation by the cattle ranchers and speculators (Hecht, 1983; Collins, 1986). Even the granting of an INCRA land title may be dependent upon the clearing of a certain proportion of the property's rainforest by the owner as 'proof' of intention to engage in productive activity. Thus, there is no inevitability about ecological deterioration, even following significant settlement; the process of environmental degradation becomes intimately bound up with the whole question of land economics, the nature of agrarian development policies pursued by government and the institutional context within which they are implemented. To an overwhelming degree it is a matter of choice exercised by commercial and State interests.

Lumbering
Cattle raising and farming together account for roughly 70% of
tropical deforestation in Brazil, with road-building a further 26%
(Davis, 1977). The last major force behind TMF destruction in
Amazonia to date is lumbering. Tropical timber is, after coffee, the
world's second largest internationally traded commodity at US$8
billion p.a., having increased rapidly from US$272 million in 1954 to
US$4·7 billion in 1979 (Goodland *et al*, 1984; Ledec, 1985). In
south-east Asia logging is the most important cause of deforestation;
in Indonesia, the world's largest exporter, the FAO has estimated
that lumbering is responsible for 80% of the million hectares deforested annually, providing 30% of all foreign exchange earned
from non-oil exports. Other countries which depend heavily on
exports of tropical hardwoods include Burma, Malaysia, the Congo.
Liberia and the Ivory Coast. In Brazilian Amazonia lumbering is still
relatively small-scale due to the diversity of tree species and lower
density of commercially valuable stands, compared with south-east
Asia where there is more uniformity. The IBDF estimates that
commercial logging is responsible for only 4% of deforestation but
this figure is likely to increase substantially as the area becomes more
accessible following extensive highway construction and industrialisation of its eastern portion, covered by the Carajás Programme. The
issue of deforestation, pig-iron production and silviculture is taken
up in a later section of this chapter.

A major impetus behind tropical deforestation lies in the demand
for hardwoods emanating from industrialised nations, both for luxury
and basic timber products. The FAO predicts that by the year 2000
tropical hardwoods production will have more than doubled, some
40% being exported to developed countries (Caulfield, 1982a).
Japan, for example, is dependent on overseas sources for two-thirds
of its timber and is the largest importer of tropical hardwoods,
taking 53%, while western Europe and the US consume 32% and
15% respectively. Japan has been praised for pursuing a 'rational'
long-term forestry strategy by conserving its woodlands, but this is
only possible at the expense of developing countries. In principle
Japan expects to be self-sufficient in wood products by the end
of the decade (Ledec, 1985) but, in the meantime, the short and
medium-term environmental cost to south-east Asian timber ex-
porters has been a heavy one for, as we have seen, much forest
cover has already been permanently lost in these countries. By the

year 2000 south-east Asia's forests are likely to be commercially exhausted.

At present about 10% of the world's industrial timber is extracted from rainforest areas but the tendency is for tropical hardwoods to replace temperate hardwoods as supplies in these latter regions dwindle in the face of rising demand, and as environmental controls are imposed. Japan is a case in point. As resources nearer to home become depleted, 'Japan is looking further afield – to Central America, Amazonia and West Africa'. Furthermore, 'Japan perceives little incentive to harvest its own forests as long as there are dependable and cheap sources of hardwoods to be exploited in the tropics' (Myers and Myers, 1982, p. 199). Of course, Japan is not alone in pursuing policies which encourage tropical deforestation for, as the Brundtland Report (1987, p. 154) notes, some industrial countries 'import unprocessed logs either duty-free or at minimal tariff rates'. The establishment in 1986 of the International Tropical Timber Organisation should in principle be seen as a valuable attempt to link conservation and development by encouraging changes in trading patterns. However, its location in Yokahama, Japan, has been likened to 'putting the fox in charge of the chickens' and has led to considerable speculation by environmentalists that the ITTO's ideals will inevitably be compromised by Japanese commercial interest in promoting tropical hardwood imports.

Brazil seems anxious to be a major future supplier of tropical hardwoods, in spite of the inherent ecological dangers. Currently Brazil is one of the six largest producers (with Indonesia, Malaysia, Philippines, Papua New Guinea and the Ivory Coast), having an 18% share of the market. Yet the IBDF wants to reserve 400,000 square kilometres and SUDAM double that area in Amazonia for commercial logging (Caulfield, 1982a). Lumbering has been responsible for many incursions into indigenous territories, a fact demonstrated in Chapter 3 by the experience of indian groups within the sphere of influence of the Carajás Programme. Although relatively small scale so far, lumbering is beginning to diminish stocks of several valuable species of Amazonian hardwoods in both lowland and upland areas.

Most logging operations in Amazonia are clandestine and small-scale but larger companies are becoming more prominent. Several lumbering projects have been approved by SUDAM, as well as a growing number under the PGC fiscal incentives scheme (see Table 2.2). Foreign multinationals have staked a claim in the industry and the US company Georgia Pacific, for example, has sixty properties in Pará totalling 500,000 hectares. Its veneer factory at Portel produces 15,000 cubic metres per year and supplies 25% of US tropical hardwood veneer needs (Fearnside, 1989). As was illustrated in Chapter 2, such priorities are evident in the emphasis given to forestry within successive agricultural development plans for the Carajás Programme. The heavy influence of Japanese advice in its design is probably significant, but should not necessarily be interpreted as foreign 'manipulation' of Brazilian policy. Lumbering was already important and the PGC also sees logging as a valuable component both for boosting timber exports as well as for supplying charcoal to numerous pig-iron smelting plants in the region, notably along the new Carajás–São Luís railway. Caulfield (1982a) cites an FAO study which observes that Brazil already uses four million tonnes of charcoal annually in the steel industry; the use of charcoal is encouraged because it reduces dependence upon imported supplies of coke and coal. Indeed, as explained below, the availability of cheap charcoal supplies is the major *raison d'être* for the establishment of pig-iron smelting and steel production in the Carajás Programme. Without such an economic advantage for domestic and foreign companies, in addition to other generous incentives, the planned industrialisation of the Carajás railway corridor would not be advantageous to investors.

The destructive impact of lumbering arises either from wholesale deforestation (clear-felling) or from the extraction of a few of the most valuable species (selective logging). In some instances, where there is a high concentration of valuable trees or where only woodchips are required, large areas may be clear-felled; this happened in the Gogol Valley of Papua New Guinea, for example, where a 618 square kilometre area was deforested to produce woodchips for the Japanese pulp and paper industry (Ledec, 1985). In Amazonia and other areas of TMF most logging is highly selective and companies extract only a few of the diverse range of species, those which have a high commercial value such as teak, mahogany, rosewood, meranti and jacaranda. However, even selective-felling can still be highly damaging if deforestation exceeds the rate of forest regrowth, if remaining species are damaged due to the use of careless cutting techniques, or if the thin topsoil is removed. Mather (1987), for example, cites the case of west Malaysia, where the extraction of

3.3% of the trees in a given area was accompanied by a total tree loss of over 50%.

It has been estimated that, 'If more careful logging techniques were employed, the damage to the residual forest could easily be cut in half (Goodland *et al*, 1984, p. 87). But while some have realised this and switched from using heavy machinery to manual methods and animal traction such as elephants, most lumber companies, in order to maximise profits, use no forest conservation techniques whatsoever. There is, of course, almost no supervision by government of such activities and the case of Indonesia, which imposes fines on companies who unnecessarily damage remaining trees, is the exception rather than the rule. In view of the foreign exchange which commercial logging generates and the opportunities which such uncontrolled operations offer for corruption most governments, including Brazil's, are reluctant to impose severe restrictions. Clearly, however, 'mining' the forest through commercial logging for short-term financial and political gain, rather than treating it as a renewable resource within a long-term perspective, will severely exacerbate the environmental dimension of the 'agrarian crisis' in the relatively near future.

Hydropower

After livestock production, settler agriculture and commercial logging, two other increasingly important sources of pressure on the Amazonian rainforest ecosystem are dams and mining, both of which are major components of the Carajás Programme. Dam construction in TMF areas is becoming increasingly popular among Third World governments anxious to harness the enormous hydroelectric potential of their rainforest hinterlands. According to Myers (1985) this amounts to some 730,000 megawatts, or 60% of the electricty-generating power of the developing world. The energy potential of the Amazon Basin is itself thought to be about 100,000 megawatts, 60% of total national capacity (Junk and de Mello, 1987). Before the inauguration in 1984 of the Tucuruí dam on the river Tocantins only seventy megawatts had been harnessed (at Curuá-Una, near Santarém and Paredão, in Amapá). Even when Tucuruí generates its full 8,000 megawatts, this will represent less than 10% of the region's potential. Although Amazonian electricity production is currently in its infancy, by the year 2000

ELETRONORTE expects to supply 40% of national demand from Amazonia.

Few dams have so far been built in areas of TMF and Brazil is something of a pioneer with Tucuruí. African dams, for example, were built largely in areas of desert and savanna. Tucuruí is by far the biggest dam ever built in a rainforest area and the fourth largest in the world, costing US$4·6 billion and flooding an area of 2,430 square kilometres. Its main purpose is to provide cheap electricity to stimulate industrial development in eastern Amazonia by attracting domestic and foreign investors. As such, it forms a key element in the Carajás Programme, supplying energy at subsidised prices to the aluminium plants of ALBRAS-ALUNORTE at Barcarena, near Belém, and ALUMAR, near São Luís, which will consume between one-third and one-half of total output (Barrow, 1986). Tucuruí also generates power for the Carajás iron-ore complex itself and (eventually) the railway connecting it to São Luís, and also supplies electricity to the city of Belém and to the national grid (Goodland, 1985, 1986a). Tucuruí is therefore, within current development priorities, a vital source of renewable energy which meets a number of crucial industrial and domestic needs.

Yet experience with other large dams in the developing world, particularly in TMF zones, as well as observation of the initial impact of Tucuruí itself since the floodgates were closed in October 1984, should sound a note of caution. This is especially so in view of the fact that Tucuruí is merely the first of a series of eight large and nineteen smaller dams in the Araguaia-Tocantins basin, which will generate some 25,000 megawatts and 'will convert the river into an almost continuous chain of lakes 1,900 kilometres long stretching from Tucuruí to within 125 miles of Brasília' (Caulfield, 1982b, p. 243). This is reminiscent of the South American Great Lakes scheme, advocated by the Hudson Institute in the 1960s, which planned to dam the River Amazon near Santarém and flood 40,000 square miles to harness hydroelectric potential (Caulfield, 1986). In addition, ten dams are planned for the Xingú basin, flooding an area of 6,000 square kilometres; the first two of these, the Altamira complex of Kararaó and Babaquara, upon which work is due to start in 1990, will have a colossal combined output of 17,000 megawatts, or over double that of Tucuruí and will cost an estimated US$10 billion. Together they will flood an area of nearly 5,000 square kilometres, including the town of Altamira, 408,000 hectares of several indigenous territories and an unknown number of riverine farmers (CPI, 1987). Altogether, about forty-three more dams are planned for Brazilian Amazonia in addition to the four already in existence. Eventually, as many as seventy dams could be built in Amazonia, flooding some 2% of the area (ELETROBRAS, 1987). In June 1986 the World Bank approved a U$500 million loan for ELETROBRAS, mainly for Amazonian hydroelectric projects, including the Altamira complex, with further such agreements being apparently under consideration (International Dams Newsletter, 1986).

Tucuruí could be considered positive from an ecological point of view to the extent that it is helping to reduce consumption of fossil fuels (equivalent to 400,000 barrels of oil a day); other advantages lie in regulating the flow of the Tocantins, reducing floods and maintaining dry season flows to aid riverine or *várzea* agriculture, as well as permitting navigation along 2,000 kilometres of the river from the sea to within 125 kilometres of Brasília. Yet, be that as it may, such dams inevitably bring with them a multiplicity of problems. Within a relatively short space of time, a number of negative social and environmental consequences have become apparent as a direct result of the Tucuruí dam and reservoir. The first and most dramatic of these has been the displacement of an estimated 25–35,000 people (60% rural), including six small towns, double the official estimate (Mougeot, 1985b; Caulfield, 1986; Goodland, 1986a). As Mougeot notes (1985b), problems arose because no planning authority was created to oversee and co-ordinate a comprehensive resettlement strategy, a task left to the ill-equipped power company, ELETRONORTE. However, such an approach is not unusual in Brazil; in the North-East CHESF (São Francisco Valley Hydroelectric Company) was charged with resettling over 70,000 people displaced by the Sobradinho dam and reservoir on the River São Francisco, creating similar social problems.

At Tucuruí the major adverse impact on the non-Amerindian population resulted from misinformation during the process of expropriation, combined with inadequate indemnification procedures which minimised compensation payments to those displaced. From 1976–82 expropriation and indemnification took place below the eighty-six metre line, well above the projected reservoir water level. In November 1982 this limit was lowered to 76 metres and those who had been expropriated were invited to reclaim their properties through written application to ELETRONORTE. Surely, one detailed study observes, 'this remedial solution arrived when most indemnification-related outmigration had taken place; it applied solely to ex-proprietors and was likely to be more accessible to well-informed individuals' (Mougeot, 1985b, p. 4).

Further problems arose from the fact that the legal concepts and procedures used for compensating displacees did not match the realities of the Amazonian land tenure situation or the region's agrarian economy. Compensation was based on the notion of individual private property, and 'landowners' with legal titles were given the choice of either a new house with land or cash indemnity for losses incurred. Non-proprietors would receive cash compensation for land improvements such as buildings, crops and fences. Yet in Amazonia such legal concepts, developed in other regions of the country, are largely irrelevant to people's needs. Land is frequently not owned *de jure* by individuals with legal titles but this does not detract from their *de facto* right to permanent occupation of the land as individuals or in groups. In this way, the numerically most important segment of the rural population (60% of displacees), namely *posseiros*, was summarily excluded from relocation provisions in the original proposals. Furthermore, the loss of a plot also signifies loss of access to the local rainforest itself, a source of many resources such as food and building materials which sustain the livelihood of peasant farmers. Thus, the legal measures adopted by ELETRONORTE at Tucuruí did less than justice to the region's inhabitants, 'where socially regulated and undocumented possession and farming of dryground, floodlands and islands, prevailed, in addition to extraction of natural resources, seasonally available in air, land and water environments that greatly extend beyond individual's own cultivated parcels' (Mougeot, 1985b, p. 5). Compensation was further minimised by scaling down permanent land titling operations in the area during the period preceding indemnification.

The indemnification process at Tucuruí was characterised by what appears to be a combination of, on the one hand, suspect attempts to minimise compensation in cash and kind and, on the other, sheer bad planning, which failed to take account of people's interests. A clear example of this was the flooding of a 100-kilometre stretch of the Trans-Amazon highway (BR 230) linking Marabá with Altamira, which partially flooded the INCRA colonisation project, PIC Marabá, resulting in the expropriation of up to 800 farmers with 100-hectare plots. Not only did initial surveys in 1979 discourage agricultural activities on the project for a five-year period, but INCRA withdrew its assistance from the entire 2,484 farms; jurisdiction of the project was transferred from INCRA, initially to the Marabá municipality and eventually to GETAT. Due to subsequent changes in agrarian legislation, dispossessed colonists had to exchange their 100-hectare plots for 50-hectare uncleared parcels of TMF. This planning error is all the more surprising since the Tucuruí dam and reservoir had been planned since at least 1968, well before the PIC Marabá was conceived and approved with the building of the *Transamazônica* in the early 1970s. This mistreatment of displaced persons by ELETRONORTE gave rise to a vociferous protest movement which, as Chapter 5 shows, had some success in obtaining redress.

One major study concludes that the authorities in charge of Tucuruí have been largely 'preoccupied with evacuating the reservoir area and relodging some of the displaced population, with limited concern to provide most with alternative means of subsistence, preserve riparian communities' access to waterway resources and care for the appropriate use of the reservoir environment' (Mougeot, 1985b, p. 13). This conforms very much to previous experience with public projects in Brazil involving resettlement. Hall (1978a) found a similar lack of official concern for those displaced by government irrigation schemes in the semi-arid interior of north-east Brazil by DNOCS during the 1970s, where those affected received little or no compensation and no plans whatsoever were made for providing alternative housing or plots of land. A similar pattern was recorded in the Sobradinho dam and reservoir project on the River São Francisco, creating the largest artificial lake in the world (surface area) and displacing over 70,000. The power authority, CHESF, only included resettlement provisions following pressure from the World Bank and national groups, but even then these were heavily criticised as grossly inadequate by the local population (CPT, 1979). Similar grievances were voiced by farmers displaced by irrigation projects run by CODEVASF (São Francisco Valley Development Company) downstream from the dam (de Barros, 1985). Here, as at Tucuruí, rigidly applied legalistic notions of private property irrelevant to people's needs, as well as many dubious official practices, resulted in the effective exclusion from any compensation of a large proportion of the 2,800 smallholders and 7,300 landless labourers and their families obliged to leave their homes.

The Tucuruí dam has also directly and indirectly affected the livelihoods and, indeed, the very survival prospects of some two hundred indians from the Parakanã and Gavião tribes, living respectively on the Pucuruí and Mãe Maria reservations. Their numbers have already been substantially reduced over the year as a result of diseases acquired through contact with settlers and highway workers. Further pressures have been generated by the partial flooding of indian lands, the routing of the main Tucuruí transmission line and Carajás railway through the Mãe Maria reserve and bisection of the indians' land by the Trans-Amazon and Belém–Brasília highways (Caulfield, 1982b, 1986; Goodland, 1986a). The Gaviões have fought long legal battles with ELETRONORTE and the CVRD to be compensated for the loss of their lands and forest resources. Only latterly, however, as a direct result of World Bank and international pressure from environmentalist and indian support groups, has financial indemnity been agreed. The details of this case are discussed in Chapter 5. Unfortunately, without the application of such outside leverage, it seems that such social and economic considerations which affect the livelihoods of substantial numbers of people, are ignored or bypassed by the Brazilian planning machine.

A series of other consequences, more strictly ecological in nature, have arisen from the creation of the Tucuruí reservoir. These are related either to limitations imposed on the reservoir's likely future performance by deforestation of surrounding areas (siltation and climatic changes), or to the effects of failing to clear vegetation from the area to be flooded (acid water, proliferation of water weeds and water-borne diseases, and anaerobic decomposition). Evidence from dams constructed in other tropical locations around the world and in Amazonia itself, together with initial observations on the impact of Tucuruí since 1984, suggest that the environmental repercussions may, despite detailed early warnings from outside specialists such as Goodland (1977), have been seriously under-estimated in the interests of commercial and political expediency. These impacts are all the more significant in view of the expansion in Amazonian hydropower development projected for the end of the century.

In the short term, the most pressing ecological problems at Tucuruí have arisen from the failure to clear vegetation from flooded areas. It is true that planners had few precedents to guide them since most large reservoirs have been built in temperate regions, in savanna grasslands or in valleys already cleared for agriculture. Yet there were sufficient examples in Latin America and indeed in

Brazilian Amazonia itself, at Curuá-Una, to give some hint of the potential dangers. Environmental impact assessments from both the World Bank (Goodland, 1977) and INPA (INPA/ELETRONORTE, 1982–84), clearly warned of the ecological consequences of not stripping the flooded area of its biomass which, it was forecast, could give rise to water acidity, disease, waterweeds and fish deaths. This seems to have prompted a decision by ELETRONORTE to undertake at least the selective clearing of some areas to protect the turbines and spillways (Caulfield, 1986), but led eventually to one of the biggest financial scandals in the history of the country. Yet preventive measures were taken too late in the project cycle to have anything but minimal impact.

The forestry authority (IBDF) tried to informally interest construction companies such as Andrade Gutiérrez and Camargo Correia, which were already engaged in the building of Tucuruí, but they declined on the grounds that extraction of the lumber was not commercially viable. When the job of clearing the forest and vegetation was finally opened to tender by the IBDF in May 1980 there was only one applicant, CAPEMI, a company with diversified interests but best known for its handling of the Brazilian Army's Pension Fund. CAPEMI was duly contracted in August 1980 and set up a joint venture (*Forestière d'Amazonie*) with the Maison Lazard Frères to provide technical assistance, which the French had acquired in south-east Asia. Under the agreement Lazard Frères would export the high-quality timber. The operation was financed by two loans totalling US$180 million from the Lazard Frères bank and the Banque Nationale de Paris, guaranteed by the government through the National Bank of Co-operative Credit (BNCC). This guarantee was issued despite the fact that the loan was equivalent to three times the size of the BNCC's capital. CAPEMI agreed to clear 65,510 hectares of both trees and vegetation, equivalent to 5·6 million cubic metres of timber, later reduced to 3·6 million cubic metres. Of course, this still represented only a small proportion of the estimated twenty million cubic metres of marketable high-quality timber waiting to be removed from the reservoir area (*Folha de São Paulo*, 5.9.82; LARR, 12.3.82: Goodland, 1985).

CAPEMI did not start its work of clearing the timber until mid-1981. Other problems soon followed, leading to long delays in meeting targets and to cost increases. Lazard Frères became disillusioned when it belatedly discovered that only 5% of the timber to be extracted was of the high quality it had expected. They also discovered that the lumber was not, after all, suited to the mechanised clearing techniques they had previously used in Asia. Furthermore, the 'experts' had not foreseen that the high water content of Amazonian trees would require an expensive drying process dependent on the use of imported chemicals which, even then, did not appear to work as well in Amazonia as it had done elsewhere. Costs and delays were further increased by the need to set up a system for transporting the felled timber. Additional questions were raised over the legality of financial transactions, the commissions charged by Lazard Frères and the refusal of the French company to accept second-grade timber.

The net result of this fracas was that CAPEMI deforested only 1,000 hectares or about 3% of the area they were contracted to clear. CAPEMI's loan of US$100 million from Lazard Frères was terminated in July 1982 and the Brazilian company went bankrupt in early 1983, owing US$4 million to its 3,000 workers. It also emerged that, in order to speed up forest clearing, the highly toxic chemical defoliant sodium pentachlorophenol (Tordon-155 or Agent Orange, used in the Vietnam War) was widely sprayed over the vegetation. Several tonnes were left behind and have subsequently been covered by the reservoir, with possibly serious environmental consequences in the future (Barham and Caulfield, 1984; LARR, 23.11.84). Reports have appeared of livestock and human deaths, as well as other health consequences, arising from the use of this herbicide in the area, for example in clearing the forest for power transmission lines (del Quiaro, 1985a). It has been estimated that if all the timber had been marketed rather being left to rot underwater, it would have represented 20% of the world's annual supply of hardwood and generated an income of US$2 billion (LARR, 12.3.82). The utilisation of this wasted resource would also perhaps have temporarily defused pressures by logging companies on other areas of Amazonian rainforest.

Although it is too soon to state categorically what the environmental consequences of Tucuruí will be, other cases of dams built in areas of tropical rainforest illustrate what can be expected as a result of not stripping the land prior to flooding. The decomposition of organic material has a crucial effect on subsequent water quality. It may become so nutrient-rich (eutrophic) and produce so many micro-organisms that the water becomes de-oxygenated and contaminated with decomposing material so that it cannot support fish. In deep, stagnant lakes such anaerobic (oxygen-free) decomposition is slow, producing foul-smelling hydrogen sulphide which increases the water's acidity. This not only kills off fish in the lake and river but erodes turbines and other equipment. At Brokopondo in Surinam repairs to damaged machinery cost over US$4 million (7% of total project costs). Evidence is also available from small dams built in Amazonia itself. At Curuá-Una near Santarém similar maintenance problems caused by excessive water acidity cost US$5 million to resolve, while at the Balbina reservoir near Manaus, formed in October 1987, corrosion problems and choking of turbines by water-weeds will require an estimated US$4·15 million annually to repair (Caulfield, 1986; Fearnside, 1989).

The risk of anaerobic decomposition at Tucuruí is reduced because the reservoir is extensive, shallow and flowing, permitting oxygenation of the waters. However, aerobic (oxygen-laden) decomposition brings its own problems of excessive weed-growth; varieties such as water hyacinths and aquatic ferns have been observed in other situations to clog turbines leading to frequent shut-downs, and to the disruption of fishing activities as water becomes de-oxygenated. Water weeds also make ideal breeding grounds for mosquitos and snails which transmit diseases suchas malaria, yellow fever, oncherciasis (river blindness) and bilharzia or schistosomiasis (which already affected 20% of Tucuruí's population even before the reservoir was created). This problem is likely to be exacerbated by the creation of a 'drawdown zone' as Tucuruí's water level falls when turbines are activated, thus regularly exposing about 900 square kilometres of temporary marshland (Goodland, 1977; Barrow, 1986).

A more important problem likely to be experienced at Tucuruí is siltation, which takes place naturally but whose pace will be greatly increased through local deforestation for lumbering, pasture formation and farming. Through engineering miscalculations, many dams have become silted up well ahead of schedule, a famous case being that of the Anchicaya Dam in Colombia, which lost 80% of its storage capacity in this way (Barrow, 1986). Similar examples are Lake Alajuela on the Panama Canal which will lose 40% of its capacity by the year 2000, Pakistan's Tarbela Dam which will, through siltation, be rendered useless within forty years and the Poza Honda reservoir in Ecuador which will enjoy a similar fate in twenty-five years' time (Myers, 1985). At Tucuruí Barrow (1986) reported, following fieldwork downstream, that the holding back of river silt by the dam has already reduced the periodic natural flooding of the valley floor, affecting fish catches, disrupting traditional *várzea* or riverine agriculture and damaging crops. Additional fears concern obstruction to migratory fish and the possible penetration of seawater into the lower Tocantins, which could affect commercial fishing and *várzea* rice cultivation (Barrow, 1986; Junk and de Mello, 1987).

Mining and charcoal production
Mining, of course, forms the nucleus of the Grande Carajás Programme, around which other activities revolve in one way or another. The extraction of iron-ore, bauxite, manganese, cassiterite and a host of other valuable minerals has, to date, had only a small direct impact on the environment, because of the limited geographical area immediately affected. Barely one hunded square kilometres (or 0·5% of the CVRD's area) will be deforested as a direct result of mining (Goodland, 1985; de Freitas, 1986). Although the discharge of toxic effluents into rivers can harm areas of TMF, this does not seem to be a problem at Carajás. The CVRD is conscious of these dangers and has spent US$34 million on building two retention dams to hold back (in settlement ponds) mineral waste washed away by the rain, on landscaping stripped areas and other measures (*Isto É*, 6.3.85). For this reason, mineral extraction is often hailed as one of the most environmentally-sound ways of exploiting the TMF, generating foreign exchange but causing relatively little damage (Goodland, 1980).

Within the 411,000-hectare area under the company's jurisdiction at Carajás, strict controls on deforestation are rigidly enforced. The forest is protected from all but the most essential destruction for mining and construction purposes. The roads display environmental publicity at two-kilometre intervals within the project perimeter and hunting of any sort is strictly prohibited, rules which are almost unheard of in Brazil; employees caught breaching these regulations face immediate dismissal. As discussed below in the following chapter, the CVRD's security forces regularly engage in cat-and-mouse tactics with invading gold-panners and small farmers, trying to prevent them damaging the environment by cutting down trees or polluting the rivers with mercury (used illegally in the gold extraction process). The project's small environmental team at Ca-

7 A series of charcoal furnaces, which will become a familiar sight along the Carajás railway corridor. Those illustrated were set up by the *Companhia Suderúrgica Vale do Pindaré* (a subsidiary of *Construtora Brasil*) in Açailândia. Their dual function is both to guarantee initial fuel stocks and to act as a demonstration unit for would-be local charcoal producers, who are expected to provide the bulk of future supplies by utilising the native Amazonian rainforest.

rajás (SUMIC-MA) takes ecological problems very seriously and this is reflected in their enthusiastic support for the botanical garden, the zoological park and the inclusion of environmental topics in the local primary school curriculum, measures whose limitations are also recognised.

Although mining operations themselves may not pose serious environmental risks, due to the limited geographical area directly affected, the scale of operations such as those in the Carajás Programme acts as an indirect stimulus to settlement and deforestation. Nowhere is this clearer than in the countryside immediately surrounding the mining project. The small adjacent town of Parauapebas, built almost from scratch from 1980 to house CVRD employees, has subsequently attracted a population of some 30,000 in search of employment and spawned the adjacent sprawling squatter settlement of Rio Verde. The surrounding hillsides have been all but totally stripped of their tree-cover to supply building materials and fuelwood, giving rise to widespread soil erosion and, according to local inhabitants, changes in the micro-climate such as higher maximum temperatures and sparser rainfall. The company town had its own housing and sanitary infrastructure but this cannot serve the presently enlarged urban area, which has no public sanitation system and almost no paved roads except the state highway which passes through it on the way to Carajás. This has been the source of much local resentment towards the CVRD which, in the eyes of the locals, has failed to meet its obligations to the town. Their hostility is further accentuated by the company's refusal to permit gold prospectors and small farmers to settle on the land under the project's jurisdiction, which is environmentally protected. Urban expansion has given rise to similar ecological problems in other nearby small towns which have grown beyond all recognition as a result of the Carajás Programme.

This chapter has outlined the major threats to Amazonia's delicate ecological balance arising from cattle ranching, pasture formation and land speculation, slash-and-burn farming by small farmers, commercial logging and dam construction from the mid-1960s until the present day. The newest and, perhaps, the gravest threat to the region's environment, however, is presented by plans to indutrialise a large part of eastern Amazonia, concentrated in the 900-kilometre railway corridor linking the Carajás mining project to São Luís. As detailed in Chapter 2, under the PGC fiscal incentive scheme it is expected that some thirty-one pig-iron smelters and mineral-processing plants will eventually be set up along the railway corridor, situated as follows: Marabá (six), Açailândia (twelve), Santa Inês (seven), Santa Luzia (one), Pindaré-Mirim (one), Rosário (four) (NATRON, 1987). By mid-1987 twelve pig-iron and five manganese/iron-alloy plants had been approved by the Carajás Interministerial Council, most of them expected to come on stream by 1990, producing about 1·3 million tonnes of pig-iron annually during this initial phase (Table 2.1). The first plant, in Açailândia, commenced production in January 1988, while two others in the same location and in Marabá were due to follow (*Isto É*, 2.12.87; *Construtora Brasil*, 1987). These first three plants will produce 250,000 tonnes of pig-iron annually during the first phase, exclusively for export overseas, while the Brazilian steel authority, CONSIDER, had in 1987

8   The effects of rampant deforestation are demonstrated around the twin towns of Parauapebas–Rio Verde, just outside the Carajás mining enclave. Removal of timber for construction purposes and domestic charcoal production have resulted in almost total loss of cover here, causing severe soil erosion, climatic changes and atmospheric pollution, which casts a permanent haze over the area.

already approved a production quota for the Carajás Programme of 1·7 million tonnes p.a. (*Jornal do Brasil*, 23.7.87).

The impact of such heavy industrial development on the rainforest environment and on the long-term livelihoods of the small farming population promises to be nothing short of disastrous. Throughout the 1970s and 1980s deforestation has been increasing at close to exponential rates in certain areas of Amazonia where cattle ranching and lumbering enterprises have been set up with the aid of official subsidies. The advent of pig-iron smelters, with their virtually insatiable demand for charcoal, seems likely to speed up the process of deforestation beyond even the most pessimistic projections of independent observers. According to figures supplied to the author by officials in Açailândia (*Construtora Brasil*, 1987) and by the CVRD itself (*Jornal do Brasil*, 5.7.87), it is estimated that charcoal accounts for between 50% and 70% of the total cost of pig-iron production.

The availability of cheap supplies of charcoal is the major *raison d'être* for the decision to transfer pig-iron smelting from Minas Gerais, where the native woodlands of the Rio Doce valley have been almost toally devastated by the iron and steel industry, to the still reasonably intact Amazonian rainforest. Eight of the twelve Carajas pig-iron smelters approved by mid-1987 were set up by companies from Minas Gerais.

A recent study by SUDAM and CODEBAR calculated that, in the short term, these twelve pig-iron projects alone will require one million tonnes of charcoal each year to fire their burners, necessitating the deforestation of 5,200 hectares of rainforest annually by 1991 (*O Liberal*, 13.4.86; *Jornal do Brasil*, 19.7.87)). In its comprehensive appraisal of the social and environmental impact of industrialisation along the railway corridor, the CVRD itself estimated that the annual charcoal consumption of the smelters will eventually be almost four million cubic metres, the equivalent of thirty-two million sacks, requiring the deforestation of 29,000 hectares of rainforest every year (CVRD, 1987). Latest estimates suggest that, if current plans are fully realised, the total number of industrial plants along the railway corridor will require a charcoal consumption of 3·8 million tonnes p.a., necessitating the annual deforestation of between 234,000 and 351,000 hectares of rainforest (Magnanini and Maciel, 1989). The then head of the CVRD's environmental division (SUMEI), Francisco de Assis Fonsêca, declared publicly in July 1987 that an 'environmental catastrophe' was imminent, predicting 'the complete destruction of the native forest' (*Jornal do Brasil*, 19.7.87).

Charcoal production on a small scale has existed for many years in the region to supply fuel for domestic cooking purposes, particularly in the countryside and even in the poorer suburbs of Amazonia's expanding urban centres where calor gas is prohibitively expensive for most. In response to the increased demand for charcoal from the iron and steel industry springing up in the railway corridor, there are likely to be three new major sources: (a) small-scale producer-peasants selling off timber from cleared farming land to supplement their incomes, (b) professional contractors or middlemen (*empreiteiros*) who collect timber by truck from farmers, some of whom may run their own charcoal ovens, and (c) industrial producers such as local sawmills and the smelters themselves who set up charcoal furnaces on a larger scale, fired by timber bought from middlemen.

The steel companies' need to guarantee regular charcoal supplies, together with the creation of a new source of profit and livelihood for larger and small producers alike, will unleash a process of uncontrolled deforestation and environmental destruction along the Carajás railway corridor the likes of which have so far not been seen in Amazonia.

Predatory destruction of the rainforest for charcoal production was, in 1987, already well in evidence, even before the first smelter came on stream. The *Construtora Brasil*'s plant in Açailândia, which is a typical case had, in August 1987, several months before its official inauguration in January 1988, some 10,000 cubic metres of charcoal stockpiled according to company officials. In Marabá, COSIPAR's plant had set aside 4,000 tonnes of charcoal ready to start production in 1988 (*Isto É*, 2.12.87). The numerous charcoal ovens being set up in the countryside to supply their prospective industrial customers, contribute further still to the permanently smoky, hazy atmosphere of eastern Amazonia, already fed by the constant burning of trees and vegetation as pastures are cleared and fields prepared for planting.

As far as peasant cultivators and other small-scale suppliers are concerned, charcoal production is seen as a valuable additional source of off-farm employment and income which could do much, at least in the short term, to alleviate their chronic poverty. SUDAM has even announced its intention of encouraging participation by farmers on colonisation schemes in the vicinity around the Pindaré area and in *bico do papagaio* settlements such as Carajás I, II and III and to encourage the setting up of charcoal production facilities there. According to the agency, an area of 2·5 hectares of forest could thus provide an annual income of £280 (*Gazeta Mercantil*, 7.10.86). Such small-scale suppliers would provide the raw material for medium-sized producers of charcoal, to entrepreneurs from the area and those from outside.

Established timber companies, such as that owned by the Galletti family in Açailândia, are currently negotiating with the iron and steel companies to adopt a new role as suppliers not just of timber offcuts but of charcoal itself. A new class of 'charcoal factory-owners' (*usineiros de carvão*) is emerging to service the industry, taking advantage of subsidised credit and other incentives through the SUDAM and PGC schemes to act as regular suppliers to the smelters, producing charcoal from timber as well as babaçú nut husks.

Several major projects approved under the Carajás fiscal incentive programme have charcoal production listed as a major activity (Table 2.2). Examples include METALTEC (Itaquí); *Agropecuária Ceres* (Turiaçú); CIPASA–*Castanha Industrial do Pará Ltda.* (Mojú); DENAM–*Dendê de Amazônia SA* (Ipixuna); and *Meape Ltda.* (Turiaçú).

During the initial phase of pig-iron production the steel companies themselves have made provisions for building up their own independent charcoal supplies. The *Cia. Siderúrgica Vale do Pindaré* in Açailândia, for example, has set up twenty-eight charcoal furnaces, each producing seventy-five cubic metres per month from sawmill offcuts. Their role is not just to supply charcoal but to act as demonstration units for other would-be producers anxious to learn the technology. COSIPAR in Marabá has set up 120 charcoal furnaces in the surrounding countryside to guarantee supplies, situated along the Trans-Amazon highway and the PA 150 highway (NATRON, 1987; *Gazeta Mercantil*, 7.10.86). As the smelters start to come on stream the price of charcoal is expected to rise rapidly. From April–May 1987 the price doubled from CrZ195 to CrZ300 per tonne as the smelters built up their stocks ready to start production early 1988 (*O Liberal*, 16.7.87). The potential profit is considerable not just for larger suppliers but also for small farmers whose meagre farm incomes could be significantly boosted.

Despite the undoubted immediate economic advantages, however, few observers have any illusions about the devastating impact on the rainforest. The history of Minas Gerais, where pig-iron production has been directly responsible for one-third of deforestation in that state (*Isto É*, 2.12.87), illustrates something of the fate which awaits Amazonia, although the effect will be more far-reaching on the delicate northern rainforest than on the more temperate woodlands of the South. Furthermore, the desperate situation of many smallholders and landless labourers in Amazonia, unable to secure a livelihood from farming alone, will encourage them to switch to production of charcoal rather than staple crops, thus accentuating environmental pressures and worsening the problem of localised food insecurity. Even steel company officials, when pressed, reluctantly acknowledge the ecological damage which will inevitably ensue from a policy of mining the TMF as a source of cheap fuel.

Serious doubts have been expressed whether, in spite of the strong incentives of large profit margins, local suppliers will actually be able to meet the smelters' demand for charcoal in the medium to long term. The Brazilian Association of Vegetable Charcoal Producers (ABRACAVE) has estimated, for example, that in Marabá the existing 400 sawmills could only supply the first three smelters, operational in 1988 (*Jornal do Brasil*, 23.7.87). A CODEBAR/ SUDAM study projected that demand for charcoal in Marabá will double from 125,000 tonnes in 1988 to 325,000 tonnes in 1991. In Parauapebas the increase is even more drastic, from 40,000 to 250,000 tonnes over the same three-year period. In Açailândia demand will jump from 159,000 tonnes in 1988 to 430,000 tonnes by 1991 (cited by Treece, 1987, p. 80). Apart from the limited capacity of local suppliers such as sawmills, the tropical rainforest is, of course, a finite resource which cannot be exploited indefinitely. A study by the German steel furnace manufacturers, KTS, predicted that, using only predatory methods and without reforestation, charcoal supplies would be exhausted within twenty years. Even this time-scale was questioned as unduly optimistic by the head of the CVRD's environmental division, who commented that the company 'should oppose the setting up of smelters based on vegetable charcoal along the Carajás railway, in the manner which they are currently being implemented' (*Jornal do Brasil*, 5.7.87).

Labour shortages could also constitute a serious bottleneck, for it is estimated that about 200,000 extra workers would be needed in the production and transportation of charcoal to meet the demand created by the first dozen smelters. This was certainly the case in northern Pará (Paragominas and Tomé Açú), where charcoal producers had to import labour (Hebette *et al*, n.d.). Such a situation could, of course, have the beneficial effect of driving up wages and perhaps slowing down the rate of deforestation. It might also, in the longer term, oblige steel companies to take more seriously the option of large-scale, mechanised plantations as renewable sources of lumber for charcoal, leaving intact the native rainforest, or what remains of it.

As if in belated recognition of the implicit environmental dangers, and in response to domestic as well as international pressure, some corrective action has been taken. The fourteenth meeting of the PGC's Interministerial Council announced in July 1987 that pig-iron projects along the railway would be obliged to undertake reforestation, although no details were given as to the nature or extent of these measures (*Jornal do Brasil*, 19.7.87, 21.7.87). The Council also contracted the Industrial Technology Foundation (FTI) to draw up a more rational strategy for the supply of wood charcoal in the PGC and advise steel companies on how to practise reforestation and forestry management. A special commission was also established to draw up guidelines for the production of charcoal, comprising the IBDF, CONSIDER and the Ministry of Agrarian Reform.

However, it is difficult to see how these ideas can be put into practise since, although a dozen charcoal-burning plants are due to come on stream in the Carajás Programme by the end of the 1980s, no study has yet been undertaken as to how reforestation could be successfully accomplished and with what varieties of tree. According to earlier versions of agricultural development plans for the Carajás Programme, charcoal was to be supplied by large eucalyptus plantations along the railway, originally some 2·4 million hectares (CVRD, 1981) but later scaled down to 700,000 hectares (PGC, 1983). However, as mentioned in Chapter 2, no comprehensive plan for the development of agriculture or forestry in the Carajás Programme has so far been approved. A recent CVRD study (1987) estimated that, in order to supply the planned smelters with charcoal using eucalyptus, a total of 2·6 million hectares of industrial plantations would be needed in the PGC. Eventually, a total of 2·6 million hectares of industrial plantations would be needed in the PGC (Rankin, 1985). Yet because tax incentives for logging in Amazonia are directed towards extraction and processing rather than sustained yield forestry, no permanent, large-scale, sustainable commercial timber operations exist, merely small experimental areas totalling a few hundred hectares. Furthermore, soils within the Carajás Programme area are generally too shallow to allow the setting up of large pine and eucalyptus plantations (Valverde, 1989).

Amazonia's largest and best-known such forestry experiment has been undertaken on the 1·6 million-hectare Jarí agroforestry enterprise, set up in 1968 by the American shipping and industrial mangnate, Daniel K. Ludwig. Jarí was eventually sold in 1982 to a consortium of Brazilian companies, headed by the mining magnate Augusto Antunes. Three varieties of eucalyptus and pine tree (*gmelina arborea*, *pinus caribaea* and *eucalyptus deglupta*) were planted from 1970–86 over a total area of 75,000 hectares to supply Jarí's cellulose factory with pulp (Fearnside, 1987b). Originating in India, *gmelina* was imported to Brazil after a brief trial in Nigeria but had never been planted on a large scale. The failure to carry out a proper soil survey and other tests led to poor yields and necessitated the conversion of 47,000 hectares of *gmelina* at Jarí to pine and eucalyptus (Pinto, 1986c). Severe problems were encountered with these imported varieties in terms of poor soil fertility, intolerance to drought and vulnerability to pests and fungus disease, which reduced yields and increased costs. Attempts to introduce homogenous varieties in place of rainforest have met with similar problems elsewhere in Amazonia. At Fordlândia and Belterra, for example, as Dean (1987) has shown, South American Leaf Blight took on epidemic proportions and was a major factor frustrating attempts to set up rubber plantation, rendering them uneconomic.

At Jarí several areas of plantation have been abandoned and production has fallen well short of expectations. It was anticipated that by 1989 as much as 50% of the cellulose factory's timber requirements would have to be met from outside. Another problem is vulnerability to world market prices. In the case of Jarí, Ludwig based his original calculations on a future world price for cellulose of US$700 per tonne, whereas in practice it had not (by 1987) surpassed US$267 on international markets, and US$331 in Brazil itself. Hence, cellulose production had to be heavily subsidised by Jarí's other activities, especially kaolin production and mechanised rice farming. In addition the IBDF provides financial incentives to 6,000 hectares of silviculture plantations, while Jarí also receives other benefits in terms of exemption from Brazilian income tax and import duties (Fearnside, 1987b, 1988).

The implications of Jarí for the Carajás Programme are clear. Twenty smelters would require plantations totalling thirty-five times the area of those managed at Jarí. The economic and ecological obstacles encountered by Ludwig and his successors would be correspondingly magnified, especially as the managerial expertise and level of investment typical of Jarí would be difficult to replicate on the necessary scale. A further problem likely to be encountered in the Carajás area is that eucalyptus plantations are likely to lower the water table significantly and modify the local flora and fauna (CVRD, 1987). The CVRD's observations reflect a growing worldwide concern over the suitability of eucalyptus for Third World silviculture despite its growing use for fuelwood and pulp production. Eucalyptus has been labelled a 'socially inappropriate species' by the Environmental Defence Fund, due to its side effects in draining soil nutrients, depleting water supplies, increasing soil erosion and displacing indigenous varieties (Joyce, 1988). As one observer put it:

...there is reason to speculate that the silviculture plantation of Carajás may either never be established or, if established, that they may fail biologically and/or economically. In either case, the wood to meet needs for fuel and other uses would continue to be harvested from the native forest for which no sustained yield management currently exists. (Rankin, 1985, p. 387).

The reduced yields, inflated costs and environmental consequences of such large-scale operations led one seasoned commentator (Fearnside, 1987b, p. 307) to note that, 'not even the continuous dedication of Jarí to silviculture, nor the significant elimination of operational losses can be interpreted as meaning that large forestry plantations are now a viable model for the economic development of Amazonia'.

Another notable silvicultural experiment approaching full operation is the 80,000-hectare *Amapá Florestal e Celulose* (AMCEL), set up in the early 1970s by the Antunes mining group, CAEMI, in Santa Isabel, Amapá, to produce wood-chips from Caribbean pine. Reputedly the 'world's biggest pine plantation' (*Financial Times*, 3.3.88), AMCEL has been providing vital supplies, amounting to 400,000 tonnes a year, to meet timber shortages at Jarí, 200 kilometres upstream. When the second phase of the scheme is completed in 1990, AMCEL will annually export 500,000 tonnes of wood-chips to pulp producers in Scandinavia and Japan, by which time it is expected that 84,000 hectares will have been established; 7,000 hectares will be cut and replanted every year. Of the US$72 million cost, US$14 million is being lent by the International Finance Corporation (LACR, 14.5.87). Notwithstanding the promising start made by AMCEL, the technical problems and subsequent financial losses experienced by Jarí (US$47 million in 1985) bear testimony to the fact that it is proving far more difficult and expensive to establish and maintain large-scale silvicultural operations in Amazonia than many planners and industrialists imagine.

But even assuming that knowledge of suitable techniques did exist, along with genuine environmental concern amongst industrialists and policy-makers, as well as adequate technical and human resources to tackle reforestation, a major problem would remain for the steel companies: replacing the native rainforest would destroy the very cost advantage which drew them to Amazonia in the first instance. In Minas Gerais state, where the iron and steel industry has been established for decades, only 20% of its charcoal is supplied by plantations, the remainder being brought from distances of up to

1,000 kilometres. Abundant supplies of cheap charcoal is one of the major pillars supporting industrialisation of the Carajás railway corridor. This fact was underlined by the German firm *Korf Tecnologia Siderúrgica* (KTS) in its report to the CVRD, which states categorically that if charcoal is produced from native rainforest the rate of return is positive but using trees from reforested areas produces a negative return for the companies involved (*Jornal do Brasil*, 7.7.87, 11.3.88). An environmentally-rational policy would have to plan such investment well in advance and make provisions for plantations to gradually supply the necessary timber for charcoal production, leaving most of the virgin rainforest intact so that sustainable development options could be explored at a later date. Unfortunately no such provisions for reforestation have yet been made, and the most likely outcome in the short term is that the already fast pace of forest destruction will be increased further still, subject to no effective controls. The extent of the subsidy and encouragement given to iron and steel producers in Carajás by allowing them to exploit the native rainforest is clearly demonstrated by the cost savings involved. Charcoal produced in this way costs US$17 per tonne, compared with US$80 per tonne if timber from plantations is used, rendering pig-iron production under the latter option uneconomic at current world market prices (Valverde, 1989). It should be noted that economically viable, non-destructive fuel alternatives such as coke or *babaçú* husks, all but ignored so far by companies, have not been seriously considered.

Even if private companies were willing to invest in reforestation, the KTS study contends that forestry techniques are not sufficiently advanced to undertake large-scale replanting in the short term (EDF, 1987). Replanting tropical rainforest on a sustainable basis is a very expensive business; Daniel Ludwig's Jarí scheme reputedly absorbed over US$ one billion and even then suffered from low yields (Rainkin, 1985, Pinto, 1986c). Carajás smelters are unlikely to voluntarily adopt environmentally appropriate practices in view of the greater profit margins to be enjoyed from the cheaper but rather more destructive technique of simply mining the rainforest. As such, initiatives are conditioned by a distorted market benefiting from large subsidies through the fiscal incentives scheme, in which short-term profit is the guiding principle and in which ecological considerations are of the lowest priority. The most pessimistic scenario from an environmental standpoint sees the smelters in Amazonia as esentially medium-term enterprises which will be closed down as soon as their cheap sources of charcoal have been exhausted.

Apart from drastically speeding up the rate of deforestation, pig-iron smelting is liable to generate significant industrial pollution. In two planned industrial poles, Açailândia and Parauapebas, both situated in valleys, frequent temperature inversions take place when, during the 'winter' or rainy season, cold air masses trap the warmer, moist air along with any industrial by-products in the atmosphere. Because these centres were planned with regard to logistical and strategic considerations only, a situation will be created similar to that in the notorious city of Cubatão, in São Paulo state, which enjoys the dubious reputation of being the most polluted place on Earth. Dense industrial smog and acid rain are probable consequences, it is officially suggested, for this part of Amazonia (CVRD, 1987).

The smelter furnaces are supposed to filter out toxic substances from the smoke which will be produced. The already unclean atmosphere will, it seems, become progressively more polluted by a combination of industrial, agricultural, lumbering and charcoal-producing enterprises, representing a danger to people's general health as well as to local air traffic. There is an increasing incidence, for example, of near crashes at local airports such as Marabá due to the runway being obscured by smoke and fog, confusing incoming pilots. Near crashes involving even commercial jets landing in the smog of eastern Amazonia are becoming common (O Liberal, 18.8.87).

Furthermore, although the steel companies, as well as the CVRD itself at its iron-mining complex at Carajás, take great pains to ensure that toxic effluent is removed and prevented from polluting the surrounding countryside, there is no guarantee that these measures will be totally effective. Officially the iron-ore tailing ponds are considered completely safe for a twenty-year period but CVRD officials have privately admitted that that their working life may be as short as five to ten years. Furthermore, leakage from the ponds of water with a high iron content has already shown signs of polluting nearby streams (Secrett, 1987). A further problem suggested by the CVRD (1987) is a lowering of the water table in Açailândia, which is fed by a small affluent of the River Cajuapara, due to the large quantities of coolant required by the smelters.

Apart from the side effects of iron-ore mining, another source of environmental danger arises from marine pollution and its negative impact on the artisanal fishing industry of São Luís and the coastline of northern Maranhão, where an estimated 60,000 fishermen earn their living (Galvão, 1984). No systematic research has been undertaken on this aspect of the Carajás programme but field evidence indicates that ecological damage has affected the livelihoods of urban and coastal dwellers as well as rainforest populations. This is due in part to the growth in sea traffic with the building of new port installations. In early 1987 a 350-tonne oilspill from a Korean tanker, the 'Hyunday New World', polluted beaches on São Luís island and disrupted the artisanal fishing industry for months (CPP, 1987). Fishermen and ex-fishermen in São Luís complain that catches have dropped substantially as a direct result of pollution arising from port construction and related activities such as the building of the ALUMAR aluminium plant. This factory has already had severe repercussions on the local ecosystem, generating clouds of aluminium hydroxide which have ruined farmers' crops as well as causing serious respiratory illnesses and skin complaints. The plant will also create an estimated 410,000 tonnes of waste 'red mud' that will need to be carefully disposed of if the entire local ecosystem of coast and mangrove swamps is not to be totally disrupted (Galvão, 1984).

One disillusioned fisherman, evicted from his village and resettled miles away from the beach on high, infertile ground complained bitterly that, 'the sea is polluted by construction operations and catches are a fraction of what they once were' (Hall, 1986a). Another report stated that, 'when the aluminium smelting plant came on stream villagers started complaining of an increase in skin irritations, respiratory complaints and dying crops. They also reported an increase in dead fish in the estuaries' (Oxfam, 1987). The USIMAR steel plant to be built in São Luís and the METALMAN manganese processing factory under construction in nearby Rosário, both funded by the Carajás Programme (Table 2.1), are widely expected to degrade the local ecology. Timber from surrounding swamplands will be cut down to supply the plants with charcoal and poisonous effluent will be discarded into the rivers, killing off the fish and possibly ruining the livelihoods of over 4,000 families. Following the mass evacuations, which involved over 20,000 local people, as well as the negative environmental impact of Carajás-related industrialisation on the livelihoods of fishermen around São Luís, the infant mortality rate amongst the low-income population doubled from 84 to 164 per thousand (Galvão, 1984).

Social disruption as a result of the Carajás Programme has been no less traumatic than the ecological damage caused. The ALUMAR factory alone, which occupies one-sixth of São Luís island's 60,000 hectares, displaced 7,000 families of small farmers and fishermen (Galvão, 1984). Although the plant created 2,000 jobs, most of these skilled and semi-skilled workers have been brought in from other regions, creating much resentment in the city. Overall the net increase in local unemployment has been considerable. These developments have galvanised local communities into action and, in co-operation with the Fishermen's Commission of the Catholic Church (CPP) and other human rights organisations, a vigorous campaign has been mounted locally and nationally in an attempt to ameliorate their worst effects (*Jornal de Hoje*, 1.8.87; CPP, 1987). At one stage the 'Committee for the Defence of the Island of São Luís', a local pressure group formed to defend inhabitants' interests, staged a series of marches and demonstrations in São Luís (see Chapter 5). Their attempts to give the campaign nation-wide publicity, however, were rather frustrated by lack of media coverage orchestrated, it is alleged, by the powerful industrial lobby.

If planners have shown relatively little consideration for small farmers and fishermen, many of whose livelihoods will be disrupted or destroyed by developments in the region, their concern for its potentially negative effects on the animal population is even less pronounced. The consequences of Amazonian settlement for plant species have been discussed briefly above, but another important aspect is the impact of port and associated industrial developments upon marine wildlife. The coasts of Pará and Maranhão possess some of the most extensive mangrove formations in South America and are 'of outstanding importance as a wintering area for shorebirds' (Morrison *et al*, 1986, p. 5). Without operational guidelines for the Ponta da Madeira port at São Luís, for controlling industrial growth and for dealing with accidents such as that involving the Korean Tanker referred to above, experts have warned that this region of high biological productivity will be under grave threat.

Environmental management and control for Carajás

Steps have been taken to incorporate ecological considerations into the management of mining operations in the PGC. The CVRD, which is responsible for the iron-ore mining complex at Carajás, the port at Itaquí in São Luís and the 900-kilometre railway linking the two, created an 'independent' environmental group in 1980 to advise the company on such aspects (Goodland, 1985; Carvalho and Borgonovi, 1986; de Freitas 1986). The Environmental Study and Assessment Group (GEAMAM) is composed of nine senior scientists and experts on Amazonia, linked directly to the presidency of the CVRD, and had a budget of US$53 million for the period 1983–87. GEAMAM prepared a set of environmental guidelines to be followed by all contractors relating to wildlife, tree removal, fires, soil erosion and fire prevention, etc. The group meets at three-monthly intervals and makes recommendations on appropriate environmental action to two Internal Environmental Commissions (CIMAs). These were established in 1981 for the mine and the port site, with shared responsibility for the railway, and they attempt to make sure that GEAMAM's guidelines are followed. In theory, the CVRD also works closely with government agencies for the environment such as the Special Environmental Secretariat (SEMA) and the forestry commission (IBDF), and related bodies such as FUNAI, EMBRAPA, the CNPq and INCRA.

The company has undertaken a sophisticated publicity campaign throughout the 1980s, professing its concern for environmental conservation within its area of direct jurisdiction. A glossy brochure for English readers wrote, 'Through its experience in the south of Brazil, CVRD has become sensitised to the ecological issues of mining projects and has developed an expertise on environmental assessment and management practices' (1984a, p. 3). The company has been anxious to convey an image of concern for social and ecological repercussions; in its document entitled 'CVRD Cares' (CVRD, 1984b) the company wrote that, 'One of CVRD's greatest concerns is the protection of ecosystems over the area's construction and future operations. In Carajás, along the railroad and at the port, every care was taken to preserve the environment' (CVRD, 1985, p. 14).

Thus armed, the CVRD has taken a number of steps and initiatives designed to minimise the adverse impact of mining on the Amazonian environment, bearing in mind the fact that a balance 'must be sought between exploitation of rich natural resources and conservation of nature' (de Freitas and Smyrski-Shluger, n.d., p. 20). The first of these is ecological zoning, based on surveys conducted by the Ministry of Mines and Energy, to facilitate planning and conservation. However, this is a very recent development and has been started only after construction of the iron-ore mine and other projects was well under way. Based on these maps, observation areas will be set up along the railway and in the mining zone. Tracts of virgin forest are being purchased for research, experimentation and the preservation of native species; one example is an area of 10,000 hectares in Buriticupú on the upper Pindaré river. In addition, GEAMAM has suggested the creation of a 48,000-hectare buffer zone around the mining area, as well as areas around the railway and the port, in order to minimise ecological damage. A plant nursery has been set up to provide seedlings for future use, while plans are under way for replanting the first site where strip mining will be completed. Steps are also being taken to guard against pollution of local towns by mineral dust and against marine pollution at the port complex. As mentioned above, mining slurry will be held back by retention dams into settling pools, filtered and then recycled for use at the plant (Goodland, 1985). The CVRD's involvment with indian support work is described in Chapter 3.

However, despite these laudable (official) organisational objectives and the strong conservation efforts of serious-minded individuals within the CVRD, a question mark must be raised over the probable effectiveness of such policies in significantly reducing environmental degradation. Not for the first time in tropical rainforest development programmes, and certainly not the last, short-term profit-maximisation is likely to take precedence over any longer range ecological considerations. It is an open secret that environmental experts within the CVRD have had an uphill struggle to convince their engineering colleagues in the organisation that conservation is a subject to be taken seriously. An article in the CVRD's own environmental journal in March 1986 appealed for greater recognition to be given within the company to the importance of ecological issues, and to the need for action to be taken where necessary to 'correct distortions' produced by company practices (Carvalho and Borgonovi, 1986, p. 21).

Nominally, at least, the CVRD itself has little direct influence over investments outside its area of jurisdiction beyond the boundaries of the mining enclave at Carajás. Although in theory responsible for conservation along the railway, which is administered by the CVRD, the company has no direct control over the establishment of industries such as pig-iron smelters, which are vetted by the Interministerial Council. It is left to individual investors to follow whatever legal guidelines exist. Industrial project proposals applications are supposed to include an environmental impact statement, yet these declarations are either omitted or so superficial as to be meaningless. In the case of the SIMARA smelter in Marabá, for example, the relevant section was left blank on the proposal presented to the Interministerial Council (EDF, 1987). One ecologist has noted that, 'No project approved under the Programme has had adequate pre-project botanical and zoological surveys carried out before starting' (Secrett, 1987, p. 62). During an interview the Secretary of Planning for Pará openly admitted that the COSIPAR smelter in Marabá and, indeed, the entire new industrial zone of that city,had been set up without the required environmental impact assessment (RIMA) having been carried out (*Isto É*, 2.12.87). In addition, the Brazilian forestry authority (IBDF) is responsible for monitoring environmental affairs but the organisation is weak institutionally, is seriously understaffed and is denied the funds and the political support needed to do its job properly. The agency has, for example, only twenty inspectors for the whole state of Pará.

Yet the CVRD does in practice exercise a large degree of control over investment decisions in the whole PGC area, and not just within its own mining projects. The iron and steel companies currently involved in the wider programme have sited their plants based on information and technical assistance supplied by the State mining enterprise. As the owner of the railway and sole supplied of iron-ore to the smelters, the CVRD could, if it chose, have a much greater say in reducing the adverse environmental consequences of mining and processing. Despite the organisation's official commitment to the environment in its public statements and publicity documents, however, reality falls far short of the rhetoric. Nevertheless, the organisation is not monolithic and not all employees share the same short-sighted, purely commercial vision.

The CVRD's environmental division has tried to draw the attention of policy-makers and the wider public to some of the crucial issues and dangers involved. In September 1986, for example, the company's environmental division, GEAMAM, helped to fund an international conference on 'Economic Development and Environmental Impact in the Brazilian Humid Tropics', held in the city of Belém, at which experts from all over the world highlighted a series of ecological problems in Amazonia, such as deforestation and air pollution, likely to be exacerbated by current investment patterns.

CVRD engineers were accused, for example, of connivance with iron and steel companies in the siting of pig-iron smelters, with no consideration of likely environmental impact. A subsequent conference policy statement noted that, 'The industrialisation of the region was not preceded by an economic and ecological survey (and) we dispute the type of industrialisation being set up.' It went on to recommend that 'industrial policy for the region be carefully reconsidered, when involving the use of charcoal of native origin (as well as) revision and restriction of the concession of fiscal incentives', urging the evaluation of 'non predatory alternatives' (CVRD/SEMA/ IWRB, 1986, pp. 5–6). Despite the gravity of the subject and the strength of these recommendations, company policy has not been modified in response to criticisms. The CVRD's top management chose to ignore the problems raised, going so far as to walk out before or during particularly sensitive debates on ecological questions (GEAMAM, 1987).

To re-emphasise the point, the conference was followed by publication of a three-volume, multi-disciplinary study organised by the company's Superintendency for the Environment (SUMEI) which focused on the social, economic and ecological consequences of environmentally inappropriate investment patterns in the seventeen municipalities along the Carajás railway (CVRD, 1987). While recognising that many of the root causes of environmental degradation are beyond the ability of the CVRD to influence, it suggests quite strongly that the company could do far more than it has done so far to ameliorate the programme's adverse impact on the region's natural resources and population. The towns of Açailândia and Parauapebas are highlighted, owing to the proposed concentration of pig-iron smelters there, although a total of eleven urban centres are mentioned as having adverse environmental indicators. The implicit suggestion appears to be that the CVRD could, if it wished, use its strong economic and political leverage to have these industries sited in alternative areas and run along different, more appropriate lines. Whether this most recent study will influence policy-makers in this direction remains to be seen; yet past experience does not augur well for the likelihood of more ecologically-sound development given the current priorities of the CVRD and other industrial participants. The sacking of the CVRD's outspoken chief environmental co-ordinator, Maria de Lourdes Davies de Freitas, in April 1987 is perhaps indicative of the company's attitude towards serious environmental control.

If internal criticism of environmentally inappropriate investment strategies usually falls on deaf ears in Brazilian corridors of power, external pressure can sometimes be more effective. The strong US environmental lobby has for some years now been trying to persuade the World Bank to monitor more carefully the social and ecological impact of major development programmes in Brazil with which it is involved. In the case of the POLONOROESTE programme for developing the north-west frontier zone of Rondônia, world-wide protests at its negative impact on indigenous populations as well as other adverse consequences resulted in a significant delaying of funds at one stage (see Chapter 5). In August 1982 the Bank made a loan of US$304,500,000 to the CVRD towards the cost of setting up the Carajás iron-ore mine and processing facilities, the railway and building of the new Ponta da Madeira port in São Luís. Section 3.10 of the Loan Agreement stipulates that 'the Borrower shall take all action, as shall be required to ensure that the execution and operation of the Project are carried out with due regard to ecological and environmental factors. . .' over an area included in the radius of one hundred kilometres from the iron mine and railway (EDF, 1987, p. 1). A similarly strong protest movement to that mounted against POLONOROESTE is being organised in the case of Carajás by an international consortium of twenty-nine environmental and indigenous rights groups, calling upon the World Bank to oblige the CVRD to honour its loan contract agreement. In an open letter to Bank President Barber Conable in August 1987 the group urged the organisation to 'halt all industrial projects using wood-derived charcoal in the project area, and to assist the Brazilian authorities in evaluating and promoting alternative development options for the area that will not cause massive deforestation', and also calls for the protection of the Gurupí Forest Reserve and the demarcation of other indian areas such as that of the Guajá (EDF, 1987, p. 7).

European environmentalists have also been engaged in a strong campaign since 1980 to put pressure on the EEC to withhold funding for the scheme pending satisfactory provisions for tackling social and ecological problems. In September 1982 the European Community approved a loan of US$600 million for the CVRD's Carajás mining project, the largest single outside investment. In exchange, one-third of the iron-ore from Carajás would be supplied to steel industries in five European countries, amounting to 13·6 million tons annually over fifteen years, totalling US$270 million (Treece, 1987). From the outset, however, European NGOs (non-government organisations) challenged the loan and in 1982, 1983 and 1984, the General Assembly of NGOs passed motions calling attention to human rights violations and environmental damage caused by the PGC. Despite the increasing weight of evidence as well as numerous motions and questions tabled in the European Parliament and the EEC Commission, which was challenged over its refusal to take the NGO recommendations seriously, Mr. Ortoli, speaking for the Commission in 1984 at the European Parliament insisted that, '. . . the project is not having the ecological and social consequences referred to' (quoted by Treece, 1987, p. 24).

Loan disbursements have been continued unhindered and the Commission has consistently refused to undertake its own independent evaluation of the socio-environmental impact of Carajás, placing its faith instead on quarterly World Bank reports. Somewhat belatedly, the Committee on the Environment, Public Health and Consumer Protection of the European Parliament reported that future projects in Latin America funded by the EEC should include environmental impact assessment studies, whose results would have a strong bearing on decision-making. A major independent study of the Carajás Programme by Survival International and Friends of the Earth, published in September 1987, castigated the EEC for its 'complacency over the impact of the Carajás Project (which) can no longer be reasonably sustained. . . in this European Year of the Environment' (Treece, 1987, p. 27). An open letter from the two organisations to M. Jacques Delors, President of the Commission of European Communities, dated 1 October 1987, urged the EEC to take corrective measures to demarcate indian lands and draw up an Environmental Master Plan to protect the region against the impact of the PGC, which was labelled 'an environmentally unsound regional development programme of disastrous proportions' (Survival International, 1987a). Survival International's bulletin (1987b) called upon members of its support group to write protest letters to the EEC and World Bank and the subject was considered important enough by one major British newspaper to give the story a front page lead (*The Independent*, 24.9.87). However, with practically the entire EEC loan having been disbursed by this stage, environmentalists' protests have not apparently had much immediate impact on Carajás development policy. In the longer term, however, they have undoubtedly helped to create a much greater general awareness of the PGC's actual and potential ecological dangers.

5

Social conflict and peasant resistance to land-grabbing

The heightened agrarian crisis in Brazilian Amazonia has placed peasant farmers in an increasingly precarious situation. Development strategies for the region have consistently marginalised small farmers. At best, the State provides little support for migrants' efforts to establish a stable livelihood on the frontier; at worst, official strategies are activity hostile to their interests. Generous official subsidies are granted to the very commercial and speculative enterprises which sustain this crisis by monopolising access to land and inducing environmental degradation, while small cultivators are left to fend for themselves against encroachment by commercial groups. If large numbers of peasant farmers have managed to survive in Amazonia it is despite, rather than because of, government policies. Yet it would be a mistake to think that small farmers and indians have always accepted the passive role of victim in this struggle. Resistance to land-grabbing has become a major social phenomenon in Amazonia, particularly within the 10% of Brazil covered by the Carajás Programme, scene of the longest-standing and most violent confrontations. The growing intensity of open social conflict in this region reflects an on-going struggle by disadvantaged and unprotected groups engaged in the defence of their livelihoods and, indeed, their very right to exist.

The scale of popular reaction may be gauged by the extent of violence in Amazonia, described in Chapter 3, and reflected in the escalating death toll from land conflicts. This has been due partly to the use of more violent tactics by land-grabbers to evict peasants, but is primarily the result of increased resistance by small farmers themselves,'unwilling to submit to such tactics. Peasant resistance was particularly marked in the late 1970s and early 1980s during the

period of political liberalisation (*abertura*) under Presidents Geisel
and Figueiredo but has, ironically, been especially intense since the
advent of a civilian administration. Deaths not only of peasant
farmers but also of hired gunmen, at the hands of their intended
victims, have seen a large increase since 1985, the annual toll in Pará,
for example, tripling within the space of only two years.

Peasant opposition to land-grabbing, or *grilagem*, takes many
forms, varying considerably in both nature and scale. Resistance
may be highly institutionalised and orchestrated through the rural
union movement or political parties. On the other hand, it may
consist of isolated battles by families or communities against individual *grileiros*, or manifest itself as spontaneous, mass occupations of
private estates. Falling somewhere between these two extremes,
the struggle may involve some articulation of peasant and indian
interests through the radical Catholic Church and Brazilian non-
government organisation (NGOs) working directly with community
groups, perhaps in association with rural unions. After examining
how semi-subsistence, peasant farmers in the Carajás region have
fought to defend their land rights, the significance of this resistance
will be assessed in relation to the longer-term development of the
region.

Institutionalised peasant opposition

Brazil has a long history of peasant revolt and protest, going back
to colonial days and the oligarchic domination of rural barons or
coroneis in the sugar and cocoa monocultures of the North-East.
Armed resistance to Portuguese, Dutch and French colonisers by
indian tribes, as well as the setting up of communities by runaway
slaves (*quilombos*) are only two of the earliest manifestations of
resistance to oppressors. The messianic movements of Canudos in
Bahia (1893–97) and Contestado (1912–16) in Paraná and Santa
Catarina, both violently crushed by the Brazilian army, are other
early examples of popular protest (Vilaça and Albuquerque, 1965;
Queiroz, 1965). Throughout the period of the New Republic under
Getulio Vargas Brazil saw numerous peasant struggles in which
small farmers armed themselves against richer and more powerful
interests seeking to displace them from the land (MST, 1986). For
example, from 1945–48 peasant farmers along the newly constructed
Rio–Bahia highway at Teófilo Otoni in Minas Gerais fought land-

grabbers seeking to evict them as property values rose, a foretaste of what would happen in Amazonia on a much wider scale. In Porecatú, Paraná, some 1,500 peasant farmers battled for five years against *grileiros* along the River Paranapanema, before the area in question was finally expropriated and redistributed in 1951. In 1957 similar resistance was mounted by 4,000 armed peasants in south-west Paraná against land-grabbers and police, until in 1964 President Goulart created the Executive Group for the Lands of South-West Parana (GETSOP) to title the occupants. Within Amazonia itself, the Trombas revolt of 1952–58 arose along the *Transbrasiliana* highway, forerunner of the Belém–Brasília, between migrant farmers from Maranhão and Piauí on the one hand, and land-grabbers on the other. In 1954 the peasantry took to arms and, three years later, the army was sent in to confront them. Apparently the state governor eventually agreed to recognise the peasants' claim in exchange for PCB (Communist Party of Brazil) support of his son's candidacy to political office.

During the 1960s peasant militancy grew with the spread to thirteen states of the *Ligas Camponesas*, the only peasant organisation which wanted to remain independent of the Ministry of Labour and which operated outside the State-directed Confederation of Rural Workers. The peasant leagues were the first to really challenge the power of large rural landowners. Several land occupations which took place in Pernambuco were subsequently legalised by state governor Cid Sampaio. Estate occupations were organised by the movement of landless peasants in Rio Grande do Sul (MASTER), set up by the PCB, but these petered out by 1962 when Brizola left the state governorship. It has been estimated that, by the early 1960s, up to 500,000 peasants had been organised into rural unions or leagues, although their effectiveness was limited then, as now, by internal ideological conflicts, and lack of overall co-ordination amongst locally-organised groups as well as by the relative absence of linkages with political parties at national level.

Military intervention in 1964 brough swift represson of both urban and rural unions, as well as attempts to diffuse conflict in the countryside through programmes of colonisation and irrigation. Yet agrarian development policies in the North-East, Centre-South and in Amazonia have, as we have seen, exacerbated rural tensions and failed to address the basic questions of polarised access to land and other resources. The late 1970s and 1980s have witnessed a marked increase in open peasant resistance and protest. In 1979, for example, 20,000 sugar-cane workers went on strike for higher wages in Pernambuco, the first such action since 1964, while in September 1987 a similar strike of 250,000 members of fifty-four unions in Pernambuco paralysed 90% of sugar estates in the region and won substantial wage increases (Sigaud, 1980; FETAPE/CONTAG, 1987). In August 1978 some 12,000 banana workers in São Paulo stopped work in protest at not having been paid for sixteen months, while in March 1980 over 700,000 small producers of soybean demonstrated in Rio Grande do Sul in favour of higher farmgate prices. Other protest movements have involved grape and tobacco producers in the South, as well as vigorous campaigns in several parts of the country against the treatment meted out to victims of hydroelectric schemes summarily displaced from their lands without adequate compensation; examples include Itaipú on the Brazil/Paraguay border, as well as Sobradinho and Itaparica in the São Francisco valley (LAB, 1982; Pandolfi, 1985).

The largest and best articulated rural workers' action has undoubtedly been the Movement of the Landless (MST), supported by the Catholic Church and the PT (Workers' Party). Its major guiding principle, set out in 1984, is that 'Land should belong to those that work it to support peasant farmers and their families' (MST, 1986). Although it has twelve member states and its first national congress in 1985 drew together 1,500 representatives from all over Brazil, the movement is undoubtedly strongest in the Centre-South. By 1986 the MST had organised seventy-seven occupations in the states of Rio Grande do Sul (twelve), Santa Catarina (eight), Paraná (fourteen), Mato Grosso do Sul (nine), São Paulo (seventeen), Espírito Santo (twelve) and Rio de Janeiro (five), involving a total of 9,000 families in dispute over 151,000 hectares (MST, 1986). Later figures (INESC, 1988) put the total number of peasant families in MST-oganised camps at 13,000. The largest single occupation, at the Campamento Uní in Rio Grande do Sul, had mobilised some 9,000 landless peasants. More recently, in November 1987, the MST organised a simultaneous occupation of three estates in Rio Grande do Sul owned by prominent PDT politicians (*Isto É*, 2.12.87). Fearful of losing its independence, the organisation keeps at arm's length from the official union hierarchy (CONTAG) and political parties. Its national co-ordinating body, which meets twice annually has set out careful guidelines for organising occupations, tackling legal problems, organising community meetings and mobilising support.

Yet while it is true that there has undoubtedly been a substantial increase in organised peasant protest in many parts of Brazil, the same cannot be said of eastern Amazonia, where small farmer resistance to land-grabbers has remained, on the whole, fragmented and disorganised, if on the increase. However, before considering these more spontaneous, although sometimes very effective, forms of social protest, the role of institutionally-directed action within the Carajás Programme area will be examined. These include the rural unions (STRs), the Catholic Church, Brazilian and foreign non-government organisations, and political parties. In practice these bodies often work together so that, for example, STRs frequently collaborate closely on land rights issues with Catholic Church groups, such as the CPT and CIMI. There is also a large overlap between union membership and that of community religious groups (CEBs), since the radical clergy has done much towards strengthening associate participation and the representation of STRs in dealing with the major concerns of land and security. Co-operation also extends to Brazilian and international NGOs, which are in close contact with the Church and the union movement, and play an important role at national, regional and local levels.

In many developing countries small farmers and rural workers form a strong electoral base for political parties. A striking feature of Brazilian politics, however, is the almost total exclusion of the peasantry, perhaps one-third of the population, from effective representation via the party system. Traditionally, during periods of electoral democracy, the rural vote in Brazil has been carefully manipulated by landowning political bosses through a combination of coercion, patron-clientage and vote-rigging. The Left in Brazil, particularly in the North and North-East, has not traditionally looked towards the countryside for support. The Brazilian communist Party (PCB), founded in 1922, is Stalinist and based its revolutionary ideals on appeals to the nascent urban working class in the large cities of the South such as São Paulo, competing initially with the anarchist movement for control of the trades unions. Its rival, the pro-Chinese splinter Communist Party of Brazil (PC do B), was set up in 1962, and originally numbered only a few hundred members. It then called for revolutionary peasant action but 'succeeded in gaining no significant adherents among the labor movement or the student organisations, the centers of radical leftist organisation' (Skidmore, 1967, p. 279); and, least of all, it should be added, among the peasantry itself. As if in belated recognition of its shortcomings, the Moscow-line PCB stated in 1984 at its national congress that, 'we have in the past under-estimated the very important rural front...one of the chief obstacles to the revolution' (cited by Hebette, 1983, p. 17).

Within eastern Amazonia political representation of the peasantry has been relatively small-scale and fragmented, through the Maoist PC do B, the Workers' Party (PT) and the Revolutionary Movement of 8 October (MR8). The MR8 was founded in 1968, named after the date on which Che Guevara was killed, and is composed mainly of dissident PCB members. It based its tactics on the formation of the rural cell (*foco*), rather than mass party organisation, as a catalyst of popular revolution (Flynn, 1978). The PC do B was behind the ill-fated Araguaia guerrilla movement (already referred to in Chapter 1), initiated in April 1972 and finally crushed by the army in January 1975, whose sixty-nine members managed to mobilise some 20,000 troops against them. Under Brazil's current post-military democracy, these parties today have only a sporadic and tenuous representation in rural Amazonia.

They have been judged as politically significant in the sense that, for the first time, they provide some peasant leaders with a voice at national level, On the other hand, they have also been severely criticised for attempting to manipulate the peasantry opportunistically without understanding its problems, leading to open discord among rival groups competing for hegemony in the countryside and to overall political fragmentation within the region (Hebette, 1983; Souza Martins, 1988). This political disunity is reflected in the internal divisions within the rural labour movement itself, discussed below. A rural population traditionally mistrustful of the State and of politicians in general, at whose hands peasants have suffered rather than benefited, has become generally disillusioned with this political in-fighting. In such circumstances the peasantry has either tended to rely far more on the Church and union movement as twin pillars of support in the escalating battle for survival, and/or to carry out its own spontaneous and individualised opposition.

The Catholic Church is still, arguably, the most important single institutionally organised source of opposition to land-grabbing in eastern Amazonia and, indeed, over much of Brazil. Religious community groups (CEBs) have existed since 1960 but expanded rapidly after the 1964 coup when, for many years, the Church presented the only semblance of structured opposition to the military dictatorship, often exercised under a thin façade of evangelism. There are now some 80,000 such 'base communities', guided by lay or clerical agents, with a membership of around two million (LAB, 1982). Based on a radical Christian interpretation of the Church's role adopted after the second conference of Latin American bishops (Vatican II), held in 1968 in Medellín, Colombia, it made a commitment to serving the immediate needs of poor and oppressed groups. The ideas expounded in the encyclical *Populorium Progressio* and the conclusions of the Medellín conference became a guiding light for the socially aware Latin American Catholic Church.

In Brazil opposition to the military regime and to landowning elites was at first isolated and voiced only by leading dissidents such as Dom Helder Câmara, archbishop of Olinda and Recife, in the North-East. However, these ideas soon gained wider support, especially in the Amazon region, which was entering a period of aggressive development and growing rural violence from 1966 onwards. Dom Pedro Casaldáliga, bishop of São Félix do Araguaia in northern Mato Grosso, was at the forefront of this struggle. 'Liberation theology' is now espoused by a large section of the Brazilian Catholic Church, promulgated through parish-level discussion and action groups and expounded by such thinkers as Leonardo Boff (1984). Freirian techniques of popular education (Freire, 1970) and 'consciousness raising' have also been widely used by lay and church pastoral workers. More often than not, however, the external threat posed by land-grabbers and their violent methods have provided the major stimulus which has galvanised hitherto passive communities into action.

The Church in Amazonia has often been condemned, with some justification, for exercising political tutelage over indian and peasant groups, what one observer has called 'progressive *coronelismo*' (Souza Martins, 1988). Yet in many areas of the country, including the Carajás Programme, the radical Church and CEBs have been of crucial importance not just in generating a greater 'awareness' among groups of threatened farmers but, perhaps more importantly, in creating the self-confidence necessary as a basis for collective action in pursuit of social justice. Other important functions have been those of providing strategic support to farmers' groups in the form of legal aid, and in bringing to the public notice the innumerable abuses committed against the peasantry by land-grabbers, hired gunmen and the police. In Amazonia, as elsewhere, commissions set up by the national bishops' conference (CNBB) to fight for peasant and indian rights, such as the CPT and CIMI, have played a central role in publicising the struggle for land and the resulting rural violence. The CPT was established in 1975 following a crisis meeting of Amazonian bishops in Goiás which recommended the creation of 'land commissions' in each diocese to undertake educational campaigns and provide legal advice to victims of the worsening land situation in Brazil, especially in Amazonia (CNBB, 1976).

Were it not for information supplied by the extensive CPT and CEB network, often in collaboration with the more committed rural unions, many of the dozens of major incidents and hundreds of violent deaths in Amazonia would never, given the region's relative isolation, have become public knowledge. In Acre, for example, the Church publicised land conflicts and campaigned for *posseiros'* and rubber tappers' legal rights in their struggle against the ranching front as it penetrated the state during the mid-1970s (Bakx, 1987). The Catholic Church has sent innumerable protest notes to the government and published regular bulletins and reports on land conflict situations, including all of the major incidents which have occurred in the Carajás area highlighted in this volume. While the political importance of the CEBs and the Church as a pro-peasant lobby should not be exaggerated, given its own internal frictions between traditionalists and radicals, neither should its importance in mobilising people's thoughts and actions at local and regional levels in conflict-ridden eastern Amazonia be underestimated. The Church has also, through its community education and action programmes, helped to strengthen the rural union movement in the Carajás region, so that today syndicates in Amazonia are far more representative and committed to peasant interests than at any other time.

In Amazonia rural trades unions have, until the 1980s, had a marginal impact upon forms of peasant protest, but their influence is undoubtedly becoming more significant. Brazil's labour code (CLT), introduced in 1937, is closely modelled on Mussolini's *Carta del Lavoro* and most trades unions have traditionally been under the direct control of the Ministry of Labour. Brazilian unions, both urban and rural, are in the main not the product of a class struggle but have been created from above by central government as corporatist institutions essentially under State auspices. During the democratic phase of Brazilian politics from 1945–64, unions in

Brazil were controlled by five federations, the largest and most powerful of which was the National Confederation of Industrial Workers (CNTI), founded in 1946 (Flynn, 1978).

There were, during the 1950s and early 1960s, various attempts to create alternative trades unions organisations to those officially sanctioned by government. Any such pretensions were firmly quashed after the events of 1964 when the CLT laws were applied with renewed vigour. Since the late 1970s two trade union congresses have been formed which are recognised *de facto* by government. The CUT represents democratic or opposition unions and is linked to the PT and the progressive Church. The other major opposition group, originally called CONCLAT, was renamed in 1986 as the CGT and is linked to the PMDB (Party of the Brazilian Democratic Movement) and the PC do B. The CONCLAT/CGT has always been accused by the CUT of being unrepresentative and amenable to State and management manipulation (*'pelego'*). This CUT–CGT ideological split divides the union opposition structure in Brazil at present, with both sides fighting for hegemony.

The National Confederation of Agricultural Workers (CONTAG) was founded during the Goulart government in 1963, and currently has 2,600 STRs with eight million members, organised into twenty-two federations. According to Grzybowski (1987) it fits the corporatist mould described above and, although CONTAG grew in size considerably after 1964, the relationship of its regional federations with the rural population is consideral paternalistic, with most unions adopting a purely welfare role. CONTAG's national leadership is allegedly more radical than its regional federations but has its hands tied by its political links with and financial dependence upon government. Its political links with the PMDB and PCB may have undermined its radical stance on major issues and, accordingly, CONTAG adopted a policy of full support for the government's agrarian reform plan (PNRA), which is opposed by many unionists as irrelevant for solving Brazil's problems of rural inequality and landlessness. A further source of tension is the CGT-CUT split which cuts through the whole rural union movement and the effects of which can be felt at the local level.

The Carajás Programme area, scene of Brazil's most violent rural conflicts during the 1980s, is covered by the state-wide rural union federations of Pará and Maranhão. In the 1960s and 1970s rural unions in Pará were organised by the establishment Church, supported by the State and by the literacy movement, MEB, along the corporatist lines established by Vargas. By the late 1970s rural unions in Pará had come under considerable pressure from peasant groups engaged in bitter land struggles, aided by the radical Catholic Church, embryonic political parties and human rights bodies such as the SPDDH, Pará's human rights organisation. This articulation started in the areas of Santarém and southern Pará but has now become far more widespread due in large part, it is argued, to the vital support given the rural union movement by these other institutions (Hebette, 1987).

The number of rural union branch offices has spread significantly, along with the commitment of a small but growing minority of STRs towards defending the interests and land rights of the mass peasant membership. In Pará, for example, following political liberalisation since 1980, the union movement has steadily gained strength, with the formation of nine municipal branches in key Carajás areas, where some of the most violent clashes have occurred; these include Marabá, Xinguara, Sao João do Araguaia, Nova Jacundá and São Félix do Xingú (CPT–Marabá, 1987). Some of these are CGT-affiliated while others are CUT-dominated, underlining the continuing problem of ideological schisms and conflicts within the union movement. In February 1986 committee elections for the Pará federation (FETAGRI) were narrowly won by the CUT faction, giving rise to optimism about the commitment of rural unions in that state to the interests of small producers. In its most recent phase, the union movement is concerned not just with the problem of access to land, but also with broader questions of agrarian policy and sustainable development (Hebette, 1987). The situation in Maranhão is rather more conservative (FASE, 1987) and, of 130 STRs in the state, just a handful is considered 'authentic' or *combativo*; only one of these, the union in Imperatriz which has CUT and PT affiliations, lies in the Carajás area.

Throughout eastern Amazonia the radical clergy and lay members of the Catholic Church have, via the community groups or CEBs, sucessfully helped the 'authentic', CUT-affiliated wing of the rural union movement to recapture the leadership of crucial STRs in areas of violent conflict. Although, since 1987, there have been indications of a certain withdrawal by the Church from such controversial areas as land conflicts, it still exercises a strong formative influence on the STR movement, especially where other forms of leadership are

9 Protest at social and environmental disruption caused by the Carajás Programme and associated government policies against small farmers is often well-organised. This demonstration in support of the ill-fated agrarian reform, at Açailândia in August 1987, illustrates the strength of feeling among peasant farmers from the Carajás area. The banners declare 'Agrarian reform; who needs it, does it', 'Rural workers of Açailândia against the pig-iron smelters, they bring unemployment to the region', and 'Against land-grabbing and the *latifúndio*'.

absent. Vatican pressure on the Brazilian Church to play a less active role in 'political' issues, accounts to some extent for the more cautious attitudes of many church members evident in the regions, especially at archdiocesan CPT level. In Maranhão, for example, there has allegedly been a renewed concentration on evangelising and pastoral work at the expense of involvement in land conflicts. Conservative dissidents have established branches of the São Paulo-based Rural Evangelisation Movement (MER) in four municipalities. However, it is debatable how far radical church workers at community level will allow themselves to be dictated to by the Catholic hierarchy and most will probably discreetly carry on with their work. Another reason for any diminution of direct Church intervention in rural areas is likely to be the strengthening of the STR movement itself.

If there has often been close collaboration between the Church and rural unions locally, at regional and national levels these religious and civil bodies have also come into profound conflict with each other. The Church/CPT raises doubts about CONTAG's legitimacy with its mass membership, criticising its moderate and pro-government position on land issues. On the other hand, CONTAG accuses the Church of being ignorant of rural questions and of having its own hidden political agenda. Grzybowski (1987) accuses the Church of having a distorted and narrow vision of social issues in the country-side, treating the land issue as 'sacred', to the exclusion of other concerns such as the plight of rural wage-labourers. He concludes (p. 70) that, 'Despite the political weight of the CNBB and its bishops, despite the heroic efforts of its priests, nuns and pastoral workers, the Church is a partial and filtered representation of a diversity of movements and rural workers' demands'. Be that as it may, however, there can be no doubt that in the Carajás region of Amazonia, while perhaps not the decisive factor, Church support for the union movement has been of central importance in articulating a growing peasant resistance to land-grabbing.

An area in which trades union activity may well flourish within the Carajás Programme is among charcoal producers. As Chapters 2 and 4 of this book have shown, it is estimated that within the next few years some 200,000 small, independent suppliers of charcoal will emerge, producing a large proportion of the annual one million tonnes required to fuel the first dozen pig-iron smelters to come on stream along the railway corridor. Apart from its potentially devastating environmental consequences, as cheap fuel is extracted from the native TMF with little or no reforestation taking place, a further effect could be to encourage the formation of associations of small charcoal producers (Hebette *et al*, n.d.). Based on pre-existing community traditions of self help, such as *mutirão, caixas agrícolas* or mini co-operatives, and informal rules prohibiting the sale of land to outsiders, these associations could help to eliminate exploitative intermediary *empreiteiros* and gain some bargaining power to maintain high prices for charcoal.

Smallholders in the Carajás area are known to be concerned about the dangers to environmental equilibrium posed by the penetration of lumber companies and this could serve as a basis for group resistance. However, small producers in Minas Gerais have not been able to organise themselves in such a fashion, while the one attempt which occurred in Paragominas, Pará, was soon crushed by sawmill owners who cut off supplies of raw material offcuts. Even if independent producers did successfully organise themselves, possibly with the help of the STR movement, there is no tradition in Pará of landless wage-workers' union activity due to the isolation of rural enterprises such as lumbering and cattle ranches, as well as a long history of brutal repression and connivance of the judiciary with police and landowners in Amazonia against rural labourers.

Non-government organisations have played a central role in publicising developments in the Carajás region, both in Brazil as well as internationally. Unencumbered by the political constraints which severely limit the ability of more enlightened government and company officials to openly voice their reservations, often deeply felt, over the social and environmental impact of the PGC, members of national and foreign NGOs have been close allies of rural unions and the Church in their protest campaigns. Brazilian NGOs have often formed the crucial link between between local communities in conflict with land-grabbers and supporting organisations such as the rural syndicates and the CPT. International NGOs are playing an increasingly important role in highlighting the situation of peasants, indians and their environment on a world-wide basis, as well as supplying vital financial, logistical and moral support.

Committed Brazilian NGOs have been active in poor rural and urban communities since the early days of military rule, practising a form of community education and mobilisation (*educação popular*) based heavily on Freirian methods. Despite, or perhaps to some extent because of, the rapid growth of rural violence in Amazonia, NGOs have been relatively slow to expand their activities in the region. However, Brazil's major organisation of this kind, FASE, with some twenty teams nation-wide, has been influential. FASE has a regional office in Belém and four local offices in the heart of the Carajás Programme, in São Luís, Marabá, Imperatriz and Abaetetuba. The organisation has had many years' experience in eastern Amazonia and has developed close links with local communities under threat, liaising closely with the Church and CPT. On the doorstep of the Carajás iron-ore complex, CEPASP (Centre for Education, Research and Union Advice) performs a similar role in the Marabá area. In addition to these two bodies, which undertake grass roots as well as more general lobbying work, the National Movement for the Defence of Human Rights (MNDDH) has a branch in Belém active in campaigning against rural violence. In April 1986, for example, it organised a mock 'Land Trial' (*Tribunal da Terra*) in Belém which highlighted the gravity of the problem in southern Pará, in view of, 'the slowness, inefficiency and dependence of the judiciary' (MMDDH, 1986).

While national NGOs have been playing an increasingly important role, however, their impact in relation to the Carajás Programme has, arguably, been limited. They face many problems; resources are limited, both human and financial, and there are other pressing concerns. Yet these obstacles are compounded by the failure of NGOs to co-ordinate amongst each other even their relatively limited activities. Unfortunately, ideological differences among Church, unions and NGOs, especially during the post-1985 era of party democracy, frequently undermine whatever cohesiveness this broad front might acquire during times of crisis. However, there now is a much greater awareness among Brazilian NGOs of this problem and efforts are being made to overcome this barrier to greater unity of action.

European and North American NGOs have been of absolutely fundamental importance in sustaining protest campaigns against the Carajás Programme, both in Brazil and overseas. Firstly, they have provided the funds to enable organisations such as FASE and CEPASP to continue their activities. Secondly, at the level of campaigning, they have also been quite effective in creating a global awareness of the scheme's inherent social and ecological dangers, while applying pressure on key funding institutions, such as the EEC and the World Bank, in an attempt to modify their policies. It is in these two areas, then, that the unique contribution of foreign NGOs to the development effort can be seen. Without this support, those of local funding and international lobbying, the scale of institutionalised protest against the impact of Carajás is likely to have been much smaller than has proved to be the case so far.

The EEC Development Fund is the largest single investor, national or foreign, in the Carajás Programme. Its US$600 million loan for the iron-ore complex and associated infrastructure was approved in May 1982 and the agreement signed in September of that year. This loan, the first by the Fund to a non-EEC country, was motivated by the Community's desire to secure guaranteed supplies of iron-ore; accordingly, contracts were signed with the CVRD for deliveries of over thirteen million tonnes a year over fifteen years, meeting 50% of European needs, which in the words of the then Vice President of the Commission, would be under 'favourable pricing conditions which will contribute to preserving the competitiveness of the European steel industry' (quoted by Treece, 1987, p. 17). Announcement of the EEC loan also paved the way for a further US$150 million from private German banks. Given the EEC's total failure to undertake any prior social or environmental impact assessment of the Carajás Programme, NGOs immediately voiced protests against the potentially disastrous consequences for the rainforest and its inhabitants.

In April 1982 the General Assembly of European NGOs passed a motion calling upon the EEC to impose conditions for protecting the Amazonian environment and indigenous groups to be affected. At a subsequent meeting in February 1983 between the EEC, World Bank, CVRD, and the French *Centre de Recherche et d'Information pour le Développement* (CRID), the recently signed CVRD/FUNAI Accord for protecting indian rights was acknowledged, but CRID drew attention to the lack of any provisions for the much larger mass of small farmers or for environmental protection. Consequently, at the next General Assembly of European NGOs, in April 1983, a second motion was passed calling for the loan to be suspended until adequate provisions in this respect could be made. Simultaneously, questions were tabled at the European Parliament challenging the Commission to justify its actions. Marijke Van Hemeldonck, of the Netherlands, for example, drew attention to the situation, '. . . tens of thousands of small farmers are violently driven away, the rights of indians are not respected, the ecological balance of the Amazon forest is broken, national and international speculators in land are in control over the complete area'. She continued with the perhaps rhetorical, if justified, enquiry, 'Does the Commission know about this dramatic situation?' (Hemeldonck, 1983).

Dissatisfaction with inadequate proposals by the CVRD for dealing with these controversial issues in its document 'Carajás Iron Ore Project–CVRD Cares' (CVRD, 1984b), led a third meeting of the European NGOs, in April 1984, to pass yet another motion drawing attention to the environmental destruction, illegal eviction of peasant farmers and abuses of indian rights currently occurring in the project area, demanding a response and appropriate action from the Brazilian government and the European Commission (NGO, 1984).

However, the EEC stubbornly refused to acknowledge the problems and, flying in the face of all the accumulated evidence to the contrary, the Commission flatly declared in June that, '. . . the project to exploit the Carajás iron-ore deposits is being carried out in a manner which may be considered satisfactory' (quoted by Treece, 1987, p. 24); accordingly, a second instalment of the loan was disbursed.

Later that year two Euro-MPs, Anthony Simpson of the UK and Willy Kuijpers of Belgium, made a five-day visit, sponsored by the Liaison Committee of NGOs, to the 'parrot's beak' area together with six Brazilian federal deputies, seven bishops and journalists, to take a first-hand look at the Carajás Programme. They heard for themselves horrific tales of evictions, house-burnings, physical violence and all manner of aggression committed by the police in conjunction with local landowners. On the eve of the visit a local parish priest, Father Jósimo Tavares (subsequently murdered by landowners' hired gunmen, in May 1986) and a lay worker, Lourdes Goi, who had both helped organise the trip, were arrested on trumped-up charges (*The Guardian*, 12.12.84). Simpson was appalled and wrote that, 'From what I have seen and heard, there is clearly evidence of eviction and violence against the peasants on a wide scale' (Simpson, 1984, p. 4). Upon their return, the two MEPs tabled a motion at the European Parliament calling upon the Council of Ministers and the Commission to express its grave concern to the Brazilian government, which was itself invited to take corrective action (Treece, 1987). The intention was also announced of setting up an office in Brasília for liaison between the European Parliament and the Brazilian Congress over the application of EEC funds in Carajás (*Folha de São Paulo*, 6.12.84).

The lack of corrective action has spurred NGOs towards further efforts aimed at pressurising the PGC's major funders, as well as the Brazilian government and the CVRD. In August the US-based Environmental Defence Fund (EDF) and twenty-nine NGOs from around the world publicly denounced the World Bank for its 'involvement in an ecologically disastrous plan to convert 58,000 square miles of pristine Brazilian Amazon tropical forest – an area larger than the state of Wisconsin – into charcoal for pig-iron smelters' (EDF, 1987). In an open letter to the President of the Bank, Barber Conable, the EDF accused the CVRD of failing to honour clauses in the Loan Agreement regarding environmental protection, and made detailed criticisms of indian reserve violations and violence against small farmers.

Two months after these public criticisms of the World Bank in the US, European NGOs renewed pressure on the EEC. In September 1987, as already stated in Chapter 4 two British organisations, Survival International and Friends of the Earth, published their detailed study of the PGC's impact on Amazonian indians and environment, focusing on the EEC's key role, and its responsibilities, as the major outside investor. The report spelled out the harmful impact of the various components of the scheme and claimed that the EEC, 'has effectively washed its hands and renounced its duty to the environment of the region and to the people whose lives are being disrupted as a result of its support for the scheme' (Treece, 1987, p. 10). The document made a call for undisbursed World Bank and EEC funds for Carajás to be reallocated to an emergency and long-term development programme which would avoid previous pitfalls. A front page story in *The Independent* newspaper (24.9.87) highlighted the report, warning of the dangers of non-sustainable development in Brazil. This was immediately followed up on 1 October by a letter to Jacques Delors, President of the EEC, drawing attention to the Commission's responsibility to see that all possible steps are taken to bring about environmentally sound and socially just development within the Carajás Programme (Survival International, 1987a).

Sustained NGO pressure has produced some results. The EEC was faced with little choice but to commission a study, in January 1988, of the broader impact of the Carajás Programme on the region and its population. In March of the same year the World Bank formally registered its concern about the effects of the PGC (*Latinamerica Press*, 14.4.88). However, as far as can be ascertained, NGO pressure has not so far led to significant modifications in the design or execution of the Carajás Programme. The strong American environmental movement was successful, in March 1985, in halting disbursement of US$256 million of a US$434 million World Bank loan for the (US$1·6 billion) POLONOROESTE scheme in Rondônia pending the inclusion of safeguards over indian land rights. The programme has been labelled by its critics as an 'ecological, human and economic disaster of tremendous proportions' (Rich, 1985, p. 695) because of the irrevesible damage done to the region by indiscriminate deforestation and the violent rural conflict associated with land-grabbing. Such unprecedented action on the Bank's part, representing the first time its loans had ever been frozen for environmental reasons, was only made possible due to a unique coalition of very different interests in applying pressure on the organisation. Environmentalists and anthropologists had their humanitarian and developmentalist reasons for questioning the Bank's involvement, while right-wing politicians in the American Congress were anxious to curb its spending in the Third World as a matter of principle. Even so, the delay was purely temporary and it is a moot point whether it has actually improved implementation of the programme.

Yet the persistence and potential impact of NGOs' concerted action against multilateral funding bodies should not be lightly dismissed. This is perhaps illustrated by the experience of the Inter-American Development Bank (IDB), whose policy in Amazonia has come under increasing scrutiny. Dissatisfaction with the inadequacy of safeguards in its loan project for the paving of the BR 364 highway in north-west Brazil prompted retaliatory action by NGOs. A successful campaign was mounted for the suspension of the loan, pending inclusion by the Brazilian government of measures to protect the land rights of indian groups in Acre. At the same time, however, in the face of current legislation which is attempting to legitimise access by commercial interests to indigenous territory for mining purposes (such as the designation of indian 'colonies', for example) caution has to be exercised in the drawing of broader conclusions about the power of outside organisation to influence official policy-making through such initiatives.

It seems that, in the case of Carajás, there is probably less leverage to be had against the major foreign funding institutions. This is partly due to the fact that virtually all of the original loans had (by 1988) been disbursed. Another consideration, however, is that major creditors are not likely to jeopardise relationships with the Brazilian government by raising such problems at this stage. The World Bank has, under duress, exerted some pressure in this direction, but the EEC in particular is reluctant to be seen as interfering in Brazil's 'internal affairs', particularly when its steel industry will become so heavily dependent upon that country's iron-ore. For the Brazilian government to make major concessions to such outside pressure groups would, of course, be at odds with the central role of Carajás industrialisation in its regional development strategy. Similarly, neither the CVRD nor the pig-iron smelters will readily yield to any attempts by NGOs, national or foreign, to slow down their activities in the region. Commercial profits and political gain appear to be the major priorities for the PGC, regardless of wider or longer-term repercussions, a recurring theme in Amazonia's development.

Despite these considerations, however, there can be little doubt that NGOs' potential in terms of more effective lobbying has not been fully realised. Unfortunately, international NGOs suffer from the same malaise as their Brazilian counterparts in being unable to liaise effectively enough to execute a timely and united strategy. By the time such co-ordination is achieved the loans have already been disbursed and there is little possibility of obliging aid bodies to rethink their policies or build in more effective safeguards at the key project appraisal and design stages. All too often, such corrective measures that are eventually authorised take the form of half-hearted monitoring or ex-post evaluation, which is little better than rubber-stamping. By this stage all the major parameters have been set and there is very little that can be done to bring about major changes, should they be deemed necessary. Yet both North American and, in particular, European NGOs have learnt from experience and, as the examples cited above show, they have improved their capacity for more effective lobbying. This is being achieved at several levels: more sophisticated educational and fund-raising campaigns directed at the donating public, raising overall awareness of the issues, an improved organisational capacity for information-gathering and net-working amongst interested parties, and a higher degree of political skill when dealing with official aid bureaucracies. Some indication of this enhanced capacity was given in September 1988, when Brazilian and international NGOs mounted a strong lobby concerning official Amazon development policies and their negative socio-ecological impacts, at the annual meeting of the IMF/World Bank in Berlin.

Spontaneous forms of popular resistance in Carajás

It is customary to equate strong opposition by the 'victims' of hostile development policies with well-organised, often highly institution-alised structures such as trades unions, political parties or, in Brazil's case, the radical Catholic Church. It is frequently assumed that, in the absence of such leadership, effective protest against powerful land-grabbers and socially negative large-scale public projects is doomed to failure. Politicians, church and union leaders, each cultivating their own spheres of influence, are prone to dismissing more spontaneous and smaller-scale protests as insignificant and irrelevant, on the grounds that the politically 'unarticulated' peasantry can only have a significant impact when guided by a firm institutional hand. Yet the experience of Amazonian settlement and, more recently, the Greater Carajás Programme, serves to dispel this myth. While the positive attributes of peasant protest articulated through unions, under the watchful eye of parties, the Church and NGOs cannot be denied, in eastern Amazonia and, indeed, in other parts of Amazonia, other form of popular dissent have arguably been far more important as vehicles through which disaffected small farmers have sought to defend their interests.

During the initial stages of frontier colonisation in the 1960s and early 1970s, there was relatively little opposition to land-grabbing. This was partly because the competition over access was less intense than nowadays, the number of settlers involved far smaller and the frontier thus far more open. Such apparent passivity can also be attributed, however, to the lack of a strong tradition of peasant resistance, in part a product of the partriarchal and paternalistic agrarian systems which many migrants had left behind, especially in the North-East. Immediate repression by the military regimes during this period of anything resembling rural protest movements would also have discouraged peasant opposition to corporate and commercial interests, particularly in view of the sensitivity of such issues following the Araguaia guerrilla war of the early 1970s, which took place in what today is the heart of the Carajás Programme.

However, since the late 1970s this picture has changed considerably. There has been a clear breakdown in traditional forms of patron-clientage in the countryside, which accompanied the increasingly violent struggle over land during the process of migration and resettlement. Long-standing ties involving economic, social and even political obligations of the sort normally associated with plantation agriculture and ranching in the rest of the country hold little attraction for either side in the tense rural areas of Amazonia. Furthermore, the increasingly interventionist role of the State has eroded the power base of local landed oligarchies (as has occurred in the 'Brazil-nut polygon' of southern Pará), hastening the demise of these older patron-client relationships.

Even before the military handed over the reins of power to a civilian administration in 1985 there had, as shown in Chapter 3, been a major escalation of land conflicts all over Brazil, particularly in eastern Amazonia. This indicates not simply a greater use of violent tactics by large landowners on a supposedly apathetic but more numerous peasantry. On the contrary, it is far more suggestive of a conscious decision by threatened groups of small farmers and indians to actively resist encroachment upon their territory. Fed up with being constantly evicted by *grileiros* and their hired gunmen, unhappy with the government's failure to intervene on their behalf, various forms of non-institutionalised peasant protest and resistance have emerged.

Informal, spontaneous peasant resistance to land-grabbing in Amazonia has a longer history than is generally imagined. A case in point is the setting up of a 'peasant republic' in Trombas, Goiás during the early 1960s, supported by the Maoist PC do B, in which *posseiros* organised collectively to resist pressures from the first major wave of large-scale land speculators and *grileiros* (Souza Martins, 1989). In Acre, from 1974–76, peasant farmers and rubber tapper groups organised foci of resistance (*empates*) to prevent ranchers and their hired hands from cutting down rubber trees and thus destroying their major source of income. From 1970–78, for example, it is estimated that some 10,000 rubber tappers and their families were violently evicted from their lands. This growing spirit of co-operation and collective resistance led, in 1985, to the First National Congress of Rubber Tappers in Brasília and the subsequent formation of the National Rubber Tappers' Council (CNS). Co-operatives have been organised with the help of the CPI and *Projeto Seringueiro*, while some rubber tappers' land claims have already been recognised: in February 1988, the Acre state government set up the first 'extrac-tivist reserve' of 100,000 hectares for the exclusive use of traditional rubber tappers (*Latinamerica Press*, 16.6.88).

The CNS has been actively campaigning for the government to formulate a specific policy of extractivist reserves in Amazonia for rubber tappers, within the agrarian reform plans. Such a reformed policy, it was argued, would bring numerous benefits to the region; it would regenerate inadequate and stagnant domestic rubber pro-duction by offering small, independent producers protection from the deforestation and pressure on land that comes with large-scale commercial lumbering and cattle ranching, it would promote a sustainable form of land-use and support one-third of the region's population, thus reducing rural–urban migration (Bakx, 1987, 1989). In association with the Union of Indigenous Peoples (UNI), the CNS has now formed an 'Amazon Alliance of Peoples of the Forest' to campaign for this goal.

Significantly, the tappers' action has gained considerable momentum since then and they have been successful in halting deforestation of rubber plantations in the Xapurí region of Acre. Unfortunately, their very success has prompted increasingly violent reaction from large landowners in the region, backed up by the UDR, culminating in the brutal murder of Francisco ('Chico') Mendes, the movement's leader, in December 1988. Yet this assassination has probably done more than any other single repressive action against peasant farmers to focus world media attention on the social and ecological plight of Amazonia, mobilising international opinion against current destructive strategies and putting pressure on the Brazilian government and multilateral aid agencies to support more sustainable development policies.

The rubber tappers' example is very relevant for other groups of small farmers and extractivists in Amazonia, for it demonstrates the potential impact on State policy of grassroots collective action. In the words of Gradwohl and Greenberg (1988, p. 151), 'The growth of political power is an important step towards the achievement of land tenure and the preservation of the rubber tappers' way of life'. Such a degree of co-operation and concerted action has not been present in the Carajás area of eastern Amazonia, in part because of the different nature of the rural economy in the Carajás region where no single commodity, such as rubber, provides a common bond among dispersed groups of peasant producers. Being predominantly recent migrants from north-east and central Brazil they are still engaged in traditional, short-cycle, food crop production, as well as limited extractive activities such as Brazil-nut production. However, other kinds of less well articulated resistance are becoming more widespread: numerous localised, estate-level land conflicts due to small farmers resisting eviction; campaigns, demonstrations and marches on official installations; and, perhaps most significantly, peasant occupations (*invasões*) of large estates as small producers attempt to carry out their own unofficial 'land reform'.

The more aggressive stance taken by the peasantry in Amazonia in defence of its interests is reflected particularly well in the growing number of estate occupations. Whereas land-hungry small farmers would previously have allowed themselves to be dispossessed of their settled plots, or denied access to under-utilised areas, many communities of peasant cultivators will now not accept such a passive role. In addition to protecting what is theirs already, they are going further still, seeking to weaken the landowners' monopoly over land in eastern Amazonia by appropriating areas of idle property to practise subsistence agriculture. In southern Brazil the MST has become a well-articulated social movement which, with strong Church backing, had by 1988 alone organised over eighty land occupations involving some 13,000 peasant families. The movement consists primarily, although not exclusively, of landless farmers resisting proletarianisation as agriculture in the region has become mechanised for large-scale soybean and wheat production and landownership has become increasingly concentrated.

In Amazonia the picture is a contrasting one of disorganised protest. The rubber tappers' movement in Acre cited above has acquired a degree of organisational sophistication and solidarity but, generally speaking, small farmers in northern Brazil lag way behind their southern counterparts in this respect. Land invasions are far more sporadic and isolated from each other, involving dozens rather than hundreds of families. However, despite their smaller scale and comparative lack of regional organisation when compared with the MST in the South, estate occupations in Amazonia, including those within the Carajás area, are growing sufficiently in scale and number to constitute both a serious challenge to large landowners and a kind of unofficial land reform. Not only are significant areas being informally redistributed in this fashion, but occupations also force the State's hand, obliging the authorities to declare them priority areas under the agrarian reform (PNRA). Although there are no precise estimates available, evidence culled from a variety of sources would suggest that, in Maranhão and Pará, up to 6,000 peasant families (50,000 people) are involved in these *invasões de terra*.

Part of GETAT's titling work was, in effect, merely legalising this occupation process, although overall land distribution by the agency was highly inegalitarian. It has been shown conclusively that, during its seven-year existence, GETAT merely reinforced the existing polarised structure of ownership. Only a relatively small area has been appropriated by peasant farmers through occupations or handed over to the victims of rural violence; a mere 7% of the total land area titled by the organisation went to farmers with fifty hectares or less. Most lands acquired without proper title or by legally dubious means are occupied by *latifúndia*; 51% of the land titled by GETAT was in farms of over 300 hectares, with one 400,000 hectare estate taking up 12% of the total (Wagner, 1985; MIRAD/INCRA 1987). The move by small farmers to occupy large holdings, both traditional Brazil-nut and rubber estates, as well as the more recently introduced cattle ranches has, of course, inevitably helped to generate higher levels of open social conflict as the struggle for land has intensified.

One of the major foci of peasant occupations in Amazonia is the 'Brazil-nut polygon' (*polígono dos castanhais*), an area of around one million hectares, which is the world's major source of this product, located in the municipalities of Marabá, Xinguara and São João do Araguaia in southern Pará, within the notorious 'parrot's beak'. Local sources estimate that, from 1981 to 1988, of 202 Brazil-nut estates, forty-three had been partially occupied by over 2,000 families, covering one-fifth of the total area. It has been calculated that each occupation involves an average of one hundred familes or 600–700 people; the total number of squatters in this case could therefore be up to 20,000 (CPT–Marabá, 1987; Hebette, 1988). These 200,000 hectares were subsequently expropriated under the agrarian reform law. The occupations took place along the eastern and western borders, and would have been more extensive but for the fact that the southern and northern limits were blocked by the Bamerindus estate and GETAT/INCRA colonisation schemes. Specific cases of land occupations reach the public's notice when violent confrontations involving multiple deaths ensue, such as those on the Fazendas Ubá, Princesa and Pau Ferrado (listed on Table 3.1, and described in more detail below). Another case is that of the Fazenda Niteroi, whose 3,000 hectares were occupied by 200 peasant families (*Isto É*, 26.6.85).

The roots of these tensions go back to the early part of the century. Until the 1920s there was relatively free access but from 1930 onwards the local landed oligarchy, in particular the Mendonça and the Mutran families, sought to monopolise the extraction of and trade in Brazil nuts, as well as to exercise political control over the rural population (Emmi, 1985, 1986). This was achieved by the granting of concessions to smaller local landowner/merchants who effectively held small-scale extractors in debt bondage through their control over the commerce in nuts and supply of food and other necessary goods. Armed guards (*fiscais*) employed by the estate-owners kept out potential intruders. By 1954, when these estates were all in private hands, Pará state law no. 913 formalised the situation by granting long-term leases (*aforamentos*) to current occupiers, by law limited to 3,600 hectares but illicitly expanded well beyond this size, reaching as much as 20,000 hectares. Until the early 1970s the forest cover of this region was intact and the low-density population lived by a combination of hunting, prospecting and nut extraction.

Under the Plan for National Integration (PIN) during the 1970s, however, the economic and political power of the Marabá landed elite came under challenge from three sources. Firstly, lands occupied by Brazil-nut estates were acquired by corporate investors such as Bamerindus, benefiting from tax incentives to set up cattle ranches and lumbering enterprises. Secondly, State companies such as the CVRD and other firms involved in the Carajás Programme, as well as federal bodies such as GETAT and the military apparatus have, since the 1970s, eroded the oligarchs' power-base. Finally, and crucially from the point of view of this discussion, during the 1980s land-hungry peasant farmers expelled from other zones have occupied the Brazil-nut estates in ever-larger numbers, competing both with the traditional landowners as well as the newer lumbering, cattle and purely speculative enterprises set up by outsiders.

Such 'invasions' are usually condemned in the state press by estate-owners as the work of 'bandits' in the pay of unscrupulous rival merchants out to steal the nut harvest. While there may be some truth in this, the majority of such 'bandits' have been officially identified by the Land Institute (ITERPA) as legitimate *posseiros* or peasant farmers in search of land to cultivate (*Província do Pará*, 17.7.85). The net result of this gradual erosion of traditional structures and landholdings in the 'Brazil-nut polygon' has been a dramatic rise in social conflicts, known locally as the 'Brazil-nut estate war' (*a guerra dos castanhais*), as well as mounting destruction of the magnificient *castanheira* trees and a sharp decline in regional nut output.

Incursions by small producers into the *castanhais*, the only available land in the area, have accelerated for several reasons. Far more migrants were attracted to gold panning at the Serra Pelada mine and to construction of the Carajás railway than could possibly be absorbed by these enterprises. The only alternative in the region for desperate job-seekers was farming and, since most were of rural origin anyway, the pressure on land received a strong impetus.

Peasant farmers have also been supported in their struggle by the committed Marabá rural union, as well as the CPT at both local and regional levels. In addition, the then PMDB governor, Jader Barbalho, openly attacked the traditional PDS (Social Devocratic Party)-affiliated oligarchy of the region, essentially a political on-slaught but carried out on the grounds that they were extracting far more from the state in subsidies than was contributed in taxes. The state government went so far as to declare the peasant invasions of Brazil-nut estates legitimate, dismissing as nonsense the owners' allegations that they were under attack by 'bandits' (*Província do Pará*, 4.2.84). The announcement the following year by ITERPA that all areas illegally taken over by the Brazil-nut estates beyond the 3,600 hectare limit would be expropriated for the purpose of resettling small farmers also helped to reinforce the legitimacy of peasant occupations. Subsequent expropriation in 1988 under the PNRA of 200,000 hectares, one-fifth of the total, illustrates the potential of such collective peasant action.

Initially, peasant occupations in the 'Brazil-nut polygon' were totally disorganised affairs, easily broken up by estate guards, with police connivance. However, groups of small farmers soon learned to plan their actions and take necessary precautions. Participants in the movement later recounted their experiences during such occupations, when the group would literally dig itself in and organise its defence with 'military discipline' (Hebette, 1987, p. 12):

> When we were expecting an attack we all had a meeting in the village. The women looked after the children and the food for the men, and we went to the trenches. Sometimes a colleague would try to escape, pre-tending to be ill, carrying children, cattle, losing his chickens on the road...but we made them return to the trenches. Those who were too afraid had to help the women fetching water and preparing food for the others. This was our system of working.

Those who were poorly organised became easy targets. In February 1987 seventy settlers on land near the *Bamerindus* estate came under surprise attack by a group of gunmen and military police:

> We had been there for one year and five months. We had only trouble; gunmen, soldiers. The last time ninety-two soldiers came and grabbed everyone from the Monte Santo area, they arrested and beat everyone, crammed us on top of a lorry....What we ended up with was this; prison and defeat at the hands of the landowner and the police...because there was no way we could stay on that land...so we came to this other area (Hebette, 1987, p. 14).

In other parts of the region also, peasant farmers have not only fought encroachments onto their lands but have taken to occupying *latifúndia*. One such area is along the 165-kilometre Pará state highway PA 150, built to serve the construction of the Tucuruí hydroelectric scheme. According to extensive field research in 1981, of the 1,200 families of small farmers who had settled there over the years few had been evicted, despite violent persecution (Hebette, 1983). On the contrary, they had become united by the struggle and firm in their resistance. The Gleba Pitanga, a 150,000-hectare estate, was occupied despite police intervention and, eventually, the occupants were titled by GETAT. In Maranhão two similar cases were reported in July 1987: the 3,000-hectare Fazenda Jiboia near Imperatriz was occupied by 200 landless workers, the fifth *invasão* in the space of a month, while the neighbouring 5,000-hectare Fazenda Itaçira was invaded by 300 farmers. In the Santa Luzia region several other estates were reported as having been occupied (*Jornal do Brasil*, 22.7.87). These are but a few examples of the dozens of such occupations which have taken place.

The heavy concentration of rural violence at the centre of the Carajás area, around the infamous 'parrot's beak', was described in detail in Chapter 3. It is the longest-settled and most intensively disputed part of 'Legal Amazonia' where, in many instances, peasant cultivators have taken a firm stand against *grilagem* rather than allow themselves to be indiscriminately evicted. Evidence to support this argument lies in the fact that, while most fatalities in such conflicts are still peasant farmers, rural labourers and union activists, an increasing number consists of estate owners and their hired gunmen. According to an official survey by the Ministry of Agrarian Reform, in 1986, twenty-eight of the 200 *pistoleiros* recruited to drive out small farmers were themselves killed by their intended victims (MIRAD, 1987).

In a situation of virtually open warfare between *latifundistas* and peasant farmers in Amazonia, it is not surprising that 'bandit' figures have emerged from the ranks of the oppressed. In north-east Brazil during the 1930s and 40s the activities of outlaws such as José Virgulino Ferreira (*Lampião*) are thought by some observers to have been inspired by a concern for defending the interests of the poor against exploitative landowners (Facó, 1976). In eastern Amazonia a similar 'Robin Hood' legend surrounded the figure of *Quintino*, an illiterate peasant who gave up farming in 1979 to do battle with land-grabbers and their gunmen in the Gleba Cidapar area (del Qiaro, 1985b). He survived for six years, supported in his guerrilla war by the local peasant population, until being killed in a police ambush in 1985. While such tactics are of doubtful long-term relevance in the struggle over land, this phenomenon is significant in revealing the fact that hard-pressed *posseiros* will increasingly resort to whatever means are at their disposal to defend their livelihoods, which in this context means securing right of access to land.

General patterns and trends in rural violence were discussed in Chapter 3, which listed some of the major incidents surrounding the struggle over access to land in the Carajás Programme area (Table 3.1). Yet it is important to go beyond de-personalised statistics, to illustrate the human dimension of these bloody conflicts. The many personal tragedies which aggregate figures conceal constitute the most distressing, yet the most easily forgotten aspect of Amazonia's agrarian crisis. Because of the difficulties of communication in Amazonia and relatively poor coverage by the media for a number of reasons, firsthand accounts of land conflicts are difficult to obtain without painstaking field research such as that carried out by Branford and Glock (1985), Esterci (1987) and Amnesty International (1988). In order to illustrate the intensity of competition over land, four of the cases mentioned in Table 3.1 above will be described in more detail. They are among the best-known examples in southern Pará and all involve peasant occupations of large estates. Their unifying characteristic is that they are all illustrative of small farmers' determination to fight back against the seemingly inexorable monopolisation of land by *latifundiários* in eastern Amazonia.

1 Fazenda Castanhal Ubá

In June 1985 this Brazil-nut estate in São João do Araguaia, became the scene of the Carajás region's most infamous peasant massacre. In April of that year about one hundred peasant families had settled on part of its 4,000 hectares. In an attempt to clear them off, Edmundo Virgolino, a traditional Marabá landowner, hired the services of a notorious local gunman already implicated in several murders, Sebastião Pereira Dias (nicknamed 'Sebastião da Terezona') who, together with three henchmen, went on a shooting spree. To start with they shot dead two *posseiros* alongside the Trans-Amazon highway and set fire to their hut. Further on they killed two more farmers and a thirteen-year old pregnant girl, and burnt down their houses. Five days later the same gunmen murdered the community spokesman and informal leader, José Pereira da Silva ('Zé Pretinho'), as well as another farmer. The community leader's wife later told researchers (Hebette, 1987, p. 16), under great stress, what happened on that day:

> When they arrived... they entered and kept asking, 'Where is Zé Pretinho?' So I got up and thought of warning him that gunmen were here but they stepped in front of me and said he was under arrest. I heard when he asked them why. Then the gunman told him to shut up and told me to get his clothes ready. When I turned round I found the barrel of a pistol at my head and didn't know what to do. I went outside and thought of getting the children from the house. They were all inside the house... they started shooting and I couldn't get in anymore.... They shot him five times... and the boy kept saying, 'daddy, get up daddy'... I was eight months pregnant but lost the child.

Altogether, eight villagers from the community of São Domingos were killed in cold blood. The incident in this case was reported nation-wide (*Isto É*, 26.6.85) due to the coincidental presence of two reporters in the area. Previously that year, no fewer than fifty-five had already died in land conflicts in Pará, a 300% increase on 1984 (CPT Norte II, 1985). The landowner behind the massacre, Virgulino, was eventually arrested but released soon afterwards with no charges having been brought (CPT Norte II, 1987), an already familiar pattern repeating itself yet again. Due to pressure from the CPT and the efforts of a judge who personally ordered his re-arrest (for he had escaped from custody) in the face of police prevarication, the gunman, 'Sebastião da Terezona' was, in mid-1988, due to be put on trial (Amnesty International, 1988). However, pre-trial proceedings had to be extended due to irregularities in post-mortem examinations.

2 Fazenda Princesa

On 27 September 1985 five peasant farmers were kidnapped by three gunmen in the pay of the estate owner, Marlon Lopes Pidde, and taken to his headquarters, where they were physically tortured, including being tied up over ants' nests, and finally shot dead. Their bodies were then weighted down with stones and dumped in the adjacent River Itacaiunas. The irony of this example is that the victims had not in fact occupied the estate at all, but had been resettled by GETAT on land bordering the *fazenda* (CEPASP, 1986). As far as can be ascertained the perpetrators of this crime have not been brought to justice. The Pará Secretary of Justice rejected several requests for assistance to arrest the landowner, who has been formally charged with the crime, but who fled to neighbouring Goiás where he was known to be living in the state capital (Amnesty International, 1988).

3 Fazenda Castanhal Pau Ferrado

For several years a prolonged dispute involving a series of armed clashes had taken place between the landowner, Col. Eddie Castor da Nóbrega and his gunmen on the one hand, and peasant farmers on the other. In 1984 two henchmen and four farmers died; at one stage a detachment of military police was fired upon and a soldier wounded (*Província do Pará*, 28.1.84). From January to April 1985 a further five fatalities were incurred on either side (CPT Norte II, 1985; *Província do Pará*, 14.4.85). State Deputy and lawyer Paulo Fontelles, himself murdered by landowners' hired assassins in June 1987, denounced the Fazenda Pau Ferrado in the State Assembly as one of several in the region which maintained private militia to evict peasant farmers (*Jornal do Brasil*, 16.5.87).

4 Fazendas Agropecus and Forkilha

A particularly detailed investigation of this case by the Agrarian Reform Ministry (MIRAD/SEPLAN, 1987d) has enabled an accurate picture to be drawn up. Ownership of the two properties in question, located in São João do Araguaia, was claimed by Tarley de Andrade but, in November 1985, a small area was occupied by one hundred *posseiros*. The landowner invited them to a meeting to discuss the matter, where they were met by a battalion of military police who kidnapped them and dumped them one hundred kilometres away.

In March 1986 the farmers returned and settled on part of the Fazenda Agropecus which had, in the meantime, been authorised by the IBDF to cut down mahogany in a 2,000-hectare sector. The farmers denounced the landowner to the IBDF for exceeding this limit and for removing lumber from the lands upon which they had settled. The military police sent to enforce the law in fact oversaw the *fazendeiro*'s illicit lumbering operations and even helped drive the timber trucks. In March four unidentified persons (probably rural workers) were killed on the 25,000-hectare Fazenda Agropecus; later that year, in August, two gunmen met the same fate and in October two military policemen died in conflicts (MIRAD, 1987). Soon afterwards GETAT reached an agreement with the two parties that a small area of the estate would be expropriated in order to legally resettle the *posseiros*. As they had been unable to farm their plots that year following their eviction and were penniless, they requested the right to sell the timber felled on the land they had occupied. On 19 December 1986, following a heated argument between the landowner and a group of farmers, shots were exchanged, resulting in the death of the estate owner and his driver.

The father of the deceased landowner, Jairo de Andrade, local treasurer of the landowners' lobby, the UDR, sent for the Security Police (DOPS) from Belém, assisted by the direct intervention of the Minister of Justice (CPT Norte II, 1987). Following the illegal arrest (for no warrant was issued until ten days later), on 6 January 1987, of seven peasant farmers they 'disappeared' for ten days and, it was later revealed, had been subjected to various tortures under interrogation, including electric shocks. Amnesty International concluded (1988, p. 71) on the basis of extensive evidence that they, 'may have been tortured, or otherwise ill-treated, in order to obtain confessions of guilt', were held incommunicado and were denied medical assistance. When MIRAD drew up its account of events, on 20 February 1987, over a month after their imprisonment, *Habeas Corpus* requests for the seven were still being judged in the state capital, Belém. The Ministry of Agrarian Reform itself condemned the prosecution as, '...yet another political move of the UDR against rural workers' (MIRAD/SEPLAN, 1987d, pp. 8–9). By early 1987 the death toll on the Fazendas Agropecus and Forkilha totalled twelve *posseiros*, fifteen lumber workers and the landowner himself.

A noteworthy feature of these cases is the sheer determination of peasant farmers to fight for the right of access to land in the face of such odds. Lacking a strong tradition of collective action, small farmers have nonetheless managed to make significant gains in many instances despite the combined opposition of private landowners, police, judiciary and even central government. From the small settlers' point of view, their more active role in resistance to land-grabbing, estate occupations and the open social conflict which necessarily ensues has not been in vain. *De facto*, large areas of under-utilised estates have been informally 'expropriated' by virtue of their permanent occupation through direct peasant action. In spite of bureaucratic procrastination and intense political opposition, these changes are slowly being formalised under the agrarian reform, albeit on a limited scale compared with the problem of landlessness at national and even at regional levels. Most of the estates identified as the scene of bloody clashes between *posseiros* and *latifundiários* were, in May 1988, targeted for expropriation by MIRAD, including all except one or two of those lised in Table 3.1, as well as the four case studies described above. These benefited almost 3,000 small farmers and their families and involved the transfer of nearly 250,000 hectares, a substantial area by any yardstick. However, it seems unlikely that sufficient social pressure will be generated in other areas of eastern Amazonia to prompt similar State intervention on peasants' behalf.

Even powerful State enterprises are not immune from popular demands and the CVRD itself has come under strong pressure, both from land-hungry peasant cultivators as well as gold prospectors (*garimpeiros*), to provide access to its 411,000-hectare mining enclave near Marabá, which is fast becoming a privileged island of conservation within a sea of environmental destruction. Apart from essential deforestation necessitated by mining operations and road-building, the rainforest is preserved intact and strictly no outsiders are allowed to settle, not just for ecological but also for general security reasons. This point is vividly brought home when entering the project by road. All vehicles must pass through a single checkpoint resembling a frontier post where prior authorisation issued by the CVRD in Rio, Belém or São Luís is inspected. Day workers at the poject returning home to the adjacent twin town of Parauapebas–Rio Verde, are routinely searched (presumably for stolen goods) by security guards. All visitors, including academics and journalists, are carefully vetted by the company but are courteously received and assisted through a highly efficient public relations department. These elaborate security precautions create the strong impression of a 'State within a State', reinforcing the acute distance which exists, whether measured in economic, social or ecological dimensions, between the privileged *Serra* and the adjacent area. This undoubtedly fuels the animosity which exists between the local community and the CVRD enclave.

Security at the Carajás mining project is, justifiably from the CVRD's point of view, a crucial issue. The existence of the mine has literally transformed the local economy and attracted thousands of job-seekers from all over north and north-east Brazil. Tension in the area is high, primarily due to widespread unemployment, as operations have come on stream and infrastructural projects are completed. According to company officials, the CVRD employed a peak of 22,500 at Carajás but, by 1987, this figure had declined to 7,000 (CVRD–Carajás, 1987). The reserve army of unskilled and semi-skilled labour which comprises the local population in part continues to seek work at the mine through sub-contractors but many turn to farming or prospecting as the only alternatives. Company officials at the mining complex live in constant fear of land invasions and security forces play a cat-and-mouse game with land-hungry peasants to prevent their farming the land. In April 1987 the CVRD took legal action to evict 200 squatter families from the eastern border zone, where they had occupied a four-kilometre strip. Although they were duly and peacefully escorted out by the state military police, the difficulty of protecting this huge area is illustrated by the fact that, four months later, the evicted families had returned.

In addition to suffering sporadic occupation by small farmers, the CVRD protected zone is continually occupied by an unknown number of prospectors. At Salobo there are rich deposits of copper, which is often mined in association with gold. As gold-panning at Serra Pelada has become more restricted, so the mining enclave has become an increasingly attractive source. The deposits of Serra Pelada were discovered in the late 1970s and, by 1980 when the federal government intervened, some 30,000 prospectors from all over Brazil had descended on the area. The task of organising the mine was given to Col. Sebastião Rodrigues de Moura (nicknamed 'Major Curió'), who had taken part in the Araguaia anti-guerrilla campaign during the early 1970s as a sergeant in the national secret service (SNI) and who had also already been involved in such matters when dealing with the south-west Paraná revolt of 1957–64 (MST, 1986). Mineral rights at Serra Pelada are owned by DOCEGO, a subsidiary of the CVRD, under the authority of the Ministry of Mines and Energy.

There had always been strong rumours that, eventually, Serra Pelada would be taken over by the Ministry for mechanised production (Kotscho, 1984). Major Curió had forestalled such attempts by persuading President Figueiredo, during a 1983 visit, of the valuable social role performed by the mine in employing some 80,000 people with 500,000 dependent on its activities. Once unemployed, these ex-*garimpeiros* would prove a formidable pressure on land and other mineral resources in the immediate vicinity, especially the CVRD's own enclave. The State mining enterprise, along with local politicians and landowners are desperate to avoid such further confrontations given the already worsening pressure on land from peasant occupations. Curió was later elected a Pará federal deputy for the PDS largely on the strength of this support, both from the Pará landowning political elite as well as the eternally grateful prospectors themselves.

In 1984 when the government did eventually close Serra Pelada temporarily to small prospectors with the intention of turning it over to mechanised production, over 2,000 *garimpeiros* marched along the PA 275 approach road to Carajás, burning property on the way. They camped for five days outside the project gates until, finally, Congress revoked the law and reopened the gold mine (CVRD–Carajás, 1987). Company officials acknowledge the presence of prospectors in the region as a significant pressure group. The CVRD's security patrols have regular confrontations with invading prospectors, when it is common for shots to be exchanged as the well-organised *garimpeiros* beat a strategic retreat, only to return when the heat has died down. Such problems for the CVRD at Carajás are intensified when perennial problems at Serra Pelada, such as popular discontent over unsafe working conditions which have killed and maimed hundreds since 1982, threaten to erupt into yet more marches upon the mining enclave, threatening the security of company installations.

It is little wonder, then, that CVRD security personnel at Carajás regard themselves as being on what is virtually a permanent war-footing. The vulnerable northern and eastern borders are dotted with observation posts, while office maps indicate the exact location of known prospectors' sites and peasant occupations in what is called, significantly, 'The Defence Plan for Carajás' (CVRD/SUMIC, 1987). Despite the fact that the CVRD has attempted to gain the confidence of locals by building a hospital and school in Paraua-pebas, animosity between town and company is reflected in the fact that officials must travel in unmarked cars to avoid being attacked, a regular occurrence at one time. The most imposing CVRD-funded construction is, not unsurprisingly in this social climate, the police station, strategically situated near the closely guarded main checkpoint.

The strength of gold prospectors as a social force, and the sensitivity of the subject to the authorities is also illustrated by a major incident which took place on 29 December 1987. A group of 1,500 unarmed *garimpeiros* and their families from nearby Serra Pelada staged a demonstration at Marabá on the two mile-long bridge which carries the Carajás railway across the River Tocantins, in support of their demands for safer working conditions. It was reported that 300 military police, ordered in by state governor Hélio Gueiros, blocked off the two ends of the bridge and moved in, without any warning, indiscriminately firing upon the crowd with guns and tear gas. Up to thirty people were reported killed; some were simply shot while others jumped, or were pushed, 250 feet below to their deaths in the river. According to eyewitnesses, many bodies were washed away, while 'most of the corpses were piled on trucks and taken to an unknown location' (*The Independent*, 7.1.88). 'Police were seen throwing into the river the bodies of at least two people with bullet wounds, a pregnant woman and a small boy'. Later on, 'military police shot at a group of prospectors near the bridge and killed four of them'. An eyewitness who told television reporters that he had seen eight corpses under the bridge was himself murdered two days later by unidentified men. After two weeks, with ninety-three people still missing, Justice Minister Paulo Brossard refused to authorise an official enquiry, a position which remained unchanged in view of President Sarney's concern that the Pará state governor's political support for his efforts to secure a five-year term of office should not be jeopardised (*The Guardian*, 14.1.88; LAWR, 28.1.88).

As the above accounts demonstrate, small farmers and prospectors have resorted increasingly to various forms of social protest as a means of defending their livelihoods. Historically, the indigenous population has been the worst victim of Amazonian colonisation. The long Brazilian tradition of encroachment upon indian territory is continued in the Carajás Programme. The lands of thirty-four indigenous groups with a population of over 13,000 inhabit the iron-ore project area. Although twenty-three of these groups were included in a US$13·6 million Accord signed in 1982 by the CVRD, FUNAI and the World Bank, there are many flaws in the agreement and its execution (as shown in Chapter 3). In addition, several tribal groups have been fit to take direct action in protest at illegal incursions upon their lands by outsiders.

In May 1985, for example, 200 Xicrín-Kayapó took over the Maria Bonita open-cast goldmine in southern Pará, expelling no

10 The extent of local hostility among small farmers in the Carajás region to the negative repercussions upon them of the Programme is well-captured by this banner at the Açailândia demonstration in 1987, which proclaims defiantly and unequivocally that 'The Carajás project is a plague upon us'.

fewer than 5,000 prospectors who had illegally trespassed on to land the indians claimed as their reserve (CEDI, 1987). They refused to leave until their royalty of 0·1% of gross revenue was increased and the 1978 demarcation of their reserve was ratified by Congress. The occupation terminated two months later on the understanding that mining would cease once the 3·3 million hectare reserve was eventually ratified. The same group took further action that year, in August 1985, when seventy indians occupied a 4,000-head cattle ranch, the Fazenda Gran Reatã, near Marabá, following a four-year dispute with the alleged owner, who was accused of illegally settling on reserve land. By 1987, however, although the occupation had finished, the estate was still operative (CEDI, 1987; Treece, 1987).

One of the most vehement and well-publicised recent indian protests in eastern Amazonia involved the 200 or so Gavião in their battle to expel small farmers or *posseiros* from part of their 62,000-hectare Maē Maria reserve near Marabá, which is bisected by the

Carajás railway. This case has been well documented by CEDI (1985, 1987). Situated within the 'Brazil-nut polygon', the conflict has its origins in the 1920s and 1930s when local landowning families were granted leaseholds on the estates for nut extraction and commerce, which they came to monopolise. The Queiroz family acquired some 8,000 hectares or more in this fashion. In 1943 the Gavião were allocated an area by the government which, by 1966, following agreements with Queiroz for additional concessions to facilitate riverine access, amounted to 52,000 hectares. Tensions rose significantly only after the influx of small farmers which followed the construction of the PA 70 road in 1964, as part of the new official drive to develop Amazonia. Dozens of *posseiros* settled on Gavião and Queiroz land and, in 1979, a peasant farmer was killed in clashes with the estate-owner. In 1977 the Gavião contracted a survey and discovered that 3,000 hectares had been occupied by *posseiros*, this influx having been facilitated by the building of the then new PA 150 highway as well as the Tucuruí transmission lines and access roads through indian territory. Although the makings of a serious conflict were already visible, subsequent developments aggravated the situation.

In 1981 GETAT decided, for reasons best known to itself, to resettle forty-six peasant families on Gavião territory along its southern boundary by the River Tocantins, on the 'Loteamento Flexeiras'. Construction of the Carajás railway between Parauapebas and Sao Luís, which bisected Gavião territory, required the redemarcation of the Mãe Maria reserve. This was carried out in 1982 and ratified in 1986, extending Gavião land to 62,488 hectares; the lands belonging to J. A. Queiroz were purchased by the CVRD for the equivalent of some £140,000. Protracted negotiations between the tribe, FUNAI and the CVRD also took place throughout this period. The indians were anxious to gain fair compensation for the deforestation and general disruption to their lives caused by the railway and rail traffic. In September 1984 after talks with FUNAI and the CVRD they obtained extra compensation for long-term projects but the invasion of their land continued. The CVRD built more surveillance posts but these were destroyed by settlers and the guards attacked. Finally, fed up with the delays and official procrastination, the Gavião threatened on several occasions to occupy the railway line and prevent the laying of tracks unless their demands were met.

The constant pressure exercised by the Gavião to defend their livelihoods and territorial integrity, undoubedly helped by indian support groups as well as the key role of the World Bank as a major funder of Carajás and initiator of the 1982 Accord, was consistent throughout the struggle, although problems remain. By August 1985 thirty-eight of the forty-six colonists originally resettled by GETAT in 1981 were still farming their fifty-hectare plots on the 'Loteamento Flexeiras', as well as about 500 other squatters who entered the reserve subsequently. At this stage, the Gavião were again threatening to hold up construction of the railway, due to be inaugurated by President Figueiredo in February 1985, to disrupt traffic on the BR 222 highway and to damage the ELETRONORTE power transmission lines from Tucuruí. These threats were withdrawn when, at a meeting with FUNAI, GETAT and MIRAD in Marabá in December 1985, the Gavião received firm promises that the trespassers would be resettled on two nearby estates to be expropriated under the recently-announced agarian reform.

Patiently, the indians waited for the promises to be fulfilled but, over a year later, the situation had not improved. In order to force the government's hand, therefore, in March 1987 the Gavião carried out their oft-repeated threat to obstruct the Carajás railway. Rail traffic was permitted to continue only after talks had taken place in Brasília between the chief, Krokrenu, and the then Minister of Agrarian Reform, Dante de Oliveira (*Província do Pará*, 26.3.87). However, illegal peasant incursions into the Mãe Maria reserve continue, as do attmepts by neighbouring estates to increase the areas under their control at the expense of Gavião territory; CEDI (1985), for example, quotes several such proven cases.

By late 1987 little progress had been made towards resettling the Mãe Maria *posseiros*. The Fazenda Ubá, scene of one of the region's most bloody land conflicts, and which had been identified for expropriation, had in fact been sold off to the Itaminas Group, whose company, COSIPAR, would use the estate as a source of charcoal for its new pig-iron smelter at Marabá. The other area proposed for resettlement, the Fazenda Araras, was in the process of being expropriated and plots demarcated, and was completed only in early 1988 (Ferraz and Ladeira, 1988). However, such was the delay that, in July 1987, in an attempt to force the government's hand, forty-six families from Mãe Maria left the area to take up temporary residence at INCRA's Marabá office while awaiting relocation on Araras. The occupation of INCRA/GETAT installations was not a new tactic; the previous year some 600 peasant farmers and their families had taken similar action following their explusion from two estates, Pedra Furada and Agua Fria, which were also due to be expropriated under the agrarian reform (*O Liberal*, 16.12.86).

The Gavião were not the only indians within the Carajás Programme area to take such action. Also included (belatedly, in 1985) in the 1982 Accord signed by the CVRD and FUNAI was a group of 340 Apinayé from the village of Sao José in northern Goiás, supported by 140 indians from other tribes (CEDI, 1987; Ferraz and Ladeira, 1988). Under the demarcation procedures the Apinayé, through the CVRD and its anthropologist consultants, claimed 148,000 hectares but FUNAI proposed a much smaller area of 101,000 hectares. In support of their demands the indians at one stage, in 1983, occupied the FUNAI office in the local town of Araguaina. When this failed to produce the desired results the Apinayé laid out their own territorial markers and, finally, blocked the Trans-Amazon highway in protest at official delays. In 1985 an area of 142,000 hectares was eventually demarcated, excluding a large portion of their traditional lands, and an estimated 8,000 *posseiros* were due to be resettled. In a continuing climate of tension between the indian population, local landowners allied with the police force, and peasant farmers seeking to retain their plots while rejecting 'derisory' compensation from FUNAI, the Apinayé are continuing their struggle for what they see as their territorial rights.

Another instance of popular protest, this time on a much larger scale, is afforded by the construction of the Tucuruí hydroelectric project on the River Tocantins. Designed to supply the Carajás Programme's aluminium smelters and other industries, as well as feeding the national grid, Tucuruí is the world's largest such scheme in a tropical rainforest. It is the first and the largest of twenty-seven hydroelectric projects planned for the Araguaia-Tocantins Basin. Apart from its environmental consequences, considered in Chapter 4, the Tucuruí reservoir displaced an estimated 25,000 to 35,000 people, most of whom were poorly treated by ELETRONORTE. The company's original proposals for compensation and for relocating the displaced rural and urban populations left much to be desired. According to at least one detailed study, it was part of ELETRO-NORTE's policy to keep such payments to an absolute minimum

11 Land conflicts have caused the displacement of thousands of small farmers in eastern Amazonia, where officially-subsidised investments, both industrial and agro-livestock, are concentrated. This group of *posseiros* from the heart of the PGC area took refuge at GETAT headquarters, Marabá, in July 1987, after being forced to abandon their farmland on the Fazenda Mãe Maria following a dispute involving the estate-owner and the Gavião tribe.

(Mougeot, 1985b, 1987). However, a wave of popular protest among those affected by the scheme forced ELETRONORTE to reconsider its plans.

Objections were first voiced by villagers in two small communities to be flooded, Itupiranga and Repartimento, who in 1980 sent a protest note to the company, two years after the expropriation survey had been carried out. They objected to the company's failure to indemnify them for the forthcoming loss of their lands. Subsequently, demands focused more on the provision of replacement lands and support rather than simple monetary compensation. In 1982, with CPT support, 400 peasant farmers camped for three days in front of ELETRONORTE's office in Tucuruí demanding, 'land in exchange for land, houses for houses and fair compensation' (Hebette, 1983, p. 6). Only seven months later, in April 1983, there was a second encampment of 2,000 people in Tucuruí, which lasted four weeks, followed by a third in September 1984, lasting forty days, which aroused much local concern and jolted officials into action. The state police tried to disrupt the protest with violent tactics, blocking off roads and dispersing crowds with teargas, but the pressure of public opinion obliged the authorities to allow shipments of food and medicines through to the demonstrators. By this time not only the CPT but rural unions, human rights organisations, NGOs and other bodies had lent their support to the movement, which reached such a pitch that ELETRONORTE and the other parties involved were obliged to negotiate in Brasília with the people's representatives.

At the end of the day, however, although the protestors managed to win only limited concessions, it should be stressed that any gains were achieved almost entirely on the strength of popular demands upon the authorities, not upon official benevolence. Three new villages were built (Novo Abreu, Novo Repartimento and Cajazeiras), additional houses were constructed in existing communities, roads and wells were provided, while additional compensation was authorised in some cases. Larger areas were set aside for relocating displaced farmers, but plots were limited to fifty hectares. As already explained in Chapter 4, these provisions were highly inadequate and failed to compensate the majority for the losses incurred. Despite this, however, another result, according to local research (Hebette, 1983), is that these years of protest have increased the ability of the peasantry to organise itself against such threats.

No doubt the Tucuruí experience will provide useful lessons for future campaigns involving populations displaced by dam-building in the region, which will increase substantially this century. ELETRONORTE has identified sixty-three sites for electricity-generating reservoirs along the Araguaia-Tocantins and major Amazon tributaries, which could flood up to 100,000 square kilometres of rainforest, displacing as many as 156,000 people from their homes (Mougeot, 1989). The Santa Izabel reservoir upstream from Tucuruí will displace an estimated 60,000, while the Xingú river complex will have equally disastrous repercussions on the local population of indians and small farmers. The five dams for the Xingú basin will flood 18,000 square kilometres and, despite the alleged low population density, will displace upwards of 60,000, including seven indian tribes. The first of these will be the Kararaó and Babaquara dams

(known as the Altamira hydroelectric complex) and are due to come
on stream in 1998 and 2001 respectively (CPI, 1987). If, as one analyst has commented (Mougeot, 1985b, p. 13), 'more participatory
and compensatory strategies' by ELETRONORTE are desirable,
then popular mobilisation will have to play an even greater role in
obliging planners and policy-makers to take their demands seriously.

Brazilian NGOs, supported by overseas development and human
rights organisations have, at the time of writing in 1988, started
to campaign more forcefully and systematically against component
projects in the Carajás Programme. This is with the dual objective
of, firstly, exerting pressure on planners and policy-makers and,
secondly, mobilising affected communities, both with the objective
of modifying project design, and to ameliorate potentially negative
socio-environmental impacts. Bearing in mind the lessons of past
experience, they are aware of the fact that, unless such popular
pressure is brought to bear from a very early stage in the project
cycle on ELETRONORTE and other official institutions involved,
the likelihood is that provisions for indemnification and relocation
will almost certainly be highly inadequate. Experience with the first
components of the Carajás Programme, such as Tucuruí where only
limited compensation was granted, even after strong (if belated)
popular protests, bears witness to the negligent characteristics of
Brazilian government planning for Amazonia.

In São Luís also, the somewhat tardy and limited scale of public
protests against the Carajás Programme has produced a similar
outcome. Over 20,000 small farmers and fisherpeople were displaced
by the building of the CVRD and ALCOA company installations
(which occupy almost 20% of São Luís island's surface area), while
pollution produced by the ALCOA refinery and smelting plant has
seriously affected local fish catches, on which a population of over
60,000 fisherpeople along the north Brazilian coastline depend for a
livelihood. As already shown in Chapter 3, only a small proportion of
those afected received proper compensation, while the vast majority
was unceremoniously evicted from their homes, virtually without
opposition.

A protest campaign was organised by a local pressure group, the
'Committee for the Defence of the Island of São Luís' which had
some success, both nationally and overseas, in publicising the social
and ecological disruption caused by ALCOA. Newspaper reports,
radio programmes and even television documentaries in Europe and

the USA highlighted the people's plight. However, these tactics have elicited little or no positive response from either the company or the Brazilian authorities. This is due partly to the general lack of accountability which characterises the Brazilian planning process. In this context, since there was no multilateral development bank funding of ALCOA, the potential for applying pressure on Brazilian decision-makers to introduce more effective compensatory measures and build in greater social or environmental safeguards, was reduced to almost zero. In other cases, such as those of the POLONO-ROESTE prgramme and the Itaparica dam in Bahia-Pernambuco, protests to the World Bank by affected groups have produced significant modifications in project design. Another important consideration in the case under discussion, however, is the fact that the impact of the publicity campaign was itself severely muted by what amounted to a news blackout imposed by most local and southern newspapers, an indirect form of official censorship (English, 1984; Galvão, 1984). Naturally, this prevented the Committee's voice from being heard as widely as it might otherwise have been.

Chapter 3 of this volume considered the various manifestations of rural violence and social conflict produced by the struggle for land in eastern Amazonia, with particular reference to the Carajás Programme. The above pages have subsequently tried to paint a broad picture of the principal means used by peasant farmer and indian groups in the area to defend their livelihoods in the face of growing pressure from State-backed development interventions. A variety of institutional channels such as political parties, rural unions, the Catholic Church and NGOs was cited, as well as increasingly important non-institutional action, including peasant occupations and even banditry. It is undoubtedly a highly diverse mixture of groups with frequently conflicting interests. Observers (e.g. Hebette, 1983; Souza Martins, 1984, 1988; Grzybowski, 1987) have already made the point that there is little ideological cohesion or fundamental agreement among the major institutional opponents of government policy towards Amazonia; namely, the political parties, rural unions and the Church. Indeed, there are deep internal divisions within all of these organisations which have severely undermined their ability to exert pressure on official planners and decision-makers in favour of disadvantaged groups. Similarly, the traditionally localised and fragmented nature of peasant resistance to land-grabbing, as reflected in violent confrontations with hired gunmen, precludes their being properly labelled as 'social movements', given their lack of political organisation.

Yet it would, perhaps, be premature to dismiss recent events in Anazonia, and especially in the Carajás Programme area, as totally insignificant from a wider political standpoint. There are signs, for examle, of a much greater level of organisation and articulation among peasant groups, indians and mineral prospectors than has been seen in the past. The number of CUT-affiliated rural unions in Pará prepared to resolutely defend their members' land rights has grown significantly since the early 1980s. Further evidence for this may be found in the 'unofficial' land reform taking place as thousands of peasants families have occupied large estates and dug their heels in against all manner of violent repression from a coalition of landowners, gunmen and police. The well-organised MST has representatives in Amazonian states and although the movement has so far not managed to significantly extend its activities to northern Brazil, its influence is being increasingly felt in that region.

Whereas in the past the pressures placed on peasant farmers would, in most cases, have elicited little or no response from the victims, nowadays the picture is rather different. Not only is it peasant farmers and indians who are dying in land conflicts but so are landowners and their henchmen. Frustrated with the government's procrastination in implementing the agrarian reform, such as it is, landless farmers are increasingly predisposed towards taking possession *de facto* of under-utilised estates and worrying about the legal consequences later, defending their plots with their lives if necessary. Such actions in Amazonia are generally not premeditated but are, rather, the result of sheer pressure of common circumstances on a hard-pressed peasantry struggling to survive against tremendous odds. In the longer run, however, it is quite possible that the involvement of the Church, the MST and rural unions in this process could eventually turn what is presently an apparently haphazard eruption of estate invasions into an organised force for longer-lasting change, along the lines of what has happened in southern Brazil over the past five years. A similar precedent is to be found in the case of Acre, where a previously disunited peasantry was, as mentioned above, driven to seek greater organisational unity.

It is, of course, a matter of conjecture whether either of these paticular 'movements', in the South and in Acre, will last. In the case of peasant farmers within the sphere of influence of the Carajás

Programme it is also debatable whether the currently fragmented if increasingly extensive direct action by farmers' groups, in the form of armed resistance and land occupations, will cyrstallise into a more unified struggle. The million or so families of poor farmers in the PGC region are occupationally diverse and geographically scattered; they have no effective political representation at national level. On the other hand, they do enjoy the support of institutions such as trades unions and NGOs, assistance which can variously be interpreted either as enlightened guidance or as tutelage. Although they have, with increasing determination, united temporarily on a local basis in pursuit of immediate interests, it is questionable whether such a diverse group could ever constitute a united, class-based socio-political movement. Given this fact, combined with the peasantry's lack of political participation on a wider scale many observers are, perhaps understandably, pessimistic about the ability of these dispersed groups of poor farmers to exert pressure on the State to significantly modify its policies towards the development of Amazonia and the Carajás area.

While it would, however, be highly premature to dismiss open protests by indians, peasant farmers and gold prospectors as insignificant or marginal in view of their successes to date, another vital dimension of this whole debate should not be forgotten. Although the examples cited above of collective, confrontational action taken by small producers are those which attract most publicity, much resistance takes place which is rarely noticed or acknowledged. If violent peasant rebellions and land conflicts attract most outside attention, they are not necessarily the most effective in the longer term at winning concessions or territory for poor groups. A less obvious and more durable struggle finds expression in 'everyday forms of peasant resistance' (Scott, 1986) characterised not by revolts, revolutions or mass demonstrations but, rather, by a constant struggle between oppressor and oppressed.

In the Carajás region, for example, pitched battles between small farmers and gunmen, blocking of the railway line by indigenous groups and marches by gold prospectors on CVRD installations have attracted most media attention. Yet in the longer run it is possibly the least-publicised, piecemeal and far more widespread process of peasant land occupation and fragmented, localised conflict, requiring little or no collective organisation on a broad scale, which has arguably won most ground for this class. By undertaking a *de facto* land redistribution in many areas, the peasantry has, in no uncertain terms, made its political presence felt; not depending on formal structures and outside funding initially, but relying on its own spontaneous adaptation to harsh circumstances. By presenting government and *latifundiários* with a *fait accompli*, such forms of popular resistance by the Amazonian peasantry have forced the State to formally recognise their permanent presence and to accomodate their interests. These spontaneous forms of land struggle may then become better articulated into more cohesive movements. The cases of Acre's extractivist reserves, as well as the limited land redistribution within the Carajás Programme near Marabá, given impetus by the rural union movement, may be cited as small but significant steps in this direction. To what extent this will result in far-reaching changes remains, however, an open question.

6

Carajás – development for whom?

Since its official inception in 1980 the Greater Carajás Programme has, by any yardstick, had a substantial and dramatic impact on the people and environment of eastern Amazonia. The foregoing chapters in this book have attempted to show that, although the development of Amazonia throughout the 1960s and 1970s already followed Brazil's modernisation strategy of growth, the PGC has accelerated and severely exacerbated the worst social and ecological consequences of this model. Notwithstanding the much-vaunted macro-economic and political benefits accruing from the Carajás Programme to both domestic and overseas investors alike, it is highly debatable whether the scheme has improved the livelihoods of the estimated five million rural dwellers who currently inhabit the one-tenth of Brazil's national territory thus encompassed. This final chapter will trace the diverse interests served by the Carajás Programme, with particular reference to the key role of the Brazilian State, drawing out important policy implications for the future of eastern Amazonia. It will be suggested that, in agronomic terms, more sustainable development options exist for the Amazon which would allow the region to generate a more stable livelihood for the vital and enduring small farmer population. In the context of a large and increasingly resistant peasantry which will not, as many expect, fade into oblivion, the Brazilian State has a potentially key role to play in facilitating their economic progress. More than this, the government is under a clear obligation to plan development interventions in the interests of this group, whose well-being it has so far neglected. Before exploring these arguments, however, the scheme's major impacts to date will be reviewed.

The principle argument pursued so far in these pages has been that the specific pattern of industrial and agro-livestock investments in the Carajás Programme has grossly exacerbated a situation of already severe agrarian crisis over a large part of the Amazon Basin. This crisis is reflected in worsening social and environmental conditions for the majority of the rural population, making it increasingly difficult for small farmers to earn their living from the land in a secure and non-destructive manner. Without doubt these trends have been emerging throughout the 1970s, largely as a consequence of official policy. On the one hand successive governments have, for economic and political reasons, generously subsidised land acquisition in Amazonia by commercial and speculative interests. At the same time, however, they have also encouraged land-hungry peasant farmers expelled from the North-East and South of Brazil to settle the frontier as a solution to mounting social problems in these regions, avoiding the need to consider more fundamental structural reforms, while simultaneously 'securing' and occupying the Amazon frontier for geopolitical reasons. Yet although this dual-pronged strategy of Amazonian settlement may have conveniently achieved a number of sometimes apparently contradictory goals, it has produced a struggle amongst competing interests over access to land which has had serious consequences for Amazonia and its peoples. The Carajás Programme, rather than being used as an opportunity for ameliorating this agrarian crisis, has merely aggravated it. This is evident from the above analysis of trends within eastern Amazonia in a number of key socio-economic and environmental indicators since its inception in 1980; namely, rural violence, landownership and employment patterns, food security and ecological destruction.

To briefly recap on the evidence, the most sensational aspect of agrarian crisis in the Carajás Programme area is undoubtedly the rapid escalation in rural violence since the early 1980s. As land conflict has increased in the region the number of resulting deaths has leapt dramatically from a handful in the 1960s to about sixty in 1984, over one hundred in 1985 and almost 200 by 1986 (two-thirds of the total for Brazil), of which nearly half occurred in the state of Pará alone, and seventy within the very heart of the Carajás Programme area itself. In fifteen major on-going land 'battles' in the Carajás region during 1985–87, for example, some sixty peasant farmers and twenty-four gunmen were killed. Despite an official 1982 accord signed by the CVRD, the World Bank and FUNAI, the 13,000 indians in thirty-four tribal groups within the direct sphere of influence of the Carajás railway (only twenty-three of which were included in the agreement) have suffered numerous invasions of their territory by mining companies, cattle ranchers, loggers, by encroaching small farmers and by various infrastructural components of the Carajás Programme such as the railway, the Tucuruí dam, power lines and official colonisation schemes. One half of the reserves remain either undemarcated or unratified, while recent legislation has opened the way for mining companies to gain easier entry to indian lands. Several murders of well-known human rights activists in the area have focused international attention on the issue, notably the assassination in May 1986 of Father Jósimo Tavares, co-ordinator of the CPT in Marabá, and that of Paulo Fontelles, a lawyer representing rural union interests, in June 1987. In addition, of course, official data and other sources reveal a rising tide of intimidation, kidnappings, rapes, use of torture and slave labour, illegal arrests, house-burnings and evictions against recalcitrant peasant farmers. So great has been the escalation of rural violence in Brazil, especially in eastern Amazonia, that Amnesty International (1988) saw fit to highlight the situation in a special report which, significantly, emphasises the role of official connivance by the police and judiciary with land-grabbers against peasant farmers.

Fatalities and the use of more violent tactics by land-grabbers have undoubtedly been exacerbated by the fact that small farmers have, in recent years, shown greater resistance to intimidation. This is reflected not only in the rise in deaths of hired gunmen killed in land conflicts, but also in active estate occupations or 'invasions' of unproductive *latifúndia* which, at the heart of the Carajás Programme area itself, in the 'Brazil-nut polygon', involve over 10,000 people and, more broadly within the PGC's area of jurisdiction, probably double this figure. Neither is the CVRD's 411,000-hectare mining enclave of protected rainforest exempt, as farmers and gold-panners engage in a continuous struggle with security forces for access to this privileged area, surrounded by what is rapidly becoming a wasteland of ecological destruction. While more effective trades union organisation and Church or NGO backing may in part be directly responsible for this more active stance, there is undoubtedly a rising tide of spontaneous, if fragmented, organised peasant resistance at estate level in direct response to continued land-grabbing tactics employed by larger proprietors. The artificial 'closing' of the local frontier in eastern Amazonia has become increasingly unacceptable to the mass of small cultivators.

However, as Chapter 3 showed in some detail, land concentration is becoming inexorably more severe in Amazonia generally, and especially within that substantial portion covered by the Carajás Programme. This has been the result of both direct and indirect effects of the PGC. Investors in both industrial and agro-livestock projects have been heavily subsidised, resulting in the concentration of land into larger units. The numerous pig-iron smelters and other industrial plants set up along the Carajás–Sao Luís railway will further encourage this process, as will charcoal production by a variety of commercial suppliers anxious to meet the factories' voracious appetite for fuel, to be produced as cheaply as possible through indiscriminately chopping down the rainforest. Tax incentives through the Carajás Programme (and SUDAM) for cattle ranches, ethanol distilleries, lumbering, charcoal production itself and other forms of agribusiness have further stimulated the concentration of rural production into larger units. Furthermore, agricultural development plans formulated, with Japanese technical assistance, should they ever be implemented, will exacerbate land concentration due to their emphasis on large-scale, capital-intensive methods. Indirectly also, the PGC has had an impact on landownership patterns by causing upward pressure on land values arising from the sheer scale of infrastructural and other investments. Within the context of Brazil's macro-economic situation, land acquisition in Amazonia has, since the early 1970s, become a profitable hedge against inflation, which was running at over 1,000% p.a. by mid-1988.

Analysis of the most recent census data illustrated the extent to which Brazil's highly skewed land distribution has become duplicated in eastern Amazonia, with 0·1% of properties occupying some 30% of farmland generally in the region. In central areas of the Carajás Programme such as Açailândia, Marabá, Xingú and Pindaré, where PGC-financed industrial, agro-livestock and forestry projects are being set up, land concentration was found to have reached even more intense levels. Large estates are steadily expanding their area of influence, generating unprecedented levels of rural violence and growing landlessness as the class of independent smallholders is reduced in relative size and the ranks of wage-labourers are swelled. Temporary work on estates, on construction projects and in gold-panning has provided some short-term alleviation but the long-run trend seems to be towards structural unemployment and permanent dispossession of a large sector of the rural population which currently gains a livelihood on the land in Amazonia even if, as will be argued below, total proletarianisation is unlikely. GETAT during its seven years of activities in land-titling and colonisation, merely reinforced existing landownership patterns rather than making any redistributive contribution. Any remaining hopes of significant advances in this field were dashed when Brazil's new constitution, approved in September 1988, effectively ruled out compulsory expropriations under the country's agrarian reform.

The social multiplier effects of these pronounced trends in rural violence, land access and employment patterns are far-reaching. While the broader and more subtle impacts of schemes such as the Carajás Programme on people's lives often goes unrecorded, wilfully or otherwise, many firm indicators do exist. Graphic accounts of specific incidents of conflict in the countryside provided by fieldworkers, journalists and other researchers, many of which have been referred to in these pages, leave little room for doubting the extent to which thousands of lives have been disrupted. The scale and intensity of rural violence, as well as forced population displacements (including 30,000 in Sao Luís and up to 35,000 at Tucuruí), and the pace of out-migration, offer some clear pointers to the profound and not always welcome changes currently taking place.

Another is that of worsening food security, the growing inability of people to feed themselves adequately. This is evidenced in the region's urban squalor, with its high levels of unemployment, infant mortality and malnutrition and can be clearly observed in towns such as Parauapebas, Marabá, Açailândia, Imperatriz and Tucuruí as their populations have been swollen in the space of a few years from several hundred to many thousands, largely resident in sprawling slum settlements. The squeeze on peasant agriculture in eastern Amazonia as a result of land concentration and the dispossession of the staple-food producing small farmer class, effectively mirroring national trends, has not only created a regional food deficit and reduced supplies of basic commodities such as corn and cassava. The consequent reduction in farmer incomes under such volatile circumstances has also made people poorer, even allowing for off-farm income, thus reducing effective demand for essential foods, while expulsion from the land has deprived many of a domestic source of staples.

The last major indicator of worsening agrarian crisis in the area, dealt with at length in Chapter 4, is environmental destruction, brought about almost entirely through extensive deforestation. An indication of the seriousness of this problem is given by the fact that the proportion of 'Legal Amazonia' deforested has quadrupled in the space of a decade, from 2·4% in 1978 to around 10% in 1988. In certain parts of eastern Amazonia, at the heart of the PGC, the figure is much higher, with levels of over 30% recorded in some municipalities. Whereas small farmer colonisation has accounted, in one way or another, for perhaps one-third of deforestation generally in Amazonia, in the Carajás heartland in particular it is the least demographically intensive forms of settlement, such as cattle ranching, pasture formation and lumbering, which have so far been the major culprits. These officially subsidised activities are responsible for most of the rainforest depletion currently taking place. To this already grim picture the Carajás Programme has added another critical factor in the environmental equation, which promises to be the most destructive of all: a series of over thirty pig-iron smelters and other mineral processing plants along the railway corridor. The dozen schemes which had been approved by the Carajás council by 1987 will alone, it has been officially calculated, require the removal of over 5,000 hectares of forest annually to supply the one million tonnes of charcoal required to fire their burners.

If there are short term economic gains to be made by both smaller and large-scale producers alike, the ecological and social consequences of this pattern of forest-use will be nothing short of catastrophic in the medium to long run. The combined effects of industrial, agro-livestock and lumbering activities currently being financed by subsidised domestic and international capital are likely to turn a large part of eastern Amazonia into unproductive scrubland. Much of the region has already gone down this road, yet the pace of ecological destruction will undoubtedly show a marked rise by the early 1990s. The first traces of this decline are already clearly evident: soil erosion, compaction and leaching, a greater propensity to flooding, siltation of rivers and dams, widespread pasture degradation, atmospheric pollution arising from forest burning and charcoal production, as well as local and even wider regional, national or global climatic changes.

Although environmental controls exist on paper, in practice they are ignored in the interests of short-term economic and political expediency. For example, although legislation requires that pig-iron smelters make provisions for obtaining half of their charcoal supplies from plantations, none has made such plans. Furthermore, none of the twelve smelters approved by mid-1987 had carried out the required environmental impact assessment. As Chapter 5 demonstrated, strong concern has been expressed at the negative socioecological repercussions of the Carajás Programme not just by Brazilian organisations but also by a wide range of European and North American environmental and other pressure groups. Feelings ran high enough to lead the CVRD's own environmental protection group, GEAMAM, to protest publicly about the company's policy in Amazonia and its lack of controls on predatory rainforest depletion for industrialisation purposes. Environmental protection measures have been built into the new Brazilian constitution concerning, amongst other aspects, the responsibilities of government towards this area, the duty of companies to undertake impact assessments and the provision of special ecological guidelines for Amazonia and coastal areas. However, while it remains to be seen whether such measures will be implemented, past practices do not augur well for Amazonia's fragile future.

Carajás, the peasantry and the Brazilian State

This volume has been concerned primarily with tracing the major social and environmental impacts associated largely, although by no means exclusively, with the Greater Carajás Programme. It is often taken for granted that these trends are the somehow inevitable 'price of progress'. Indeed, some policy-makers go even further to suggest, flying in the face of all the evidence, that current official strategies can ameliorate Amazonia's agrarian crisis. The history of the PGC shows that such complacency is totally unwarranted, and a major purpose of this book has been to focus in some detail upon the nature and direction of socio-environmental change in this region. However, while the gravity of Amazonia's crisis should certainly not be underestimated, neither should it lead to total despair. This study, which has highlighted the negative effects of growth policies upon the people and environment of Amazonia, will also suggest that there is no inevitability in this situation. The direction of development can and must be modified if social and ecological disaster within the next few decades is to be averted. A glimmer of hope for the future may be derived from a brief consideration of the key roles played by two major actors in this drama: the Brazilian State and the Amazonian peasantry.

Contending theoretical explanations of the causes of continued underdevelopment in Brazilian Amazonia, as well as the respective roles of State and peasantry, may be conveniently grouped into three broad categories: the logic of capital model, the institutional-incorporation argument and a more pluralistic analysis. Each of these places differing emphases on explaining agrarian crises, such as that presently characteristic of Amazonia, in terms of a variety of factors; for example, dominant global and domestic class interests linked to the spread of capitalism, the variable role of the State machine in determining development policy, the continued existence of the Amazonian peasantry, and the influence of intermediary organisations as active bargaining forces negotiating with a range of private and government bodies. In terms of this present debate, it is pertinent to ask which of these best explains the pattern of agrarian development within the Carajás Programme, what the implications are for official development interventions in the region and, most importantly, what are the implications for its rural population of some five million.

The first model, that of the logic of capitalism, essentially subsumes both rural development patterns and State policy to external forces. Agrarian crisis is seen as the result of dependent and uneven capitalist expansion at the periphery, causing social polarisation, depeasantisation and proletarianisation. Although the peasantry is functionally integrated into the commodity market through sales of crops and cheap labour to supply capitalist enterprises, as well as via the purchase of basic goods and services, it is excluded from the mainstream consumer economy in a process of what de Janvry (1981) calls 'functional dualism'. State power-holders and policy-making merely serve dominant class interests, ensuring the long-term survival of capitalist accumulation. Occasionally, however, the State may be forced to intervene temporarily, in apparent opposition to these elite groups' interests, in order to deal with temporary crises by promoting reformist programmes. But such relative State autonomy is short-lived and, in many ways, illusory; the class structure, both domestic and international, and the need to resolve the contradictions of capitalism, are seen as the driving forces behind State action.

Analysis of the origins and direction of the Carajás Programme have tended to adopt such an approach, generally arguing that the pattern of Amazonian development has been distorted by an alliance of domestic and dominant foreign industrial capital, both commercial and aid-funded. Showing obvious concern at the apparent ease with which successive Brazilian administrations have allowed international investment in Amazonia to take hold, inflating the foreign debt, IBASE (1983) objected to Brazil 'mortgaging its future' to overseas interests while the majority of its citizens was excluded from decision-making. In a similar vein, Pinto (1982) criticised the PGC as a 'Trojan horse' for foreign interests which is 'attacking the heart of Amazonia', while Cota (1984) accused the Programme of being an 'unarmed invasion'. Perhaps the most systematic analysis from a dependency perspective is that of Neto (1988, 1989) who is of the opinion that regional development policy for the region has been determined almost exclusively by the global corporate strategy of foreign mineral groups, particularly the aluminium transnationals such as ALCAN and foreign consortia such as the NAAC (see Chapter 2), precluding the formulation of a locally-determined, self-sustaining strategy, and relegating the Brazilian government to an essentially passive role.

In terms of Amazonian rural development within this model, the 'Junker' road of agrarian transformation is frequently posited as explanatory of events in that region. This aruges that the State, reflecting the interests of domestic and foreign capital, is fundamentally antagonistic towards small farmer interests and, in designing policies of Amazonian occupation, is concerned primarily with closing the frontier to peasants, eventually expelling them from the land and reserving it for exploitation by large commercial and speculative interests within a process of capitalist expansion (Cardoso and Muller, 1977; Becker, 1982; Branford and Glock, 1985). The long term outcome, according to these analyses, seems to be the inevitable disappearance fo the peasantry, which would be transformed either into urban migrants or members of a wage-earning proletariat. Given current levels of violence in Amazonia, the rapid pace of urbanisation and land concentration, combined with the apparent lack of State intervention in favour of small farmers, this theory certainly invites serious consideration as a plausible explanation.

A similar conceptualisation, not quite so Leninist in its prognostications, views Amazonian settlement as a reproduction of Brazil's *latifúndio-minifúndio* complex. This is essentially a hybrid process of primitive accumulation which leads to some polarisation and 'differentiation' of the peasantry, but at the same time allows the peasant mode of production to co-exist with large, capitalised estates. The purpose of this articulation of different modes of production is, firstly, to supply urban areas with cheap food and, secondly, to create a 'reserve army' of seasonal labour serving Amazonian estates, clearing the forest ready for appropriation by private capital and providing temporary wage-workers for other productive purposes. By being kept continuously on the move in search of new areas to occupy, the peasantry is denied longer-term, permanent access to land and is also weakened politically (Oliveira, 1987). The legal and administrative apparatus of the State is mobilised towards this end, encouraging both violent and non-violent means to perpetuate a 'closed' form of frontier occupation in which a subordinate peasantry is reproduced, characterised essentially by non-capitalist relation-ships (Velho, 1976; Foweraker, 1981). Some observers, such as de Janvry (1981), reject the idea of a durable specific peasant economy or simple commodity mode of production articulated to capitalism arguing that, under the capitalist mode in Latin America, subsistence and semi-subsistence farmers are essentially a transitory phenomenon. Implicitly, in the 'articulated modes' analysis, the future of the peasantry is still uncertain, although some variants envisage an enlarged and diversified small farm sector as a function of capitalist expansion on the frontier (e.g. Sawyer, 1979). Within this paradigm also, the State is largely reduced to being a passive tool in the hands of capitalist interests, with little power to intervene on behalf of the mass of small, migrant farmers to promote broader development goals.

However, the 'logic of capital' argument appears to be funda-mentally flawed in assuming total passivity both of the State and of the peasantry. Analysis of developments in the Carajás Programme area shows, on the contrary, that both have exercised a major influence on the nature and direction of change in Amazonia. By ignoring the crucial role of political intervention and State develop-ment ideology on the one hand, as well as the widespread response by small farmers in defence of their threatened livelihoods on the other, this concept offers only a very partial explanation of policy-formulation and related developments. As Long (1988) points out, it cannot explain the true extent of such dependence nor account for those circumstances in which the State may operate autonomously. By treating the States as a monolithic entity, neither can the theory offer any insight into the variable socio-political composition of the bureaucracy and how this can influence policy.

The second model, that of institutional-incoporation, offers an alternative explanation, based on the overriding role of government as the major agent of development. In this Weberian conceptualisation, the spatial expansion into the countryside of urban-based institutions, the commercialisation of production, as well as the spread of 'rational' science, technology and communications, lead to an increasing centralisation of State control over the rural economy. Government agencies and policy are not simply derivative of class relationships but have a distinctive, if variable, autonomy of their own (Benvenuti, 1975; Pearse, 1975). Yet this institutional-incorporation model, while going some way towards offering an additional explanation to that of capitalist expansion, still has major drawbacks. Like the first approach, it assumes a relatively monolithic State apparatus united by a common rationality among politicians, planners and technicians in which little or no allowance is made for internal goal conflict. Also, farmers' decision-making is assumed to be gradually taken over by the State, as well as by the increasing penetration of agribusiness, undermining their independence and allowing little possibility of autonomous action.

Criticisms of the capital subsumption and State institutional control models have been partially met by the third or pluralistic, more actor-oriented approach. This type of analysis, of which there are several, generally attributes somewhat different roles to both the peasant farmer class and the State apparatus to which it relates. Rather than assuming a helpless peasantry faced by overwhelming outside forces, it is seen as responsive to changing circumstances, thereby actively moulding the process of change and interacting with institutions and individuals at all levels. Groups may in fact cope differently in similar structural circumstances, giving rise to contrasting social patterns. In other words, there is no inevitable uniformity or linear progression, either in the nature or direction of change, or of State action. Bottom-up pressure upon and negotiation with policy-makers, as well as competition amongst bureaucrats themselves, will produce different solutions in different situations.

Grindle's (1986) analysis of agrarian change patterns and the role of the State in Latin America has important implications for development policy in Amazonia. It focuses in particular upon the

variable autonomy of State planners and technicians in the formulation and implementation of government policy, soundly rejecting the
passive role attributed to the State by the capitalist model. Arguing
that State intervention in markets for land, labour and capital has
been fundamental in determining official economic policy, resource
allocation and conflict resolution, Grindle suggests that in Brazil and
other countries a powerful public bureaucracy has emerged with its
own specific interests. However, the parallel expansion of the State
alongside the spread of agrarian capitalism has favoured a powerful
export-oriented, landowning elite of capitalist entrepreneurs which
has formed a strong political lobby to guarantee privileged treatment
by government.

Simultaneously, Grindle argues, the State has become preoccupied with the failure of agricultural modernisation to alleviate
mass poverty, and has thus intervened with compensatory programmes in order to avoid facing the problem of structural reforms;
in Amazonia, POLONOROESTE, directed colonisation, the agrarian reform plans and GETAT land-titling could be interpreted in
this light. Such a 'new dualism' in State policy, at once favouring
agrarian capitalism and yet promoting piecemeal, poverty-alleviation
is, according to Grindle, the product of increasing State concern
with worsening socio-economic indicators such as rising poverty
levels, increased rural-urban migration, declining staple food production and increased food imports. The State apparatus may also,
exercising its autonomy, pursue policies which are sometimes opposed to dominant class interests. However, in Amazonia at least, it
will be argued that State interests and those of private capital, more
often than not coincide in their pursuit of short-term economic and
political gain, to the detriment of long-run social and environmental
considerations.

Before examining the decisive role of the Brazilian State in
moulding the Carajás Programme and its *latifúndio*-biased model of
rural development, the issue of the peasantry needs to be briefly
reconsidered. It was concluded above that several key social and economic indicators, such as land concentration, growing landlessness and rural violence lent some credence to theories which suggest,
implicitly or explicitly, either the gradual disappearance of the semi-
subsistance farmer class as proletarianised labour (the 'Junker'
road) or at best, its marginalisation as a politically disenfranchised,
permanently mobile and subservient category (the centre-periphery,

articulated modes of production model). Such essentially unilinear analyses are, however, oversimplified and do justice neither to the peasantry itself nor to progressive planners and policy-makers. While in Brazil the capitalist transformation of agriculture and its direct integration into industrial development has been evident, especially in the Centre-South, in Amazonia this process is in its infancy. There are several reasons for suggesting that the transformation of the peasantry in the Amazon Basin will follow a more multidimensional route than in other areas of the country, allowing or even encouraging the presence of both capitalised and semi-subsistence small farmers on a large scale.

There is ample evidence that the State and allied commercial interests support the formation of a class of small, capitalised family farms not operating within the logic of primitive accumulation serving the cities, but increasingly integrated with agroindustrial enterprises oriented towards export markets (see Chapter 1). Colonists on private colonisation schemes in Pará and Mato Grosso are producing cash crops such as cocoa, coffee, pepper, rubber and other forest products, either as independent farmers or as outgrowers for larger industrial concerns, usually through co-operatives which provide access to official subsidies and other support. While such 'modern', small farms are becoming an increasingly viable and permanent feature of Amazonia's agrarian structure they are, however, in a small minority and most cultivators lack such privileges.

Yet even as regards the mass of subsistence and semi-subsistence farmers there are good reasons for believing that these groups also have a longer-term place in Amazonian development. This could arise in the first instance from the market segmentation effects of Brazil's post-1964 agricultural policies, which have favoured rapid expansion of the export crop sector but, at the same time, come to rely increasingly for staple food supplies on non-capitalised family labour (Goodman, 1986). This role has possibly been enhanced by recent reductions in the level of subsidies to large farmers as a component of structural adjustment agreements with the IMF and World Bank. The practice of risk-aversion strategies by peasant farmers such as mixed cropping and falling back on labour-intensive methods have helped to absorb worsening rural-urban terms of trade. Together with the limited employment-generation capacity of Brazil's cities, the variable demand for estate labour and the attraction of supplementary income-generating activities such as gold-panning, it could thus be concluded that, 'Concentrations of impoverished, small-scale producers will continue to characterise the Brazilian agrarian structure, constituting a source of small marketed food surpluses and, more significantly, a reserve of labour' (Goodman and Redclift 1981, p. 183).

However, it would be a grave oversimplification to assume that all, or even most, small farmers in Amazonia live severely impoverished lives, barely surviving at the economic margin. Certainly, policy-makers with an interest in encouraging the capitalisation of agricultural production and occupation of the area by other groups have in the past tried to promote the image of semi-subsistence farmers as 'backward', ignorant of appropriate production techniques and, to boot, prone to bouts of tropical 'laziness'. Yet it is not quite so easy to distort reality with such gross misjudgements. Anthropological research undertaken in eastern Amazonia serves to dispel these myths. Small squatter cultivators have been shown to farm more efficiently, using traditional techniques, than more recent migrants from the South adopting mechanised, capital-intensive methods (Andrade *et al*, 1983). Rather than conforming to the popular image of subsistence producers barely scraping a living from the soil and able to meet only immediate family needs, this class is, in fact, usually well-integrated into the market through a highly structured chain of intermediaries (Santos *et al*, 1985; SMDDH, 1985). Furthermore, as Wagner (1985) has demonstrated, communal land-use practices facilitate production and group survival while attempting to minimise environmental degradation through shifting cultivation.

Yet while the adaptive capacity and economic role of the specific peasant economy of eastern Amazonia helps to explain its continued existence, settlement patterns in the region suggest another major reason for the longer-term persistence of the peasant mode of production, which has little to do either with cash cropping or local demand for wage-labour arising from capitalist penetration, or with market segmentation effects of government agricultural policy. The resilience of small cultivators in eastern Amazonia and the refusal of the peasantry to vacate the land upon demand is driven increasingly not by macro-economic forces alone, but also by the quest for social reproduction and survival in the countryside. This is well-illustrated by the growing number of cases (as detailed in Chapters 3 and 5) in which peasants and indian groups are offering fierce resistance to land-grabbers, centred in particular on the Carajás region, leading to a mounting annual death toll over the past few years. This fight for survival is indeed not unique to Amazonia, and has parallels in the North-East where, as in Amazonia, the limited scope of differentiation has allowed wider socio-political organisation and land occupations to take place, forming a significant movement in localised areas (Henfrey, 1988). Implicitly, therefore, the 'safety-valve' function of Amazonian colonisation, which has long been recognised by government planners as crucial for the success of Brazil's economic model, is itself reinforced by the independent political actions of the peasantry, both institutionalised and in more fragmented forms, as it struggles to survive, against all the odds, by virtue of its own social dynamic.

Thus, in assessing the relevance of theories of small farmer development in Amazonia, few useful insights are to be gained from Leninist and neo-Marxist paradigms, which view the peasantry as totally subservient to capital, destined to disappear altogether. A multidimensional analysis will offer scope for the formulation of development policies in the region as a whole, and the Carajás area in particular. Similarly, by adopting a more pluralistic frame of analysis with regard to official policy formulation, it becomes evident that neither should the distinct pattern of State intervention in Amazonia be viewed in a unilinear fashion. The State has served no single set of interests in Amazonia. On the contrary, settlement strategies since the mid-1960s and, more recently, in the Carajás Programme itself, have conveniently fulfilled a wide variety of economic, social, political and geopolitical goals, of both government and private groups, in Brazil and overseas. Many parties are reaping short to medium term advantage through access to cheap raw materials and heavily subsidised government funding, ensuring quick profits, while other investors are purusing longer-term strategies of diversifying production to stengthen their global competitiveness. An examination of the specific and complementary range of objectives behind the PGC will underline the diversity of actors and their varied motives for involvement in this scheme.

As already mentioned, contemporary analyses of the Carajás Programme have tended to focus upon the extent of foreign domination of policy-formulation, implying that the Brazilian State is a weak partner. While Japanese, American and European investors pursue their own global strategies, Brazilian planners are implictly portrayed as powerless, having somehow forfeited the destiny of Amazonia to foreign transnational corporations at the expense of national interests. However, this dependency-type perspective, while partially valid, is questionable as a full representation of reality. Although there can be no doubt that foreign interests have benefited substantially, from the point of view of the Brazilian State itself, Carajás has clearly served a number of purposes; otherwise there would have been little point in extending such generous incentives to attract foreign investors.

Successive governments have, for example, made no secret of the fact that the PGC was expected to help service the huge foreign debt. According to (perhaps over-optimistic) early plans it was estimated that the US$40 billion in direct investments would generate US$17 billion annually in foreign exchange from a combination of industrial and agro-livestock enterprises (IBASE, 1983). This concern was reiterated on many occasions by government officials in the early 1980s, especially by Planning Minister, Delfim Neto. While the figure for export earnings would undoubtedly have to be revised downwards today, in view of reduced iron-ore and aluminium production levels due to low world demand, as well as the failure of grandiose agricultural plans to be realised, debt-servicing continues as a major perceived advantage of the programme. There are other positive aspects of the PGC from a State perspective.

The State mining company, the CVRD, has played the key role in designing and implementing Carajás industrial development policy. The CVRD is among the top companies in the developing world, with assets of over US$2·6 billion and profits in 1986 of US$341 million (*South*, 1987) and is the world's major company in the oceanborne iron trade (Trebat, 1983). Its formative influence in drawing up plans for the PGC, with Japanese technical assistance, was demonstrated in Chapter 2. This powerful enterprise had a clear interest in transferring iron-ore production from Minas Gerais to Amazonia, to exploit the rich ferrous mineral reserves in the Carajás hills, taking advantage of heavily subsidised electricity prices and infrastructural developments. Abundant and cheap supplies of charcoal, obtained from cutting down the native rainforest, will permit an economically feasible integrated iron and steel industry to be set up in the region. This was a crucial factor in encouraging the switch to Amazonia from the South, where timber has become scarce and expensive after decades of deforestation.

Linked to the CVRD's desire to expand its activities in eastern

Amazonia, the Brazilian government was, by the close of the 1970s, looking for an additional strategy to livestock production as a means of developing the region and integrating it more effectively into the national economy. Cattle ranching had proved of very limited use in this respect, its export potential much lower than had been anticipated, its environmental and social consequences little short of disastrous, and the subsidised credit provided, as subsequent evaluations proved, subject to gross misuse. Although the expansion of mining activities in eastern Amazonia had formed part of government policy since the mid-1970s, the advent of the Carajás Programme concept offered the Geisel and Figueiredo administrations an opportunity of undertaking what seemed to be an 'integrated' regional development strategy which would also help deal with the mounting debt problem.

Another perceived advantage from the government's point of view was the creation of jobs in the industrial and agricultural sectors, rather optimistically put at one million in early projections (IBASE 1983). From a social perspective this investment programme was also expected to help absorb excess labour from other regions of the country, thus continuing Amazonia' long-established 'safety-valve' function. Despite many warnings from outside observers, however, planners failed to recognise the fact that a parallel consequence would also be increased levels of unemployment and social conflict resulting from the escalating land struggle in the region prompted by the Carajás complex of projects.

If macro-economic and regional development objectives were of paramount importance to the State as inspirations for the Carajás Programme, political goals were of no less consequence. The history of official thinking on Amazonian frontier occupation during the 1970s illustrates in no uncertain terms the extent to which governments were content to pursue economically and environmentally irrational policies of support for widespread cattle ranching in the Amazon Basin, which can only be explained in political terms. There has always been a strong alliance between government and private interests in the occupation of Amazonia with industrial, agrarian and construction companies being able to strengthen their influence over policy-making for the region (Bourne, 1978; Pompermeyer, 1984; Grindle, 1986).

Chapter 1 demonstrated that such pressure from private companies was of considerable importance during the mid-1970s in

consolidating official policy in favour of agribusiness, livestock production and land speculation. These were given access to subsidised
credit and other generous incentives, while attempts were simultaneously made to discredit programmes of government-supported
directed colonisation in favour of poorer groups. The State was
happy to buy political support from landholding and commercial
elites by offering huge amounts in subsidised funding for pasture
formation and livestock production, rationalised as part of an
agribusiness strategy of development. About 90% of these units
failed miserably as productive enterprises, their prime function
being as a speculative hedge for wealthy elites against the country's
rampant inflation. This strong linkage between the economic and
political dimensions of official policy-making for Amazonia thus
offers some explanation for the State's pursuit of seemingly ill-advised
policies in the region.

Thus, despite the adverse social and environmental impacts associated with the Carajás Programme, significant benefits have accrued
to the Brazilian State. Clear linkages can be seen between the interests of private capital, motivated by commercial profit, and the
policies of successive governments, driven by macro-economic and
broader political objectives. In this scenario, negative social and
ecological impacts acquire only a secondary importance and become
an acceptable price of development, at least in the short term. In
pushing forward with a 'modernising' growth strategy in eastern
Amazonia, latterly abandoning any pretence at even small-scale
compensatory, poverty-focused projects such as colonisation or land-
titling, or even limited agrarian reforms, the State has consciously
opted for a policy which ignores the needs of the majority of small
farmers and places its faith in commercial elites as the most appropriate catalysts of regional development.

Expansion of government involvement in Amazonia through the
Carajás Programme is consistent with the generally enlarged role of
the Brazilian State in directing and planning national development.
The high degree of State intervention in Brazil's economy has been
well documented, a process which started with the *Estado Novo*
and was consolidated during twenty-one years of military rule
(Baer, 1975; Flynn, 1978; Ianni, 1986). The expanded role of Brazilian State enterprises as key agents of government development
policy, for example, has been highlighted as a key factor in that
country's rapid economic growth in recent years (Trebat, 1983).

Centralised control over Amazonian development, as shown in Chapter 1, got seriously underway in the early 1960s with the construction of the new capital city and the Belém–Brasília highway, and took a quantum leap during the following decade with the advent of SUDAM, the Programme of National Integration (PIN) and POLAMAZONIA as an integral part of the Second National Development Plan (PND II). Many studies have documented the State's expanded economic and political role in Amazonia itself over the past two decades (Cardoso and Muller, 1977; Bunker, 1985; Grindle, 1986). However, their interpretations of the significance of this expanded role differ somewhat, a theme which is taken up below.

The Carajás Programme, with its influx of State enterprises and bureaucracies, undoubtedly represents a significant extension of government influence. Such a measure of centralised direction is necessary in order for the State to realise its macro-economic as well as socio-political objectives through development of the Amazon Basin. In exercising such guidance within a particular framework of industrial and agricultural development, the social and environmental costs have been considerable. To the extent that this is a path consciously chosen by government, these far-reaching consequences themselves represent an enlarging of the State's sphere of influence, for without such intervention through a whole range of stimuli to large-scale extractive and commercial settlement, the picture in Amazonia would today surely be very different.

The broadening and intensification of opposition, through a variety of social movements and forms of resistance, to the State's predatory use of the Amazonian environment is a firm indication of growing popular dissent. Another clear illustration of frustration with the pattern of State encroachment has come not from the most obvious victims of goverment policy, but from traditional regional interest groups. Many of these have seen their power base gradually eroded as official bureaucracies have increased their control over the area and its resources. Emmi (1985), for example, in her study of the relationships between landownership and political power in the Marabá area of Brazil-nut estates, demonstrates this well. Until the early 1960s land in the 'Brazil-nut polygon' was monopolised by a handful of traditional families, but their properties and power have declined considerably with the arrival of State enterprises such as the CVRD and others which form part of the Carajás Programme.

Such elites manage to diversify their economic activities sufficiently to retain a degree of wealth and influence but the State, by virtue of its expanded role, has been decisive in altering the socio-political structure of the region.

Growth of the State's powers to mobilise Amazonia's resource-base in the interests of 'national development' is also illustrated by conflict between local and central government over division of the fiscal revenues arising from development schemes, as well as the issue of land rights. Decree-law 1164 of 1.4.71, for example, placed under INCRA jurisdiction all land in Amazonia within a 100-kilometre radius of federal highways, effectively removing from regional control, for example, about 70% of the area of Pará. A further piece of government legislation (Decree-law 1473 of 13.7.76) transferred from the state of Pará to AMZA the 411,000 hectares now occupied by the CVRD Carajás mining enclave, depriving the state government of tax income from mining operations. A vigorous campaign has since been mounted by Pará's politicians to obtain suitable compensation from Brasília on the grounds that, in the words of the then governor, Jader Barbalho, 'we have lost all our rights over the Carajás mineral reserves' (*O Liberal*, 7.5.85). Efforts by regional groups to regain control over resources are also reflected in the periodic, if futile, attempts by local politicians to have the PGC Interministerial Council in Brasília abolished and its decision-making powers transferred to SUDAM, based in Belém (*O Liberal*, 23-23.8.85).

State governors have also been attempting to re-establish their control over local developments through greater participation in the Carajás Interministerial Council, which has ultimate responsibility for vetting and monitoring all projects approved under the PGC fiscal incentive scheme. Originally governors were not included as members of the Council but, following the change to civilian rule in 1985, those from Pará, Maranhão and Goiás were each given a place. However, their role was purely advisory and they had no voting rights on the Council. This gave rise to a campaign for a change in the rules to grant these three state leaders appropriate decision-making powers along with ministers, following the practice in regional development bodies such as SUDENE and SUDAM (*O Liberal* 19.4.86).

While there is little doubt, then, that the Carajás Programme forms part of the Brazilian State's greatly expanded development role in eastern Amazonia, simultaneously generating opposition and countervailing pressure from various affected groups, the precise extent and nature of central government control is still highly debatable. A major question, however, concerns the extent of government influence over current events in the region. Is the current scenario, with its attendant agrarian crisis,a carefully scripted drama being played out along pre-established lines, or has the State unthinkingly created a situation over which it has lost control? This question has already been partially answered above when it was suggested that the PGC is part of a wider macro-economic and political strategy whose benefits, in the minds of key government decision-makers such as the PGC Interministerial Council, outweigh any social or ecological disadvantages. The agrarian crisis, in these terms, in seen as a necessary and inevitable cost of developing the region. While some of these adverse consequences might have been unforeseen, the general pattern had been well established in the 1970s and could only have been expected to worsen. Planners and politicians have not lacked adequate information upon which to base their investment policies. These have been, for the most part, conscious decisions over development priorities taken with full knowledge of the probable outcomes.

A second and parallel set of issues concerns the problem of identifying whose interests are being represented by the State machine in Amazonia, and the vexed question of whether the State exercises autonomy of decision-making in the process of regional development. The notion of State interests being totally subservient to the logic of capitalist expansion was discussed above and rejected as a useful theory for explaining the history of Amazonian settlement. It was suggested instead that the State has played a powerful and largely independent interventionist role in eastern Amazonia in pursuit of several goals; these include the generation of foreign exchange for debt servicing, the need of the CVRD, Brazil's State mining enterprise, to obtain cheap raw material supplies, and the expansion of mining activities to complement livestock production as a vehicle of regional and national economic growth. It has played an active rather than passive role in moulding the pattern of Amazonia's development. At the same time, however, it was recognised that pressure from overseas interests has acted in favour of defining development goals as a function of transnational mineral companies' global strategies. It is a moot point whether this has actually undermined Brazilian development choices in Amazonia, or simply fitted into an existing set of national priorities.

Yet although a strong case can be made for the concept of a powerful autonomous Brazilian State exercising increasing influence and control over Amazonian development as a component of national growth strategy, with the Carajás Programme forming a significant part of this wider picture, the argument is certainly not as straightforward as appears at first sight. While convenient as a theory, in practice it is virtually impossible to disaggregate public from private interests or to ascertain the extent to which official policy-making has been conditioned by the profit motives and production strategies of commercial enterprises. Private companies undoubtedly form an immensely powerful lobby in Brazil which has exerted considerable pressure on government in favour of prioritising commercial activities in Amazonia, such as the federal road-building programme, private colonisation, cattle ranching and, latterly, mining. In practice it is difficult to firmly allocate prime responsibilities for particular strategies, due to the blurring of boundaries between private and public sectors. It is an open secret, for example, that many politicians and members of the executive have strong business and family links with the construction industry, creating an in-built bias towards a particular kind of modernisation path in Amazonia based on large-scale, capital-intensive projects, as well as towards widespread corruption in the allocation of lucrative building contracts. Thus, rather than there being any fundamental conflict of purpose among State, domestic and foreign interests in Amazonian development over the past two decades, the notion of a 'triple alliance' (Evans, 1979) of largely coincidental, if occasionally diverging, interests is perhaps more appropriate.

From the point of view of the present analysis, a relevant issue is the extent to which progressive elements within the State apparatus are able to influence the formulation and implementation of policy initiatives which attempt to ameliorate the harsh impacts of mainstream activities, as manifested in Amazonia's emerging agrarian crisis. Based on the notion that the State is not a monolithic block acting along unified lines, areas may be highlighted in which particular government bodies have attempted, even if not always very successfully, to encourage more rational, less destructive development practice. Identifying these genuinely 'progressive' State components and distinguishing these from organisations set up purely for cosmetic purposes becomes a formidable task. The history of reformist or nominally redistributive measures in Amazonia is certainly not encouraging.

Several observers have suggested that much State intervention in Amazonia since the 1970s has been prompted by dissatisfaction with the failure of modernisation strategies to alleviate mass poverty (Bunker, 1985; Grindle, 1986). Compensatory programmes and projects were thus designed to help tackle this problem by targeting vulnerable groups, usually with substantial foreign aid funding. A popular model is that of integrated rural development, as conceived for the poorest regions, the North-East (POLONORDESTE and, more recently, the *Projeto Nordeste*) and north-west Amazonia (POLONOROESTE), both supported by the World Bank (World Bank, 1981a, 1983; CEPAC, n.d.). Not only have such programmes helped to diffuse demands for land reform but, in the case of POLONOROESTE, they have also served the State's geopolitical aims of consolidating Brazilian occupation of frontier zones, as with the recent *Calha Norte* scheme. By their very nature, such interventions have increased further still the State's direct influence over the national economy and society.

As far as the Carajás Programme is concerned, it is difficult enough to identify genuinely compensatory programmes which address the region's serious social and environmental problems. In this respect, the State's record is extremely poor; the cynical observer could be forgiven for believing that the only concern of government in the PGC is to generate as much revenue as possible, as quickly as possible, regardless of these wider costs. However, while this is probably a fair judgement of many key decision-makers' priorities at the highest levels within government and State enterprises active in the PGC, it by no means reflects the whole picture. Central government, or some more progressive elements within it, have been mindful of the longer-term deleterious effects of ceaseless rural violence and ecological destruction. Several State interventions in the Carajás area could be cited as examples of well-intentioned, if largely ineffective, attempts by government planners to tackle these growing problems; these include the activities of GETAT and the agrarian reform (PNRA) dealing with land issues, the *Carajás Agrícola* scheme and the work of environmentalists within the CVRD.

As Chapter 3 explained in some detail, GETAT was set up in 1980, attached to the National Security Council, as part of an attempt to diffuse land conflict in the extremely violent core of the Carajás Programme area centred around the 'parrot's beak'. Although GETAT granted 60,000 property titles involving an area of seven million hectares, the organisation was roundly condemned for distributing land highly unequally, consolidating a traditionally inegalitarian structure. Its resettlement schemes have fared little better, although they have offered a small avenue of mobility for peasant farmers. The 1985 agrarian reform law was a modest if promising initiative, intended ostensibly to redistribute under-utilised areas to landless farmers, yet this also has been rendered all but useless. Not only have large landowners used the PNRA as an excuse for selling off poor quality land but right-wing UDR pressure has weakened the relevant legislation to such an extent that, under the new constitution, it is a mere shadow of its former self. Furthermore, while the bureaucracy has been mainpulated to generate inertia and deliberately slow down the progress of 'sensitive' expropriations, those committed and reformist-minded elements of MIRAD and INCRA have been successively weakened and marginalised, problems compounded by a turnover of four MIRAD ministers in less than three years. Thus, although progressive State managers have had some success in tackling the land question this has, predictably, been very limited.

More specifically linked to the Carajás Programme itself, another area in which some attempt was made to devise a more balanced development programme was the Ministry of Agriculture's *Carajás Agrícola* plans, published in 1983, discussed at length in Chapter 2. While the proposals were clearly biased towards large-scale, capitalised production, provisions were made for accommodating smaller farmers. The failure of this plan to receive serious consideration by the Planning Ministry, despite any intrinsic faults in its design, illustrates the low priority attached by central government to systematic agricultural development in Amazonia, and of the limited powers of technicians who adopt an unconventional approach to this question. Bearing in mind the fact that the PGCA would have had to be reformulated in order to perform a more reformist role the State, nevertheless, has forfeited a unique opportunity for drawing up and implementing a pioneering initiative for helping in a small way to address the region's agrarian crisis.

One critical area on which progressive State managers have left their mark is environmental conservation. The CVRD's active environmental division, GEAMAM, has been a vociferous critic of company policy in this regard. As Chapter 4 demonstrated, members have not hesitated to chide the State company for its failure take environmental issues seriously. Many believe, for example, that although the company has no direct control over the activities of steel companies setting up pig-iron smelters along the railway corridor, the CVRD could do much more than it has done so far to ensure that minimal guidelines are followed to protect the rainforest. But despite forceful criticisms of their own company's attitudes, backed up by extensive and well-documented research into environmental impacts, GEAMAM's experts have been able to exert little influence on industrial policy for the Carajás region. Once again, critical social and ecological issues brought to the fore by State groups have been, to all intents and purposes, ignored by mainstream decision-makers, whose overriding concern is to implement as quickly as possible this strategy of Amazonian modernisation.

As if in belated recognition of the need to plan more rationally for the use of Amazonia's resource-base, the Executive Secretariat of the PGC issued further policy guidelines in 1985. While maintaining the existing emphasis on large-scale, export-oriented ventures, these new proposals stressed the crucial role of 'integrated planning' based on systematic, regional socio-economic studies, which would encourage the use of technology appropriate to the tropics, would reformulate the fiscal incentive scheme along more 'distributive' lines and would incorporate 'community participation' in the planning process to encourage the balanced growth of both industry and agriculture in the Carajás region (PGC, 1985b, pp. 15–20). While there is no sign at present of such rhetoric becoming reality, one step in this direction has been taken with the move to prepare overall guidelines which would serve as a basis for planning the overall development of a major part of the Carajás Programme.

This Master Plan, or *Plano Diretor*, embraces the 10% of the PGC area along the railway corridor (95,000 square kilometres) in which industrial, infrastructural and agricultural investments are concentrated. It is designed to guide industrial policy and social development in order to promote 'self-sustaining growth with (income) redistribution' (SEPLAN/PGC 1987, p. 4). The document recognises the limitations of past Amazon Basin development strategies based primarily on cattle ranching, accepting the need to encourage investments both for domestic and overseas markets. At the same time, however, it warns against predatory exploitation of Amazonia's natural wealth for purely short-term gain, and calls for a more rational use of resources.

Attributing a high priority to meeting the basic needs of the local population to land access, to employment creation and local self-determination, the plan suggests a greater decentralisation of decision-making. In order to help achieve these aims, it is proposed to introduce community participation through a variety of formal and informal channels. As something of an innovative planning initiative it clearly attempts to critically analyse the PGC's role and impact but, at the same time, recognises that planners at regional level can themselves do little without policies from central government which would support this concept of optimal resource-use within a more democratic planning framework. However, although this example appears to show that progressive State managers are, once again, attempting to make their influence felt in the policy-making process, it remains to be seen whether this results in significant changes in direction for the Carajás Programme. The fact that in mid-1988, eight year after the advent of the PGC, this Master Plan still existed only on paper and had not yet been formally adopted, is perhaps itself indicative of the low priority afforded by key decision-makers in the State to attempts at planning for socially and environmentally-sound development in the region. This pessimistic scenario could and, indeed, must change if Amazonia is to fulfil its true potential.

Carajás–development for the people?

Two major points have emerged from the foregoing discussion which are of crucial importance for future policy-making and implementation in the Greater Carajás region. Firstly, there exists a semi-subsistence farming population of some five million in eastern Amazonia which will not disappear in the foreseeable future. Although both Marxist and neo-classical modernisation analyses are based on the premise that the peasantry has no long-term prospects, as land becomes increasingly concentrated and production more capitalised, experience in Amazonia suggests otherwise. Not only does the large population of small farmers perform key macro-economic roles which will guarantee its preservation for a good while yet; its own social dynamic of resistance to land-grabbing and its struggle for self-preservation in the face of extreme adversity is becoming increasingly apparent. Any moves by policy-makers towards planning for more sustainable forms of development in the Carajás region will have to take account of this fact. The design and execution of large-scale projects in the region, either as if the peasantry did not exist, or as if it constituted a temporary and inconvenient obstacle to mainstream development activities, is no longer acceptable to the victims of this process or, indeed, to many of the planners involved.

This leads on to the second major point for consideration, namely, that the Brazilian State is not simply the passive tool of dominant domestic or international class interests. Successive governments and their commercial allies have, since the 1960s, had clear motives for pursuing the settlement and investment strategies witnessed in Amazonia. Despite the current global wave of criticism against State-led development as inefficient and international pressure in favour of decreasing levels of government intervention (IDS, 1987), there is no sign of a free market model being applied to Amazonia. The Brazilian State continues to play a leading role in development policy formulation and implementation in the region, through a variety of special programmes and fiscal measures which subsidise capital investment, as well through a large degree of increasingly centralised institutional control over regional activities.

The Carajás Programme is a prime example of this expanded government role. Despite aggravating the agrarian crisis, many advantages have accrued to the State from its investment strategies in the region during the 1980s. Yet it is also clear that not all planners share the same perspective on how best to tap the area's resources for national and regional development. The main thrust of policy-making has been short-sighted in its failure to take due account of the negative social and ecological consequences which have resulted from the drive to industrialise the Carajás railway corridor in the shortest possible time-span. In this sense the PGC and, indeed, most development strategy for Brazilian Amazonia has been moulded by governments which have chosen to allocate rents or benefits according to the distribution of political power rather than on the basis of broader considerations. This strategy has clearly been at odds with any pretensions towards economic efficiency or sustainable development. Although the State has perhaps acted rationally within its own narrow terms of reference, it has 'failed' to promote progress in the sense of encouraging a more rational resource-use which would spread these benefits to the wider population.

Increasingly, however, the wisdom of this approach is being questioned. This is due partly to doubts raised by progressive State managers themselves over critical issues such as deforestation and environmental pollution associated with the PGC's haphazard industrialisation strategy, reflected in proposals for a Carajás Master Plan, as well as in growing public debate of the issues. In addition, vociferous Brazilian and foreign lobbies have raised the public profile of the PGC and, by applying pressure through multilateral development banks and raising questions in the EEC parliament, have obliged planners to reconsider some current practices, notably concerning indigenous affairs. Clearly, then, the Brazilian State can exercise autonomy in decision-making and is susceptible to both internal and outside influence. While the extent and effectiveness of such pressure is highly debatable, it does suggest some room for manoeuvre in catering for the needs of the Carajás region's rural population of five million, hitherto largely ignored by policy-makers, in the design of rural investment programmes.

The notion of settling the Amazon Basin in a more carefully planned and systematic fashion to accommodate, on a sustainable basis, a much larger proportion of Brazil's landless farming population than current development strategy allows, still tends to be dismissed by government technicians and planners as romantic nonsense. Most official development practitioners still hold the view that progress in Amazonia can be achieved exclusively through the application of capital-intensive techniques in large-scale industrial and agro-livestock units, geared primarily to serving export markets. No clearer example of this philosophy exists than in the Carajás Programme itself. Yet research has demonstrated unequivocally that there are alternative methods which could be harnessed to at least complement, if not actually subsitute, the prevailing model; thus, many of the worst excesses of current development practices in eastern Amazonia could, in theory, be avoided as long as appropriate political and institutional support were forthcoming. Although an exhaustive survey of environmentally appropriate, sustainable development practices for Amazonia is beyond the scope of this book, even a brief survey of the growing practical experience in this field for Amazonia will illustrate the agronomic potential which exists, but is largely untapped and ignored by the State planning machine.

The Brazilian State's anti-peasant bias was, perhaps unwittingly, reinforced by ecologists during the 1970s who challenged developers' early assumptions about Amazonia's apparent fertility, suggesting instead that the deceptively verdant rainforest canopy hid soils which were essentially too infertile for widespread agriculture. Large-scale settlement and crop production would induce major permanent damage to the ecosystem, transforming it into a 'red desert' (Goodland and Irwin, 1975). The tropical rainforest, it was suggested, should be left intact and development efforts transferred elsewhere to less environmentally problematic regions such as the savanna grasslands of the central plateau, or *cerrado* (Goodland, 1980). Yet an increasingly large body of multi-disciplinary applied research is demonstrating that these early prognoses were perhaps over-pessimistic and that, in fact, much more scope exists for the widespread practice of small farmer agroforestry than had previously been thought possible.

Investigations and experiments carried out in a variety of Amazonia's numerous micro-ecosystems have shown that 'sustainable development' is indeed possible. The concept of sustainability is crucial; it refers to the farming or forest system's ability to support its human managers, as well as supplying commercial customers, maintaining both productivity and livelihoods on a long-term basis without incurring irreparable damage to the ecosystem (Redclift, 1986, 1987). Sustainability thus signifies social as well as ecological soundness. Clearly, current models of developing Amazonia do not fall into this category. Their inherent lack of sustainability is well illustrated by the agrarian crisis which has gripped eastern Amazonia and the Carajás Programme area, leading to a spiral of increasing land concentration, rural violence, poverty and permanent environmental decay. Yet a shift in the way the State utilises Amazonian territory in pursuit of national growth could help avoid the worst excesses of current land-use patterns in the region. This notion is not based on a blanket condemnation of 'cash crops' as the source of all evil, and concentration on staple commodities as the sole solution to the small farmer's plight. Apart from helping to meet local and regional food requirements, the more widespread use of appropriate agricultural and silvicultural systems should be capable of generating a commercial surplus of industrial and food crops for export.

Provided that security of land tenure and minimal institutional support are supplied to peasant farmers by the State on a broader and more committed front, there is every reason to expect that

Amazonia could offer far more sustainable options for forest management and agricultural expansion. Although official development planners and politicians have been dismissive of traditional farming systems in Amazonia, such judgements have been premature and sweeping. While bias in favour of capital-intensive farming has been largely inspired by political factors, it has also rested to some extent upon sheer ignorance of the enormous potential for economic and social progress offered by more indigenous, locally-adapted methods. As well as successful examples of natural forest management, applications of appropriate farming methods compatible with the rainforest environment are far more common than is generally recognised by planners. However, although these experiences remain relatively small-scale, they could be widely replicated over much larger areas of the Amazon Basin.

Of central concern to the one million small cultivators and their families living primarily off the land in eastern Amazonia, is the potential for sustainable agriculture, both on the fertile alluvial floodplains, or *várzeas*, and the upland *terra firme*. The critical point has been made that, as long as certain basic principles are observed concerning integration with the forest, crop diversity, nutrient recycling, weed and pest control and, most importantly, adaptation to local conditions, 'the intensive use of small plots...can be applied to almost any tropical environment' (Gradwohl and Greenberg, 1988, p. 105). This is as true for the Amazon Basin as elsewhere. As Furley (1989) and others have pointed out, although only some 7% of Amazonia has no fertility problems whatsoever, physical conditions in the region are generally favourable for agro-pastoral and silvicultural development provided that drainage is adequate and soil conservation is practised. Considerable potential therefore exists for increasing crop production on Amazonia's varied soils using low-input technologies which combine traditional (indigenous or *caboclo*) methods with new techniques.

Although the *várzeas* cover only 2% of Amazonia, they have considerable agricultural potential and it has been estimated that, with proper flood control, small farmer production of irrigated rice, tree crops, food crops and jute, as well as water buffalo and fish, could be substantially increased without damaging the environment (Barrow, 1985). Field research has shown that, in spite of natural obstacles and their exclusion from official support programmes such as PROVARZEAS, Amazonian riverine farmers have frequently been successful in sustaining production systems based on forest management, conventional crops and forest-extracted products such as fruits, timber, medicinal plants and wild game (Barrow, 1988; Gradwohl and Greenberg, 1988). However, although floodplain agriculture has been practised in Central and South America for centuries, and appeals have been made to successive Brazilian governments for Amazonian *várzea* farmers to be given greater support, there has so far been little official response.

The record of State-sponsored small farmer development is little better for the 70% of Amazonia which consists of *terra firme*. These upland areas have predominantly poor, acidic soils (oxisols and ultisols), with very fertile patches an exception, in which the ecological balance has in the past been maintained by low-population-density agroforestry and shifting cultivation. Indigenous groups and indian-descended (*caboclo*) farmers achieved widespread sustainability until the region was opened up for development from the mid-1960s onwards, and, indeed, continue to do so in many still isolated parts. However, as Chapter 4 demonstrated, the system of slash-and-burn farming is rapidly becoming destructive under the joint pressures of population and commercial occupation, while indian land and culture is under constant threat. Agricultural research and development in Brazilian Amazonia has paid scant attention to the productive potential of small-scale, locally adapted techniques; agricultural development plans for the Carajás Programme are a prime example of such neglect.

However, an abundance of research evidence now supports the notion that a combination of indigenous and scientifically-adapted agriculture could support a much larger rural population than many policy-makers suggest. Opinions to the contrary are expressions of political priority rather than agronomic reality. Many examples exist, both in Amazonia and elsewhere, of how rural production can be made sustainable in areas of tropical rainforest. These include not only long-established extractive and agroforestry activities, but also sedentary agriculture and even livestock production. Involving not just indian groups but also peasant farmers, small-scale commercials producers and even extensive cattle ranchers, socially and environmentally sound practices already exist on *terra firme* lands which could be more widely replicated under appropriate circumstances.

New settlers in Amazonia have, for over sixty years, been clearing upland forest for the growing of annual crops such as rice, beans, corn, cassava and yams. Under intensive, uncontrolled occupation, with inappropriate techniques transferred from other regions of the country, often compounded by harrassment from land-grabbers, yields soon decline after a few harvests, game is hunted out and the farmer is obliged to move on, setting in motion a process of potentially destructive shifting cultivation. In contrast, non-destructive agroforestry has long been practiced by Brazil's Amerindian and *caboclo* population. This enables them to grow a wider range of annuals and perennials such as fruit and tree crops, while maintaining soil fertility and facilitating forest regeneration (Barrow, 1985, 1988). Many examples can be cited which demonstrate sustainable agroforestry practices in fragile areas of tropical rainforest.

Studies of the Kayapó tribe in southern Pará, for example, have shown how careful species classification and forest management have enabled them to satisfy their basic food, fuel, construction and medicinal needs while preserving the region's ecological balance (Posey, 1983, 1985; Anderson and Posey, 1985). This principle could certainly be diffused and it has been suggested that, 'there is little to prevent the Kayapó's efficient and sustainable agriculture from being fruitfully applied in other parts of the world' (Gradwohl and Greenberg, 1988, p. 125). This type of swidden-fallow management is also used by the Bora people of Peru's Amazon Basin, as well as in other regions of Central America and Africa (Denevan *et al*, 1984; Richards, 1985; Gradwohl and Greenberg, 1988), while the sustainable use of forests is also well-illustrated by Brazil's own 'extractive reserves' set up by rubber tappers in the western state of Acre. The *caboclo* inhabitants of the River Amazon's estuary floodplain have also shown great adaptability to their environment, combining rational forest management and extracted products such as fruits, palm hearts and honey with conventional staple food crops.

Great potential also exists for extending complementary, non-agricultural, extractivist activities, which account for up to one-third of household income in rural Amazonia (Hecht, 1988). For example, the cultivation and use of the *babaçú* palm, which grows widely in the transition zone between north-east Brazil and the Amazon Basin, in the state of Maranhão as well as in Goiás and, indeed, in other countries such as Bolivia, Colombia and Mexico, could be expanded in the region (Anderson, 1985; May *et al* 1985; Hecht *et al*, 1988a). *Babaçú* palm is closely integrated with pastoral activities and shifting cultivation, and in many tropical areas is a key component of the peasant household economy. Since it is suitable for areas of marginal soils and sparse population, research strongly suggests that it could make a significant contribution to the design of sustainable rural development in Amazonia.

Although there is ample scope for improving techniques of shifting cultivation in association with extractivism and other silivicultural activities, it has also been demonstrated that, generally speaking, more sedentary forms of agriculture are viable in Amazonia under the right conditions. Even if, due to the policy bias in Brazilian agriculture, these examples are at present few and far between, it is recognised that low-cost, low-input technologies can stabilise smallholders farming, increasing productivity and improving standards of living. However, new forms of production do need to be carefully tailored to particular micro-environments in the region based on principles such as site-specific crop patterns and soil management, minimal use of chemical fertilisers and machinery, knowledge of local soil patterns and maintenance of organic litter (Charlton, 1987; Furley, 1989). Techniques of fertility restoration through fallow management, improved tillage and the use of intercropping are all techniques which have produced very positive results in tropical rainforest areas.

One of the best-known examples of successful, small-scale commercial agroforestry can be seen at Tomé Açú, south of Belém (Barrow, 1989; Gradwohl and Greenberg, 1988). Established in 1924, Tomé Açú, now with two 'satellite' communities, has several hundred smallholders, each cultivating plots of between twenty and eighty hectares. Through a process of carefully studied land management, fast-growing annual crops such as cotton, rice and beans are intercropped with perennial vines such as black pepper and passion fruit, as well as tree crops such as cocoa, oil palm and rubber. The co-operative, CAMTA, has been instrumental in providing support to the farmers for marketing, which includes the sale of products in the USA and Europe, and for agricultural experimentation. While the success of Tomé Açú is often attributed primarily or even solely to the innate entrepreneurial talents of its Japanese-descended population, one researcher concluded that, 'there seemed to be nothing unusual about Tomé Açú's agricultural practices that would prevent their being replicated elsewhere in Amazonia by other migrant groups with different backgrounds' (Barrow, 1988, p. 17).

Results of the Yurimaguas experiments in Peruvian Amazonia have also been encouraging in this respect, showing that low-fertility ultisols can produce sustainable yields of rice, maize, groundnuts and soya under careful farm management and site-specific fertiliser regimes (Nicholaides *et al*, 1983; Charlton, 1987). In contrast, studies of private colonisation in southern Pará (Butler, 1985; Moran, 1987, 1989) have made it clear that its indifferent economic performance and highly varied farmer yields owe much to migrants' failure to adapt agricultural practices to the Amazonian environment, as well as to poor management and overall planning. Smaller-scale examples of successful agroforestry are also to be found in the Zona Bragantina area, near Belém, as well as near the cities of Manaus, Santarém, Monte Alegre and Cametá.

However, although such techniques offer considerable potential for combining commercial profitability with sustainability, agroforestry is a complex and intricate form of land-use which is dependent upon several preconditions for success (Anderson, 1987). Not only does it require high inputs of both labour and capital, but it is vulnerable to fluctuating world commodity prices and pest attacks. A highly risky enterprise, its widespread transferability in Amazonia has been questioned by many observers, who stress the need for continued research into less capital-intensive agroforestry systems than that of Tome-Açú, for example, which would be more suitable for poorer, isolated rural communities.

The most roundly condemned form of Amazonian settlement has undoubtedly been cattle ranching facilitated by SUDAM and, latterly, even Carajás tax credits. As the largest single activity on cleared Amazonian land, its disastrous environmental and social impact on the region has been widely documented (see Chapters 3 and 4). With its high rate of pasture degradation and abandonment, livestock production in Amazonia has itself been described as a type of shifting cultivation. Research has suggested, however, that if properly implemented its effects need not be so catastrophic. Careful grazing management, it has been argued, could render cattle-raising economically viable (as opposed to concealing a merely speculative investment in land) and could even be used to upgrade depleted areas and increase carrying capacity (Falesi, 1976; Alvim, 1980).

However, research currently under way in the Paragominas area of Pará has shown that reclamation of degraded pastures is proving exceedingly difficult (Gradwohl and Greenberg, 1988), although experiments in Roraima with grassland improvements have proved more promising (Barrow, 1988). Most observers, however, see little future for the expansion of cattle ranching as a sustainable activity in ecological terms. Recent work on this area based on simulations has tended to confirm the suspicion that, even though livestock activities could be profitably expanded in Amazonia without subsidies given favourable pricing conditions, this would be at the cost of extensive land clearance and overgrazing (Hecht *et al*, 1988b). Socially, of course, as experience over the past two decades has demonstrated, the spread of huge livestock enterprises would merely benefit large landowners, increasing the pressure on smallholdings further still, without offering compensatory employment opportunities.

If any single message has emerged from this growing body of research, it is that there exists no single solution, no panacea for sustainable development in the region. This can only be achieved through adapting techniques to a wide range of agro-ecosystems, which will involve shifting cultivation and sedentary methods, annual and perennial crops, silvicultural plantations, extractivism and possibly even some pasture formation. Neither should the importance of wage labour, albeit largely seasonal and temporary, be underestimated as an increasingly important source of off-farm income under conditions of precarious agricultural production. Studies of waged activities in various parts of Amazonia (Hecht, 1988), for example, show that it can account for up to 80% of household income. Although there are, in practice, various ways in which sustainable income-generation may be promoted in the Amazon Basin, it would be highly misleading to suggest that technical improvements alone will be adequate; they are a necessary but, on their own, an inadequate basis for broader development without the institutional and political support necessary to make successful experiments replicable on a wider scale. The enormity of this task is awesome given both the physical and political constraints which exist upon progressive development practitioners, both within and outside the State machine, in their attempts to challenge the current settlement model and its neglect of smallholders. The list of essential prerequisites would have to include security of land tenure (titled or otherwise), guaranteed minimum commodity and crop prices, adequate support in the form of credit, proper extension advice and other farm inputs, a sound marketing system, as well as farmer participation in the design of appropriate rural strategies.

While many of these principles have elsewhere been expounded as necessary preconditions for successful, poverty-targeted development (Shaner *et al*, 1982; Chambers, 1983; Richards, 1985), in Brazil they remain, at best, marginal to the declared priorities of official policy. Agricultural commodity prices, for example, are not only determined by the vagaries of fluctuating world markets but are also artificially depressed by the government to keep urban food prices down. Furthermore, even when crop production can be successfully sustained, unless surplus extraction through traditional mechanisms of unequal exchange can be controlled, peasant households may become decapitalised and the incentives to continued farming removed, diverted perhaps to mini-land speculation. Even land reform, often highlighted by critics as the major obstacle to the expansion of peasant farming activities in Brazil, will be of limited use to small cultivators unless they receive complementary support to strengthen their productive capacity in the long term.

It has often been suggested that the biggest single short-term contribution to reducing environmental decay and encouraging more sustainable forms of land settlement would be for the Brazilian government to suspend SUDAM tax subsidies to pasture formation and cattle ranching. However, the continued political importance of State support for the livestock sector and the businessmen who invest in it, despite the negative economic and socio-environmental consequences, is reflected in the latest development plan for Amazonia under the New Republic. This envisages increases in credit available through POLAMAZONIA, FINAM and other special programmes, although with 'adjustments' to improve their efficacy (Brazil, 1986, pp. 129–53). The political sensitivity in Brazil of the subject is also well-illustrated by President Sarney's declaration, in July 1987, that he did not 'even want to hear' about the possibility of abolishing these subsidies (*Isto É*, 15.7.87).

Yet the reduction of fiscal incentives, while in itself probably a crucial first step, would not necessarily stop pasture formation in Amazonia. Large enterprises derive institutional rents not just from tax incentives but also from other factors such as rising land values under hyperinflation and cheap credit politics. It should also be borne in mind that small-scale land speculation, without the benefit of State subsidies, is quite widely practised by peasant households as a survival strategy and one of the only means of capital formation in the absence of supportive agricultural policy or other stable employment opportunities. As far as the Carajás Programme is concerned, its own fiscal incentive scheme for livestock as well as charcoal production for mineral processing, discussed at length in Chapter 4, is clearly at odds with any notion of sustainable development. The belated preparation of a so-called 'Master Plan' for the Carajás railway corridor has done little to temper such misgivings.

While technical solutions for sustainable development are probably within the grasp of forward-looking planners, the emergence of broader socio-political conditions which would allow these solutions to be applied are only at an embryonic stage. Without major political support, at both domestic and internationals levels, for a broad strategy of sustainable development in Amazonia, the livelihoods of the rural poor are unlikely to see substantial improvements. There is little indication that progressive State managers are strong enough to bring about such a policy swing, although pressure from concerned national and overseas organisations may be starting to have some impact on decision-making in the Carajás Programme and other parts of Amazonia. At the same time, the vast majority of Amazonia's peasantry remains marginalised by the formal party system and even the trades union structure, leaving small farmers with little direct influence on planning through such institutional channels.

The victims of this development pattern have not accepted their fate altogether passively. They have, rather, engaged in various forms of social protest against the actions of the State and its allied commercial interests, questioning the fundamental premises upon which current Amazon development strategy is based. At the same time, the need for such countervailing action is a sad comment on the role of official policy-making for Amazonia and its failure to cater for peasant farmer and Amerindian needs. Yet in leaving their mark as a force to be reckoned with, the victims of this model have made a lasting contribution towards ensuring a more promising future for the Carajás region. This should entail not, as many planners would have it, the wholesale extinction of small cultivators as archaic obstacles to commercial and industrial expansion, but their full incorporation into Amazonian and Brazilian development strategy.

Bibliography

The Agribusiness Council (ed.) (1975), *Agricultural Initiative in the Third World*, Lexington Books, London.

Almeida Jnr., J. M. C. de (ed.) (1986) *Carajás: Desafio Político, Ecologia e Desenvolvimento*, CNPq/Brasiliense, São Paulo.

Alvim, P. (1980), 'Agricultural Potential of the Amazon Basin', in Barbira-Scazzocchio (ed.), pp. 27–36.

Amnesty International (1988), *Brazil: Authorized Violence in Rural Areas*, London.

Anderson, A. (1972), 'Farming the Amazon: The Devastation Technique', Saturday Review, V, Part 55, pp. 61–64.

Anderson, A. (1987), *Forest Management Issues in the Brazilian Amazon*, Consultancy Report to the Ford Foundation, Museo Goeldi, Belém.

Anderson A. and S. (1985), 'A Tree of Life Grows in Brazil', *Natural History*, 12, pp. 41–46.

Anderson, A. and Posey, D. (1985), 'Manejo de cerrado pelos índios Kayapó', *Boletim do Museo Paraense Emílio Goeldi*, II, 1, pp. 77–98.

Andrade M., Santos, M. and Nutti, M. (1983), 'Estrutura Agrária e Colonização na Fronteira Amazônica', *mimeo*.

Asselin, V. (1982), *Grilagem: Corrupção e Violência em Terras do Carajás*, Vozes/CPT, Rio de Janeiro.

Baer, W. (1975), *A Industrialização e o Desenvolvimento Econômico do Brasil*, Fundação Getúlio Vargas, Rio de Janeiro.

Baer, W. (1986), 'Growth With Inequality: The Cases of Brazil and Mexico', *Latin American Research Review*, XXI, 2, pp. 197–208.

Baer, W. *et al.* (eds.) (1978), *Dimensões do Desenvolvimento Brasileiro*, Editora Campus, Rio de Janeiro.

Baiardi, A. (1982), 'O que se espera da agricultura', *Ciência Hoje*, I, 3, November–December, pp. 42–43.

Baker, G. (1973), 'Good Climate for Agribusiness', *The Nation*, 5, pp. 456–462.

Bakx, K. (1987), 'Planning Agrarian Reform: Amazonian Settlement Projects, 1970–86', *Development and Change*, XVIII, pp. 533–555.

Bakx, K. (1989), 'The Shanty Town, Final Stage of Rural Development? The Case of Acre', in Goodman and Hall (eds.), forthcoming.

Barbira-Scazzocchio, F. (ed.) (1980), *Land, People and Planning in Contemporary Amazonia*, Centre of Latin American Studies, University of Cambridge.

Barham, J. and Caulfied, C., (1984), 'The problems that plague a Brazilian dam', *New Scientist*, 11 October.

Barrow, C. (1985). 'The development of the *várzeas* (floodlands) of Brazilian Amazonia', in Hemming (ed.), pp. 108–127.

Barrow, C. (1986), 'The Impact of Hydroelectric Development on the Amazon Environment, With Particular Reference to the Tucuruí Project', *mimeo*. Paper presented to the Brazil Workshop seminar, London School of Economics and Political Science, 21 November.

Barrow, C. (1988), 'Environmentally Appropriate, Small-Farm Strategies for Amazonia', *mimeo*, Centre for Development Studies, University College, Swansea. Also included in Goodman and Hall (eds.), forthcoming 1989.

Batista, D. (1976), *O Complexo da Amazônia*, Conquista, Rio de Janeiro.

Batista Filho, M. (1985), 'Panorama alimentar e nutricional do Brasil', in Minayo (ed.). pp. 32–47.

Becker, B. (1982), *Geopolítica da Amazônia*, Zahar, Rio de Janeiro.

Benvenuti, B. (1975), 'General systems theory and entrepreneurial autonomy in farming: towards a new feudalism or towards democratic planning?', *Sociologia Ruralis*, XV, 1–2, pp. 47–62.

Boff, L. (1984), *Do Lugar do Pobre*, Vozes, Petrópolis.

Bonfim, S. (1958), *Valorização da Amazônia e Sua Comissão de Planejamento*, SPVEA, Coleção Araujo Lima, Rio de Janeiro.

Bourne, R. (1978), *Assault on the Amazon*, Gollancz, London.

Branford, S. and Glock, P. (1985), *The Last Frontier: Fighting Over Land in the Amazon*, Zed Press, London.

Brazil (1971), *I Plano Nacional de Desenvolvimento (1970–74)*, IBGE, Rio de Janeiro.

Brazil (1983), *Programa Grande Carajás Agrícola: Versão Preliminar*, Ministry of Agriculture, Brasília.

Brazil (1986), *I Plano Nacional de Desenvolvimento da Amazônia, Nova República*, SUDAM, Belém.

Brundtland Report (1987), *Our Common Future*, Oxford University Press, Oxford and New York.

Bruno, E. S. (1967), *História Geral do Brasil*, Cultrix, São Paulo.

Bunker, S. (1985), *Underdeveloping the Amazon: Extraction, Unequal Exchange and the Failure of the Modern State*, University of Illinois Press, Urbana and Chicago.

Burger, D. and Kitamura, P. (1987), 'Importância e viabilidade de uma pequena agricultura sustentada na Amazônia oriental', in Kohlepp and Schrader (eds.), pp. 447–461.

Butler, J. (1985), *Land, Gold and Farmers: Agricultural Colonization and Frontier Expansion in the Brazilian Amazon*, Ph.D. thesis, University of Florida.

Camargo, J. (1973), *Urbanismo Rural*, INCRA, Brasília.

Campanhole, A. (1969), *Legislação Agrária*, Editora Atlas, São Paulo.

Cardoso, F. H. and Muller, G. (1977), *Amazônia: Expansão do Capitalismo*, Editora Brasiliense, São Paulo.

Carneiro, R. (ed.) (1986), *Política Econômica da Nova República*, Paz e Terra, Rio de Janeiro.

Carvalho, J. C. M. and Borgonovi, M. N. (1986), 'Cinco anos de atividades sobre a conservação do meio ambiente na CVRD. Participação do GEA-MAM e das CIMAs', *Espaço, Ambiente e Planejamento*, I, 3, March, pp. 3–22.

Caulfield, C. (1982a), *Tropical Moist Forests*, Earthscan, London.

Caulfield, C. (1982b), 'Brazil, energy and the Amazon', *New Scientist*, 28 October.

Caulfield, C. (1984), 'The $62 billion question', *New Statesman*, 23 March.

Caulfield, C. (1986), *In the Rainforest*, Pan Books, London.

CEDI (1985), *Povos Indígenas do Brasil. Vol. 8, Sudeste do Pará (Tocantins)*, São Paulo.

CEDI (1987), *Povos Indígenas do Brasil – 85/86*, São Paulo.

CEPAC (n.d.), *Projeto Nordeste: A Proposta Regional*, Teresina.

CEPASP (1986), 'Questões Fundiárias', mimeo., Marabá.

Chambers, R. (1983), *Rural Development: Putting the Last First*, Longman, London.

Charlton, C. (1987), 'Problems and prospects for sustainable agriculture in the humid tropics', *Applied and Geography*, VII, 2, pp. 153–174.

Cleary, D. (1986), 'The Social and Economic Implications of the Amazon Gold Rush', mimeo. Paper presented to the Brazil Agrarian Change Workshop, Institute of Latin American Studies, University of Liverpool, 19 December.

CNBB (1976), *Pastoral da Terra: Estudos do CNBB*, Edições Paulinas, São Paulo.

CNBB (1986), Telexed statement on land reform and rural violence, Brasília, 13 May.

CNI (1969), *A Indústria Brasileira e a Amazônia*, Edição do Serviço Social da Indústria, Departamento Nacional, Rio de Janeiro.

Coelho, J. (1985), *Por Qué Reforma Agrária?* Fundação Joaquim Nabuco, Recife.

Collins, J. (1986), 'Smallholder Settlement of Tropical South America; The Social Causes of Ecological Destruction', *Human Organization*, LV, 1, pp. 1–10.

Construtora Brasil (1987), Interview with company staff, 14 August.

CONTAG (1986), Official agreement between CHESF and rural workers affected by the Itaparica dam, dated 6 December, accompanied by letter dated 11 December.

Correio Brasiliense, Various reports.

Correio do Tocantins, 'CEDERE I, CEDERE II, CEDERE III', 8 August, 1987.

Costa, G. (1987), 'Brazilian Foreign Policy Towards South America During the Geisel and Figueiredo Administrations', mimeo. Paper presented to the Brazil Workshop seminar, London School of Economics and Political Science, 20 March.

Costa, J. M. da (ed.) (1979), *Amazônia: Desenvolvimento e Ocupação*, IPEA/INPES, Rio de Janeiro.

Cota, R.G. (1984), *Carajás: A Invasão Desarmada*, Vozes, Petrópolis.

CPI (1987), 'Hydroelectrics of the Xingú and Indigenous People', *mimeo.*, São Paulo.

CPP (1987), Archival data, São Luís.

CPT (1979), *As Ilhas de Resistência: Os Lavradores no Vale do Rio São Francisco*, Secretariado Nacional, Goîania.

CPT (1986), 'Projeto Carajás II e III: Menina dos Olhos do GETAT', *mimeo.*, Marabá.

CPT–Marabá (1987), Interview with staff, 11 August.

CPT Norte II (1985), 'Violência no Campo: Recorde de Violência: 55 Mortos, Janeiro à Junho de 1985', *mimeo.*, Belém.

CPT Norte II (1987), 'Marcha Lenta da Reforma Agrária no Pará e Balanço da Violência no Campo', *mimeo.*, Belém.

CVRD (1979), *Corredor de Carajás: Projetos Potenciais*, n.p.

CVRD (1980), *Amazônia Oriental: Um Projeto Nacional de Exportação*, n.p.

CVRD (1981a), *Amazônia Oriental: Plano Preliminar de Desenovlvimento*, n.p.

CVRD (1981b), *Projeto Ferro Carajás*, Rio de Janeiro.

CVRD (1984a), 'Carajas Iron-Ore Project: Industry and Environment', *mimeo.* Paper presented at UNEP *World Industry Conference of Environment Management*, Versailles, November.

CVRD (1984b), 'Carajás Iron-Ore Project. CVRD Cares: the essential human, environmental and social work undertaken by the CVRD', *mimeo.* Paper presented at the Commission of the European Communities, Brussels and Luxembourg, 21 February.

CVRD (1984c), *Aptidão Pedoclimática: Zoneamento Por Produto*, Rio de Janeiro.

CVRD (1985), *Carajás 1985*, Rio de Janeiro.

CVRD (1986), 'Carajás: Manganês do Azul', *CVRD Revista*, VII, 24, June.

CVRD (1987), *Estudo Impacto Ambiental e Desenvolvimento Sócio-Econômico ao Longo da Estrada de Ferro Carajás*, CVRD/SUMEI, Rio de Janeiro.

CVRD–Carajás (1987), Interview with security personnel, 5 August.

CVRD/SEMA/IWRD (1986), 'Recommendations of the Seminar on Economic Development and Environmental Impact in Areas of Brazilian Humid Tropics', *mimeo.* Held in Belém, 29 September–4 October.

CVRD/SUMIC (1987), *Anexo 1 ao Plano de Defesa de Carajás*, Carajás, 19 May.

Davis, S. (1977), *Victims of the Miracle*, Cambridge University Press, Cambridge.

Dean, W. (1987), *Brazil and the Struggle for Rubber*, Cambridge University Press, Cambridge.

de Barros, H. O. M. (1985), 'Modernização Agrícola no Baixo São Francisco', *Cadernos de Estudos Sociais*, I, 1, January–July, pp. 97–113.

de Freitas, M. de Lourdes Davies and Smyrski-Shluger, C. M. (n.d.), 'Brazil's Carajás Iron-Ore Project–Environmental Aspects', *mimeo.*, CVRD, Rio de Janeiro.

de Janvry, A. (1981), *The Agrarian Question and Reformism in Latin America*, Johns Hopkins University Press, Baltimore and London.

del Quiaro, R. (1985a), 'Brazil to drown forest in herbicides', *New Scientist*, 14 February.

del Quiaro, R. (1985b), 'Amazon war gives birth to a Robin Hood legend', *The Observer*, 7 July.

Denevan, W. *et al.* (1984), 'Indigenous Agroforestry in the Peruvian Amazon: Bora Indian Management of Swidden Fallows', *Interciência*, IX, 6, November–December, pp. 346–357.

Dória, P. *et al.* (1978), *A Guerrilha do Araguaia*, Alfa-Omega, São Paulo.

dos Santos, B. A. (1986), 'Recursos Minerais', in Almeida Jnr. (ed.), pp. 294–361.

Dumont, R. and Cohen, N. (1980), *The Growth of Hunger*, Marion Boyars, London and Boston.

The Economist, Various reports.

EDF (1987), 'EDF, World Environmental Community Denounce World Bank Involvement in Amazon Deforestation Plan', *News Release*, 7 August, Washington D.C.

ELETROBRAS (1987), *Plano 2010*, Brasília.

EMATER (1986), Interview with officials, Belém.

EMBRAPA (1982), *Projeto Grãos*, Brasília.

Emmi, M. F. (1985), *Estrutura Fundiária e Poder Local: O Caso de Marabá*, M.Sc. thesis, Núcleo de Áltos Estudos Amazônicos, Universidade Federal do Pará, Belém.

Emmi, M. F. (1986), 'Os castanhais do Tocantins: Da terra livre ao controle oligárquico', *O Liberal*, 13 July.

English, B. A. (1984), *Alcoa na Ilha*, Cáritas Brasileira, São Luís.

Estado do Maranhão, Various reports.

Esterci, N. (1987), *Conflito no Araguaia: Peões e Posseiros Contra a Grande Empresa*, Vozes, Petrópolis.

Evans, P. (1979), *Dependent Development: The Alliance of Multinational, State and Local Capital in Brazil*, Princeton University Press, Princeton, New Jersey.

Facó, R. (1976), *Cangaceiros e Fanáticos*, Civilização Brasileira, Rio de Janeiro.

Falesi, I. (1976), 'Ecosistema de Pastagem Cultivada na Amazônia Brasileira', *Boletim Técnico I*, EMBRAPA, Belém.

Falesi, I. (1986), Interview at EMBRAPA, Belém, 8 April.

Falesi, I., Freire, E. and Teixeira Silva, L. (1986), *Levantamento de reconhecimento de media intensidade dos solos e avaliação da aptidão agrícola das terras da area da Estrada de Ferro Carajás*, CVRD, Belém.

FASE (1987), Interview with staff, São Luís, 19 August.

Fearnside, P. (1979), 'Cattle Yield Predictions for the Trans-Amazon Highway of Brazil', *Interciencia*, IV, 4, July–August, pp. 220–225.

Fearnside, P. (1983), 'Development Alternatives in the Brazilian Amazon: An Ecological Evaluation', *Interciencia*, VIII, 2, March–April, pp. 65–78.

Fearnside, P. (1984a), 'Brazil's Amazon Settlement Schemes', *Habitat*

International, VIII, 1, pp. 45–61.

Fearnside, P. (1984b), 'A Floresta Vai Acabar?', *Ciência Hoje*, II, 10, January–February, pp. 43–52.

Fearnside, P. (1985a), 'Deforestation and Decision-Making in the Development of the Brazilian Amazon', *Interciencia*, X, 5, September–October, pp. 243–247.

Fearnside, P. (1985b), 'Agriculture in Amazonia', in Prance and Lovejoy (eds.), pp. 393–418.

Fearnside, P. (1986a), 'Spatial Concentration of Deforestation in the Brazilian Amazon', *Ambio*, XV, 2, pp. 74–81.

Fearnside, P. (1986b), 'Agricultural Plans for Brazil's Grande Carajás Program: Lost Opportunity for Sustainable Local Development?' *World Development*, XIV, 3, March, pp. 385–409.

Fearnside, P. (1986c), *Human Carrying Capacity of the Brazilian Rainforest*, Columbia University Press, New York.

Fearnside, P. (1987a), 'Frenesí de desmatamento no Brasil: a floresta Amazônica irá sobreviver?' in Kohlepp and Schrader (eds.), pp. 45–57.

Fearnside, P. (1987b), 'Jarí aos dezoito anos: Lições para os planos silviculturais em Carajás', in Kohlepp and Schrader (eds.), pp. 291–311.

Fearnside, P. (1988), 'Jari at Age 19: Lessons for Brazil's Silvicultural Plans at Carajás', *Interciencia*, XIII, 1, January–February, pp. 12–24.

Fearnside, P. (1989), 'Environmental Destruction in the Brazilian Amazon', in Goodman and Hall (eds.), forthcoming.

Ferraz, I. (1982), 'Os Índios Pagam Primerio e Mais Caro', *Ciência Hoje*, I, 3, November–December, pp. 51–53.

Ferraz, I. (1986), 'Programa Grande Carajás: Avaliação e Perspectivas', *mimeo.*, Centro de Trabalho Indigenista, São Paulo.

Ferraz, I. and Ladeira, M. (1988), 'Os povos indígenas na Amazônia Oriental e o Programma Grande Carajás: Avaliação e Perspectivas', *mimeo.*, Centro de Trabalho Indigenista, São Paulo. Paper presented at the 46th International Congress of Americanists, Amsterdam, July.

FETAPE/CONTAG (1987), 'Zona Canavieira Pernambuco, Campanha Salarial 1987, Informe 1 & 2', *mimeo.*, October–September.

Financial Times, Various reports.

Fleuret, P. and A. (1980), 'Nutrition, Consumption and Agricultural Change', *Human Organization*, XXXIX, 3, pp. 250–260.

Flynn, P. (1978), *Brazil: A Political Analysis*, Ernest Benn, London.

Folha de São Paulo, Various reports.

Foweraker, J. (1981), *The Struggle for Land: A Political Economy of the Pioneer Frontier in Brazil From 1930 to the Present Day*, Cambridge University Press, Cambridge.

Freire, P. (1970), *Pedagogia do Oprimido*, Paz e Terra, Rio de Janeiro.

Furley, P. (1989), 'The Nature and Sustainability of Brazilian Amazon Soils', in Goodman and Hall (eds.), forthcoming.

Furtado, C. (1968), *The Economic Growth of Brazil*, University of California Press, Berkeley and Los Angeles.

Galvão, J. G. (1987), 'Os Incentivos Fiscais na Amazônia: Resultados e Problemas dos Projetos Agropecuários', *Dados Conjunturais da Agro-*

pecuária, IPEA, Brasília, July.

Gasques, J. G. and Yokomizo, C. (1985), 'Avaliação dos Incentivos Fiscais na Amazônia', *mimeo.*, IPEA, Brasília.

Gazeta Mercantil, Various reports.

GEAMAM (1987), Interview with personnel, CVRD, Rio de Janeiro, 21 July.

George, S. (1976), *How the Other Half Dies*, Pelican Books, London.

George, S. (1984), *Ill Fares the Land*, Institute for Policy Studies, Washington D.C.

GETAT (1986a), 'Ação do GETAT 1985', *mimeo.*, Marabá.

GETAT (1986b), Interviews with personnel, Marabá, 14 April.

Ghai, D. and Radwan, S. (1983), *Agrarian Policies and Rural Poverty*, ILO, Geneva.

Gistelninck, F. (1986), Interview at INCRA, São Luís, 19 April.

Gistelninck, F. (1987), Interview, São Luís, 20 August.

Gistelninck, F. (n.d.), 'Regularização Fundiária, Região Alto Alegre', *mimeo.*, São Luís.

Gomes, M. P. (1984), 'Quarto Relatório Sobre as Reservas Indígenas Turiaçú, Carú e Pindaré e Seus Problemas Perante a FUNAI e o Projeto Carajás', *mimeo.*, UNICAMP, Campinas, São Paulo, 20 August.

Goodland, R. J. A. (1977), *Environmental Reconaissance of Tucuruí Hydro Project*, ELETRONORTE, Brasília.

Goodland, R. J. A. (1980), 'Environmental Ranking of Amazonian Development Projects in Brazil', *Environmental Conservation*, XVII, 1, Spring, pp. 9–26.

Goodland, R. J. A. (1985), 'Brazil's environmental progress in Amazonian development', in Hemming (ed.), pp. 1–35.

Goodland, R. J. A. (1986a), 'Environmental Aspects of Amazonian Development Projects in Brazil', *Interciencia*, XI, 1, January–February, pp. 16–24.

Goodland, R. J. A. (1986b), 'Hydro and the environment: evaluating the trade-offs', *Water Power and Dam Construction*, November, pp. 25–29.

Goodland, R. J. A. and Irwin, H. S. (1975), *Amazon Jungle: Green Hell to Red Desert?*, Elsevier, Amsterdam.

Goodland, R., Watson, C. and Ledec, G. (1984), *Environmental Management in Tropical Agriculture*, Westview Press, Boulder, Co.

Goodman, D. (1978), 'Expansão da Fronteira e Colonização Rural: Recente Política de Desenvolvimento no Centro-Oesto do Brasil', in W. Baer *et al.* (eds.), pp. 301–337.

Goodman, D. (1986), 'Agricultural Modernisation, Market Segmentation and Rural Social Structures in Brazil', *mimeo.*, Dept. of Economics, University College, University of London.

Goodman, D. and Hall, A. (eds.) (1990), *The Future of Amazonia: Destruction or Sustainable Development?* Macmillan, London, forthcoming.

Goodman, D. and Redclift, M. (1981), *From Peasant to Proletarian: Capitalist Development and Agrarian Transitions*, Blackwell, Oxford.

Gradwohl, J. and Greenberg, R. (1988), *Saving the Tropical Forests*, Earthscan, London.

Graziano da Silva, J. (1981), *A Modernização Dolorosa*, Zahar, Rio de Janeiro.

Graziano da Silva, J. (1985), *Para Entender o Plano Nacional de Reforma Agrária*, Brasiliense, São Paulo.

Graziano da Silva, J. and Kohl, B. (1984), 'Capitalist Modernisation and Employment in Brazilian Agriculture, 1960–75', *Latin American Perspectives*, XI, 1, Winter, pp. 117–136.

Graziano da Silva, J. *et al.* (1980), *Estrutura Agrária e Produção de Subsistência na Agricultura Brasileira*, Hucitec, São Paulo.

Grindle, M. (1986), *State and Countryside: Development Policy and Agrarian Politics in Latin America*, Johns Hopkins University Press, Baltimore and London.

Gross, D. and Underwood, B. (1971), 'Technological Change and Caloric Costs: Sisal Agriculture in North-East Brazil', *American Anthropologist*, LXXIII, 3, June, pp. 725–740.

Grzybowski, C. (1987), *Caminhos e Descaminhos dos Movimentos Sociais no Campo*, Vozes, Petrópolis.

GTPI (1985), 'Sobre a Participação de Antropólogos na Assessoria de Órgãos Públicos ou de Projetos de Desenvolvimento Regional', *mimeo.*, Águas de São Pedro, São Paulo.

Guanziroli, C. (1984a), 'Política Agrária do Regime pós-64', *mimeo.*, IBASE, Rio de Janeiro.

Guanziroli, C. (1984b), 'Informações Básicas Sobre a Estrutura Agrária Brasileira, *mimeo.*, IBASE, Rio de Janeiro.

The Guardian, Various reports.

Guimarães, A. P. (1968), *Quatro Séculos de Latifúndio*, Paz e Terra, Rio de Janeiro.

Hall, A. (1978a), *Drought and Irrigation in North-East Brazil*, Cambridge University Press, Cambridge.

Hall, A. (1978b), 'Irrigação para vencer a sêca: O caso do nordeste brasileiro', in W. Baer *et al.* (eds.), pp. 265–281.

Hall, A. (1981), 'Irrigation in the Brazilian North-East: Anti-Drought or Anti-Peasant?', in S. Mitchell (ed.), pp. 157–169.

Hall, A. (1986a), Interviews with fishermen in São Luís, Maranhão, April.

Hall, A. (1986b), 'More of the Same in Brazilian Amazonia: A Comment on Fearnside', *World Development*, XIV, 3, March, pp. 411–414.

Hall, A. (1987), 'Agrarian Crisis in Brazilian Amazonia: the Grande Carajás Programme', *Journal of Development Studies*, XXIII, 4, July, pp. 522–552.

Hall, A. and Midgley, J. (eds.) (1988), *Development Policies: Sociological Perspectives*, Manchester University Press, Manchester.

Harris, N. (1987), *The End of the Third World*, Penguin, Harmondsworth.

Harriss, J. (ed.) (1982), *Rural Development: Theories of Peasant Economy and Agrarian Change*, Hutchinson, London.

Hebette, J. (1983), 'A resistência dos posseiros no Grande Carajás', *mimeo.*, Núcleo de Áltos Estudos Amazônicos, Universidade Federal do Pará, Belém.

Hebette, J. (1987), Untitled paper, *mimeo.*, NAEA, Federal University of

Pará. Included in Goodman and Hall (eds.), forthcoming.

Hebette, J. (1988), 'A luta sindical em resposta às agressões dos grandes projetos na Amazônia Oriental brasileira', *mimeo.*, Núcleo de Altos Estudos Amazônicos, Universidade Federal do Pará. Paper presented at the 46th International Congress of Americanists, Amsterdam, July.

Hebette, J. and Açevedo-Marin, R. (1979), 'Colonização espontánea, política agrária e grupos sociais', in Costa (ed.), pp. 141–191.

Hebette, J., Menezes, M., and Guerra, G. (n.d.), 'Estudos Sobre os Impactos Sociais da Produção de Carvão Vegetal no Projeto Grande Carajás', *mimeo.*, Belém.

Hecht, S. (1981), 'Deforestation in the Amazon Basin: Magnitude, Dynamics and Soil Resource Effects', *Studies in Third World Societies*, XIII, pp. 61–108.

Hecht, S. (1983), 'Cattle Ranching in the Eastern Amazon: Environmental and Social Implications', in Moran (ed.), pp. 155–188.

Hecht, S. (1984), 'Cattle Ranching in Amazonia: Political and Ecological Considerations', in Schmink and Wood (eds.), pp. 366–398.

Hecht, S. (1985), 'Environment, Development and Politics: Capital Accumulation in the Livestock Sector in Eastern Amazonia', *World Development*, XIII, 6, June, pp. 663–684.

Hecht, S. (1988), 'Contemporary Dynamics of Amazonian Development: Reanalyzing Colonist Attrition', *mimeo.*, Graduate School of Planning, UCLA, California.

Hecht, S., Anderson, A. and May, P. (1988a), 'The Subsidy From Nature: Shifting Cultivation, Successional Palm Forests and Rural Development', *Human Organization*, XXXXVII, 1, Spring, pp. 25–35.

Hecht, S., Norgaard, R. and Possio, G. (1988b), 'The Economics of Cattle Ranching in Eastern Amazonia', *mimeo.*, Graduate School of Planning, UCLA, California.

Hemeldonck, M. V. (1983), 'Oral question with debate by Mrs. Marijke Van Hemeldonck to the Commission of the European Communities, according to article 42 of the Regulations', *mimeo.*, Brussels, 7 November.

Hemming, J. (ed.) (1985), *Change in the Amazon Basin (Vol. I, Man's Impact on Forests and Rivers; Vol. II, The Frontier After a Decade of Colonisation)*, Manchester University Press, Manchester.

Henfrey, C. (1988), 'Peasant Brazil: Struggle and Change in the Paraguaçú Valley, Bahia', *mimeo.* Paper presented at the 46th International Congress of Americanists, Amsterdam, July.

Homem de Melo, F. (1985), 'A questão alimentar no Brasil sob o ponto de vista macroeconômico', in Minayo (ed.), pp. 39–47.

Ianni, O. (1979a), *Ditadura e Agricultura*, Civilização Brasileira, Rio de Janeiro.

Ianni, O. (1979b), *Colonização e Contra-Reforma Agrária na Amazônia*, Vozes, Petrópolis.

Ianni, O. (1986), *Estado e Planejamento Econômico no Brasil*, Civilização Brasileira, Rio de Janeiro.

IBASE (1983), *Carajás: O Brasil Hipoteca Seu Futuro*, Achiamé, Rio de Janeiro.

IBASE (1984a), 'Agricultura no Brasil. Produção Para Consumo Interno x Produção Para Exportação', *mimeo.*, Rio de Janeiro.

IBASE (1984b), 'Dossiê Amazônia', *mimeo.*, Rio de Janeiro.

IBASE (1984c), 'O Capital Japonês no Brasil', *mimeo.*, Rio de Janeiro.

IBGE (1975), *Censo Agropecuário. VII Recenseamento Geral – 1970*, Rio de Janeiro.

IBGE (1984), *Censo Agropecuário. IX Recenseamento Geral do Brasil – 1980*, Rio de Janeiro.

IBGE (1987), *Sinopse Preliminar do Censo Agropecuário*, Rio de Janeiro.

IDCJ (1980), *A Preliminary Study of Regional Development of the Carajás Corridor in Brazil*, Tokyo.

IDS (1987), 'The Retreat of the State?' *IDS Bulletin*, XVIII, 3, July, Institute of Development Studies, University of Sussex, Brighton.

ILO (1977), *Poverty and Landlessness in Rural Asia*, International Labour Office, Geneva.

INCRA (1974), *Estatísticas Cadastrais, Vol. 1. Recadastramento 1972*, Brasília.

INCRA (1985), *Estatísticas Cadastrais, Vol. 1, Recadastramento 1978, Brasil e Grandes Regiões*, Brasília.

INCRA (1985), *Estatísticas Cadastrais, Anuais (Dados Preliminares)*, INCRA /MIRAD, Brasília.

INCRA (1986), *Estatísticas Cadastrais Anuais (Dados Preliminares)*, INCRA/ MIRAD, Brasilia.

INCRA (1987), Interview with Head of Colonisation Dept., Marabá, 12 August.

INCRA–Belém (1986), 'Areas Prioritárias Para o Pará', *mimeo.*, INCRA, Directoria Regional Norte, DR-01, Belém.

INCRA–Marabá (1987), Interviews with group of *posseiros* displaced from the Fazenda Mãe Maria, 10 August.

The Independent, Various reports.

INESC (1988), Untitled document, Brasília.

INPA/ELETRONORTE (1982–84), *Estudos da Ecologia e Controle Ambiental na Região da UHE Tucuruí: Relatórios Setoriais*, INPA, Manaus.

International Dams Newsletter, I, 5, September issue.

Isto É, Various reports.

Jaguaribe, H. *et al.* (1986), *Brasil 2000: Para Um Novo Pacto Social*, Paz e Terra, Rio de Janeiro.

Jarvis, L. (1986), *Livestock Development in Latin America*, World Bank, Washington D.C.

JICA (1983), *The First Progress Report For the Study Related to the Regional Development Plan of the Greater Carajás Program of the Federative Republic of Brazil*, March.

JICA (1985), *The Study Related to the Regional Development Plan of the Greater Carajás Program of the Federative Republic of Brazil (Phase II), Summary Report*, JICA and Executive Secretariat of the PGC, Brasília, July.

Jornal de Hoje, Various reports.

Jornal do Brasil, Various reports.

Jornal do Comércio, Various reports.
Joyce, C. (1988), 'The tree-that caused a riot', *New Scientist*, 18 February, pp. 54–59.
Junk, W. and de Mello, J. (1987), 'Impactos ecológicos das represas hidrelétricas na bacia Amazômica brasileira', in Kohlepp and Schrader, (eds.), pp. 367–85.
Katzman, M. (1977), *Cities and Frontiers in Brazil*, Harvard University Press, Cambridge, Mass.
Kinzo M. D. (1986), *Small Producers and the State: Agriculture on the Amazon Frontier*, Ph.D. thesis, University of Manchester.
Kleinpenning, J. M. G. (1975), *The Integration and Colonisation of the Brazilian Portion of the Amazon Basin*, Institute of Geography and Planning, Catholic University, Nijmegen.
Kohlepp, G. and Schrader, A. (eds.) (1987), *Homem e Natureza na Amazônia*, ADLAF/Forschungsschwerpunkt Lateinamerika, Geograpisches Institut, Universität Tubingen.
Kotscho, R. (1984), *Serra Pelada: Uma Ferida Aberta na Selva*, Brasiliense, São Paulo.
LAB (1982), *Brazil: State and Struggle*, Latin America Bureau, London.
LACR, *Latin America Commodities Report*, Various issues.
LAER, *Latin America Economic Report*, Various issues.
Lanly, J. (1983), 'Assessment of the forest resources of the tropics: review article', *Forestry Abstracts*, 44, pp. 287–318.
Lappé, F. M. and Collins, J. (1977), *Food First: The Myth of Scarcity*, Souvenir Press, London.
LARR, *Latin America Regional Report* (Brazil), Various issues.
Latinamerica Press, Various reports.
LAWR, *Latin America Weekly Report*, Various issues.
Ledec, G. (1985), 'The Political Economy of Tropical Deforestation', in Leonard (ed.), pp. 179–226.
Leonard, H. J. (ed.) (1985), *Divesting Nature's Capital*, Holmes and Meier, New York and London.
Lipton, M. (1982), 'Game against nature: theories of peasant decision-making', in Harriss (ed.), pp. 258–268.
Long, N. (1988), 'Sociological perspectives on agrarian development and State intervention', in Hall and Midgley (eds.), pp. 108–133.
Magalhães, A. *et al.* (1985), 'Os Povos Indígenas e o Projeto Ferro-Carajás: Avalição do Convênio Companhia Vale do Rio Doce', *mimeo.*, December.
Magnanini, A. and Maciel, N. (1989), 'Parecer Técnico', in Pressburger, (ed.), pp. 26–28.
Mahar, D. (1979), *Frontier Development Policy in Brazil: A Study of Amazonia*, Praeger, New York.
Martine, G, (1980), 'Recent Colonization Experience in Brazil: Expectations Versus Reality', in Barbira-Scazzocchio (ed.), pp. 80–94.
Martine, G. (1987), 'A Evolução Recente da Estrutura de Produção Agropecuária: Algumas Notas Preliminares', *Análise dos Dados do Censo Agropecuário de 1985*, July, IPEA, Brasília.
Mather, A. (1987), 'Global Trends in Forest Resources', *Geography*,

LXXII, 1, pp. 1–14.

Mattos, R. and Guanziroli, C. (1985), 'Marabá: a Luta Pela Terra, A Luta Pela Vida', *mimeo.*, IBASE, Rio de Janeiro.

May, P., Anderson, A., Frazão, J. and Balick, M. (1985), 'Babassú palm in the agroforestry systems in Brazil's Mid-North region', *Agroforestry Systems 3*, ICRAF, AF Systems Inventory Project, pp. 275–295.

Médici, E. G. (1970), 'Visão do Nordeste', Speech at SUDENE, Recife, 7 June.

Melby, J. (1942), 'Rubber River: An Account of the Rise and Collapse of the Amazon Boom', *Hispanic American Historical Review*, XXIII, pp. 452–469.

MINAGRI (1987a), Interview with staff, Ministry of Agriculture, Brasília, 29 July.

MINAGRI (1987b), Interview with staff, Ministry of Agriculture, Brasília, 31 July.

Minayo, M. C. de Souza (ed.) (1985), *Raizes da Fome*, FASE/Vozes, Petrópolis.

MIRAD (1985a), *Proposta para a elaboração do 1 Plano Nacional de Reforma Agrária da Nova República – PNRA*, MIRAD/INCRA, Brasília, May.

MIRAD (1985b), *Plano Nacional de Reforma Agrária – PNRA*, MIRAD/INCRA, Brasília, 10 October.

MIRAD (1986a), *Plano Regional de Reforma Agrária – PRRA Pará*, MIRAD/INCRA, Brasília.

MIRAD (1986b), *Plano Regional de Reforma Agrária – PRRA Maranhão*, MIRAD/INCRA, Brasília.

MIRAD (1986c), *Plano Regional de Reforma Agrária – PRRA Goiás*, MIRAD/INCRA, Brasília.

MIRAD (1986d), *Conflitos de Terra*, Coordenadoria de Conflitos Agrários, MIRAD/INCRA, Brasília.

MIRAD (1987), *Conflitos de Terra*, Coordenadoria de Conflitos Agrários, MIRAD/INCRA, Brasília.

MIRAD/INCRA (1987), 'Primeiro Relatório da Comissão MIRAD/INCRA Responsável Pela Coordenação da Ação Fundiária Emergencial na Região do Araguaia–Tocantins', *mimeo.*, MIRAD/INCRA, Brasília.

MIRAD/SEPLAN (1987a), 'Dossiê Sobre a Atuação do GETAT e a Sua Extinção', Secretaria Geral MIRAD, Secretaria de Planejamento, Coordenadoria de Programação e Projetos, *mimeo.*, Brasília, February.

MIRAD/SEPLAN (1987b), 'Avaliação da Intervenção Fundiária do GETAT (1980–87)', Secretaria Geral MIRAD, Secretaria de Planejamento, Coordenadoria de Programação e Projetos, *mimeo.*, Brasília, April.

MIRAD/SEPLAN (1987c), 'Levantamento de Processos de Desapropriação sob Jurisdição do GETAT, Realizado em Marabá, Dias 22 e 23 de março de 1987', Secretaria Geral MIRAD, Secretaria de Planejamento, Coordenadoria de Programação e Projetos, *mimeo.*, Brasília.

MIRAD/SEPLAN (1987d), 'Relatório sobre os conflitos na Faz. AGRO-PECUS que ja resultou na morte de 12 posseiros, 15 madereiros e 1 fazendeiro (Tarley de Andrade)', *mimeo.*, Brasília, 20 February.

Miranda, M. (1988), 'A ação federal/estadual da apropriacao da terra: a colonização no corredor da E.F. Carajás', *mimeo.*, Dept. de Geografia, Universidade Federal do Rio de Janeiro. Paper presented at the 46th International Congress of Americanists, Amsterdam, July.

Mitchell, S. (ed.) (1981), *The Logic of Poverty: The Case of the Brazilian Northeast*, Routledge and Kegan Paul, London.

MNDDH (1986), *Tribunal da Terra*, 18–20 April. Pamphlet, Belém.

Momma, A. (1987), *Ferrovia Norte-Sul. Um Sistema de Transportes Para o Desenvolvimento Regional*, Ministry of Agriculture, Brasília.

Moran, E. (1981), *Developing the Amazon*, Indiana University Press, Bloomington, Indiana.

Moran, E. (1982), 'Colonisation in the Transamazon and Rondônia', in Schmink and Wood (eds.), pp. 285–303.

Moran, E. (ed.) (1983a), *The Dilemma of Amazonian Development*, Westview Press, Boulder, Co.

Moran, E. (1983b), 'Growth Without Development: Past and Present Development Efforts in Amazonia', in Moran (ed.), pp. 3–23.

Moran, E. (1987), 'A produção agrícola em um projeto de colonização em Carajás', in Kohlepp and Schrader (eds.), pp. 353–366.

Moran, E. (1989), 'Private and public colonisation schemes in Amazonia', in Goodman and Hall (eds.), forthcoming.

Morrison, R., Ross, R. and Antas, T. (1986), 'Distribuição de maçaricos, batuíras e outras aves costeiras na região do salgado paraense e re-entrâncias maranhenses', *Espaço, Ambiente e Planejamento*, I, 4, April.

Mougeot, L. (1985a), 'Alternative migration targets and Brazilian Amazonia's closing frontier', in Hemming (ed.), Vol. II, pp. 51–90.

Mougeot, L. (1985b), 'River Impoundment Related Population Displacement in Brazilian Amazonia: the Tucuruí Resettlement Program (TRP), 1976–84', *mimeo*. Paper presented at 45th International Congress of Americanists, Bogotá, Colombia.

Mougeot, L. (1987), 'O reservatório da usina hidreléctrica de Tucuruí, Pará, Brasil: uma avaliação do programa de reassentamento populacional, (1976–85)', in Kohlepp and Schrader (eds.), pp. 387–404.

Mougeot, L. (1989), 'Forced Population Resettlement in Brazilian Amazonia: Greater State Concern for its Development Potential', in Goodman and Hall (eds.), forthcoming.

MST (1986), *Construindo o Caminho*, Movimento dos Trabalhadores Rurais Sem Terra, São Paulo.

MST (1987), *Assassinatos no Campo: crime e impunidade, 1964–86*, Global Editora, São Paulo.

Mueller, C. (1987), 'A Evolução Recente da Agropecuária Brasileira Segundo os Dados dos Censos Agropecuários', *Análise dos Dados do Censo Agropecuário de 1985*, IPEA, Brasília, July.

Myers, N. (1980), *Conversion of Tropical Moist Forests*, National Academy of Sciences, Washington D.C.

Myers, N. (1985), *The Primary Source: Tropical Forests and Our Future*, Norton, London.

Myers, N. and D. (1982), 'Increasing Awareness of the Supranational Nature of Emerging Environmental Issues', *Ambio*, II, 4, pp. 195–201.

Nation, J. and Komer, D. (1987), 'Rainforests and the Hamburger Society', *The Ecologist*, XVII, 4–5, pp. 161–169.

NATRON (1987), *Apreciação Crítica da Área de Influência da E.F. Carajás, Setor Industrial*, CVRD, SEPLAN/PGC, June.

Neto, F. (1988), *National and Global Dimensions of Regional Development Planning: A Case-study of Brazilian Amazonia*, Ph.D. thesis, London School of Economics and Political Science, University of London.

Neto, F. (1989), 'Development of Planning and Mineral Mega-Projects: Some Global Considerations', in Goodman and Hall (eds.), forthcoming.

Neto, M. (1982), *Os Lucros da Fome: O Mito da Escassez de Alimentos*, Achiamé, Rio de Janeiro.

NGO (1984), 'Motion de l'Assemblé Generale des ONG Européenes (Avril 1984)', *mimeo.*, Brussels, 12 April.

Nicholaides, J. *et al.* (1983), 'Crop Production Systems in the Amazon Basin', in Moran (ed.), pp. 101–153.

O Globo, Various reports.

Oldfield, M. (1981), 'Tropical Deforestation and Genetic Resources Conservation', *Studies in Third World Societies*, XIV, pp. 277–345.

O Liberal, Various reports.

Oliveira, F. de (1987), *A Economia Brasileira; Crítica à Razão Dualista*, Vozes, Petrópolis. Originally published in 1972.

Ortiz Mena, A. (1975), 'Agroindustry and the Development of Latin America', in The Agribusiness Council, pp. 139–157.

O Senhor, Various reports.

OXFAM (1987), 'Pollution and Industrialisation Hit the Small Fishermen', *mimeo.*, Oxford.

Pacey, A. and Payne, P. (eds.) (1985), *Agricultural Development and Nutrition*, Hutchinson, London.

Pacheco de Oliveira, J. (1988), 'Segurança nas fronteiras e o novo indigensimo: formas e linhagem do projeto Calha Norte', *mimeo.*, Rio de Janeiro. Paper presented at the 46th International Congress of Americanists, Amsterdam, July.

Pandolfi, M. (1985), 'Lutas Sociais no Sertão de Pernambuco', *Cadernos de Estudos Sociais*, Fundação Joaquim Nabuco, I, 1, January–June, pp. 53–67.

PCN (1985), 'Desenvolvimento e Segurança na Região ao Norte das Calhas dos Rios Solimões e Amazonas; Projeto Calha Norte', *mimeo.*, Grupo de Trabalho Interministerial, Brasília.

Pearce, D. (1986), 'The Sustainable Use of Natural Resources in Developing Countries', *Discussion Paper 86–15*, Dept. of Economics, University College, University of London.

Pearce, D. and Myers, N. (1989), 'Economic Values and the Environment of Amazonia', in Goodman and Hall (eds.), forthcoming.

Pearse, A. (1975), *The Latin American Peasant*, Frank Cass, London.

Pereira, A. (1986), *Ethanol, Employment and Development: Lessons from Brazil*, ILO, Geneva.

Pereira, P. de Assis (1987), 'A Nova República e a Reforma Agraria', *mimeo.*, IBASE, Rio de Janeiro.

PGC (1982), 'Scope of Work for the Study Related to the Regional Development Plans of the Greater Carajás Program of the Federative Republic of Brazil', *mimeo.*, Executive Secretariat of the PGC/JICA, Brasília, 4 February.

PGC (1984a), *The Greater Carajás Programme: Legislation and Norms*, SEPLAN, Brasília.

PGC (1984b), 'Terms of Reference for the Study of the Selected Sub-Regions in the Greater Carajás Program Area', *mimeo.*, Brasília, January.

PGC (1984c), *Aptidão Pedoclimática: Zoneamento Por Produto*, MINAGRI/ EMBRAPA, Brasília.

PGC (1985a), 'Reunião em 20.12.85. Projetos Aprovados', *mimeo.*, Conselho Interministerial do Programa Grande Carajás.

PGC (1985b), 'Programa Grande Carajás: Análise da Situação Atual e Novas Diretrizes', *mimeo.*, Executive Secretariat of the PGC, Brasília.

PGC (1985c), *Programa Grande Carajás: Histórico, Objetivos, Atividades e Legislação*, Brasília.

PGC (1986), 'Plano Operativo do Programa Grande Carajás Para 1986', *mimeo.*, Executive Secretariat of the PGC, Brasília, February.

PGC (1987), 'Projetos Integrantes, Posição em 30.12.87. Atualizado em 27.7.87', computer print-out, Executive Secretariat of the PGC, Brasília.

PGC (n.d.), 'Plano Operativo Para 1987', *mimeo.*, Executive Secretariat of the PGC, Brasília.

Pinto, L. F. (1982), *Carajás, O Ataque ao Coração da Amazônia*, Editora Marco Zero, Rio de Janeiro.

Pinto, L. F. (1986a), 'As imagens do saque', *O Liberal*, 25 January.

Pinto, L. F. (1986b), 'O ritmo das motosserras', *O Liberal*, 26 January.

Pinto, L. F. (1986c), *Jarí. Toda a Verdade Sobre o Projeto Ludwig*, Editora Marco Zero, Rio de Janeiro.

Pinto, L. F. (1987a), 'Associação entre CVRD e japoneses na origem do projeto da ferrovia', *O Liberal*, 13 July.

Pinto, L. F. (1987b), 'A viabilidade de uma ferrovia que não é o melhor meio de transporte', *O Liberal*, 14 July.

Pinto, L. F. (1987c), 'Carajás: o laboratório da nova ferrovia', *O Liberal*, 17 July.

Plumwood, V. and Routley, R. (1982), 'World Rainforest Destruction – the Social Factors', *The Ecologist*, XII, 1, pp. 4–22.

Pompermayer, M. (1979), *The State and Frontier in Brazil*, Ph.D. thesis, Stanford University, California.

Pompermayer, M. (1984), 'Strategies of Private Capital in the Brazilian Amazon', in Schmink and Wood (eds.), pp. 419–438.

Portela, F. (1979), *Guerra de Guerrilhas no Brasil*, Global, Rio de Janeiro.

Posey, D. (1983), 'Indigenous Ecological Knowledge and Development of the Amazon', in Moran (ed.), pp. 225–257.

Posey, D. (1985), 'Nature and indigenous guidelines for new Amazonian development strategies: understanding biological diversity through ethno-ecology', in Hemming (ed.), Vol. I, pp. 156–181.

Prance, G. and Lovejoy, T. (eds.) (1985), *Amazonia: Key Environments*, Pergamon, Oxford.

Pressburger, T. (ed.) (1989), *Inquérito Civil Programa Grande Carajás*, Instituto Apoio Jurídico Popular, Rio de Janeiro, January.

PRODIAT (1982–85), *Projeto de Desenvolvimento Integrado da Bacia do Araguaia-Tocantins*, Ministério do Interior, Brasília.

Província do Pará, Various reports.

Queiroz, M. I. P. de (1965), *O Messianismo no Brasil e no Mundo*, São Paulo.

Railway Gazette International (1984), February issue.

Rankin, J. (1985), 'Forestry in the Brazilian Amazon', in Prance and Lovejoy (eds.), pp. 369–392.

Redclift, M. (1984), *Development and the Environmental Crisis: Red or Green Alternatives?* Methuen, London.

Redclift, M. (1986), 'Sustainability and the Market: Survival Strategies on the Bolivian Frontier, *Journal of Development Studies*, XXIII, October, pp. 93–105.

Redclift, M. (1987), *Sustainable Development: Exploring the Contradictions*, Methuen, London.

Reis, A. C. F. (1974), 'Economic History of the Brazilian Amazon', in Wagley (ed.) pp. 33–44.

Reis, A. C. F. (1982), *A Amazônia e a Cobiça Internacional*, Civilização Brasileira, Rio de Janeiro.

Resende, G. Castro de (1988), 'External Adjustment and Agriculture', *mimeo.*, IPEA/INPES, Rio de Janeiro.

Rich, B. (1985), 'The Multilateral Development Banks, Environmental Policy and the United States', *Ecological Law Quarterly*, XII, pp. 681–745.

Richards, P. (1985), *Indigenous Agricultural Revolution*, Hutchinson, London.

Rocha, J. (1982), 'Brazil buys dream of American billionaire', *The Observer*, 24 January.

Rosillo-Calle, F. and Hall,D. (1988), 'Brazil finds a sweet solution to fuel shortages', *New Scientist*, 19 May, pp. 41–44.

Rossato, A., Hanrahan, P., Chaves, J. and Krautler, E. (1987), 'Carta das Igrejas de Marabá, Conceição do Araguaia, Cametá e Xingú aos irmãos do Brasil', *mimeo.*, Belém, 5 April.

Saint, W. (1982), 'Farming for Energy: Social Options Under Brazil's National Alcohol Programme', *World Development*, X, 3, March, pp. 223–238.

Salati, E. (1987), 'Amazonia: um ecosistema ameaçado', in Kohlepp and Schrader (eds.), pp. 59–81.

Salati, E. and Voge, P. (1984), 'Amazon Basin: A System in Equilibrium', *Science*, 225, pp. 129–137.

San Martin, P. and Pelegrini, B. (1984), *Cerrados: Uma Ocupação Japonesa no Campo*, CODECRI, Rio de Janeiro.

Santos, M., Andrade, M. and English, B. (1985), 'Os Impactos Sociais da Implantação do Projeto Carajás, *mimeo.*, São Luís.

Sawyer, D. (1979), *Peasants and Capitalism on an Amazon Frontier*, Ph.D. thesis, Harvard University, Cambridge, Mass.

SBPC (1982), 'O Programa Grande Carajás', *Ciências da Terra*, 3, March–

April, pp. 36–46.

SBPC (1983), *O Programa Grande Carajás e a Crise*, 35th Annual Meeting of the Brazilian Society for the Progress of Science, Belém, July.

Schmink, M. and Wood, C. (eds.) (1984), *Frontier Expansion in Amazonia*, University of Florida Press, Gainesville, Florida.

Scott, J. C. (1986), 'Everyday Forms of Peasant Resistance', *Journal of Peasant Studies*, XIII, 2, January, pp. 5–35.

Secrett, C. (1987), 'Greater Carajás: Sustainable Development or Environmental Catastrophe?' In Treece, pp. 58–91.

Sen, A. (1981), *Poverty and Famines: An Essay on Entitlement and Deprivation*, Clarendon Press, Oxford.

SEPLAN/PGC (1987), *Plano Direto da Estrada de Ferro Carajás, Vol. I. Termos de Referência*, Rio de Janeiro, July.

Shaner, W. *et al.* (1982), *Farming Systems Research and Development Guidelines for Developing Countries*, Westview, Boulder, Colorado.

Sigaud, L. (1980), *Greve nos Engenhos*, Paz e Terra, Rio de Janeiro.

Simpson, A. (1984), 'Visit to North Goiás and South Pará Provinces', *mimeo.*, n.p.

Sioli, H. (1985), *Amazônia. Fundamentos da Ecologia da Maior Região de Florestas Tropicais*, Vozes, Petrópolis.

Skidmore, T. (1967), *Politics in Brazil 1930–64: An Experiment in Democracy*, Oxford University Press, New York.

Skillings, R. and Tcheyan, N. (1979), *Economic Development Prospects of the Amazon Region of Brazil*, School of Advanced International Studies, Johns Hopkins University, Baltimore.

SMDDH (1985), 'Levantamentos de dados sobre as consequências da implantação do programa Grande Carajás', *mimeo.*, Sao Luís, April.

Smith, N. (1982), *Rainforest Corridors: The Transamazon Colonization Scheme*, University of California Press, Berkeley, California.

Sorj, B. (1980), *Estado e Classes na Agricultura Brasileira*, Zahar, Rio de Janeiro.

South, Various reports.

Souza Martins, J. de (1984), *A Militarização da Questão Agrária no Brasil*, Vozes, Petrópolis.

Souza Martins, J. de (1986), *Os Camponeses e a Política no Brasil*, Vozes, Petrópolis.

Souza Martins, J. de (1988), 'Impasses políticos dos movimentos sociais na Amazônia', *mimeo.*, Universidade de São Paulo. Also included in Goodman and Hall (eds.), forthcoming.

Speller, P. (1987), 'The Role of the State in the Settlement of Northern Mato Grosso', *mimeo*. Paper presented to the Brazil Workshop seminar, London School of Economics and Political Science, University of London, 6 March.

SPVEA (1955), *Primeiro Plano Quinquenal*, 2 vols., Belém.

SUDAM (1968), *Primeiro Plano Director, Triênnio 1968–70*, 3 vols., Belém.

SUDAM (1971), *Plano de Desenvolvimento da Amazônia (1972–74)*, Belém.

SUDAM (1976a), *Programa de Polos Agropecuários e Agrominerais da Amazônia, POLAMAZONIA; Carajás*, Belém.

SUDAM (1976b), *II Plano de Desenvolvimento da Amazônia (1975–79)*, Belém.

SUDAM (1985), *Relação de Projetos Aprovados*, Belém.

The Sunday Times (1986), 'Civil war looms as church fights the landowners', 25 May.

Survival International (1987a), 'Open letter to M. Jacques Delors, President, Commission of European Communities', London, 1 October.

Survival International (1987b), 'Brazil. The Greater Carajás Programme. Massive Agro-Industrial Scheme Devastates Indian Lands', *Urgent Action Bulletin*, BRZ/11/OCT.

Tambs, L. (1974), 'Geopolitics of the Amazon', in Wagley (ed.), pp. 45–87.

Tavares dos Santos, J. (1988), 'A colonização agrícola, uma solução para a crise agrária brasileira', *mimeo.*, Universidade Federal do Rio Grande do Sul. Paper presented at the 46th International Congress of Americanists, Amsterdam, July.

Thomas, V. (1982), *Differences in Income, Nutrition and Poverty Within Brazil*, World Bank Staff Working Paper No. 505, Washington D.C.

Timberlake, L. (1985), *Africa in Crisis*, Earthscan, London.

Trebat, T. (1983), *Brazil's State-Owned Enterprises: A Case-Study of the State as Entrepreneur*, Cambridge University Press, Cambridge.

Treece, D. (1987), *Bound in Misery and Iron: The Impact of the Greater Carajás Programme on the Indians of Brazil*, Survival International, London.

Tudge, C. (1977), *The Famine Business*, Faber and Faber, London.

Valverde, O. (1989), 'Parecer Técnico', in Pressburger, (ed.), pp. 17–23.

Veiga, J. S. da (1975), 'Quand les multinationales font du ranching', *Le Monde Diplomatique*, September.

Veja, Various reports.

Victoria, G. and Vaughan, J. (1985), 'Land Tenure Patterns and Child Health in Southern Brazil: The Relationship Between Agricultural Production, Malnutrition and Child Mortality', *International Journal of Health Services*, XV, 2, pp. 253–274.

Vidal, L. (1988), 'Os Índios da Amazônia, Um Desafio Recíproco', *mimeo.*, Dept. of Anthropology, University of São Paulo. Paper presented at the 46th International Congress of Americanists, Amsterdam, July.

Vilaça, M. V. and Albuquerque, R. C. de (1965), *Coronel, Coroneis*, Tempo Brasileiro, Rio de Janeiro.

Wagley, C. (ed.) (1974), *Man in the Amazon*, University of Florida Press, Gainesville, Florida.

Wagner, A. (1985), 'Estrutura Fundiária e Expansão Camponesa', *mimeo.*, Rio de Janeiro.

Wagner, A. (1988), 'A intervenção governmental face aos conflitos agrários na região Amazônica', *mimeo.*, Rio de Janeiro. Also included in Goodman and Hall (eds.), forthcoming.

Wetterberg, G. (1981), 'Conservation progress in Amazonia: a structural review', *Parks*, VI, 2, pp. 5–10.

Wood, C. and Schmink, M. (1978), 'Blaming the Victim: Small Farmer Production in an Amazon Colonization Project', *Studies in Third World*

Societies, VII, February, pp. 77–93.

Wood, C. and Wilson, J. (1984), 'The Magnitude of Migration to the Brazilian Frontier', in Schmink and Wood (eds.), pp. 142–152.

World Bank (1981a), *Brazil: Integrated Development of the Northwest Frontier*, Washington D.C.

World Bank (1981b), *Accelerated Development in Sub-Saharan Africa*, Washington D.C.

World Bank (1982), *Economic Development of Tribal Peoples: Human Ecologic Considerations*, Office of Environmental Affairs, World Bank, Washington D.C.

World Bank (1983), *Rural Development Programs for Brazil's Northeast: An Interim Assessment*, Washington D.C.

World Bank (1986), *Poverty and Hunger: Issues and Options for Food Security in Developing Countries*, Washington D.C.

WRI/IIED (1986), *World Resources 1986*, World Resources Institute/ International Institute for Environment and Development, Basic Books, New York.

WRI/IIED (1987), *World Resources 1987*, World Resources Institute/ International Institute for Environment and Development, Basic Books, New York.

Index

Postscript

Since the text of this book was completed in September 1988, the Greater Carajás Programme (PGC) has come under the influence of significant economic and political changes, both within and outside Brazil. In particular, awareness of the socially and environmentally damaging consequences of poorly planned and executed regional development initiatives has been substantially heightened. The potentially harmful effects of government-backed settlement strategies have been amply illustrated in the 1980s by the much-criticised North-West Frontier Development Programme (POLONORO-ESTE), as well as by the disastrous official policy of encouraging cattle ranching and logging in Amazonia generally.[1] The debate over accelerating Amazonian deforestation, its negative impacts on people and ecology, as well as its contribution to global warming has, over the past two years, been the subject of increasingly intensive and condemnatory media coverage. This has involved in-depth analyses by major newspapers and international journals,[2] as well as a spate of books and a major TV documentary series on the subject.[3] Pivotal events such as the murder of rubber-tappers' leader Francisco 'Chico' Mendes in December 1988, the Altamira meeting in February 1989 of 3,500 Amerindians opposed to the construction of the Xingú hydro-electric complex, and the World Bank's almost simultaneous postponement of the US$500 million second power sector loan for Brazil, have also helped to put Amazonia's development problems in the spotlight.

Growing controversy surrounding Carajás and other Amazonian development programmes has led to a number of potentially important policy changes over the past two years. In October 1988, in response to mounting criticism at home and abroad over the government's failure to tackle worsening environmental problems, President Sarney announced the 'Nossa Natureza' (Our Nature) conservation programme. Entering the statute books in April 1989, this involved the creation of IBAMA, the new National Environment Agency (*Instituto Brasileiro do Meio Ambiente e Recursos Renováveis*), which absorbed the IBDF, SEMA and the environmentally-related activities of six ministries. It also included a ban on the export of unprocessed timber, an agro–ecological zoning project for Amazonia and a commitment to create 'extractive reserves' for rubber-tappers in Acre, the first of which was approved by presidential decree in January 1990 (of 2,000 square miles, in the Juruá valley, Acre). Perhaps the most surprising move, however, was the introduction of a 90-day suspension of fiscal incentives, later extended, for the three regional development agencies (SUDAM, SUDENE and SUDECO) as well as for the PGC. This last measure was highly significant in view of President Sarney's adamant refusals on past occasions to address the issue of tax breaks for ranching enterprises, which critics have consistently identified as a major cause of land speculation and environmental destruction in Amazonia.

Despite these promising beginnings, however, major progress came about only with the advent of a new government in March 1990, headed by President Fernando Collor de Mello. Important policy changes were signalled by the appointment of José Lutzenberger, an agronomist and outspoken critic of past government policies, to lead the new Special Environmental Secretariat, attached directly to the office of the Presidency. Three months later, President Collor launched 'Operation Amazonia',[4] through which IBAMA hoped to cut down Amazonian deforestation by 30% from the 1989 figure of 60,000 square miles. Using a quick-response strategy based on the identification of illegal activities through high-definition satellite imagery, coupled with the use of helicopters, 300 IBAMA inspectors set off on a campaign to catch and prosecute those responsible for illicit logging, gold prospecting, deforestation and charcoal production. By October, after only four months' operations, IBAMA had achieved an apparently impressive degree of success, having imposed over 2,200 fines and closed 88 illegal logging operations. This led the organisation to claim that its new policy had reduced the rate of deforestation by 50% compared with 1989 (*O Globo*, 15.9.90). Critics allege, however, that this reduction was due primarily to unusually heavy rains over this period and that IBAMA's actions themselves had only a marginal impact.

Within this more environmentally-sensitive context, the Carajás

Programme has attracted its share of international attention. This is especially so with regard to the core iron-ore mining project and linked pig-iron smelters, which are having the most dramatic consequences in the region compared with other PGC industrial and agricultural components. Lutzenberger indicated the extent of official concern by acknowledging that the pig-iron smelters and other factories along the 900-kilometre railway linking the Carajás iron-ore mine to the coast 'represent a threat to the forests of the region'. His assertion is borne out by the fact that, in 1989, charcoal production to serve the four operational smelters in Marabá and Açailândia was alone responsible for the destruction of over one million trees covering 11,600 hectares of rainforest (*Veja*, 20.6.90). Recent projections bear out earlier misgivings over the potential destructiveness of these highly subsidised industrial activities along the Carajás railway corridor. Anderson,[5] for example, suggests on the basis of his own careful estimates that, to produce the required three million tonnes of charcoal every year to supply the planned total of 34 smelters, would create an annual demand for fuelwood of 14 million tonnes, destroying 1,500 square kilometres of rainforest a year in the process.

However, such a doomsday scenario seems increasingly unlikely. Only four of the twelve pig-iron smelters which were expected to be operational by 1990 had actually started production by the end of that year. The decision to invest in Carajás was originally taken by iron and steel manufacturers (mainly from Minas Gerais) based largely on the availability of generous official subsidies and cheap charcoal produced from the native rainforest. The gradual withdrawal of financial assistance under President Collor's macroeconomic austerity programme, together with stricter enforcement of environmental legislation, has made Amazonia a decidedly less attractive proposition. In July 1989, the SIMARA pig-iron smelter in Marabá was fined the equivalent of US$0.5 million by IBAMA for buying illegally cut timber and was eventually forced to suspend operations. Acknowledging the extent to which its existence depended on the availability of cheap rainforest timber, SIMARA's manager declared at the time that 'The smelter has become unviable. As soon as we can, we shall get rid of it' (*Veja*, 20.6.90). The COSIPAR smelter in Marabá was fined US$25,000 for similar offences but is still operational, and IBAMA has started to punish illegal charcoal operations which use native rainforest rather than sawmill offcuts. In late 1989, IBAMA mounted an intensive aerial survey called 'Operation

Carajás' to ascertain the causes of intensive deforestation in the area associated with projects benefitting from SUDAM, SUDENE and PGC fiscal incentives.

The Collor government has tightened up considerably on appraisal procedures for pig-iron smelters and other industrial establishments in the PGC area, with legislation having been introduced in 1990 by the President's Regional Development Secretariat to reduce the risks of deforestation and industrial pollution. IBAMA's requirement that each project appraisal should include an environmental impact assessment (RIMA) is now being more rigorously enforced, whereas previously it amounted to little more than an irritating formality for entrepreneurs which was often ignored altogether. Regulations now stipulate that new iron and steel projects within the Carajás Programme, in order to become eligible for fiscal incentives, must not utilise charcoal derived from native rainforest and must plan to become self-sufficient, from the commencement of production, on fuel extracted from associated timber plantations. Further prerequisites include the use of energy-saving and pollution-reducing technology.[6] As a direct result of these measures, only eight of the remaining thirty unconstructed pig-iron smelters which had originally been approved by the PGC are currently eligible. It is, furthermore, questionable how many of these eight will be implemented since, in this new climate, potential industrial investors appear increasingly reluctant to become embroiled in such controversial, environmentally sensitive undertakings. In addition, as explained below, the sheer economic feasibility of smelters in Amazonia is increasingly uncertain under these more rigorous conditions.

A new manganese ferrous-alloy plant due to open at Marabá in 1991, PROMETAL, has taken a more progressive path. It has opted for coal as a fuel rather than local charcoal, in order to avoid these problems and to facilitate negotiations with the now perhaps somewhat more ecologically-tuned European and US commercial banks (*Jornal do Brasil*, 26.8.90). The Brazilian government has also taken other less punitive and more positive steps towards encouraging sustainable forms of industrial development at Carajás. During a visit to the iron-ore mine in July 1990, for example, President Collor announced a plan to establish 'forestry poles' along the Carajás railway corridor (*Programa de Polos Florestais na Amazônia Oriental*), costed at US$1.2 billion (*O Globo*, 15.7.90). Yet as far as charcoal is concerned, it has been clearly demonstrated that the use of plantation timber would make pig-iron smelting uneconomic, pushing up production costs beyond the market price.[7] While there is obviously some virtue in reforesting this already severely degraded area, Japanese and German commercial interest in cellulose production along the corridor and the likely prevalence of single-tree species such as Eucalyptus could create other grave social and environmental problems.

Environmental issues are therefore being taken seriously by government perhaps for the first time in Brazil's history. As mentioned above, at the level of policy formulation and, increasingly, at the level of implementation, this commitment is reflected in developments within Amazonia generally, including the Carajás Programme. A similar concern has also manifested itself in the policies of major outside funders such as the World Bank, which has effectively admitted its institutional culpability in exacerbating, unwittingly or otherwise, the adverse trends explored in this book, and has taken steps to strengthen environmental analysis and control in Brazil. Early in 1990, for example, the Bank approved a 'National Environmental Project' for Brazil, with an initial funding of US$117 million, to assist the new government's efforts in this area. This will involve protecting conservation areas in Amazonia and elsewhere, strengthening IBAMA and state environmental agencies, and supporting Brazil's new 'National Environmental Programme' (*Programa Nacional do Meio Ambiente* – PNMA). However, little such systematic consideration has been given so far, either by aid donors or the Brazilian government, to dealing with the related but specifically social impacts of Carajás and similar large-scale projects.

Despite some progress towards ameliorating and controlling the environmental impacts of programmes such as Carajás, serious problems remain. IBAMA can never, with the relatively limited resources at its disposal and the political context within which it operates, hope to effectively police a region as vast as Amazonia. The Environmental Secretariat also faces formidable obstacles; strong political pressures from a whole range of vested interests (military, commercial and state government-level), public spending cuts and lack of co-operation from other government agencies. Furthermore, as explained at length in this volume, the major forces which drive poor migrants and attract speculative investments to the region have their roots in the very structure of the Brazilian economy and society. Land concentration, landlessness and poverty still fuel the migration of small farmers to the

Amazon frontier, while Brazil's rampant inflation increases the financial attractiveness of land speculation. One discouraging move in this field is the recent proposal by a special presidential commission, co-ordinated by the Regional Development Secretariat, that the fiscal incentive funds for Amazonia (FINAM) and the North-East (FINOR), currently suspended, should be converted into highly subsidised loan schemes, administered by the regional development banks, such as BASA.[8] The transfer of project appraisal from regional development agencies to banks on the grounds of financial competence could, however, have serious repercussions in terms of environmental and social impacts.

The question of land distribution is in the eyes of many observers a continuing obstacle to development for the majority of the rural population. Yet the 1985 agrarian reform programme (PNRA), which was intended to provide some relief despite being hamstrung as the result of political pressures from the landowners' lobby, has slowed to a virtual halt under the Collor administration. In the states of Maranhão and Pará, for example, covered by the Carajás Programme, one million hectares were expropriated by the Sarney government but less than one-third of this land has so far been put to use under the reform. In Brazil overall, the equivalent of US$ 1 billion compensation in the form of bonds is still owed to expropriated landowners (*Veja*, 23.5.90 and 3.10.90).[9] Collor's government has itself carried out no expropriations nor resettled any farmers, but has merely granted property titles to those who benefited from the PNRA under the Sarney administration. According to INCRA president, José Reinaldo Vieira da Silva, a new phase of the agrarian reform will have to wait until late 1991, pending a review of past interventions under the PNRA.

Rural violence is another indicator of agrarian crisis which has shown little sign of diminishing in recent years. Although national figures for 1989 show a reduction in deaths arising from land conflicts compared with the previous year,[10] there is little such sign of improvement in the Carajás region. Land disputes in both states of Pará and Maranhão showed a significant increase in 1990 over the previous year, and in June the rural workers' union leader of Marabá was murdered in such a conflict. In a move which relects the continuing struggle for land in Eastern Amazonia, some 500 landless families occupied the protective 'green belt' around the Carajás iron-ore mine and have refused to move until they are resettled on farmland elsewhere (*Jornal do Brasil* 6.6.90). Small farmers' desperation is also revealed by their occupation of several local INCRA offices in protest at the organisation's failure to resettle them under the agrarian reform.

In conclusion, therefore, although some promising initiatives have been taken with regard to correcting problems either caused or exacerbated by the Carajás Programme, and there have been significant developments within the broader Amazonian context, hopes that dramatic improvements can be expected in the near future should be tempered by extreme caution. The PGC experience has one redeeming virtue, however; it has provided a salutary, if expensive, lesson to policy-makers over the dangers inherent in any narrow-minded, strictly sectoral approach to regional development which ignores wider social and ecological repercussions. It has, furthermore, served as a shocking reminder of the consequent need to calculate in advance the full costs likely to be incurred. National planners in Brazil as well as international aid donors, who bear a large part of the responsibility for supporting and legitimising such grandiose projects, must learn constructively from these profound errors, whether of judgement or omission. The survival of the world's largest remaining tropical rainforest, and the livelihoods of those people who live there, will surely depend on it.

Anthony Hall,
London, December 1990

Notes

1   See chapter 4.

2   See, for example: 'The Month Amazonia Burns' (cover story), *The Economist*, 9–15 September 1989; 'Amazon in Peril: The World's Biggest Rain Forest is Shrinking Fast' (cover story), *Newsweek*, 30 January 1989 and 'Torching the Amazon: Can the Rain Forest be Saved?' *Time*, 18 September 1989.

3   Recent books include: S. Hecht and A. Cockburn, *The Fate of the Forest: Developers, Destroyers and Defenders of the Amazon*, Verso, London, 1989; A. Revkin, *The Burning Season: The Murder of Chico Mendes and the Fight for the Amazon Rain Forest*, Houghton Miflin Co., Boston and Collins, London, 1990; A. Shoumatoff, *The World is Burning*, Little, Brown and Co., Boston, 1990 and A. Cowell, *The Decade of Destruction: The Crusade to Save the Amazon Rain Forest*, Henry Holt and Co., New York, 1990. Adrian Cowell also produced an updated version of an earlier series of documentaries with the same title, which was shown simultaneously on BBC television and on US public television in September 1990. Significantly, the Carajás iron-ore

project and its socio-ecological impacts came under close examination in one of these programmes.

4   Ironically, 'Operation Amazonia' is the same title given to the first major Amazon development drive by the (post-1964) military regime, set up in 1966 to build highways and attract commercial enterprises such as cattle ranches to the region with generous fiscal incentives granted through the newly created regional agency, SUDAM. That particular 'Operation Amazonia' certainly took no account of environmental concerns. See chapter 1, pp. 6–9.

5   Anthony Anderson, 'Smokestacks in the Rainforest: Industrial Development and Deforestation in the Amazon Basin', *World Development*, Vol. 18, No. 9, September 1990, pp. 1191–205.

6   Secretariat for the Environment, Decree No. 99, 353 of 27.6.90 and *Portaria* No. 140 of 23.11.90. Approval of new smelters is subject to their involvement in the Integrated Plan for Forestry–Industry (*Plano Integrado Floresta–Indústria* – PIFI).

7   See Anderson, *op cit.* and chapter 4.

8   *Folha de São Paulo*, 10.9.90 and *O Globo*, 23.9.90.

9   Anthony Hall, 'Land Tenure and Land Reform in Brazil', in R. Prosterman, M. Temple and T. Hanstead (eds.), *Agrarian Reform and Grassroots Development: Ten Case Studies*, Lynne Reinner Publishers, Boulder, Co. and London, 1990, pp. 205–32.

10   *Informa*, No. 37, CNRA/IBASE, Rio de Janeiro, 1990.